FIRE IN
MY SOUL

ALSO BY JOAN STEINAU LESTER

The Future of White Men and Other Diversity Dilemmas

Taking Charge: Every Woman's Action Guide to Personal, Political and Professional Success

ELEANOR HOLMES NORTON

FIRE IN MY SOUL

JOAN STEINAU LESTER AS AUTHORIZED BY
ELEANOR HOLMES NORTON

ATRIA BOOKS

New York   London   Toronto   Sydney   Singapore

ATRIA BOOKS
1230 Avenue of the Americas
New York, NY 10020

ISBN: 0-7434-0787-3

First Atria Books hardcover printing January 2003

10   9   8   7   6   5   4   3   2   1

ATRIA BOOKS is a trademark of Simon & Schuster, Inc.

Printed in the U.S.A.

For information regarding special discounts for bulk purchases,
please contact Simon & Schuster Special Sales at 1-800-456-6798
or business@simonandschuster.com

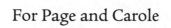
For Page and Carole

Contents

PART FOUR:
"TILL VICTORY IS WON"
241

"The arc of the moral universe is long, but it bends toward justice."
THEODORE PARKER, 1810–1860, UNITARIAN MINISTER AND ABOLITIONIST ORATOR

*F*ire in My Soul is an important book about a remarkable woman, born to the human rights struggle that challenged and changed our country. Eleanor Holmes Norton has always been enmeshed in America's contradictions. She was born a black child in the nation's capital when it was a segregated Southern bastion. She grew up in the city that symbolized freedom and democracy, when our government denied its citizens self-government at home and representation in the Congress. And she became a young woman when we all lived in a man's world.

This book tells the fascinating story of how Eleanor has challenged every barrier designed to contain her and others like her. The capitol and the rest of the country are no longer segregated by law, because her generation of activists—adults and students—would no longer have it. The man's world is opening to women because Eleanor and her generation of feminists insisted. The District of Columbia has a home-rule government, and the woman the city has chosen to bring complete self-government and full congressional voting representation is Congresswoman Eleanor Holmes Norton, the city's native daughter.

Eleanor was one of the generation of students who went South, inspired by Martin Luther King Jr. and his philosophy of direct action and nonviolent resistance. I met Eleanor when she was a young woman, and learned that she had gone to Antioch College, where both my sister and I had attended. The friendship between Eleanor and me, however, has been based on more than an old school tie. For us both, our non-conformist college suited our mutual understanding that there was work to be done in a world that needed changing.

With great skill, Joan Steinau Lester uses one exemplary and complicated life to tell the story of a remarkable generation. The author captures Eleanor, fighter for great causes and mediator among diverse groups, part activist, part intellectual. She shows how Eleanor rose from the Civil Rights Movement to enforce the laws she struggled in the Movement to achieve. She takes Eleanor from a foot soldier in the Student Nonviolent Coordinating Committee to the first woman to chair the U.S. Equal Employment Opportunity Commission, and from the segregated schools of the nation's capital to the House of Representatives.

Fire in My Soul captures Eleanor's life as it tracks and embraces the great movements for justice of our time. Racial justice has been Eleanor's anchor, but she has used her experience as a black woman in America to set sail to many other shores of injustice as well. As Eleanor says, and as Martin Luther King Jr. believed, "Human rights is all or nothing." *Fire in My Soul* is the story of a woman who has lived her credo.

—Coretta Scott King
Founder, The King Center
Atlanta, Georgia

In October 1991 law professor Anita Hill stunned the nation by charg-ing that Clarence Thomas, President George Bush's nominee to the U.S. Supreme Court, had sexually harassed her.

Seven congresswomen strode to the Capitol to demand the Senate hear Hill's account. One was Eleanor Holmes Norton, Thomas's prede-cessor as chair of the Equal Employment Opportunity Commission, where she had authored the very harassment guidelines he was accused of breaking.

When the women climbed the long Capitol steps, Norton's erect pos-ture, radiating force, said it all. At the Senate, she and her counterparts insisted on a hearing for Hill. Norton said then, "If nothing happened and the whole thing went away, the guidelines weren't worth the paper they were written on."

The hearing electrified the nation: Hill's dismissive treatment res-onated with women accustomed to being disbelieved. And Norton, who has found one flash point after another—from arguing free speech for the most notorious segregationists of her day to battling for the dis-enfranchised citizens of Washington, D.C.—had once again helped shape a pivotal moment.

I first met Eleanor Holmes at Antioch College in 1958, when she was a worldly twenty-one to my green eighteen. Just after the height of the Red Scare, I was thrilled to meet a real-live radical. Not to mention a Negro. This smart-talking, fast-walking woman fascinated me, as she did much of the campus.

Eleanor was skinny and firm and knew what she wanted. I felt fat and round, though photos of the time show me as slender as she. Confused and formless, I felt shapeless, whereas she seemed all form and shape, a steely diamond ready to cut to her clear-eyed goals.

I was flattered when she sought my company; on long walks we dis-cussed politics and life. Soon she went off to Yale Law School; coinci-dentally, I worked in New Haven and joined her on civil rights picket lines. One Saturday afternoon, picketing Woolworth's, I invited the mostly black demonstrators over to my small apartment for a party. Minutes after they arrived, carloads of police filed in to clear the mixed-race group. On Monday morning I was evicted. Eleanor said, "Fight it!" That hadn't entered my mind.

In the forty years since, her strongly expressed opinions—on everything from free speech to war, vitamins to welfare—have both educated and infuriated me, sometimes simultaneously. Passionate, ever ready to argue and armed with statistics to back a point, she'll take on any subject. Her vehement views still rankle, but ultimately, I've discovered, Eleanor is usually proven right.

In writing her biography, my overarching questions were: How did this ebullient debater escape the limitations typically imposed on women to become a national figure? What circumstances molded this "force of nature"? And who, deep down, was she?

My research followed all the usual trails of archives and interviews: scores with Eleanor, almost a hundred with colleagues, family and friends. Their cooperation as I probed, month after month and year after year, rewarded my quest. I have satisfied myself, at least, with answers. To convey them, I have made generous use of Eleanor's strong voice. Publicly, we still have heard too few voices of African-American women, civic thinkers, and actors; this one I could hardly hold back. Thus I have woven her direct quotations liberally into the traditional biographical form, joining, I hope, the best of my critical eye and others' perspectives to her first-person story.

During this four-year project I also got a windfall: glimpses of the pure, sweet core referred to by several of her closest friends and relatives. On my birthday this year, I was astonished to pick up the phone and hear a soft alto voice singing "Happy Birthday, dear Joan." Like other groundbreaking women of her generation, Eleanor has had to be armored and tough, buttressing her naturally argumentative character. But it has been a gift to witness the warrior's complexity.

I am also inspired by how closely she has stayed the course, lo these forty years. She has never let go of her original goals, or her passion to fulfill them. "It is people like Eleanor who keep my eye on the prize," affirms Peabody Award winner Charlayne Hunter-Gault, herself no novice at equity efforts.

Twinned with Norton's extraordinary story is that of her city, Washington D.C., home to her family for four generations. The

District's own long travails, as a unique federal enclave fighting for self-government, congressional representation and statehood, are entwined with those of its embattled delegate. That she is now her city's voice in Congress is a miracle match.

Over time she will be dissected with other questions; her life will flow from many pens. Let legal scholars, civil rights historians, political scientists and others examine this fertile ground. This is her story as I am privileged to be the first to tell it.

It begins in the late 1850s, deep in the heart of a Laroline, Virginia, plantation, where Richard John Holmes was enslaved with his siblings and parents, Richard and Ann. Our fragmentary knowledge suggests this tale of escape, fleshing out the bare fact of flight handed down in family lore.

Part One

"FULL OF THE FAITH THAT THE DARK PAST HAS TAUGHT US"

*A*ll signs were propitious: the plantation owner was away, the overseer and *"ole miss"* were both in bed with flu, and there was enough moonlight to illuminate the path, but not so much to make him an easy target. Young Richard John Holmes had waited years for this moment. He summoned his will and put a piece of salt herring and ash cake into a bandanna. He slipped his worn Bible into his pocket along with a tiny compass, telling only those who needed to know, so others would not be laden with his secret—forbidden knowledge that could bring any punishment. So many people had recently made the clandestine journey north, especially from Virginia, that measures had tightened. But Richard Holmes had resolved to go, and this would be the night.

All day he gave penetrating looks at friends, longing for good-byes, wishing he could take them with him. Most of those he'd known since childhood had been sold off in recent years, going down with thousands of others into the vast cotton fields of Georgia, Alabama, Louisiana and the Mississippi delta.

Late in the evening Richard crept away, leaving behind the landscape of his birth, fleeing those who fettered his body, but not his ever-active mind. All night he kept to small back roads, some no more than trails, wading through water whenever he could to throw off bloodhounds; he walked 'til morning, when he lay warily in damp bushes near a dirt road, trying to sleep. But as the sun slowly crossed the sky he was alert. Even this little road could carry the ever-present bounty hunters and slave traders.

When dusk finally blanketed the road, Richard left his hiding place and walked again the second night, guided by stars and hearsay. He knew how to read the night and assess weather for direction. His fellow captives had pieced together enough information from conversations overheard and from skilled slaves—harness-makers, tanners and blacksmiths sent out to work on neighboring plantations—that Richard Holmes had a detailed map in his head. He knew what spots to avoid. And although literacy for slaves was illegal, he'd learned to read from a woman who worked in the house, where the white children showed her their daily lessons.

Late on his second night out, Richard made his way to a large house where a cook stayed up, baking and waiting. While the owners of the household slept upstairs in their beds, she took up a plank in the kitchen floor and hid him in a tiny space lined with a quilt, hushing him as she hurried him into his hiding place.

Richard slept fitfully all day, and by night was ready to set out again, this time carrying a small bundle of biscuits and a scrap of dried pork, wrapped in old cloth. He walked again through the starry night, each footstep carrying him farther away from all that he knew.

And so he traveled, walking by night, sent from one refuge to another. He shivered in rain, walked across creeks, was dazed with fatigue. Just before dawn one morning, faint with thirst, Richard Holmes saw the dark waters of the Potomac River. It looked exactly as he'd heard it would: muddy and marshy, with narrower spots where brush grew into the water. He crept toward its banks crouching low, for the waning moon still cast his shadow. Spying no one, he paused, then saw the Long Bridge. His heart contracting as much from fear as chill, he managed to keep his wits about him and stole toward it. Reaching its entrance, he stood resolutely and began to walk, not daring to run, should anyone see him at this early hour.

For ten agonizing minutes Richard moved rapidly, his heart thumping with fear and exertion. As the sky crackled pink and dew shimmered on the grass, his heart leapt, this time with joy, when his feet touched land. A shiver went through his body; he stepped off the road into an alley in Southwest Washington, sobs racked his body and he sank to his knees, thanking the Lord who brought him through.

CHAPTER 1

The Ancestors

I am not what you call me. I am what I respond to.
AFRICAN PROVERB

The city into which Richard Holmes stepped was a city of contradictions. In the heart of world democracy, human slavery was legal. The recently passed Fugitive Slave Act of 1850 had ensured his vulnerability to recapture, for crossing a state line was no longer sure protection: those who captured fugitives would be rewarded and harboring refugees was a crime. If found, Richard Holmes could legally be whipped, resold or even executed.

"Nor do I exaggerate how I understand my great-grandfather came here," his great-granddaughter Eleanor Holmes Norton says 150 years later, shaking her head in her plush congressional office. "Walked off a plantation in Virginia, walked across the bridge. My grandfather told me this story, told it with enormous pride, and passed that pride on to us.

"Richard walked across the District line, because there you could get work, and the white man couldn't get you unless he could find you. They were building Washington and hired people off the streets every day. My grandfather says that, moreover, under the law, you could come here and get your slave and take him back. The city was swarming with all kinds of blacks: you couldn't tell one from another because Washington had a large number of free blacks. And white people would come from all over looking for their slave."

In the bustling Washington of the 1850s, Richard Holmes, like thousands of fugitives before him, made his way in a shadow economy. Southwest Washington was home to large numbers of fugitives; twenty-seven neighborhood churches provided relief, and the area housed many stops on the Underground Railroad. Escaped slaves were welcomed in this part of town. Probably living in a one-room shanty with a dozen others, he soon found work, according to Eleanor, on a construction gang.

"Remember, he came to a city where the Capitol *itself,*" she roars, "was built in part with slave labor, and blacks free and slave were used throughout the city to build the official buildings and develop the historic streets. Tough as it was, it beat working for nothing as a slave in Virginia." Foremen on construction sites, needing ready and cheap workers during a building boom, often didn't ask questions—especially when they could pay a fraction of what they'd pay their white workers or even their slave labor, hired from local owners.

Depending on the kindness of others and his own well honed wits, crafted for survival, Richard made his way in the city. After only a few weeks, another day came for which he had rigorously prepared. According to family history, handed down generation by generation, while Richard shoveled mud on the side of a road a white man stalked up and shouted, "Richard!"

Richard didn't flinch, didn't so much as move a muscle; he simply kept shoveling. His former owner accosted the foreman:

"That's my nigger! I'd recognize that nigger anywhere!"

"Looks to me like he ain't *your* Richard," the foreman replied. "He didn't answer to you. I saw him. He didn't pay you no mind."

Rebuffed by the insistence of the foreman, the white man finally gave up. With no way to prove his ownership of this particular disinterested black man, he wandered away. Perhaps he had made a mistake.

So Richard Holmes was, by his own hand, a free man.

"It's enough to inspire anybody," Eleanor says. "My great-grandfather clearly had been waiting for that day. Yes, he had disciplined himself to know the day could come and he told himself, 'Wait for that day.' And when that day comes, make sure that you do not know who that man is. He must have practiced the inner discipline not to instinctively respond, even to what every human being responds to: his name! Here's a man who thought ahead."

When Richard Holmes arrived in the 1850s, Washington was a city mired in muddy streets and controversy. Founded as a grand symbol of the new republic, the city plan called for magnificent boulevards laid like wagon spokes, ending at public squares designed to inspire patriotic pride. Yet Congress wouldn't pay to finish the splendid boulevards or maintain the inspirational squares. Author Charles Dickens had recently ridiculed the District as "a City of Magnificent Intentions," laid out with "broad avenues that begin in nothing and lead nowhere."

The federal government charged with running the city had a history of rebuffing local requests. Streets were dim; in order to save money, municipal streetlights were lit only when Congress was in session. President Jefferson said early in the century, "We cannot suppose Congress intended to tax the people of the United States at large for all the avenues in Washington." Yet the District was not allowed to tax its natural base, government property.

The battle over local control, one that Richard Holmes's great-granddaughter would someday lead, had raged since Congress granted the city its charter in 1802, with a mayor appointed by the president. In the decades since, every power had been contested, from the authority to regulate schools to control the noisy pigs, cows and geese that roamed the town. And although the streets were full of mud in the 1850s, Congress repeatedly turned down petitions to pay for street-cleaning, for fear, as one congressman warned, of giving an "opening wedge to future demands." The contest escalated. Representatives defended their home interests versus those of the federal District, which would have no advocate in Congress for another hundred years.

In the 1850s Washington was a rough city, with plentiful gambling and drinking. But it was starting to fulfill its promise. After a fire in its library, Congress spent unprecedented money to install citywide water pipes and funded 800 gas lamps, to be lit year-round. Though unpaved streets abounded and the Mall—a touted city park—was only partially complete, Congress began to lay the framework for a modern city.

And its construction required labor.

Richard Holmes emerged into Washington history during a propitious era of growth. Yet the issue of slavery was even more contentious than local control. Washington had accepted the laws of its neighbors—Virginia and Maryland—along with the land they'd ceded to make the federal District just fifty years before. Wedged between these two slave-holding states, the capital was a battleground. Linked to the South as a slave territory, Washington was at the same time uniquely open to the influence of Northern abolitionists and free-state congressmen.

On the eve of the Civil War, the status of blacks—both free and slave—was a sizzling issue. In the District, local newspapers warned about the "unsettling influence" of "free negroes," with their ambiguous status. By the time Richard Holmes arrived as part of a great migration, Washington severely restricted mobility and occupations. City codes with almost impossible restrictions—monetary bonds to ensure good behavior, registration with the mayor, character testimonials from whites, curfews and certificates of freedom always at hand—had been passed, modified, loosened and tightened during the previous decades. Nat Turner's 1831 rebellion in neighboring Virginia had not been forgotten; white fears brought corresponding restraints. In 1835, after the so-called "Snow riot," in which whites demolished black churches, schools and businesses—including a restaurant owned by Beverly Snow, a free black woman—the right of black people to own businesses was terminated. While the restrictions were difficult to enforce, by the 1850s almost three-quarters of all free black people in Washington could find work only as laborers and domestics.

"Oh, they had slave blocks all downtown," says Eleanor. Congressional policy was noninterference with slavery in the District. In 1850 the slave *trade* was finally eliminated in the federal city, but this "compromise" included tough provisions for the return of fugitives like Richard Holmes. Violent clashes increased, with some whites and blacks physically resisting the efforts of traders and bounty hunters to seize people on Washington streets. Yet the District would hold onto slavery itself until 1862. If slavery was repugnant, becoming a haven for "free negroes" was worse, in the eyes of many whites. Public opinion was shaped by the city paper, the *National Intelligencer,* which continually raised the specter of black "mobs" emigrating from neighboring slaveholding states if there were to be emancipation in the District. "No asylum for free negroes!" it thundered. Attacks on blacks increased.

Yet in this perilous situation Richard Holmes prospered. After he had been in Washington just a few years, in 1861 the Civil War erupted. President Lincoln had predicted that: "[Slavery and freedom] are like two wild beasts in sight of each other, but chained and apart. Some day these deadly antagonists will . . . break their bonds, and then the question will be settled."

The turbulence of war stimulated even more rapid city growth, and the construction trade that was Richard Holmes's livelihood exploded.

"A stable black middle class had its root established right there," says Eleanor. "That was the beginning of federal employment, the spring-board for the black middle class. For a black person living in and around Washington, government work of almost any kind was good work, respectable work. I give a lot of credit to the government hiring black folks."

First, regiment after regiment of white soldiers, then thousands of destitute black refugees poured in. Labeled "contrabands"—literally, confiscated property, for they had stolen themselves—these fugitives arrived, as had Mr. Holmes, carrying at most a small sack with a few belongings. Hundreds came each week from nearby Maryland alone. Local whites became alarmed as people crowded into any shelter they could find: former slave pens in the shadow of federal buildings, aban-doned schools, or already-bursting tenements. Even some abolitionists urged deportation of these free "darkies," questioning how they could ever be integrated into American life.

As refugee numbers swelled, the army opened "contraband camps" on both sides of the Potomac River, housing up to ten thousand refugees at a time. Fortunately, the demand for wartime labor kept pace. The federal government hired fugitives; the need was such that wages were often above the $10 a month established by military order. But incredibly, the government also imposed a staggering $5 a month "help-blacks-in-need" tax on these very wages, a burden borne solely by contrabands, until protests eliminated it.

All during the early 1860s arguments over slavery continued in the halls of Congress. Were there any states, abolitionists asked, where a refugee could be safe from recapture or a "mistaken identity" seizure? Finally in 1864 Congress repealed the Fugitive Slave Act. And for the first time Richard Holmes was legally a free man. He no longer had to pretend to be someone else; even if he were identified he at last had the law on his side.

Richard Holmes continued to prosper, and on August 20, 1872, he married Lucy Ellen Jones, a woman with her own difficult story of the times. Daughter of a white master and black slave, a young Lucy Ellen, "very fair with straight hair," her descendants say, had been left by her father in Washington, D.C., right after the Civil War, hours after he dropped off her sister in Baltimore. Lucy Ellen never saw her sister or father again, though later she managed to reconnect with her mother and other sisters, "decidedly different in appearance." Three generations later, Lucy Ellen Holmes's great-granddaughter Eleanor would have a vehement explanation for this ancestral desertion. Upon learning the story, her unsentimental response was, "That's not abandonment! Before the war she was privileged, a house nigger. But what life could she have in the South after the Civil War? There was no space for her. He dropped her off in Washington, where there were other blacks, where people were aspiring, to give her a chance—and I'm sure glad he did!"

As the years went by, Richard Holmes took initiative of a different sort. History shrouds the exact circumstances propelling this laborer to become a student, but he attended the recently founded Howard University Ministerial School while Lucy Ellen supported him, washing, ironing and baby-sitting for the families of Washington Barracks military officers. Although he did not graduate, Eleanor's great-grandfather became minister of a small church in nearby Arlington, Virginia, to which he and his wife traveled by horse and buggy.

"Leadership appears in the family tradition. Ambition. I can only imagine him, having the guts to walk off the plantation. I see him as a kind of righteous man. The family was always religious, raising children well and right. So I just have a sense of these righteous black people who came to Washington and started churches."

Family legend variously places Lucy or her husband Richard among the founders of today's large Vermont Avenue Baptist Church; however, church records list neither as among the seven who created the church in 1866. "Founders are usually persons who sign the legal papers," Eleanor speculates. "Not everyone who helps start a church would be on the founders document."

Because Richard Holmes became a minister, he had a freedom unusual for a black man in post–Civil War Washington.

"The more segregated [the] society, the more the church was the leader in the community, because the minister, in any real sense, was the only free man. He didn't have to depend on anybody except his parishioners. He wasn't dependent on the white man."

In a sea of white control, churches formed critical networks. Ministers often took up an "after collection," a second offering distributed during the week to those most needy. In the trauma of exodus and relocation, churches stabilized communities, inspiring worshipers who sang, "Order my steps in your Word, dear Lord. Lead me, guide me, every day." Soon these anchors attracted grocery stores, cafés, barbershops and offices; community sprang to life.

In the chaos of the post–Civil War migration, much of Washington's black population viewed education—with religion—as the way to freedom. After the cultural wilderness of slavery, when literacy was severely punished, a thirst for knowledge propelled the founding of school after school. Unable to use public facilities until after the war (though they paid taxes), black Washingtonians supported more private schools than any other city. This educational emphasis would later have a direct impact on Eleanor Holmes.

"Washington's premier schools for Negroes," she would boast of her schooling in the 1940s and 1950s, "were unparalleled in the nation. Washington was a mecca for aspiring blacks. A critical mass of institutions nourished black intellectual life."

Beyond public schools, themselves unusual, Howard University, created after the war by contraband camp commander General Howard, was established in the heart of Washington's black community. A magnet for nationally renowned artists and intellectuals, Richard Holmes's great-granddaughter would grow up in its orbit, ever-aware of its luminous presence.

During these post–Civil War years Richard Holmes and his wife Lucy, remembered by a namesake granddaughter as "kind and busy, a good cook making wonderful fruit pies," had five children: another Richard, Alfred, Isaac, John—who died at age seven—and Irene. The offspring of this independent couple "were very clear that they didn't want to function in a 'less-than' role, that it was important to 'Be Somebody,'" another great-granddaughter says. "They wanted their children to excel. High academic standards were important." This drive for educational excellence—a way to escape the crushing conditions—would continue down the generations.

While the family grew and each of its members figured out how to "Be Somebody" in a culture that frustrated that possibility, official Washington swelled in size and polish. When the United States emerged as an imperial power in the 1890s its capital city correspondingly gained stature. Historian Constance McLaughlin Green describes senators of that era, "conscious of the new prestige attaching to the men who ratified or rejected international treaties, [who] abandoned the broad-brimmed hats and string ties of yesteryear and adopted high silk hats and frock coats as standard daytime attire." This was white federal Washington, with grand conventions, hotels and fine restaurants.

The other Washington, where most black people lived, was still the city of back alley shanties, desperate poverty and daily humiliations. Yet amid the indignities, a new middle class flourished. Near the end of the century, civil rights giant Mary Church Terrell wrote in her autobiography, *Colored Woman in a White World,* "There are more well-educated colored people to the square inch in Washington than in any other city in the United States."

After the war the radical Republicans who controlled Congress used the capital as a model city, legislating unprecedented civil rights. Calling this a time of "Reconstruction," they opened public accommodations. On Washington streetcar lines, for instance, the Holmes family could now ride inside the car, rather than sit on the roof in rain, snow and burning sun.

Richard John Lewis Holmes, son of the man who walked off a Virginia plantation and the woman dropped in Washington by her slave-owning father, was one of the handful who made it through the narrow Reconstruction window of the 1870s and 1880s into the new black middle class. His siblings, like others in Washington, had steady work with the federal government. Alfred mowed grass and cleared snow, Irene cleaned, and Ike, who attended Howard for several years, worked in the government printing office.

But Richard secured a plum city job. In 1902, at the age of twenty-five, he became one of only half a dozen black D.C. firefighters—a secure, high-paying position that blacks would still have trouble attaining fifty years later. Yet Richard grew frustrated. As one of the few colored men scattered throughout the Fire Department, he could not rise to become an officer; there was an unbreakable ceiling above his head.

"You could not have black men over white men in a paramilitary environment."

The post–Civil War window of opportunity was closing. Repeatedly discouraged as he sought promotion, Richard Holmes joined several others to petition the Fire Department for the first all-black company. Successful in their mission, on January 28, 1921, Private Richard John

Lewis Holmes was promoted to sergeant, paid "$1,700 per annum." Two decades later he would retire as a lieutenant.

Like his father, this Richard would live to be an old man past ninety, but he died before his granddaughter would help eliminate such segregated units as the one he proudly started; no fire department should have to be segregated for a black man to be an officer. Almost a century later, she, equally proudly, displays in her congressional office a picture of Grandfather Richard standing with his all-black firefighting company.

As the twentieth century dawned, restrictive laws everywhere eroded civil rights gained in postwar Washington. Mary Church Terrell recalls that in the 1890s "a colored person could dine anywhere in Washington." But the devastating 1896 *Plessy* v. *Ferguson* Supreme Court decision signaled the end.

The case arose from a Louisiana citizen—Homer Plessy—who refused to sit in a "colored" railroad car. He lost on appeal to the Supreme Court, which ruled that "separate but equal" facilities could be provided. The decision gave the green light to a resegregation that would stand until the firefighter Richard Holmes's granddaughter Eleanor was almost grown. Using *Plessy*, the city ignored District Reconstruction codes mandating nondiscrimination—in fact, they "lost" those codes—and created two distinct, racially divided cities.

Soon Mrs. Terrell, wife of a judge, could walk the sixteen blocks from the Capitol to the White House and find not one restaurant "in which I would be permitted to take a morsel of food if it was patronized by white people." She recalled being ravenously hungry and weary downtown, unable to replenish anywhere unless, in an occasional concession, she was offered the option of eating behind a screen. (Imagine the noted school board member, international lecturer on suffrage and president of the National Association of Colored Women, clad in her elegant attire, coming from a meeting at the Capitol. She takes off her white gloves, sits and places her napkin in her lap as a screen is placed next to her table to shield other diners from her presence.) In real life, Mrs. Terrell rarely submitted to the indignity, even when hungry or with out-of-town colleagues needing a meal.

Housing and schools resegregated, many hospitals no longer accepted black patients and most black people became even more firmly relegated to humble work. "There is no way for me to earn an honest living in the National Capital, unless I am willing to be a domestic servant, if I am not a trained nurse or a dressmaker, or unless I can secure a position in the public schools," Mrs. Terrell fumed. Teaching was often impossible since the supply of colored teachers exceeded demand.

Yet while the city soon had separate schools, churches and clubs, the turn-of-the-century black community, one third of the population, developed a vibrant cultural life with its own movie theaters—the Lincoln, the Republic, the Howard, and the Booker T—in the U Street area. Despite segregation, Washington's public schools were known as extraordinary and the city harbored a burgeoning intelligentsia. The federal government, though offering mostly menial jobs, still contributed a modicum of economic stability.

As the twentieth century opened, aspiring blacks—including Richard the firefighter and his wife Nellie, daughter of the immaculately starched midwife Matilda Jackson Coleman and her husband Frank—clustered in the near Southwest and Northwest neighborhoods. Living on a muddy street at 913 3rd St., SW, in a little four-room house, the Holmes clan expanded. First child Selena was followed by a baby boy, who, according to family lore, died from eating a piece of meat inadvertently given him too young by his father. Then Frank and another Richard were born, each exactly four years, nine months apart. On April 17, 1912, at 2:10 A.M., when his parents were thirty-five years old, the last baby, Coleman Sterling, was born.

Richard provided well for his family. Years later his ex-wife Nellie would tell her granddaughter Eleanor, "We had fifty-pound bags of flour, twenty-five pounds of sugar, kegs of every kind of food. Richard was a man who did right by his family."

And she did right by him, speaking nothing but praise for his "right-minded" ways even after they divorced, though she did later tell Vela, her daughter-in-law, that on her wedding night her husband's behavior was a shock. Richard undressed and dropped his clothes on the floor, clearly expecting his new wife to pick them up.

"Why have you left these clothes for me to hang up?" the proud woman asked her surprised husband. But she remained married to Richard for twenty-five years.

Hardworking, independent-minded folk, Richard and Nellie

Holmes were faithful Baptists like Richard's father, the man who walked away from slavery: they didn't drink or smoke. With their middle-class neighbors—postmen, teachers, shoemakers, Pullman porters, and barbers—they helped build a flourishing community that founded its own businesses and inaugurated holidays celebrating black achievements, like Douglass Day on February 14. These self-sufficient institutions at least partially protected their children from racial insults, yet Washingtonians also fought discrimination, organizing an early NAACP chapter to protest Jim Crow laws.

Within this vibrant, segregated environment, Coleman Sterling Holmes grew to adulthood. A tall, handsome young man who dressed impeccably, he both read music and played piano by ear, enjoyed fine foods and was a true son of his upwardly mobile, independent-thinking family. His father, Richard, the firefighter, got an unheard-of Mexican divorce, Uncle Ike played the violin, and Uncle Alfred had a farm in Maryland—something most blacks didn't do.

Called "Coley" at Cardozo Business High School, "the first business high school in the history of Negro education," Coleman was a member of its first graduating class. An editor of that historic yearbook, he also figured prominently in it. Coleman was everywhere: acclaimed as an oratorical contest winner, vice president of his home room, chair of the Recreation Committee, one of four student speakers at commencement and a football player who played in his own patent leather shoes because the new Athletic Association had no size elevens.

In 1931, as the Depression gripped the country, this young leader of his class determined to leave the protection of home and set off north for Syracuse University, where he had received a scholarship.

"Very unusual for that day, especially for black men," declares Eleanor about the role model who would be her father. Alone among his schoolmates, he made the arduous trip to Syracuse to begin his odyssey, constantly scraping together money for school.

During the years that Eleanor's paternal family made their way in the nation's capital, her maternal root flourished farther south. Great-grandparents Emily Johnson Fitts and William Fitts, enslaved in northern North Carolina, near Warrenton and Macon, faced different hazards. There was no possibility here of crossing a river to a city filled with free blacks and abolitionists. No chance here of passing by a town square as Frederick Douglass poured forth his vision, or stumbling into an antislavery lecture given by young Susan B. Anthony and her father. Deep in the hills of North Carolina, the black Fitts (named after their white owners) labored on the Fitts plantation, far from urban networks or hopes of flight.

But like Richard and Lucy Ellen Holmes, these were people of strong wills. Eleanor's mother Vela Holmes sits in her comfortable Northwest Washington living room and tells a tale of hardy ancestors.

During the Civil War, when the white Fitts men raced off to battle in the Confederate Army, the plantation mistress, "ole miss," was left in charge. Eleanor's mother carefully emphasizes her choice of words— "My mama, who told me this story, always called her 'ole miss,' never said Mrs. Fitts"—as she grimly recounts a story she heard many times growing up.

"I don't know whether my mama added a little juice to this or not," she says as she begins. Ole miss, anxious about her sons at war, carefully followed Confederate troop reports, foraging scraps of news from neighbors, letters from the front and deserters who rode by with tales of burning and carnage.

"Well, naturally," Mrs. Holmes explains, "they were listening for if any of their children were hurt." In fact, one of ole miss's sons was eventually wounded in the war raging nearby. She ordered her slave, Eleanor's great-grandfather, to find the wounded Confederate soldier and bring him home.

"I know the thing my mother resented the most," says Mrs. Holmes, "was that when the message reached ole miss that her oldest son had been shot, ole miss said right away, 'William, you've got to go get him, you can't let him die!' "

Mrs. Holmes grimaces. "Evidently ole miss thought my grandfather, William, was a giant."

Ordered off on this dangerous mission, William Fitts set out with two horses. When he managed to track Confederate troops and find the injured soldier, William hoisted the man onto a horse and trotted back to the plantation. Someone shot his own horse out from under him; eventually he arrived home walking, his hands pulling the bridle as he led the other horse carrying the Confederate soldier.

"My mama said," Mrs. Holmes relays, "that her mother, little ninety-pound Emily, took the roof off the house to her husband when he brought the white man home. I understand that the tiny grandmother, Emily Fitts, said to her husband William, 'Why didn't you shoot him *and* the horse?'

"After that rescue from Sherman's army, when the Confederate son got home to recuperate, he raped William's wife, my grandmother, and that baby was born. He became Shepherd Fitts, my uncle, who got to go to college and read law, because who do you think got him in there?

"His father, the white man. And you see how they tried to pay up. Human beings are peculiar beings, and the owners ran things.

"But that Emily Fitts, she raised sand," Mrs. Holmes repeats with a smile of satisfaction. "Yes she did. She had a will. And all of Eleanor's ancestors did."

After the Civil War, the black Fitts family remained near Macon, farming. Emily and William Fitts's daughter Lucinda, who would be Eleanor's grandmother, was at first thought to be lazy because she liked to read all the time.

"My mother Lucinda was a very bright young person," Mrs. Vela Holmes reminisces. "When she got to be about sixteen or seventeen, the Plummers, a historically free black family, wanted somebody to help with their children's studies. You see, they didn't have schools. So they asked my mother if she would come and live with them." In late nineteenth-century North Carolina, Lucinda Fitts became an educator, although there had been little opportunity for her own education. "The county tried to give you a certificate. That's what you strived for. Every time, you got a little bit more here, and a little bit more there too. And Mama talked about her first-grade certificate."

While Lucinda taught the Plummer children, she met a young carpenter, Mark Lynch, who came into Warrington on business and had to stay overnight, tying his horse at Plummers' livery stable. Mark's father had been another North Carolina rarity—a free black man during slavery. After courting, Lucinda Fitts and Mark Lynch married and built a house on land given them by Mark's parents, Dudley and Mary Silver Lynch.

First a son, Bernard, was born. Then on September 7, 1909, Emily and William Fitts's daughter Lucinda gave birth to a baby girl, Vela, who would become Eleanor's mother. Two more boys—Fitzhugh, and, in 1919, Nathan—completed the family.

Born less than fifteen miles from the old Fitts plantation on a

Littleton farm that raised cotton, corn, peanuts, cane, sweet potatoes, and tomatoes, Vela remembers tending "everything that grew." On the red, rocky land, everything grew but tobacco, and every crop was worked by the family. Vela's father's and mother's people all lived nearby, forming a large extended family.

Like their neighbors, Vela's family dined on food it harvested, wore clothes its women made, and relied on its men to build the shelter they enjoyed. Vela regularly ate a country breakfast: fried chicken and gravy, rice, biscuits, and corn bread—though Vela, as a girl, got only the feet of the chicken. At midday dinner, she had a pot of cabbage with potatoes and "middling meat"—pork cut from the middle, between the shoulder and the hip of the hog. At supper, the family had a light meal of fried potatoes, a fresh-picked vegetable and leftovers from midday dinner.

The family worked from before dawn until after dusk, raising crops, tending animals and making virtually everything they used. Vela's cousin Ara Walls remembers vividly, "We worked on the farm from the time you was big enough to walk. Mama put a five-pound sugar sack around your neck for cotton, Mama had her bag, you had your bag, you know you wanted to do everything your mama did. As you grew, it turned to a meal bag, and then you'd fill that up. By that time, you're almost able to have your own row in the field." The family worked cotton with a hoe, thinning seedlings row by row and "when you finished one job Papa had another one for you."

Finally Sundays came. Vela did up her hair and dressed in Sunday slippers and middy blouse, with her white pleated skirt "starched until it could stand up by itself." The family set off by horse and carriage for the little junction of Essex and Pine Chapel Baptist Church, the home church for grandfather Dudley Lynch and his six grown children, each a prosperous farmer he'd started out with a piece of land. When they'd made the journey, hoping to avoid skirt-soaking rain, Vela greeted her aunts, uncles, and cousins; together they went in to sit on the long hard benches.

Every Sunday evening when chores were done, after the family had prayed at Pine Chapel and eaten dinner, when the cows and horses were where they should be, "Papa would take his children and we'd go to his father's." Vela Holmes smiles at the memory. "Grandfather Dudley always had a hug for us. Then he would say, 'Go look up there, and whatever is in that thing bring it to me.' " Grandfather had a sweet potato treat or a piece of hard candy tucked away. "And that was what he had been saving all week for us. So you see you can't help but have a lot of affection for people like that."

Vela saw her entire family on important occasions. A few had cars; a drive across the mountain was an all-day event. On dirt roads, if it was raining, they were mired in mud. If it was dry, they got stuck in sand. But several times a year, they made it.

Mrs. Holmes reminisces, "knowing my mother's cousins, they were also slaves indentured to a similar family. In fact, they all had the same last names, as all slaves did [who worked for a family]. And it was Fitts. As I grew up I remember looking at these Fitts men, my uncles and cousins. They were tall and strong and fine-looking men. And they seemed to be very happy people."

A generation later, these hard-workers would have their legacy in Eleanor. Raised by her country mother Vela, the daughter would herself labor from dawn to dusk and beyond, just as her North Carolina relatives had done. Eleanor would emerge the heir to both sides of her family, twining the legacy of independent-minded, urban paternal ancestors with that of her even-keeled, industrious Southern roots, both sides joined by a love of education.

After Vela Lynch completed sixth grade at Jerusalem School, she left her close-knit kin to go off to Bricks Junior College, since no public high schools were open for "colored" in North Carolina. Run by people who looked white ("but known as colored," Vela recalls), the school was founded by the American Missionaries, a Northern group. The few who attended these private high schools became the educated leaders of the next generation. Amongst this vibrant group of seekers, Vela has fond memories; the boarding school also provided relief from the city school, where white children had pushed her off sidewalks.

"You'd have to hold your own," she recalls with a shake of her head, "or they'd bump you off."

After just three years at Bricks, Vela was yanked from her comfortable second home. At the age of fifteen, she was summoned by the school principal to receive fearful news: her mother was gravely ill. Vela hurried home just in time. Within days, Lucinda Lynch died, leaving four children. On her deathbed she specified that her only daughter was to be sent north, away from the harsh conditions of Southern farm life. Almost immediately, Vela was sent to Auburn, New York, to live with her mother's older sister, Elizabeth, after whom Vela Elizabeth had been named.

"It was a very heartbreaking thing," Mrs. Vela Holmes remembers, leaving her family behind on the farm. "I'll never forget the day. I had never seen all my aunts and uncles. I knew my uncle was a lawyer, his daughter had gone to Howard University, and she was supposed to be musical. She had a piano, I'd heard. But I had never seen them before. It was such a dreadful day."

The difficulty of her leave-taking was magnified by her treatment in the "colored" waiting room at the train station. Although she arrived early with her family, she was kept waiting at the ticket window until all in the white waiting room purchased their tickets, moments before the train pulled out. But the spirit of her grandmother, the indomitable Emily Fitts, came to Vela in a most unexpected form.

"My uncle Shepherd [the offspring of Emily Fitts's rape] walked by, and he hugged me and kissed me on my cheek and threw five dollars in my hand." Vela Lynch was thus fortified to start her journey alone to the chilly unknown, way up north.

On the train Vela sat in "a little cubbyhole" of a Jim Crow car, right behind the engine. "It was the only place black people were put in front of the white," her cousin says, laughing at the irony seventy-five years later. With the window open to relieve the stifling heat, smoke blew in Vela's face all the way to Syracuse, covering her with soot. Allowed in neither sleeping cars nor dining room, she sat up all night and ate food her family provided. Every few hours the young woman untied the twine around her shoe box, crammed with chicken, ham sandwiches, biscuits, cake and apples.

"Travel," Vela Holmes understates, "was very difficult then."

In Syracuse, stepping off the train with her cardboard suitcase, she was greeted warmly by Aunt Elizabeth and Uncle Alfred, thought by Vela to be a relative of Harriet Tubman. Vela arrived wearing her mother's old coat.

"I remember my aunt took that coat, sewed it, hemmed it, and I threw that thing.

" 'Aunt Elizabeth,' I said, 'I'm not going to wear this old coat!'

"So she said to me, 'Yes you will. Yes you will.'

"Uncle Alfred, who is no relation to me, said, 'Fittsie, go downtown and take her into Witherow's and get her a coat. You're not going to have her walking down Genese Street in that old coat.' " The following Saturday Vela's uncle and aunt took her into Syracuse for her first city-bought coat and a city outing.

"I was well treated," Mrs. Holmes says, her face softening as she remembers the kindness of her uncle and aunt. "They were wonderful teenage years," made more marvelous by the arrival of her brother Fitzhugh, who secured a nearby live-in job as a chauffeur.

After graduating from Central High School in Syracuse in 1930, where all the other students in her high school yearbook were visibly white, the young woman worked her way through two years at Syracuse Normal School by being "in service." Always groomed with gloves and purse, she cooked in white folks' kitchens and lived as a maid in their homes until, like her mother before her, she received her teaching certificate.

Vela began to teach in the public schools. Yet twenty-five years later another African-American woman, Marjorie Carter, would be heralded as the first to break the city's teaching color bar. Perhaps, Vela's niece Dolores Brule now speculates, "it's possible they didn't know she was African-American. If they did a face-to-face they might not have known. She was light enough that it may not have occurred to them, and if they didn't ask she may not have told. I've always thought that's what happened."

"New York State would not have had a question on the application form," Eleanor concurs. "My mother graduated from Normal School where they didn't ask you what you are, she applied for a job where they didn't ask you what you are.

"There's no question that my mother was very light, but she wasn't passing. She said, 'Here's a job, I show up for the job, hire me.' Passing was if someone asked you and you said 'No.' Passing is literally passing over; a large number did it in the oppressive climate of the early twentieth century. They lost their identity as blacks, disappeared from the black world, lost their friends."

However Vela secured her early 1930s teaching job, she found pleasure after-hours in the company of her brother Fitzhugh and his wife Gwenderlin. In 1931 she was delighted by the arrival of their first child, Dolores; Vela spent hours combing the child's hair and pushing the carriage while she talked to friends.

Soon the sedate young woman encountered a debonair student at Syracuse University, Mr. Coleman Holmes.

"One way they had of integrating everything at the university was, I think, they all assumed that the men could sing." Vela describes the fateful meeting with a wry smile.

"I had a good friend, Fanny, who [later] stood up to be Eleanor's god-mother. And she would say, 'Well, let's go on up to the university and see if these colored boys can sing. They're going to sing tonight.' So we'd go up there. They could usually sing. We'd go, and Fanny's husband Robert would go with us. He was also a friendly person and he got to know Coleman. After that, quite often, when I'd go to Fanny's house, Robert would say, 'Oh, Coleman was here. He wants to meet you.' "

Coleman Holmes was just beginning his college career when he met the light-skinned Vela Lynch. Upwardly mobile Washington had made its mark on the young man with high ambitions. "Coleman was very color-struck," his daughter Eleanor would later concede. "Part of the legacy of middle-class Washington was a pronounced color conscious-ness within the race. Although it wasn't like New Orleans, there was a color hierarchy for which Washington was well-known. Today we've gone through 'Black Is Beautiful,' but Coleman hadn't." Years later his mother Nellie would laugh about her dark brown son, "Coleman said he would never marry anybody as dark as he was."

The romance between Coleman and Vela blossomed as he struggled to complete Syracuse University.

"Lord," Mrs. Holmes exclaims, "we've had a hard way to get through school. That scholarship ran out, and before he could go back, he went to work, and he had to come back and beat it through."

On July 14, 1936, Vela Elizabeth Lynch and Coleman Sterling Holmes pledged their union in Syracuse, New York. After saying their vows the couple left for Washington D.C., where the Holmes family had estab-lished deep roots since Richard Holmes first walked across the Long Bridge from Virginia eighty years before.

In August, Coleman and Vela moved into a small apartment on Lamont Street, Northwest, and began life together in the nation's capital.

Washington, D.C., in the Depression-era 1930s was a modern city. Gas lanterns were mourned by some but had been almost universally supplanted by the new electricity that lit up nearly every building.

And it was a segregated city. Even white-owned stores in black neighborhoods wouldn't employ colored people, triggering the New Negro Alliance to form, with the slogan "Don't Buy Where You Can't Work!" Thurgood Marshall and other lawyers were filing federal complaints for access to rest rooms and lunch counters.

Coleman Holmes arrived home to the District with his shy, attractive bride as his community cheered one "first" after another: people huddled around radios to hear the news when Jesse Owens racked up four gold medals at the Olympic games in Nazi-led Berlin. They cheered as Joe Louis pounded white opponents in the boxing ring with satisfying thuds, and little boys shadowboxed like their idol. Singer Lena Horne describes the "Brown Bomber": "Joe was the one invincible Negro, the one who stood up to the white man and beat him down with his fists. He in a sense carried so many of our hopes, maybe even dreams of revenge."

In the city of his birth Coleman was well connected. Finding work as the Depression deepened was a day-to-day challenge when those "last hired and first fired" got the hardest, dirtiest work, the so-called "Negro jobs." Urban black unemployment climbed to over 50 percent; white women competed for jobs as maids and cooks. The new Social Security Board established a Bureau of Public Assistance to help an increasingly destitute populace. But Coleman's people, hardworking and self-reliant, tightened belts in a time when even porter jobs became difficult to find.

Coleman's father, Richard ("Papa"), a tall dignified man, married his second wife, Miss Olivia. The grown Holmes children—Coleman, Selena, Frank, and the third Richard—regularly went out to Papa's house for Sunday evening dinners after lengthy services at the Mt. Mariah Baptist Church. The aroma of fried chicken, ham, fresh corn and beans, black-eyed peas, greens, cornbread and sweet potato pie, all blended into one sweet smell of home. Soon, however, Coleman and Vela broke from this tradition of Holmes family life.

"In their search for upward mobility," Eleanor says, they left the clapping Baptists of their youth and on December 18, 1936, joined Saint George's Episcopal Church at 2nd and U Streets. "They always said they were determined to get out of the long day of church services." After a brief sermon the couple enjoyed their own small family dinner at home.

Coleman, a witty and sociable man, also enjoyed the fellowship at several local clubs. Coming alive at night, he played cards—whist and bridge—with his wife and other up-and-coming couples, and soon hatched plans to go to law school at night while driving a cab during the day.

The young couple sparred. Vela Lynch Holmes was still, in her husband's eyes, the North Carolina farm-girl-turned-teacher. When she scooped grease off a plate with a piece of bread he teased her about being "country."

"That's straight out of North Carolina!"

Coleman scoured secondhand stores, looking for antiques and Oriental rugs to furnish their little apartment, "to keep North Carolina from getting in here."

If Coleman was elegant, Vela was thrifty and practical, captivating her husband and friends with steady, no-nonsense ways and a friendly manner. Determined to once again make the best of another move to a strange city, Vela ignored her husband's barbs and threw herself into work and family life. She began to think about night school, perhaps at Howard, where she might complete her bachelor's degree and get a District teaching license.

Barely four months after their move to Washington, as President Franklin Delano Roosevelt was elected to a second term and cold fall rains chilled the air, the new couple got the news: Vela was pregnant.

All that winter and spring they prepared. As snow piled up around their front door, Vela put away what money she could. By the time daffodils opened, she was cutting old clothes into blankets, sewing up baby dresses and knitting tiny caps.

While Vela stitched and saved, Coleman the dreamer found the perfect name, one that honored a relative—his grandmother Lucy Ellen—and preserved tradition, but also invoked another woman, prominent and daring: the president's wife. She had begun publishing "My Day," a widely read newspaper column. This "exquisitely right name," as its holder would later declare, signified both a grounding in Coleman's family past and an anticipation of a future that would be different. In the hot, humid, early June days of 1937, Vela and Coleman anxiously awaited the arrival of their first child.

They would name her Eleanor.

CHAPTER 2

A Warrior Is Born

*Thank God I'm a Negro born in 1937 instead of 1837. Indeed, thank God that
I'm a Negro, for it is an experience in itself that gives meaning to life. There's
always a tomorrow when you're a Negro.*
ELEANOR HOLMES, ANTIOCH COLLEGE ESSAY

The sun was shining brightly on June 13, 1937, the day I was born,"
Eleanor wrote in an eighth grade autobiography. "This 'blessed
event' took place in Washington, D.C. My father named me Eleanor
Katherine. My mother would have named me had I been a boy."

Prewar Washington was strictly segregated, but people objected where
they could, filing NAACP suits or picketing movies like *Gone with the Wind*
over Hattie McDaniel's mammy role. Pressure built until a pivotal event
ignited release. When Eleanor was two years old, in 1939, the Daughters
of the American Revolution denied "colored contralto" Marian
Anderson, the classically trained diva, use of their Constitution Hall.

"Every African American sees it as one of the great moments of the
twentieth century," Eleanor describes the furious response. First Lady
Eleanor Roosevelt resigned from the DAR (which Franklin called the
BAR, for "Bitches of the American Revolution") and used her White
House connections to open the Lincoln Memorial for a concert. On a
cold day fraught with symbolism—Easter Sunday, April 9—Marian
Anderson stood dramatically wrapped in fur on the steps of the monument to the Great Emancipator. The Mall was jammed with a racially
mixed crowd of over 75,000. She walked up to six microphones and,
with her exquisite voice, sang the National Anthem.

"It somehow fits the black story," Eleanor smiles. "One of the great
lessons about racism and democracy was taught: she never said a word,
she only sang about our country."

Eleanor's relatives and neighbors shivered, wept, and were inspired
in the cold air. Thousands more listened at home. The watershed day

rippled for years. "I remember it was particularly talked about in my house," says Eleanor, echoing conversations in thousands of black homes. "You always knew about it, you knew it in your mother's womb. We talked about civil rights all the time—race, constant talk about politics at the dinner table."

"There's something larger than life about being born in the nation's capital when it was segregated, as World War II was about to liberate the world from fascism." On December 7, 1941, when Eleanor was four and a half, Japan bombed the U.S. fleet at Pearl Harbor and the country mobilized. She remembers the war coming into her grandmother's home when Aunt Selena's son walked in one day.

"We were sitting in the kitchen, and Albert opened the door. He had obviously just gotten the mail. He said, 'I'm in the army now.' And grandma said, 'Boy, what are you talking about?'"

Even in the forces fighting fascism, apartheid reigned. Many of the million black soldiers filled familiar cook and porter jobs. A handful—notably the Tuskegee airmen and Buffalo Division infantry—are remembered for combat, but even they couldn't enter a post exchange to buy coffee or a stamp. Civil rights groups drove home the irony.

In Washington, cheek by jowl with new government buildings, black people lived in shacks. "Colored" and "white" marked public benches. Some department stores, remembers a friend of Vela's, served Negroes only if a white sponsor called in advance. "My maid will be in tomorrow evening for a lamp." Then the prospective buyer had to go to the children's shoe department, where a clerk brought the desired item.

"Middle-class black parents went to great pains to indoctrinate their black children, to mitigate the effects of all this," recalls Eleanor. "They attempted to give you a feeling of specialness." And they laughed over the dinner table about their subversion of whites.

"One of the funniest stories my father told was about how somebody came across one bridge in Washington and said to him, in the deepest Southern accent, 'Boy, which way do you get to this certain place?' And my father said, 'What you do is you take this road right here, and you travel right there, across that bridge.' That was the way to go right back South! He loved to tell that story. He turned the man right around back to where he came from! You could see how few outlets there were for protests."

Civil rights leaders pressed President Roosevelt to open the services and defense firms that advertised, "Negroes hired as janitors." The president, with the fear of powerful Southern Democrats licking at his heels, had opposed all rights legislation, like the antilynching bills introduced almost every year. But when A. Philip Randolph, the legendary organizer of the Brotherhood of Sleeping Car Porters and Maids, threatened a massive march on Washington, "a hundred thousand strong," Roosevelt had a sudden change of heart. One week later, on June 25, 1941, he issued historic Executive Order Number 8802, banning discrimination in government and defense plants. The order also created a monitoring mechanism, the Fair Employment Practices Committee, the forerunner of an Equal Employment Opportunity Commission that Eleanor Holmes would one day head.

In the warm days of June 1941, when the order was announced, Vela Holmes was a printer's assistant in the Bureau of Engraving and Printing, making sixty-six cents an hour to examine crisp new money as it rolled off the press. The young mother worked the evening shift, 3:30 to 11:30 P.M., so she could be home days with her three little daughters: Portia Coleman, born a year after Eleanor, and Nellie Carol, one year later. Vela and Coleman, now a public health inspector, staggered schedules. He also drove a taxi at erratic hours. When work overlapped, they hired care from neighbors.

The growing family moved to a larger apartment at 1424 W Street, Northwest, where Vela and Coleman created a strong family unit that drew into themselves. Though Coleman was often "gone with his buddies," he and his wife played bridge or pinochle with other couples and occasionally saw horse races together. North Carolina cousins complained that Vela rarely brought her children to family reunions and wondered "if the husband has a status thing." Coleman, a proud, protective man, hated to place his daughters in situations of deference to whites, an obedience then required on Deep South trips.

Vela's Washington area relatives ascribed their lack of contact to Coleman's blunt, status-oriented personality; they sometimes visited Vela alone. Many of his local relatives were also put off by what they considered his snobbish attitude, believing that, as a college graduate, he put on airs. And Vela and Coleman *were* upwardly mobile; their choice of church, profession and neighborhood all indicate their relentless climb.

The result was that Eleanor grew up with little connection to most cousins, uncles or aunts. But for a crucial decade her parents created extended family with Grandmother Nellie, Coleman's mother and Grandfather Richard's first wife. In 1942, Coleman and Vela moved to a rented house at 712 Kenyon, Northwest, a neighborhood of well-kept homes where their large backyard met Grandmother Nellie's. She lived with her daughter Selena, also divorced. Eleanor affectionately remembers the warm home of this deeply religious woman, who was "brown like Coleman, dark brown." And "growing up in color-struck Washington, a town known for skin color prejudice, my grandmother would just laugh about how Coleman, my gorgeous, black father, was not going to marry anybody dark-skinned." In a house where Grandmother "didn't resent her color, but laughed at those who did, it was pretty hard for me to be color-struck."

Her beloved grandmother's early training to responsibility, sweetened with the small privileges of power, laid the groundwork for Eleanor's entire life. "That goes back to being a firstborn. You're supposed to take control of events. You're not supposed to let events take control of you." As the oldest of three girls, with no brothers to pluck the leadership role, she was groomed by her grandmother to be the hope of the family. Aunt Selena openly told neighbors and friends, "Eleanor is Mama's favorite."

The training was deliberate.

"My grandmother sent me to the Safeway store a block away. I must not have been more than six, at a time when to get meat you had to go to a long counter and ask for it. I got three lamb chops, brought them home, and she said, 'Well, Eleanor, tell me, did you get good lamb chops?' And I said, 'I certainly did, because when he pointed to one, I told him 'Not *that* one. I want *this* one.' "

For days, whenever Eleanor's grandmother greeted passersby in the evening, as she rocked on her front porch, she responded to their polite queries, "How are you, Miz Holmes?" with a gesture, beckoning them over.

"Come on up here. Do you know what this child did? I sent Eleanor to the store and the man tried to give her a lamb chop that wasn't good. Do you know that this child, only six years old, said she didn't want *this* one, she wanted *that* one.

"Yes indeed," the older woman boasted with a happy laugh, "Only six years old." In the joyful repetition Eleanor learned the assertiveness she was expected to show in public. "Child said she didn't want this one, she wants *that* one." At age six, Eleanor had made a white man in a Safeway do what she said to do.

To this day Eleanor credits her grandmother with formative instruction, carefully delivered in the many hours spent at the "wonderful house" with no toys or television, but "a back porch on which my dolls were kept, and upstairs another porch, enclosed and cool in summer." This grandmother with the "pretty face and soft, wonderful skin, who bragged she had all her teeth until she lost one or two at the end of her life," deliberately molded her favorite grandchild. "I was absolutely groomed, regarded as a source of great pride." Less than a year older than Portia and not three years Nellie's elder, she regarded them as "the kids."

"In the tradition in which my grandmother grew up, the oldest was given great responsibility. I'm telling you, I went over there, pulled up weeds in the garden, swept off the front yard, brushed down the stairs from the second floor to the first floor with a brush and a dustpan." Eleanor used a little shovel to put coal into the furnace by the back door. "Everybody did it. Keeping heat was a major enterprise." Or she ran upstairs to fetch a hat for her grandmother. The reward was a favorite strawberry ice cream cone or a trip to the store with Aunt Selena.

After chores were done, Eleanor sat in the living room and listened to her grandmother hum the old hymns while Aunt Selena played the piano. The sound, carried forward from another time, soothed grandmother and granddaughter alike. Together they sang at the old home church, Mount Mariah Baptist back in Southwest, where they traveled by cab on Sundays. The heavyset woman walked up the church steps laboriously on arthritic legs.

"The emotion of the black community is in the black church," Eleanor remembers, visioning dark pews inside the dim, cathedral-like stately Gothic church. "My grandmother got happy, filled with emotion during the sermon." As choir and congregation sang, the girl added her voice to her aunt's contralto and her grandmother's alto. "I come to the garden alone. While the dew is still on the roses ... And He walks with me, and He talks with me, and He tells me I am His own."

Coleman reinforced Grandmother Nellie's lessons in leadership. When Eleanor or her sister returned from the corner store with a bare loaf of bread or other unbagged item, Coleman chided, "You go back and tell the white man, 'We don't take bread without a bag.' Tell him, 'Don't send any bread that you've paid for here, without putting it in a bag!' " Eleanor reluctantly turned around, demanded her rights, and came back home with the requisite brown bag. Never tolerate less than one's due, she learned the hard way from her father's pride.

Eleanor speaks with great love about this man who stiffened her backbone, even when depicting what she calls his flaws. A "character," Coleman, talented, vocal and insistent, "was quite argumentative with his children, as well as devoted to us," Eleanor says, smiling broadly. "And my mother said I was just like him!" She laughs.

"Undisputed head of the household, his word was the last word. The house that we lived in was chosen by my father, the furniture was chosen by him. He certainly didn't trust Vela's taste. For some good reason. My mother, for example, would put on too much jewelry. 'Please Mother, take that off. You don't need but one of those things on.' I learned everything about taste from him."

The tall, large-boned Coleman, dressed to the nines, was as extravagant as he was witty and playful. When the girls played double Dutch, he'd run out to jump. He'd buy a baby grand piano, opera records and expensive antiques, while Vela bought twenty-five savings bonds a year.

"My mother wore the kind of steadiness that comes from having grown up on a farm; farm life is a very tough life. So I think the hard work part of me has a lot to do with Vela."

Coleman had urban roots and "was at pains to indicate he was a sophisticated man," Eleanor says, decades later mirroring his concern. Her eyes still shine when she describes him: "charming ... elegant ... urbane ... brilliant" and above all, worldly.

"My father was just right for a feminist family. My sense of going through the world and making it on my own comes from my father." Coleman was "forever cuddling, bundling us against the cold," Eleanor happily remembers. "I was wrapped and warm and secure. Whenever he sensed I was cold he would wrap me in greater and greater warmth."

In an effort to polish his girls, Coleman admonished, "See what your mother is doing now, putting milk bottles on the table. That's straight out of North Carolina. We do not do that." When he combed his daughters' hair, they were wreathed in Shirley Temple curls. "My father would take that straightening iron and make something perfect and unique, where our mother would put us in three braids and a barrette."

The young Vela often seemed intimidated by the dapper Washingtonian, yet sometimes she stood her ground. When she inherited a diamond ring after Uncle Henry Fitts died in Baltimore, Coleman shouted, "I'm the one that deserves that ring!" However, she refused to hand it over and wore it, though her husband screamed and threatened, stomping out, slamming doors. He was often contentious, especially after overimbibing, his daughters say. At such moments, Vela "knew how to handle him," says Portia.

But more often, she acceded. When her husband came after she decorated the Christmas tree with tinsel and recast her work, Vela moved silently away, "because he knew just how it should be," Eleanor says sharply. "She didn't react personally! Because we were family. He had artistic talent, an extraordinary aesthetic sense. Where did this taste come from? Probably from being a third-generation urban person. From having been exposed at an early age to taste, something quite possible in Washington. Blacks worked in the White House, in rich people's kitchens and homes." When dinner guests were to arrive, Coleman put the finishing touches on the table, making sure it was set just right.

In the early 1940s, Vela started school part-time while still working at the Bureau of Engraving. Teaching was highly respected though it wouldn't pay more than she already earned. The family always needed cash. Coleman was "not responsible with money, frequenting the racetrack and likely to be out in the street with his sophisticated buddies." Coming up with money for household bills and children's clothes often fell on Vela's shoulders. "We would have been more comfortable had he been better with finances. He took care of the part of the household that didn't involve credit; not only was his own record poor, but at one point he messed up my mother's credit. His father [Richard] helped her with credit. So Coleman bought food and other items where you had to pay cash."

But at five o'clock when the girls were hungry, Vela sometimes said, "Well, we're still waiting for your father to bring home the groceries." Now and then he had them; other times he promised them next day.

"We'd get a little angry at him for being late bringing home the food. But I think of my father and what people go through today who have no father, who don't bring home anything. You know it was a flaw. But he was also very affectionate.

"And he was an extraordinary cook. My mother usually cooked; when he did, it was a feast." In her descriptions Eleanor shares a common bent of daughters, particularly of that period: the tendency to adore a proud and nurturing father while casually accepting an equally devoted, less self-confident mother.

Coleman was the leader, concerned with "knowing which fork to pick up, how to hold our hands around a teacup, and the niceties that young ladies were supposed to do." For both parents, presenting a cultured, dignified appearance was critical, but to Vela internal virtues counted even more. Once when Eleanor's visiting cousin Dolores confided unhappiness with her large feet, her aunt Vela sat her down. "You are lucky to have feet that work. Big feet are a good foundation for a big life. You can't have a big house on a small foundation." Such moral lessons twined, for Eleanor, with the grand gestures of her dashing, brilliant father. Integrity was sacred; so was sophistication and pride.

Her parents' complex relationship also shaped Eleanor's view of marriage. "They were married forty years. That certainly taught me that you didn't have to be alike. They were very different people." Subtly, she absorbed the habit of turning a blind eye to transgressions and accentuating the positive.

In the fall of 1942, little Eleanor, wearing an ironed-to-within-an-inch-of-its-life plaid dress tied with a sash in back, entered kindergarten around the corner at Monroe Elementary. The public laboratory school for Miner Teachers College, it radiated racial pride. Ralph Bunche's daughter had sat in these seats. Role models like General Benjamin O. Davis and Mary McLeod Bethune, "a colored lady that talks like white people," came to speak.

"I remember being very nervous, wanting to do well in school from the beginning." The teachers set high standards, focusing on study and field trips to museums. The children knew they were in segregated schools, but sensed no lack. "Our teachers and parents never portrayed us or themselves as victims."

Every fall teachers sat students down at their desks with used texts from white schools and big soap erasers, announcing, "Let's clean them up!" With elbow grease, brown paper and glue, the students erased marks, made new covers and had new books. But, despite the second-hand texts, "This was a place where people believed that people who segregated us were inferior in some sense. Pitiful and ignorant."

In this environment, where all the students were prepared, Eleanor was more so and willing to prove her point. "I couldn't imagine going to school without doing homework. I never missed a day. You went to school!" Even at seven, classmates remember, she marshaled facts and debated anyone who disagreed, teachers or students. In her brown-and-white saddle shoes and plaits, dressed in cleanly starched dresses—some secondhand from Vela's friend Frances Nails—Eleanor was contentious and insistent. "My mother would say, 'Where did this child come from?' She didn't understand my drive.

"There's a lot to be said for how much life is a matter of will: just deciding it's going to happen and not taking 'No' for an answer.... You were reminded from the time you were a little child that you were in a segregated world, so deal with it—just try to be smarter than the rest."

An early awareness of her ability to mold circumstances to her will came when Eleanor wanted a seventh birthday party. She asked for one, the kind she'd attended at other girls' homes, with singing, presents and cake. Her parents equivocated. "They didn't say No and they didn't say Yes." Taking matters into her own hands, the six-year-old invited friends and cajoled her grandmother, announcing, "There are going to be twelve children." When Grandmother Nellie didn't forbid it either, Eleanor told her friends the time and the place, and had the glorious birthday she had imagined.

Eleanor drew significant insight from this victory, discovering that a wedge could be forced into the smallest opening; determinedly pried, it could open most situations. "I could not have made the ice cream and cake. But I knew there was going to be a cake anyway. I invited the people. It didn't take a lot more. What were they going to do? It was my birthday. Not that there was any permissiveness in my life and family. But I pulled it off."

"My elementary school days were good days," Eleanor would later boast in her eighth grade autobiography. "I remember serving as president of the Glee Club and as president of the Junior Red Cross. I also recall being treasurer of the Student Council, assistant secretary of the citywide Junior Red Cross and a junior librarian. While in elementary school I also won second place in a spelling bee, which was attended by most of the colored elementary schools, junior and senior high schools. I came out of Monroe with honors."

Fifty years later Eleanor sits in her upstairs family room, just off the phone from a constituent call. After working her usual fourteen-hour day, the congresswoman is in her accustomed spot, curled up in an easy chair surrounded by papers, books, pens, telephone. A large television blares nonstop news. "It was so colored," Eleanor comments on her eighth grade essay, "You talked about what you'd achieved, not who you were.

"I grew up before affirmative action. 'You've got to work with what you've got.' That meant education first. A lot of what the white man was doing to you, you could overcome. When we went on trips to public buildings, the teachers would say, 'Now I want to make sure that we behave ourselves, because that's what they say about Negroes, ill-mannered.' They were trying to make us conform to good behavior by invoking a racial stereotype. Well, the stereotype was outrageous, but in a real sense what they said to us had a salutary effect."

Yet there was a heavy cost to constantly proving one's worth. As Eleanor would acknowledge later in a college application, she was a tense child. Dutifully following family and school injunctions to shine, she did, but the price was her peace of mind.

In the strict environment, with dress codes mandating white shirts, ties and dresses, with spotless hallways and neatly clipped grass, Eleanor was an all-A student. "I remember blushing because when they called names to stand up, indicating the child who had done this, that and the other, I stood up a lot and was proud of it. I was told, 'You're supposed to stand up a lot.' "

Pride, discipline, faith and hope held her community together, with common values refracting from home to school. Students were hit with rulers at school for infractions just as at home. "I remember being spanked and switched with a switch from the bush by my parents and grandmother." Accountability was unavoidable. Older students watched younger ones cross streets; misbehavior could rarely be hidden. In Eleanor's close-knit neighborhood, if a child acted suspiciously, someone would come outdoors and ask, "Who is your mother?" Parents were called; concern was palpable.

School assemblies—with the Lord's Prayer, Pledge of Allegiance, flag salute, national anthem, "Lift Every Voice," and appearances by eminent Negroes—embodied the atmosphere. Patriotism, especially during and after World War II, was evidenced in the decision not to call "Lift Every Voice" the Negro national anthem; there should be but one national anthem. "We are Americans." Nonetheless they sang the stirring song so often it was impossible not to know the words by heart.

Whereas a good education was viewed as the ticket to prosperity everywhere in black America, in the District it was more available. Eleanor's pride in her hometown is unmistakable. "If you had to be black in racist America before 1960, a good place to be was Washington." High-caliber teachers with advanced degrees came to this mecca where, uniquely, they were paid as well as their white counterparts. Howard, the flagship university of black America, exerted an umbrella of influence; its scholars, also excluded from white academia, were first-rate. "Growing up black in Washington gave a special advantage. This whole community of blacks was very race conscious, very civil rights conscious."

In this education-rich environment, Eleanor pushed herself and flourished. Like her namesake Eleanor Roosevelt, who believed she was ugly and worked to make up for it by good manners and good works, Eleanor Holmes was convinced she was "not pretty, not light enough and didn't have straight hair, good hair." But at least in Washington, "brains could trump anything, even skin color."

Natural ability imposed hard work. She studied and conquered every spelling, oratorical and Negro history competition in sight, with her sisters following behind to scoop up honors in their classes. A member of all the clubs, often as president, by the time she graduated from Monroe Elementary at eleven, Eleanor was friends with everybody and on her way to being in charge. "Oh, I was a leader in everything, a natural leader."

Just as music had permeated the lives of her ancestors, so did it move through Eleanor's world. "We couldn't go to the Warner Theatre, for God's sake! We couldn't go to Constitution Hall." In Howard University's small chapel, the choir sang Handel's *Messiah* and spirituals in packed Christmas concerts. At school, hymn singing, chorus and Glee Club were daily events. At home, records, singing or the sound of Coleman's piano filled the house. "If you could hum it he'd play it: Gershwin, Rachmaninoff, everything."

The girls took piano and the three sang together, carried by Portia, "the only musical talent among us." The hit song "Now Is the Hour, We Must Say Good-Bye" was a favorite. "There was great regard for the piano as an instrument. Many children took lessons and recitals were common."

But Eleanor did not fritter away hours practicing piano. Instead, she read or, in summer, played outdoors, inventing games with her sisters and friends on the block. "I was a politician from the beginning. I played with everybody. It was important to be liked, very important to be popular. You don't get to be president of the class or an officer in clubs by staying up in your room and not playing any games."

Soon she developed her own routine, arising at 6:30 to take a bath in privacy before others awoke. Then she dashed downstairs for breakfast, a no-frills, self-made meal in the Holmes household. Usually milk on cereal sufficed.

Dinner was family time around an old dining room table picked up on Coleman's antique store wanderings. Sometimes her working parents alternated cooking, but mostly "mother cooked. My father wanted his meals cooked his way. One of the reasons I can't cook is because my father said to my mother, 'I don't want these children cooking for me.' Let me tell you though, he was an extraordinary cook. This was a Renaissance man. If he had been born today, God knows what he could have done."

With the aroma of chicken and potatoes filling the air, the three daughters told about their school days and reported on projects, while they ate with proper "young lady" manners. They also heard and engaged in active political talk. Current affairs—often racial—were thoroughly dissected.

"My parents were always politically conscious and we had a very intellectually alive household. My father was a dyed-in-the-wool New Deal Democrat." Vela, modeling independence to her daughters, "voted on occasion both Socialist and Republican in protest against the Democrats' racial policies."

Food was not overabundant, so the resourceful oldest child figured out early how to get an extra piece of chicken. Since no one liked the neck, she chortles, "I always asked for it, and got it. Just wasn't a lot of meat."

While Portia and Nellie shared a bedroom, Eleanor had her own small room at the front of the house. With the bed and wooden dresser taking up most of the space, Eleanor sat on the bed to do her homework, her thin legs dangling over the side as she sat reading, hour after hour, while her little sisters laughed and played in their room. Devouring fairy tales such as *Hansel and Gretel* and *Rapunzel*, her fertile imagination was nurtured by the rich fantasy world of myth and legend, existing adjacent to the harsher reality of the Negro history that also drew her passionate interest.

"My instincts were broader [than surrounding values]. I don't know if it came from reading. A lot of who I am came from being a first child who learned to think by herself. I embraced the basic black middle-class values, but ultimately rejected the pomp and the imitation of white people. I can only say that I had an inquiring mind and wanted to get way beyond what I could see in my all-black community."

"Part of my individualism, my apartness, began very early in life." Her skeptical approach formed before she was ten. "If you have a curious mind you may be disinclined to take things at face value." As the first child, her responsibility implied thorough investigation: "You'd better know all you can about what lies where you cannot see." Growing up with the mythology of racism around her, the gifted youngster quickly puzzled out the contradiction. Her own lived experience, with well educated parents and neighbors, was utterly at variance with the popular image of unkempt "darkies." Thus she learned the necessity of scanning all popular wisdom, assessing it for a fit with the evidence. And she trusted her own eyes first.

At the same time, "I never wanted to be rejected or alone. I always wanted to be part, if not leader, of what was happening." Simultaneously independent and enmeshed, outside home Eleanor formed a close unit with Portia and Nellie. "No one could say anything about my sisters. Don't talk to me about my sisters." Yet, just as she maintained a zone of privacy with other girls, Eleanor didn't disclose feelings to her sisters, who confided in each other, giggled and "hang on the phone with each other to this day." Eleanor kept doubts deep inside, especially as she grew older and entrusted less of her thoughts to her one confidante, Grandmother Nellie. "You could tell her things. I didn't know where babies came from. She said, 'Babies come in the same way they come out.' It was a startling revelation. Yet somehow immediately comprehensible."

But "part of being the oldest child is you don't go around saying, 'Here are my problems.' " And sharing gushy secrets was hardly suitable for a girl trained by her mother's example to maintain the dignified privacy of her emotions. Nor was it appropriate for a young achiever. Those aspects of her interior life at variance with her public self—her worries, her sorrows—were not on display. "I was a religious child. I would resolve problems, mostly having to do with school, by praying over them and thinking about them."

At home as at school, Eleanor was clear about her rights. The three girls shared one bicycle. When it was Eleanor's turn to ride, if she was inside reading, she still made her younger sisters wait to use it until she finished what she was doing.

"These are the rules," she'd proclaim. "You have to leave the bicycle alone during my time, until your turn." Her sisters argued furiously that they should split up her time. But in the end, the bicycle sat idle while the clock ticked off their big sister's turn.

By the late 1940s, Vela Holmes, like thousands of others, paid $1 annual dues to the NAACP for its "Struggle for Full Emancipation for the American Negro." Legal victories overwhelmed losses. In 1948 the Supreme Court found restrictive housing clauses unconstitutional. Yet real estate agents still showed buyers only "their kind" of neighborhood; banks didn't lend outside racially coded areas. In fact, Washington grew even more segregated. Until the black middle class started to press its new legal advantage, it essentially had to remain where it was, squeezed into narrow corridors like the Northwest area centered around Howard, Miner Teachers College, and, for Eleanor, Monroe and then Banneker Junior High. But dreams were kindled. Coleman, who always had an old car, took his family for Sunday drives through beautiful white neighborhoods and declared that someday they would have a house amongst these fine old trees and large lawns.

The push increased in every sphere.

"You couldn't go into theaters or restaurants outside of U Street, the center of black downtown. There were whole parts of Washington I'd never been inside, like the Capitol, until I came back at age forty to chair the EEOC . . . that's how much of a colony D.C. was.

"All Congress meant to me was [Mississippi Senator] Bilbo on the floor using the word 'nigger.' . . . There wasn't any Congress for me. There was no mayor, no city council, there certainly wasn't a member of Congress. I didn't have any sense of the Congress except as another discriminatory body; every committee was controlled by Southern Democrats. They were sent because of their racism, since blacks couldn't vote. As long as you talked your anti-Negro talk, you were going to be there for life. They were sent back until they gained seniority, whereas Northerners, every once in a while, got thrown out."

Eleanor may not have known about Congress but she was well aware of Mrs. Mary Church Terrell. The tall, regal woman "is who I think of as a Washingtonian. Mary Church Terrell was at once an aristocratic and militant woman, the kind of role model I had for what the civil rights movement should be about. I wanted to enlist in any movement a woman like that was running!"

When Eleanor entered Banneker Junior High in 1949, Terrell was about to make headlines. The eminent educator and rights leader would try, with three others, to eat at Thompson's Restaurant, a cafeteria near the White House. Howard students, including Pauli Murray, had unsuccessfully sat-in there six years earlier.

"We don't serve colored," the manager said once again.

Terrell sued, using the District's 1872 and 1873 open-accommodation laws. For three years a Coordinating Committee for Enforcement of the D.C. Anti-Discrimination Laws sent test-eaters to restaurants. Many opened. When Kresge's didn't, Mrs. Terrell put on her ankle-length fur coat, wrapped her head in a scarf and, cane in one hand, sign in the other, led the first picket line in a snowstorm. In eight weeks, Kresge's capitulated. Then, remembers Eleanor, "Terrell put a picket line around Hecht's department store on 7th Street, because you could go in there, use your charge-a-plate, but couldn't go to the bathroom. That was a consciousness-raising moment for me as a child." At Hecht's, musician Josephine Baker dropped by the picket line. Soon the cafeteria opened up, though without stools, forcing people to eat standing.

Eventually, Thompson's also folded. On June 8, 1953, Chief Supreme Court Justice William Douglas, in a unanimous ruling, affirmed the District's old nondiscrimination laws. When Mrs. Terrell returned to Thompson's, the manager personally carried her tray to the table.

*   *   *

But schools remained segregated. At Banneker Junior High, another prestigious colored school, Eleanor was in the top track with children of doctors and lawyers. The demands were fierce. In this high-pressure environment, Eleanor, while often strained, did what she was used to doing. Her first semester grades—seven As and one B—led the class; her ability to jump out in front of a crowd got her elected president of her class and the Honors Club.

"I have made the decision to become a journalist," she wrote in a school paper, "though knowing that Negroes have not gone in for 'big writing' as yet. That is, writing famous books, working for big newspapers, and play and poem writing is something the Negro has not done on a large scale. This is mainly, I think, because we have not had the opportunity to investigate this profession . . . However, now that we are getting more advantages every day more of us will go into the fields that prohibited us.

"I tried reading when I was four years of age and by the time I was five, it really interested me. To be another Dickens, Longfellow or Alcott is the ambition of every journalist or journalist-to-be. So is it my ambition," she wrote at twelve.

Reflecting the lack of black authors introduced at school, Eleanor didn't mention a desire to be another Richard Wright, though *Native Son* was published ten years earlier and Zora Neal Hurston's novel *Their Eyes Were Watching God,* about a woman's quest, was available.

Eleanor's narrow choice of literary role models was not surprising, for while she sang "Lift Every Voice," had black dolls and studied black heroes, black Washington surrounded its young with white literature, and society bombarded them with white images. Her birthday and Christmas cards depicted white, apple-cheeked girls, mostly blond. School scrapbooks and magazine cutouts all featured whites. The very covers of the scrapbooks came with pictures of teens, pink and smiling, pasting items into *their* scrapbooks. Sketches and models in the newspapers of her colored schools depicted only whites, as did every text she used.

"This was pre–Black Studies!" Eleanor says heatedly. "Nobody read anything but the classics. My dolls were all black because by that time there was a black doll industry. But there was no black ad industry, nobody had us read black literature. There were very few blacks who had been able to be published . . . in the fifties Wright was still a struggling author. Then, it was not exactly what you would expose junior high school students to. There was no breakthrough of that kind until the late sixties.

"Where there was black availability blacks embraced it. *Ebony* magazine, the *Afro* newspaper, black dolls. I'm running out of places that you could buy black things when I name those three."

But if her literary models were monochromatic, her political heroines were diverse: citing Mary Church Terrell as the woman she most admired, she pasted Eleanor Roosevelt's "My Day" columns in her scrapbook. At thirteen she already straddled worlds, retaining her deepest roots in one while getting ready to navigate another.

In the summer of 1950, between seventh and eighth grades, Eleanor attended an almost entirely white girls' camp. Coleman arranged for a friend to meet the gangly thirteen-year-old in New York City, seeing her onto the bus with her suitcase, headed for Fern Rock, a YWCA camp in Bear Mountain, New York.

"I was surprised, because I was desperate to go to this camp. And right away I was very, very homesick." Eleanor was racially self-conscious, as she confided in a letter to a cousin. But the two weeks were extraordinary.

"Made my first white friend, first white child I ever knew, quickly became my best friend at camp. Loved her. We hit it off immediately." For years she would correspond with Lee, from Three Bridges, New Jersey. Eleanor remembers her with a smile fifty years later. "Such a fast friend."

Utilizing a trait that would become lifelong, Eleanor overrode her intense longing for home with action. She organized a fashion show and produced a variety program, including a skit she wrote herself. The sketch, starring "Good Campers" and "Bad Campers," had a moral: cooperate with counselors, walk quietly and promptly, and pass food at meals correctly. "Lazy girls" lounged in the morning, acted rowdy and slid food along the dining table.

Camp letters from home offer further windows into Eleanor's developing values. Coleman's note, written in his elegant script, closed, "Be good. Be sensible. Be a lady and above all you do look out for yourself. Write soon. Yours truly, Daddy."

"Isn't that wonderful?" Eleanor comments today. "I love that 'Be a lady.' It came from having three daughters. My father once told me how to get out of a car with the help of a gentleman. He said, 'To keep him from looking up your dress, look him in the eye as he's helping you out.'

"And 'look out for yourself.' The whole notion was: you couldn't depend on anyone else to look out for you."

In an interview thirty years later, Eleanor would expand on this assumption of self-reliance, calling it critical to her development as a female comfortable with exercising power. "Black women are raised knowing they must work outside their homes to keep their families economically together." Her father enjoined her to the notion; her mother exemplified it. Additionally, she would cite her status as a first-born, with no male siblings who might be favored.

Vela's letters, on the other hand, instructed her daughter to experience a broader world than the northwest corridor of black Washington. "I want you to meet and understand different people. In that way you will find that people are more or less the same. As to the gum, I am sending some but feel that if they do not sell it at the canteen they do not want you to chew it. Please do not chew it where it will annoy other people. All send love to you. Yours always, Mother."

Little sister Nellie also penned a short letter: "I sleep in your bed. I sleep very well. Love, Nellie."

Though Eleanor was a budding class politician, she was also a party girl. Dancing was taught in gym—waltzing, the two-step and square dancing—along with care of teeth and hair. In junior high she began receiving frequent party invitations. "I was the president of the class, so that got you into the social mix, whether or not you were pretty." The small formal invitations, often written in rhyme, flowed weekly, with instructions for dress: "skirt and blouse" or "semiformal wear."

There'll be swimming
Supper at 6
Playing and prancing
Following that—pavilion dancing!
From 3 P.M. to 10
There'll be fun for each
The place? Of course
The Highland Beach.

The notes represented yet another aspect of a culture modeled on that of upper-class whites: the strict, prep school atmosphere, the strong parameters on "respectable" behavior, volunteer work, "coming out parties" and somewhat lavish evening events, often held in rec room basements. Most of those sending invitations were not wealthy; some were the children of Pullman porters or government workers, though others were the offspring of the black elite: doctors, teachers, ministers, or Howard professors.

Eleanor was passionate about dancing, whether slow drag or jitter-bug. At friends' houses she let the music flow through her body, moving to the Sparrows, Temptations and Drifters, all performing locally at the Howard Theatre. "Swing was very athletic and graceful, and always left much room for improvisation." In friends' basements Eleanor wiggled, swayed, and snapped to the pounding piano of young Fats Domino, Ruth Brown's upbeat "Wild Wild Young Men" and King Cole's "Destination Moon." But her favorite group was the Orioles. Their early harmonies—"Crying in the Chapel"—appeared just before the crossover, when whites began to snatch up black music.

A month before her fourteenth birthday the negotiator convinced her parents again. "Hayrides were what people did; that's another one I willed. I had parents who didn't give up a lot of money for that kind of thing: the truck, the hay, and having children over." She got Coleman to borrow a truck; perhaps, she speculates, he liked having her be part of what children of the middle-class strivers were doing. She sent out her mimeographed invitation:

My birthday time has rolled around
It might be hot here in town
So be at my house by the hour of 3
We shall go out into the country-try.
Wear skirts and shirts in a sporty way
We will ride out there in the hay
Tell "Ma and Pa" that you won't be late
For we will be back by 8.
June 16, 1951. Eleanor K. Holmes, 712 Kenyon St., NW

On the appointed day twenty-nine guests jammed the ride. (Little sister Nellie laughs plaintively, "I had to fight my way to get on.") Coleman drove the teens out to then-retired Grandfather Richard's big, sprawling house in rural Silver Spring, Maryland, where few blacks lived in 1951. There, at her formal grandfather's home, they enjoyed food and music, singing and dancing. "Oh boy, that hayride was a high point," beams Eleanor. "The boys; it was terrific. That was the point, sitting back there in the hay with boys."

Eleanor seemed to be everywhere. Known as friendly and witty, if never intimate, her academic ability was complemented by an extroverted personality. The combination of talent, drive and her social needs "set her up for extraordinary leadership," says classmate Annice Robinson-Wagner, who also remembers a tenderness to the young whirlwind.

"Eleanor had a nice concern about you. I can't remember whether it was the time I injured my ankle or whether it was the time that my eye swelled up and closed, but Eleanor insisted on making sure that I got home, walking me all the way to my house.

"I didn't forget that. I thought that was really something. You don't think about those things when you're in high school. You get home the best way you can. But it's another side of Eleanor."

Mostly, however, Eleanor was out leading. One such club was the Junior Elites, who, complete with jackets and other paraphernalia, presented a "beautifully decorated Thanksgiving basket to a lucky family," the *Banneker News* reported. "We were an elite group in the school, the people with the best marks, the leaders." The Junior Elites were in the tradition of those who, struggling to leverage sometimes illusory power, gave themselves royal titles: Nat *King* Cole, *Duke* Ellington, *Count* Basie.

"Blacks do it to this day. People named King and Queen, Duke." Yet these junior high school students did expect to rise. For them such self-naming was not illusion, but preparation for imagining themselves into posts in the new world they could see on the horizon, one in which the barriers that had kept their parents and grandparents out of power seemed sure to fall. They were primed to help bring the hurdles down.

Eleanor experienced her first electoral battle when, as an eighth grader, she managed the campaign of two students running for Student Council. In this hotly contested election, Eleanor's carefully scripted speech to a school pep assembly prefigured a lifetime of preparation for public addresses. She didn't attack, but praised her opponents. "It must be a hard decision for you to make up your minds as to whom to vote for . . . I am sure Banneker has not seen a better group of candidates. Yet one team stands out, Smith and Wines. . . . Just as we think of Banneker as the best junior high in the city, we would most certainly want only the best Student Council Officers."

A week later, the front page of the *Banneker Newsletter* showed the tall, willowy Eleanor, dressed in bobby socks and plaid dress, hair pulled back with barrettes, reaching over to shake the hands of her candidates. It was her first campaign victory.

Eleanor also honed her journalistic skills, writing a short biography of astronomer Benjamin Banneker, "a free Negro who died in 1806, and a landowner at a time when nearly all of his race were held in slavery. Not only did this cruel and inhuman system offend his sensibilities as a citizen, but it dealt him a great personal disaster." The woman Banneker loved was a slave barred from marrying him and "she destroyed herself," Eleanor concluded, having read the tragic tale for Negro History Week on WOOK radio.

She herself had heartbreak. Her beloved grandmother was stricken with cancer. All that winter of 1951 Eleanor came home every day after school to sit with Grandmother Nellie until Aunt Selena returned from work.

"I would sit there and read books," she says sadly almost fifty years later. "I always loved her and she doted on me, so I didn't think that was very much to do." When Nellie Coleman Holmes died in February, the family laid her out in her living room. With the fragrance of lilies and other aromatic flowers wafting through the familiar room, the fourteen-year-old was overcome by loss. For years, the scent of funeral flowers stayed with her. "I was old enough to understand death, but I was not ready." Already adept at solitary coping, she grieved alone.

In her ninth grade spring, Eleanor participated in a milestone event, traveling with a student delegation to a Columbia University Scholastic Press Association Convention. Addressed by a *New York Times* editor, the event offered roundtables and made available cultural events closed to her at home: a New York City Ballet, *Swan Lake,* and Cole Porter's new musical, *Out of the World.* Taking to heart Vela's advice to expand her world, she even managed a whirlwind tour that included a trip to Macy's.

The highlight was a television interview by Edward R. Murrow. Her teacher, Ms. Brooks, chose Eleanor as the black child who would literally represent the race, giving her the first in a lifetime of Sunday morning news show appearances.

"If your name was in the telephone book, you got a call from Coleman Holmes to look at Edward R. Murrow at ten o'clock. 'Eleanor is going to be on national television.'

"Do you realize what it was for a colored child to be on national television? Whenever there was a colored person on television for two seconds, shaking her booty or God knows what, 'Negro on television!' Everybody ran! You would jump out of the bathtub. So to see a familiar black face! It is hard to overemphasize what that would have meant in black Washington. National television? You couldn't get on the *local* news unless you stabbed somebody.

"After everybody he ever heard of, and some he had not, heard from my father, my family gathered in the dining room where the television stood. Then I saw my ugly self on television. I'd never seen anything that ugly in my life! They had on all the white kids. And I was the only black child, speaking up, but oh I was ugly."

Eleanor would forever after believe she looked terrible on television, but the vehemence of her response can only lead to speculation about whether the poison of Washington's color-struck message had seeped in, despite her family's efforts at rebuttal. Eleanor herself denies a connection, pointing out that "the evidence is all the other way: I married a dark man. My father was dark. My relationship to my grandmother, and everything I've done, when young or old, contradicts this armchair analysis." Yet she would continue to regard herself as different and unattractive, needing talent to be accepted.

So she persevered, leading Honors Club, reporting for the *Banneker Newsletter* and writing plays with equity themes, such as the value of the United Nations. Winning honorable mention in a *Scholastic Magazine* contest, her essay "Men Are Brothers" gave early indication of her lifelong philosophy: "I never hated a man I really knew; I never knew a man I really hated." Today Eleanor says, "I was steeped from the beginning in the belief that the superior position is one of no hatred. So if you engage in hatred, you lower yourself. We were in this way superior to white folks because we would not succumb to race hatred. . . . When I see blacks doing to them what they're doing to us I remember, 'No, no. That's what we always said we wouldn't do! Only white people do that.'"

In June 1952 Eleanor graduated from Banneker with General Scholastic Honors and the prestigious Danforth Foundation Award, given annually to a boy and girl with "outstanding qualities" in each Washington junior high. The prize was a small red leather book, *I Dare You,* whose motivational themes echoed those she'd gotten all her life: "Stand Tall, Think Tall, Smile Tall, and Live Tall." Opening with a Herman Melville quote, "What I've dared, I've willed;/And what I've willed, I'll do!" the challenge to Be Somebody reverberated from every wall of her life. Fifty years later the inspirational little book still resides on the bookshelf in her family room library.

In the fall of 1952 Eleanor entered Dunbar, a large four-story brick building fronted by trees, with high wooden windows half-covered by white-and-green window shades. The first U.S. public colored high school, it had graduated a Who's Who of distinguished black professionals. Many teachers had doctorates, some traveling abroad to gain advanced knowledge of their subjects. Brilliant scholars rebuffed at white institutions found a home at Dunbar.

"Anybody could go there," Eleanor beams. "If you aspired to go to college, you went there. It all was based on aspiration; and then it was tracked." While similar schools in all the border states existed to develop the "talented tenth," this one was famous. Families like Vela's cousins, the Ashes, moved to Washington so they could send their children to what was essentially a public prep school. Ninety percent of its graduates went to college; all the Ivy League schools recruited.

"Dunbar was, in effect, a 'white' school in a segregated system," says psychologist Dr. Kenneth Clark. "Washington had a class system among blacks of different shades and economic backgrounds. . . . Dunbar is the only example in our history of a separate black school that was able, somehow, to be equal."

"Out of slavery, lighter people got a head start," Eleanor says. "They were often house Negroes with kinship to the white families, so they sometimes knew how to read and write. The people who had done very well in the South often came from half-white families or families where some very light-skinned black had married some other very light-skinned black. A lot of the descendants of these folks ended up at places like Dunbar.

"So what? Nobody kept dark-skinned blacks out! People sometimes separated themselves out. Maybe they didn't feel comfortable being with all those high-yellow types. But by the time I got there, you could be nappy-haired; one of the brightest people in my class was a little, short, very dark girl with short hair. Nobody kept her out . . . By then, if anything, very light-skinned people, straight-haired types were in a minority."

The school was rich with history. Frederick Douglass's grandson taught American history, using his grandfather's notes. The list of graduates was a Who's Who of black "firsts" like Senator Edward Brooke and Judge Robert Terrell.

In the stiffly competitive environment, the teenager in sweater sets was in constant motion. Stepping onto the stage of a class assembly in loafers and pleated skirt, she urged classmates to "make the '55 class the best to ever enter or leave Dunbar. We can do it!" To make their mark, she warned, using words she must have often applied to herself, they'd better "get on kick now, start doing something right away."

She exhorted students from junior highs all over the city, "Get to know each other," and told them how. "Your section [home room] presidents will assist you, and there will be sophomore get-togethers. Unity and friendliness within the class is the first step we can make in order to gain recognition as an outstanding class at Dunbar." She boasted: "We are not really as unimportant as we think . . . We accept the challenge! We are going to do greater things than the great things they expect of us . . . Get spirit!"

She suggested a talent show fund-raiser and ended with appeals that anticipated her later can-do speeches. "Come on kids, get with it! Latch on, start the ball rolling! Participate, get to know classmates! Let's get going, sophomores!"

At a school where everyone wanted to get A's, Eleanor got straight A's her first semester. "Eleanor was driven," Annice Robinson-Wagner says. Oratorical competitions were a featured highlight and, like her father, Eleanor compelled an audience. In one contest, Annice remembers Eleanor, dressed in saddle shoes, circle skirt and short-sleeved blouse, eloquently comparing the Negro's ascent to climbing a ladder. In another contest Eleanor debated Home Rule: Should District citizens have the right to vote? Would that mean a change in the Constitution? She cared about winning, but was also fascinated by the issues.

During her second fall at Dunbar Eleanor left her familiar Kenyon Street home, moving to 4120 5th Street, NW, in a blizzard. The swirling snow left the indelible image of her father standing just inside the door, carefully wiping wet snow from each piece of furniture as it was carefully carried into the house.

Coleman would soon be the only person on 5th Street to firmly remove any vestige of Southern culture. He took off his porch, thereby creating "a sophisticated townhouse, the first on the block, way ahead of his time." Vela did not object although she was sole owner of their home; she did not trust Coleman to co-own it, and he was unable to get credit.

The Holmes family moved just after the first wave of Negroes pushed north in Washington. Though the newcomers carefully tended their long-awaited homes, whites fled to the suburbs. The exodus meant the city population, and tax base, shrank. Yet the city remained a gateway for job-seeking Southern families moving north, and began its transformation to becoming blacker—and poorer.

Coleman and Vela would remain in their 5th Street home until well after all their daughters left home. When they moved in 1971 to 1365 Iris Street, NW, into a house that Vela again would buy on her own (sharing the deed with Portia), they would finally live in "the most up-scale part of black Washington, the Gold Coast. And that," says Eleanor, "is the staircase of upward mobility of my family."

"Service was taught at an early age, right in school. And that led straight into the civil rights movement, because service was related to consciousness-raising about race." Eleanor fulfilled her service by teaching Sunday School at St. George's; she, Nellie and Portia often rode the bus over to 2nd and U Street, NW, since their parents rarely attended church. She raised cookie sale money as secretary of Freedmen's Hospital's Junior Auxiliary; president of the Coleman and Mary Jennings Community Service Club, she planned annual outings for orphans. Business manager for the Junior Elites and Dunbar representative at youth conferences, Eleanor even appeared on television when students questioned members of Congress. Her civic life at sixteen was a teenage version of the hectic adulthood she would soon configure.

During her last year at Dunbar Eleanor typed a three-page memo—"IMPORTANT NOTICE!"—to the Junior Elites, castigating members for allowing the club to become dormant. Demolishing excuses, she admonished, "Only 2 members took the part of the [College Board] test that requires outside study" and stated her goal: "to awaken members and officers to the responsibilities they agreed to accept." "What YOU can do" included the reprimand, "By all means, don't just sit and stare, doing nothing and showing no interest in the situation."

The memo closed, "We hope to have a meeting Saturday at which we expect perfect attendance." She created written accountability in the form of two columns, under the heading, "Please Sign." One side, which every girl initialed, read, "I agree with the points as stated in this notice and I shall give my cooperation." The other side, which remained blank, said, "I disagree with this notice. (State disagreement.)" Thus the young litigator compelled the recharging of the Junior Elites.

While Eleanor took community service and schoolwork with a seriousness few could match, invitations for evening parties flowed. "I was very much of a party girl. Wanted to go to every party every Friday night, every Saturday night. I was one of the best dancers Dunbar had ever seen. Ask my sisters. Out-dance them any day! They ain't got no rhythm," she teases.

"I felt I wasn't as pretty, so I'm sure that encouraged me to reinforce my other traits." She believed her compensatory talents—politician, scholar and "great outgoing qualities"—were proven when "a quite studious girl like me could be elected president of the class." Her dancing skills made her socially desirable, "though not nearly on the level of success of the average pretty high school girl."

Still, though Eleanor wanted popularity, she dropped one boyfriend because, she told Portia with no display of sorrow, "He has no goals." A breakup with a previous boyfriend had also elicited no visible emotion, though privately, Eleanor says, she was heartbroken. The life of a young woman on her particular fast track, when change was coming any day, allowed no time for weeping.

"I remember precisely where I was," she recalls Monday, May 17, 1954. "It was afternoon. We heard the chime that told us there would be an announcement. I remember the voice of the principal, Mr. Charles Lofton, interrupting class to tell us news of major importance. We had the right to go to any school now. We were stunned, then elated. And I remember believing that the world had changed, literally had changed."

The Supreme Court declared in *Brown* v. *Board of Education,* a case developed over years of late night labor by legal scholars at Howard and the NAACP, that segregated schooling, "separate but equal," was unconstitutional.

"I remember seeing a teacher, a woman who had taught black children for fifty years in the public school system, just breaking down crying, saying that she had lived to see the day segregation was declared illegal."

The historic importance was driven in by the mesmerizing, if unnerving, sight of strict teachers sobbing. "How things had changed, specifically, I did not know. Who could foresee that three years later Martin Luther King would lead a bus boycott that would ignite an entire movement?"

Ten years later Eleanor would reminisce in the Sunday *New York Herald Tribune,* "A joyful undertone swept through the dingy classrooms where so many colored children had come to learn what they could. Now this old school, named for a Negro poet, had been outlawed. Tomorrow, I thought, our needlessly separate world would finally dissolve itself into America."

The following spring, Eleanor's last in high school, the Willard Hotel downtown opened up and a group of Dunbar debutantes came out at a grand ball, complete with formal gowns, elbow-length gloves, corsages, and glossy photographs.

"That was black middle-class society imitating white society. But it was very exciting." Eleanor came out as a debutante at an even more select event: one of thirty young women, she was presented on April 15 by the Bachelor-Benedict Club at their annual Debutante Cotillion. Mothers were instructed to wear pastel gowns and fathers white ties for the formal presentation. At midnight the young women proceeded in a long march led by the president of the club. Eleanor, hair straightened by Coleman to perfection and dressed in long formal gloves and floor-length evening dress, was applauded in her introduction to black society, and danced until two.

That same year, there were still many places in Washington, like the White Tower, where the young debutante could not eat.

Eleanor knew she was going to college. "I came out of the womb believing you're supposed to go. That was not anything you even blinked at. The only question was, 'God, which of these schools to go to?'

"It was always the notion of, 'What is the very best you can do?' Much that has propelled my life has really been a sense that you must be treated equally." She explains her desire to leave the area, unlike her sisters who came after her. "Sometimes on a personal level perhaps I've been too insistent, to put it politely." But her father had provided an indelible example. "He brought home his insistence upon being treated with respect . . . a black man insisting in every way you could find upon your dignity." Her male classmates "went everyplace: to Amherst, to Harvard, to Yale." The women attended Vassar, Bryn Mawr and other women's colleges.

Eleanor's family finances allowed little contribution, so just as she had willed a seven-year-old birthday party into being, she found the means to go away to college. The Ford Foundation, discovering that almost no blacks attended white colleges, funded the National Scholarship Service and Fund for Negro Students. Naturally, it came to Dunbar.

Eleanor's friend Elizabeth Ann Walton had a sister at Antioch College in Yellow Springs, Ohio. The small liberal arts school, with an innovative work-study program, had few Negro students, but its high academic standard, offbeat reputation and social consciousness attracted Eleanor. Antioch represented a breakaway from the world of Washington's black bourgeoisie, although Eleanor acknowledges she had "partaken of its advantages."

Her parents, while strongly invested in middle-class dreams, encouraged independence. Both finished college at night, though "Daddy never reached his entire promise." Obtaining a law degree, Coleman never took the bar. Though paying dues to Sigma Delta Tau legal fraternity, he didn't practice law, and remained at his government job.

"You didn't see many black lawyers of his generation doing anything except low-level criminal law, and that may have deterred him from doing something with a law degree. He may have thought that by the time he got out of law school there would be more opportunities. But there weren't."

Her mother, receiving a bachelor's from Howard, had passed the District teachers' test, eliciting shouts from one end of the block to the other.

"Miz Holmes passed her exam!" She went on to establish a solid teaching career.

Eleanor had watched both parents aim high, with contrasting results. But their deep belief in schooling took root in this daughter of a family whose members, she wrote in her college application, "have striven for and obtained education against tremendous odds."

Although "my parents would not have chosen Antioch, nor did they oppose it." So rather than select "the traditional woman's or eastern college to which people like me often aspired, a school whose name would be instantly recognized," Eleanor applied to Antioch. "I anticipated, based on the way finances were when I was a child, I would have trouble getting the full freight. One of the main reasons I chose Antioch was that the work-study plan would enable me to earn money."

She was briefly angry at her father because, "frankly, I thought they could afford to give me more if he had been contributing his share. But you know, I didn't have time for that. I had to go out and find a way." With her mother's practicality she moved on, applied for scholarships, and soon committed to Antioch College.

When Eleanor left Dunbar in 1955 as a member of its last segregated class, she left a world about to vanish. With integration, suddenly there was a dispersal of the tight-knit community. Students and faculty scattered to different schools and the focus was no longer all in one place. Nellie went to Roosevelt, the high school nearest home. The sense of excellence, the competition and the spirit of the race that had combined to help produce a remarkable generation, fragmented.

People began to rely less on each other. Instead of doing things in the community, they wanted to get out of it, because now they could. As theaters, restaurants and shops opened up along with new neighborhoods, the thriving U Street business district began a decades-long decline. Dunbar students just a year behind Eleanor went to formerly all-white schools and were amazed at the laxity. White students chewed gum, talked in class and were disrespectful to teachers. Nor had they ever heard "Lift Every Voice and Sing." And so, with the passing of segregation went some black traditions of excellence. While some now mourn the demise, Eleanor scoffs, "I'm not romantic about segregation. I don't believe the Lincoln Theater—or the Booker T—was owned by black people.

"That kind of nostalgia can be debilitating. What price that kind of excellence? You have to ask yourself what exactly was lost? The endless

blacks locked out of what might have been? There's a failure to understand history as organic and the world as always becoming.

"Each period produces its own huge challenges. The breakup of segregated excellence can be lamented only in the sense that you look back
and honor those who put together excellence in a segregated environment. That kind of nostalgia keeps you from coping, unprepared to
move into the complications of a new period."

But in 1955, when Eleanor was leaving, she didn't turn back to look
at the world that was fading, for better and for worse. Her eyes were set
on a future she hoped to help create.

When the determined eighteen-year-old was about to leave home for
college she started out the door without a farewell to her sisters. Her
father, appalled, told Portia and Eleanor, who were standing near each
other, "Say good-bye." The two undemonstrative sisters did just as he
instructed. "Good-bye," they said, without touching or kissing, as
Eleanor walked out the door.

CHAPTER 3

Far from U Street

You don't so much fit in as you jump in.
ELEANOR HOLMES NORTON

On their drive to National Airport, Eleanor and her parents talked about what to expect. Coleman, "a man of many words," steadily conversed. As they parked the car, he prompted his eldest daughter to "be careful" on her first airplane trip and upon arrival at Antioch.

When they reached the plane Coleman looked for the pilot. "It's my daughter on this plane, on her way to Antioch College," he told the startled man. "I want you to know it as you take off. She's never been on a plane before and I want to make sure she gets back." The pilot agreed to keep his eye on the college-bound teen.

Thus safely shepherded and sent off with a final example of how to take charge, Eleanor, clad in a new navy blue dress, left her parents' embrace, nervously entered the plane and found her seat.

When she stepped off in Ohio she was bound for Yellow Springs, at the heart of the American counterculture. Founded in 1852, even the college's site was selected for its liberal leanings: the abolitionist town was a stop on the Underground Railroad leading from the slave states of Kentucky and Virginia to Canada. During the Civil War, when Richard John Holmes was still a fugitive in Washington, the trustees resolved that "Antioch College cannot, according to the charter, reject persons on account of their color." While not always honoring their mission, its intent was clear, and Antioch pioneered when it did take Negro students.

The school was progressive in every aspect: at the college's first commencement, three women were among the fifteen graduates. In the 1920s the school piloted alternating work and study periods ("cooperative education") and in the 1930s created student governance. Stating

"The primary mission of Antioch College is to empower students," the college was a magnet for rebels.

In 1955, Eleanor's experience with white people was limited to her two-week summer camp stint. Arriving at the virtually all-white college, she uncharacteristically confided to a friend at home that, again, she felt "very self-conscious about being a Negro." Aware in the cafeteria with wall-to-wall windows that "I was the only Negro, I was very sensitive to being in a small minority for a long time at Antioch." In the low brick library she seemed at first too timid to ask for help, according to later campus legend. Eleanor stoically searched the card catalogue alone until she was successful. However, ascribing her reticence to timidity was probably inaccurate. A proper young Negro woman schooled in careful presentation of self did not request assistance; a Dunbar graduate maintained face.

"I couldn't get out there and fall on myself," Eleanor admits. Too many believed in her. Like many of the hardworking superachievers of her generation and beyond, she carried an entire family and community. If this young woman didn't know something, she faked it. The attribution of Eleanor's reserve to shyness may be emblematic of misread cultural cues she and her fellow students sometimes exchanged. But she did appear "quiet" to many during those first months. Forced for the first time to measure herself against well prepared white students, many from New York, she initially felt out of her depth culturally, coming from what she scoffs was then "a one-horse Southern town."

The pressure to succeed had already exacted a toll.

"One of my weak points which I have steadily improved since I was a child in elementary school," Eleanor wrote in her college application, "is a tenseness from too great a desire for perfection. I am not, by any means, as tense as I once was."

College letters of recommendation confirmed Eleanor's stress: a Dunbar teacher noted that "at the beginning of the year she seemed over-anxious to succeed, but with increased confidence she has lost this tenseness and self-assertiveness." A summer employer commented, "because of her will to be a perfectionist she has a tendency to become depressed if her undertaking does not meet the standards she sets. Therefore her leadership ability is handicapped, due to the fact that she cannot . . . accept the fact that the other person has done his best."

Eleanor had dutifully added to her list of flaws, "I do not feel that I am reserved enough in expressing myself. I am sometimes too frank." That opinion would soon be shared by one Antioch employer, who commented in an evaluation that Eleanor resented being shown her mistakes and didn't hesitate to display her displeasure.

Yet despite her initial nervousness and occasionally sharp tongue, the young woman made her way on the leafy campus, impressing her peers, as she had in high school, with her drive and clear goals. The setting, with faculty on a first-name basis, allowed her curiosity free rein.

"What impressed me was Antioch's rejection of the dominant political and social culture, and its highly charged intellectual atmosphere. As I embraced the environment, being in a small racial minority became less a matter of distinction or distraction." At a conservative time, with a national atmosphere poisoned by McCarthyism and fifties conformity, Antioch's openness to a full spectrum of ideas gave vital nourishment to a young woman craving new experiences. The probing questions posed by irreverent faculty, who had just endured a congressional investigation of their "nest of free love and Reds," offered thrilling explorations of proscribed views.

Suddenly Eleanor mingled with students who grew up with access to major museums, the Metropolitan Opera, art, live theater—the best. Langston Hughes had come to the District, giving poetry readings. But even with Howard University, Washington didn't have the theaters of Harlem or the mainstream institutions—opera and great museums—of a Chicago or New York. The vibrant U Street area was just "one little street that went from Georgia Avenue to 14th Street. You're not talking about the whole wide world here.

"I have to give Dunbar credit, though. It prepared me for whatever I would meet. I never had a moment of thinking, 'Can I do this?' "

Eleanor was soon wrapped in a social circle. Later she would remember college days fondly and wistfully as a time with "friends like I haven't had since." Rooming in a small freshman house, Norment II, on the edge of campus, Eleanor was soon part of a close-knit, otherwise all-white hall. The little wooden building, with its homelike feel, fostered intimacy. In one late-evening discussion, Eleanor remembers a traumatic moment.

"Somebody said, 'Six million Jews were killed.' It was mentioned in passing, in a way that assumed everyone was aware of it."

Sitting on the floor, leaning her elbow on a bed, "It struck me like a thunderbolt because I didn't know it. I was struck dumb. It was inconceivable that 6 million people could die like that, civilians, but the fact that I didn't know it and was at the top of my class at Dunbar High School, that's what struck me. I looked around; I was the only one astonished by that. It drove home how sequestered had been my segregated world and my education."

A Norment hallmate, Shelly Eisenberg, from a self-described "New York left-wing working-class Jewish background," befriended the Washingtonian with the twin sweater sets. The two each offered the other a decidedly new perspective. At a time when women rarely created autonomous life agendas, Eleanor impressed Shelly with her drive and organization. "Eleanor knew what she was going to do and there was nothing that was going to stop her."

Shelly, a graduate of New York's Music and Art High School, introduced her friend to progressive ideas and groups like the Socialist Discussion Club. Eleanor had grown up with race pride and an awareness of racial injustice; Antioch expanded her understanding to broader concepts of equality and a range of remedies.

"Folk singing was ubiquitous throughout the campus; you sang folk songs even at meetings. I lost track of my own popular music that I loved, my black music that I later returned to. It was not a part of campus life. The music of my community was music that virtually required dancing, and that kind of dancing wasn't done on campus."

Instead, long-haired, black-clad bohemians led students in "This Land Is Your Land," union songs and long ballads of heartbreak. Trios played recorders. And the dancing was international folk.

On Friday nights "absolutely, folk dancing. That was the place to be." Outside on Red Square, a brick patio adjacent to a dorm, swaying bodies danced the night away. Students twirled their partners to great leaping polkas or stamped their feet in line dances.

"I felt about folk dancing the way I did about fast dancing in the District. When you hear a few bars you get up as if on a signal. If you didn't know the step you looked at the next person. Folk dancing was another way to move. It had its own rhythms and gyrations and extraordinary variety. I could easily get the step before the dance was over."

A record player plugged into the dorm next door played circle dances or the foot-stomping "Yellow Dog Rag." And although "it was a very white place, with very few blacks," the dancer from Dunbar adapted, leaving behind the Orioles and Faye Adams for the *hora*, Eastern European line dances and the Greek *miserlu*.

Thoroughly enjoying it all—the unfamiliar music, the intellectual discussions, the challenge—the gangly teenager focused her energies, determined "to make something of myself," as she wrote. Eleanor did not dwell on self-reflection. If she did, she might lose her sense of purpose, like many classmates who floundered in Antioch's unaccustomed freedom as they struggled to "find themselves." Coming from a family, a people, and a place that refused to "dwell," Eleanor's purpose was clear: achieve, advance the race and "do something worthwhile for humanity. There's so much around me to be done. Surely there is something I can do that would really benefit society," she wrote in a Life Aims essay. Deviation from her goal of service could waste the years she'd spent; she kept her mind clear of extraneous concerns and concluded, "whatever I set my mind to do, I can."

But she did allow herself to be influenced. She had seen friends' older siblings go away to college and noticed, to her disdain, that "most came back much like they went." As she strolled across the broad green lawns of the lovely campus day after day, Eleanor was ready to shift her views. And she did. The eighteen-year-old freshman sporting a white leather jacket with DEBS across the back, a carryover from the Junior Elites, soon evolved into the combat jacket–wearing chairman of the Socialist Discussion Club.

"Antioch pushed me, allowed me to push toward my more radical self, the part that was already very skeptical about middle-class values. There was a kind of black bourgeois approach to the world, where the next step in life is orchestrated, you were going to marry somebody successful. . . . The black middle class was narrow, proper, and unadventuresome, and I did not want to relive it."

At Antioch Eleanor found affirmation for her intimation that there was more to life than material things. Her justice concerns implied alliance with, rather than differentiation from, the ordinary Negroes from whom middle-class blacks often tried to escape. Eleanor explicitly began to discard bourgeois values of a "good" life. But while she rejected materialism, some middle-class elements would remain. She would always maintain a large zone of privacy and shrink from ever "having my business in the street."

After Eleanor was in college just six weeks a defining public event occurred. Travel for black Americans had often been difficult, even dangerous; desegregating public transportation carried a special historical charge. A hundred years before, Sojourner Truth had refused segregated treatment on Northern streetcars.

On a cool December day in 1955, the first of the month, as Mrs. Rosa Parks rode a Montgomery, Alabama, bus filling rapidly with whites, the driver routinely called back to several "nigrahs" to stand so that a white man could sit. When they didn't rise, he turned.

"You'd better make it light on yourselves and let me have those seats."

The others moved but Mrs. Parks remained while the driver left the bus. He returned with two policemen, who promptly took her to jail. Friends posted bond and this trained activist contacted her wide circle of friends, including the ready-to-go members of the Women's Political Council and an NAACP official. Four days later a citywide boycott began.

"Something different about America began to happen when the black people of Montgomery refused to board buses under circumstances that stripped them of their human pride and dignity. Americans—first blacks and then others—began to see that offenses *against* them would be rectified only *by* them, that violations of their rights would probably continue until they, themselves, took militant initiative.

"There was a cumulative effect here. They're not lonely acts that make history move. If Rosa Parks had sat down in a bus in 1945 instead of 1955 she might not have gotten out of Montgomery jail. There are moments you can light a spark and moments you can't. People get to the point where they are because events drive them that way and bring out what was always there. The ripeness of history is central to how social action takes place and presses forward."

After *Brown,* sit-ins and countless other victories had fed a growing conviction that racist laws could be changed. Independence movements in India and Africa inspired hope. Artists—Harry Belafonte, Sidney Poitier, Lena Horne and Marian Anderson—were breaking through; and a political infrastructure—the NAACP and CORE—was ready to mobilize. After President Truman's integration of the armed services, pressures grew for broader integration.

"Finally there was a critical mass of events that joined with the will that was always there. The black people of Montgomery, Alabama, took a step which set America on a new course." Until they could ride buses freely, black citizens waited for car pools, pumped up old bicycles or walked miles to jobs and schools. Within days, the boycott was almost total. "It was the first large-scale protest by blacks against the nation's oppressive racial caste system. Southern Jim Crow was shattered beyond repair."

The boycott was led by twenty-six-year-old Reverend Martin Luther King of the Dexter Avenue Baptist Church, who inspired nightly mass meetings, where singing and preaching raised peoples' spirits. Utilizing Ghandian philosophy introduced by organizer Bayard Rustin, King stretched the boycotters' idea of their purpose: not only did they stay off city buses to fight for their own rights, "but for all the people of Montgomery, black and white." The nonviolent marchers were spurs who would trigger America to fulfill its promise of brotherhood.

Despite the burden placed on a population that could ill afford to miss work, almost fifty thousand people boycotted for twelve long months, through summer heat and the chilly rains of fall. The country, electrified by the spectacle of unity in a major city, poured in support; Duke Ellington and Harry Belafonte performed at a huge New York rally. At Antioch, the college NAACP chapter led by Eleanor went to work.

"There were no other organizations like it on campuses. It was the place from which people engaged in civil rights." Students set up tables in front of the "caf," raising money for bicycles and a car for boycotters. They stood in late spring afternoons and then in fall when days grew short and cool, handing out mimeographed articles, asking for coins to drop into cans. The chapter requested support from the school's Community Council and sent a sizable contribution to Montgomery.

The boycott also inspired local actions. In spite of its liberal history, Yellow Springs, located in southern Ohio not far from Kentucky, had only recently integrated. Even the Little Art Movie Theater, showing must-see foreign films for left-leaning students, had a rope down its middle until 1952, three years before Eleanor arrived. The rope came down after an integrated group—townspeople, Antioch and nearby

Wilberforce College students—walked in together and sat randomly on both sides of the color-dividing cord.

Eleanor, "speeding a mile a minute," says one college friend, gathered a few students to plan a sit-in at a restaurant in Xenia, a particularly segregated town nearby.

"But when we showed up," Eleanor laughs ruefully, "they heard we were coming and served us." The surprised students, not sure how to celebrate such an easy victory, ate and scurried back to campus.

On November 13, 1956, the Supreme Court ruled: people could sit freely on buses. "It was a defining experience of my life," Eleanor would later write about this opening of the mass movement for civil rights. "For my father, the historical moment had been the Great Depression; for my grandfather, Reconstruction; for my great-grandfather, who walked away from slavery in Virginia and began our family in Washington, it was the Civil War."

On her college application Eleanor had written, "My interests tend toward writing, languages and politics." But by her first year she wanted to be a doctor, because, she wrote in her Life Aims essay, her father wished it. An Antioch co-op job counselor confirmed in written notes, "Her father apparently has a good deal to say in her plans." Independent though he wished her to be and fight with him though she might, Coleman's stamp of approval was important. "And then," Eleanor laughs, "every little smart middle-class black kid wanted to be a doctor."

In line with her pre-med plans, Eleanor chose a first co-op job—set up by Antioch—as an attendant at New York City's Montefiore Hospital. Just three months after she entered Antioch, on a bitter day in January 1956, Eleanor took the bus from Washington and went directly to the home of an elderly widow.

"My father found a woman at 112th Street who lived by herself in a wonderfully neat apartment." Eleanor arrived at "one of those Harlem apartments with a long hall and rooms off to the side." Her tiny windowless room was tucked away at the end of the long dark hallway, yet she remembers, "my future seemed so bright that every time I came into the apartment it seemed a bright and cheery place, even though in any real sense it was located on anything but the sunny side of the street."

On her first day she learned to catch the D train for the Bronx.

"Comfortable oxfords an asset," she would recommend to future Antiochians for, dressed in a green and white uniform, Eleanor spent eight hours on the hospital's dirty work: emptying and washing bedpans, making beds. But this mostly Jewish men's ward was a fascinating, unfamiliar environment for the eager student.

"A wonderful black nurse, super-efficient," she chuckles, "washed a black man who then died, and a Jewish man said, 'You washed him to death.'"

The startled Eleanor burst into laughter at this unfamiliar humor. Learning to savor "the wonderful quick Jewish wit of the old men," she describes "the quickness, the aptness, always to the point. I first learned the word 'kvetch' and still use it. It seemed the perfect rendition of what it was trying to convey." She cherished this humor, so different from the repartee she'd grown up with, for "nothing can hit the target like black wit." But what greater contrast than "to have graduated from Dunbar in June, and in January here I am in a ward of old Jewish men at Montefiore Hospital. That was an education in and of itself."

Taken on by the staff, they even brought her into the operating room dressed in scrubs and mask, and gave her a box to stand on so she could watch a long surgery. "There I was bobbing in the back," she recalls with delight. During an eight-hour heart operation the patient's heart briefly stopped beating; Eleanor reported the dramatic procedure to Antioch as "an awesome spectacle and unforgettable feat."

Another joy was the meals. "You could go downstairs and eat all the food you wanted, free, and saving money the way I was for school." Eleanor made the trip down to the cafeteria religiously; in twelve weeks her body swelled from 108 to 123 pounds. "Phenomenal weight gain. I did it on purpose, in reaction to how skinny I thought I was."

At the end of her stint Eleanor concluded that while the hospital "was a fairly dreary place to work, for me it was sparkling with the newness and the discovery of it, and the thought of perhaps becoming a doctor myself." But disappointingly, even with free food, the $30 weekly pay hadn't allowed savings. Not that she spent unwisely. In her windowless room where "it was hard to read because the lights weren't bright" she accounted for every cent.

"I kept a little notebook, with lined pads that opened from top to bottom, in which I kept a record. I remember one day I couldn't

account for a penny or two and just pored over it for hours until I could." Like her mother, she scrimped, worried and saved.

Back on campus in spring 1956, Eleanor started to earn a reputation as "incredibly studious, incredibly bright," according to classmates. The lean young woman in jeans took herself seriously as a student. Friendly, she didn't hang out downtown drinking at the popular Tavern or go to Com's, the "black bar" that served huge portions of fried chicken and delicious salad. "I didn't have the money to go out." One of a handful of Negroes on campus ("all very smart"), she studied, was politically active and baby-sat.

During that spring a dorm-mate "who believed I had acting ability, from the way I acted in the dorm, took me down to audition." Eleanor landed a role in a campus production of Arthur Miller's new play, *The Crucible*. A tale of the Salem witch-hunt, its plot paralleled the recent "Red Scare." Eleanor, cast as the only black Salemite—Tituba, a terrified slave from Barbados—electrified the audience when she leapt and screamed, writhing on the floor, possessed by spirits. Her stunning, emotional performance, against the backdrop of a minimalist set, astonished those who knew the studious young woman: the college reviewer called the tour de force "the high point of the play."

"Tituba was about emoting, conveying through words and emotions the terror," Eleanor recalls. "I didn't have the slightest problem to let it go and let it out." Acting in dramas since first grade had been one outlet for Eleanor's passions, ever since Mrs. Gertrude Parthenia MacBrown at Monroe Elementary created a part especially for her.

"I could never play the parts that little girls want to play. Cinderella had to be pretty and have long hair. So Mrs. MacBrown created the role of the fairy godmother's sister, and that was me. I did not fit into the typical roles ever. I had to create it, or she did. That's a metaphor for my life." Perhaps the theater gave her a vehicle to exhibit depths of feeling she usually expressed only in passionate opinions.

The Crucible carried a theme that would become increasingly familiar to the student who, even in her youthful politics, refused to be a lockstep liberal. The play warned of repressive authority, but also the dangers of herd psychology; it showed a community devastated by fear, with people unable to risk their neighbors' wrath by telling the truth.

Raised in a household of independent thinkers, Eleanor had come to her own judgments regardless of those expressed by friends, and argued

her points. Her candor was noted even as a teenager by friends who, describing Eleanor, frequently add, "She's not the sort of person you'd idly want to cross." Her passion, preparation, and willingness to not be "nice" made her a formidable opponent.

During Eleanor's first college years, the Alger Hiss case was a hot button topic. In 1950, Hiss, an alleged Soviet spy, had been convicted. His front-page "GUILTY!" verdict lent credibility to charges issued a month later by Wisconsin Senator Joseph McCarthy, who famously waved "a list of two hundred and five card-carrying Communist Party members in the State Department." The allegations of widespread infiltration later proved false, but they fanned fears of "a fifth column in our midst." By the mid-1950s the Hiss case tapped fierce emotions.

Hiss, a Harvard-educated former Roosevelt aide and United Nations founder, was vehemently defended by leftists as the victim of a witch-hunt. His accuser, Whittaker Chambers, a rumpled "reformed" Communist, was the darling of right-wing politicians.

Eleanor's friends accepted Hiss's claim that he was framed, but she didn't follow her doctrinaire peers. While she agreed there was prejudice against Hiss, several friends remember she found the famous type-writer test—in which his typewriter, alleged to have typed secret State Department reports, was identified by a peculiarity of one of its letters—"disturbing." This evidence-based habit of questioning would lead to a lifetime of critical thinking, where idealism coexisted with pragmatism. Left-wing critics would sometimes accuse her of not appreciating the larger "right-wing conspiratorial picture."

"But look at the evidence!" she'd invariably respond. To her, conspiracy talk was generally an excuse for sloppy thinking.

Eleanor was equally resistant to another aspect of Antioch's culture: "processing" experience or data. As a co-op job counselor noted in an interview, "Among other things Eleanor is one of those students who does not think she is 'learning' anything unless she is putting new *information* in her head! 'Facts' have meaning, not 'insights' or 'understanding.' We had a *long* discussion of this."

But the progressive atmosphere opened her to options she'd never considered. She began to question the spiritual beliefs which she had relied on for sustenance. "My faith was very much rooted in tradition. At Antioch I associated organized religion with conservatism and hypocrisy. I could not understand the notion that if you did not believe in Christ you were condemned to hell. Christians were the minority in the world, yet were the only people saved! Once you got to conundrums like that you could go no further.

"To be perfectly honest, at the root of it was that if you were going to be religious you ought to practice it in a serious, systematic way. I was no longer prepared to do that."

Eleanor found great pleasure in the company of the few other Negro students. At any given moment there were less than five or six on campus; she knew them all. Most were from middle-class backgrounds like her own. The vivacious and dynamic Harriet Blackburn, a Midwesterner, was, she reminisces fondly, "my boon coon." Harriet had "all the clothes, the styles and all the values of the black bourgeoisie," Eleanor laughs. "Yet we were fast friends 'cause she was a colored girl, by which I mean we were of the same culture." Though Harriet was not as political, the two went to parties and meetings or ventured—when they could find rides—to nearby Central State and Wilberforce, both historically black colleges. "We went out with guys from there, didn't go out a lot with Antioch students." Eleanor sometimes spoke at meetings of Wilberforce students; once, her friend Bob Press remembers her standing on stage, exhorting them to find their self-reliant centers and get moving. Echoing her admonitions at Dunbar High, now she lectured, "You have to pick yourself up by yourself and give yourself direction. Don't wait for the white man to do it!"

During her first spring on campus Eleanor also had a regular boyfriend. "A very smart chemist," she says, smiling. "He taught me to drive and helped with math." The good-looking graduate student who taught at Antioch was four or five years older "and browner, not dark brown but kind of nut brown, and joyous," Eleanor happily remembers. The couple spent a great deal of time together, until summer bloomed and she left for a co-op job at the U.S. Geological Survey in Washington, which "interrupted the relationship and ultimately severed it."

Living at home again after a year of being on her own showed how much she had become an Antioch bohemian. Portia teased, "There's Eleanor with her Jesus shoes [leather sandals] on." Other friends noticed how differently, in Eisenhower fifties America, she dressed and thought. But in typical Eleanor fashion, she declares emphatically, "Didn't bother me in the least.

"I did not fit the pattern, but I was absolutely a part of this environment and never estranged from it. Just like there's a part of me now that always wants to stomp and dance and talk to colored people, I had no problem living in the several worlds that were open to me, and I never felt a need to change the world that formed me, or leave the Eleanor Katherine Holmes that grew up in a segregated city.

"I simply took its good points, left what I considered its bad. I was very grateful for the good points: church, stability, family, a high social consciousness that came from the segregated environment, and an unquestioned and automatic surge towards the highest educational level attainable. When I talk about its bourgeois side, that is part and parcel of those values.

"I didn't come home and say, 'I'm different.' I came home looking for my buddies. I was thinking different things, reading different things, with a different set of social values, but 'Hey, where's the party?' "

In the fall of her second year, 1956, Eleanor returned to Antioch with greater confidence. Recommitting to plans for medical school, she took another hospital job, this time at Michael Reese Hospital in Chicago. A medical records clerk, she once again enjoyed the free lunches that came with the paycheck.

Eleanor struggled in pre-med science courses, not getting her usual A's. But she was in every social-issue club. As president of the campus NAACP chapter, Eleanor chaired meetings that filled the North Hall lounge. In spring 1957, she mobilized her group for a Washington Pilgrimage called by Reverend King, the NAACP's Roy Wilkins and the venerable A. Philip Randolph.

The march was held to force White House leadership for protective legislation. President Eisenhower, like Roosevelt twenty years before, refused to meet with civil rights leaders or tell resistant Southerners to obey new laws requiring integration. With Negroes terrorized when they tried to vote or enter schools, an outraged Martin Luther King telegraphed the White House. "If you, our president, cannot come South to relieve our harassed people, we shall have to lead our people to you in the capital in order to call the nation's attention to the violence and organized terror."

The Pilgrimage of Prayer, organized by Ella Baker and Bayard Rustin at Manhattan NAACP offices, was called for May 17, 1957, the third anniversary of the *Brown* decision. Nineteen-year-old Eleanor drove with two cars of local ministers and Antiochians: NAACP and Socialist Discussion Club members.

The trip was difficult. Their old car ran out of gas in the mountains of West Virginia; later the driver, a minister, turned off the ignition going down hills to save gas, terrifying Eleanor. One of the car's occupants, student Manuela Dobos, claims the trip was "memorable, because Eleanor wouldn't shut up, the whole trip. She didn't care who heard her or what she said when we stopped." When one of the ministers asked her to lower her voice in public, where she might offend others with her raw language or left-wing views, Eleanor responded, "What do you mean? I won't." Tension in the full car rose.

In Washington, thirty thousand people, mostly Southern, flooded the Lincoln Memorial, site of Marian Anderson's momentous concert eighteen years before. The largest interracial civil rights demonstration ever held in the capital, its program was filled with spirit: Mahalia Jackson sang and Harlem congressman Adam Clayton Powell Jr. made a "tremendously exciting speech," while a circling plane almost drowned him out. Eleanor and her friends, sitting on the grass in the afternoon sunshine of her hometown, rose and shouted each time Reverend King repeated the electrifying refrain, "Give us the ballot!" which built into a towering, rhythmical demand.

Within three days, Eisenhower sent King an invitation to meet. Soon Congress passed the first Civil Rights Act in eighty-two years, a modest bill termed by the *New York Times* "the most significant domestic action of any Congress this century."

Eleanor returned to the car energized by the fiery speeches. Stopping at a nearly deserted Howard Johnson's in Maryland, the racially mixed group was told by a waitress, "We don't serve nigrahs."

The group was stunned into silence. People stared. In whispers the marchers discussed how to respond and decided they were trying to get back to Antioch, not make a sit-in. But Eleanor did say loudly on the way out, "We're not getting served here, we'll just have to leave!"

One of the ministers turned sharply and reprimanded, "Eleanor, I'm going to have to ask you again to lower your voice and not speak so carelessly in public."

"I won't lower my voice!" she said defiantly as the group filed out. They drove away, stung by confirmation of why they had come to Washington.

In the car, the quick-tempered Eleanor was silent. Her rage at the restaurant rebuff soon found an outlet, however, in a ferocious, no-holds-barred political argument with Manuela, another Socialist Club member with whom Eleanor often furiously disagreed. Others in the car shriveled as the two shouted.

"She could really bat it out," Manuela recalls. "Whatever was on her mind she put it out there, not refraining from all the emotionality. Ellie is so much like me," she adds. "I didn't think screaming fights were unusual for a friendship."

Eleanor herself retains no image of the restaurant rejection. "I must have been so red hot mad I blurred it from my memory. It must have been that painful." This daughter of Vela had learned well to excise disturbing remembrance. Nor "dwelling" meant recalling the past in a positive light, as foundation for a positive future. This tendency would become habit, creating behavior some regard as glossing over real tragedies; others judge it an admirable pillar of her structure, one that enables her to function at full capacity no matter what may come her way. Nursing grievances was not the path this child of segregation chose as a way to move forward.

That spring of 1957, Eleanor had been at Antioch almost two years, and was torn: to be a doctor or a lawyer? A co-op counselor wrote, "Father is a lawyer who wants Eleanor to be a doctor" and noted, "Got interested in law through NAACP and Thurgood Marshall and courses in logic."

"I was totally engaged in the civil rights movement," Eleanor explains. "And there were virtually no black civil rights lawyers. Becoming somebody prestigious in my black society became quite beside the point.

"I thought lawyers engaged in winners and losers and I hated that, whereas medicine was all doing good. Ultimately what made me know I was to be a lawyer was the ripening of my civil rights consciousness, and here I was, smack dab in the midst of one of the few colleges in the United States that had any sense of social action, right as the civil rights movement underwent the great transition from law to action.

Thurgood Marshall and the lawyers opened the world. They made the nonviolent revolution occur. So lawyers were the key to the future, not doctors, as much as doctors were needed in the black community."

A unique opportunity confirmed her desire. She discovered the Encampment for Citizenship in New York City, a summer public affairs camp for young people. Obtaining a six-week scholarship, she had "a whirlpool of fun, running around New York City with socially conscious young people just like myself."

Bunking at the progressive Fieldston School, Eleanor played Joan of Arc in a group reading. She put her heart into Joan's defiant speech, and recites the words with feeling even today: "They told me you were fools, and that I should not listen to your fine words." Eleanor thrilled to the echo of the warrior who followed her own voices, dressed in men's clothing, and, thus armored, charged forward to save her country. The whole summer, a "soup of fun," with trips to the United Nations and observations of a labor management arbitration, was a preview of her life-to-be.

And she met a new boyfriend: Dick Merman, a Haverford student. For the next several years this young white man would be her guide to the wonders of New York City and adventures like camping in the Adirondacks, "where you had to bathe in cold streams and live outdoors." She shudders. "But it was so new and an experience I wanted.

"Dick was a strong presence and I was very attached to him. There wasn't much interracial dating. But as two young people who were out to see what the world was about, this was something the world was about that neither of us had known before.

"We had a great deal in common, though he was an only child from a wealthy Park Avenue Jewish family. But we went to similar schools and had values that were similar, as evidenced by his presence at the Encampment. It was one of the most joyous periods that I recall growing up." Dick would become a regular Antioch visitor; the two stayed in her friend Herschel Kaminsky's off-campus apartment.

Concluding her tale of this relationship that opened doors to so many new worlds, Eleanor adds wistfully, "Later we moved on and I lost contact."

Eleanor had one more medical job lined up. Though she had decided on law, she honored her commitment to clerk at the Department of Health, Education and Welfare, T.B. section. The five-month job was tedious; her report to Antioch struggled to find meaning in the routine work. But she found it, acknowledging a new appreciation for the labor of statisticians and the growth in her own character. "The job was an aid toward better and more discipline for me, for I learned to stick to things that I didn't especially enjoy doing."

The government job also allowed her to save money by again living with her parents. Finances continued to plague her. Yet, as in her decision to have a seven-year-old birthday party or fly off to Antioch at eighteen, now she didn't let apparent lack limit her grand plans for a major future. Her co-op job counselor wrote, "I am more and more impressed with her good sense and direct approach to problems."

Eleanor was now deeply involved in the intellectually charged campus. The political atmosphere "made me think about the roots of what I believed and why I believed it. Sloganeering was not possible at Antioch; it was all analyzing." Her family had discussed politics, but focused on current events. Now, "the intellectual basis for my politics was forming.

"Antioch drew out of me impulses that would remain: a rejection of the status quo on race and gender and even on economic matters, because of my rejection of poverty as a condition that has to be." Michael Harrington, the democratic socialist soon to be famous as the author of *The Other America,* spoke regularly at Antioch on peace, labor and civil rights. Eleanor was one of his devotees. The Hungarian Revolution "really aroused the campus in 1957. That was extraordinary, that there would be people who would rise up against the Soviet totalitarians and risk everything by throwing rocks at tanks." Eleanor joined classmates to raise funds for Hungarian students; Herschel Kaminsky recalls that "we, the noncommunist left, hoped this would set off something in Western Europe."

Classmates remember Eleanor as totally focused. When her roommate Shelly Eisenberg came back from a Pittsburgh visit to her boyfriend and, sitting cross-legged on her bed in their modern brick dorm, confided her engagement, Eleanor was appalled.

"There is more to life than getting married!" she shouted. "Are you crazy? You may never finish school. It's like throwing your life away. You can do that anytime. Tell him to wait!"

"Only a white girl could come to college and get married," Eleanor thought. "A black girl knows better. She has to take care of herself."

Nonetheless, demonstrating her intense loyalty to a friend, Eleanor was the only schoolmate to attend Shelly's Brooklyn wedding the following June. "There were all these people dancing and I was one of a kind there as I recall." Eleanor herself had boyfriends. But, she explains, "I thought men were to have fun with, not to marry, while you were in school."

Once Eleanor left science courses, she excelled in the history and philosophy pre-law required. The acting dean of students wrote in a scholarship recommendation, "Eleanor approaches her work, and her career aspirations, with a really rare quality of seriousness which does not veer into overintensity or lack of humor. . . . she is, I think, a woman who will make a really worthwhile contribution to her chosen field."

The reason for this letter to the Noyes Foundation was that Eleanor's family finances had changed. "When Eleanor first came to Antioch she needed very little scholarship assistance," another administrator wrote on Eleanor's behalf, "mostly because both of her parents were working. This still remains the situation although her mother now has the full financial responsibility for the family. I do not understand what has happened to the father and my attempts to get this clear were so painful to Eleanor that I did not pursue them. The one thing that is clear is that, although her father is still resident with the rest of the family, he takes none of the financial responsibility."

Coleman and Vela, in fact, had separated finances and bedrooms; yet they would live in the same home until Coleman's death twenty years later. Some relatives speculate the couple remained together for the sake of their daughters. Years later, long after her father's death, Eleanor dismissively gives "Coleman was a night owl" as the reason for separate bedrooms, and her parents' divided finances stemmed from "my mother wanting to make sure that Coleman's credit rating was not in the picture. Mother, thrifty to a fare-thee-well, wanted to keep Coleman's credit ratings from being searched." And that, Eleanor explains, is why Vela bought their two homes in her own name. As to the change in family finances, "I do not know."

Perhaps Eleanor's favorite job, and most significant in her development as a social activist, was a three-month stint as an investigator at the Cleveland Urban Renewal Agency. The city itself astonished her.

"The industrial might of Cleveland was right there in the middle of the city. You saw the burning steel plants really going, right there. It divided the town from one side to the other and brought with it dirt and crime. If you come from a white-collar town it was very stark and seemed to me to be a homely city."

Eleanor lived in "a glorious big room, with huge windows" in a mansion-turned-settlement house, where she got care packages from home. Aunt Selena mailed fragrant boxes of fresh-baked cookies and candies to her niece, "and of course I left them in my room during the day to eat after work.

"Crumbs and cookies. I'll never forget when I was lying on my bed one night, at the back of this very long room, watching a rat try to get into my room. I could see the shadow under my door and hear it moving back and forth, gnawing, trying to get in. Every once in a while part of the doorway light from the hall would disappear, and you knew he was there."

Too petrified to move and too proud to scream, she lay motionless.

"I was so afraid. I didn't want to call out in the middle of the night, that wasn't like me. I wanted at least to get through the night and then tell about it."

But she couldn't. After hours of watching the rat from bed, she screamed, "John!"

"This funny big black guy, bless his heart," who lived on the premises, came to the rescue and shooed the rat away. After that terrifying night, "one of the ten most frightening experiences in my life," Eleanor felt lingering dread whenever she turned out her light or needed to use the hall bathroom after dark.

Returning to campus in April 1959, she reported on "The Challenge of Integration and the Housing Problem," providing an early demonstration of her win/win philosophy. Not only did "the poorest, blackest Negro" have a stake in urban renewal, but so did members of "the great American middle class" who were "intimidated daily in the city" before their evening exodus to the suburbs.

"No suburb can afford to let the city die," she wrote, for it remained the place to work. Negro crime was basically a symptom of a failure in integration. Thus, new construction was not the solution, for, she argued, "the atmosphere of segregation must be eliminated before the resulting social blight can be eliminated."

At twenty-one, Eleanor had a penetrating analysis of a complex problem, and was already honing arguments to win allies, appealing to self-interest. Without rhetoric she pierced one of the most emotionally charged problems of the day—urban renewal, often disparaged as "Negro removal"—and wrote of a larger solution intended to benefit all parties.

By her fourth year in the five-year Antioch program, Eleanor took on the kind of broad-ranging leadership she'd shown at Banneker and Dunbar. She'd already been president of the campus NAACP and a member of Publications Board, which set policy and hired staff for Antioch publications. Now she was influential in virtually every area of campus life. A history professor would later write of Eleanor's "tremendous development during her last two years at Antioch." The switch from pre-med to history may have contributed, and she had grown from her successes in the variegated world of school and co-op jobs. Eleanor was now widely recognized as a sharp, hardworking leader. As Bob Press, co-chair of the campus NAACP, says, "I never saw her as that radical. Her strength was in seeing all sides and coming across as someone you could trust, who was going to be honest with you. She was coming from a solid base and would respect your opinion."

Eleanor was elected by the entire campus community to be one of six students on the policy-making Community Council, and then elected chair by its members. She also became a hall advisor to first-year students; by year's end she was on the hall advisor selection committee. And she joined the Civil Liberties Committee.

During her last years at Antioch, student Peter Hambright ("I knew Eleanor because she was black and I was black. There weren't that many of us") remembers her walking into the cafeteria, finding a table, "and immediately five hundred people would come and sit down, and she'd sit there and talk and everybody would listen."

In 1959, "at the end of my fourth year, I took my senior independent study at Berkeley, and wrote a lot of my thesis. I literally got there in a beat poet way. I went in a car to the West Coast with four or five Antioch students. We bought bread and bologna, stopped just to go to the bathroom and see the Grand Canyon, and I arrived in San Francisco dirty as I could be.

"Berkeley was not yet Berkeley in the 1960's sense but was on the cusp of it. We could feel it." Supporting herself with several short jobs—

psychology research assistant at the University of California and secretary at a San Francisco community chest—for five months she shared the ground floor of a North Berkeley house, "just up the hill where it starts to get steep." Her roommate was an Antioch alumna, graduate student Bette Stubing. The two were thrilled by orange and avocado trees in the yard.

After Antioch, Eleanor was often unaware of her immersion in a white world. So on a Monday morning when she set out for the bus, dressed in her workaday skirt and blouse, she called out to Bette without thinking.

"I'll be home late tonight because I have to get my hair straightened and curled."

"Straightened AND curled?" her bewildered roommate responded.

"I have to straighten it to do anything, before I can set it," Eleanor explained, while thinking, "Bette has long black hair. All she has to do is go into the shower, and I have to go through all these mechanics!"

Bette was dumbfounded.

"To have a deliberately nappy head is not possible," Eleanor spelled out, describing the lye-based "relaxer" applied to her hair, before the ends were curled back up. She would soon be "one of the first, and one of the few" to get an Afro. But in 1959 the costly, time-consuming process was a customary routine of life.

"I had to find a hairdresser every time I went on an Antioch job. What a bother. You can always find some colored people to help you find one. Hair is trouble! At least white women can just take it and tie it back. Black girls and women had to worry about being nappy. So tying it back would still be unacceptable. It costs money too. I took to wearing my hair in a kind of upsweep; that way you'd have to go less often, and wouldn't have to roll the damn stuff up all the time."

Still, the two women reveled in their newfound bohemia. Jumping into radical circles, Eleanor soon met Young People's Socialist Alliance member Bob Martinson, later a well-known sociologist.

"I was very thick with him, saw him almost every day, often with Bette, who was later to marry Bogden Denich. Bogden and Bob would come over to eat with us."

The women, both twenty-one, were dazzled by the two charming thirty-year-olds, political honchos in West Coast radical circles who were equally interested in the bright, attractive women. Over spaghetti dinners in one or another of their flats, decorated with the de rigueur madras bedspreads and Chianti bottles topped with dripping candles, Eleanor and Bette listened to war stories about McCarthyism, demonstrations gone awry and strategies for organizing. The four sweethearts, as in love with politics as with each other, stopped in after meetings for pitchers of beer at clubs like the Blind Lemon and the Steppenwolf, Berkeley bars with a Greenwich Village atmosphere and decor. "I had a ball," Eleanor reminisces happily. "I was writing a senior thesis, I was working, I had this boyfriend and we were very much of the same ideology and philosophy. It was a wonderful, happy time. I hated to leave."

But leave she did, returning in January 1960, for her final college spring. She now chaired the powerful Publications Board, served on the Student Personnel Committee and resumed leadership of the NAACP, along with her studies. The Eleanor of junior high and high school days who walked off with most of the honors had resurfaced in this white environment, far from U Street. She'd made it in the wide world, or at least this little progressive corner of it. Now she would apply to law schools.

In a letter of recommendation an Antioch administrator wrote, "She is tenacious. She does not mind long hours of hard work. . . . She writes well, and speaks and thinks well on her feet. She is one of the most effective defending speakers I have ever heard—whether on an unpopular NAACP position or about a proposed editor."

Another concluded, "She is realistic about herself, her excellent capabilities and her handicaps, including that of being a Negro woman, without the slightest defensiveness."

She also impressed students. David Crippens had heard about Eleanor Holmes, the talk of the campus. "It was Eleanor this and Eleanor that." To the impressionable and inspired seventeen-year-old from Nashville, "she was bright, she was a Negro, *and she was not afraid of anything*. If you didn't know what you were talking about, she could—and would—totally cut you apart." In his eyes Eleanor stood ten feet tall, the smartest human being he'd ever met, a spellbinding speaker who had read everything and done everything. "She spoke as a true intellectual who more than held her own with the great intellectuals of the campus. For a little Southern boy like me, I thought, my goodness." He had never seen a black woman speak with such surety that even whites elevated her. She carried herself differently from women he'd known. But "she wasn't trying to be white, she was just being who she was, true to herself." In the debating society that was Antioch, Eleanor's surety about who she was and what she wanted, evident since earliest childhood, was now even more solid. If she battled internally, few knew it.

Eleanor was on her way to legendary campus status. Her certainty and zeal to convey opinions were unusual; but joined to her self-confidence was a loyalty and concern for others—even if expressed briefly and brusquely—that would be a lifelong trait. She also had a quick wit that sometimes softened her determined "rightness." The party girl from Dunbar who delighted in the Jewish humor she learned at Montefiore still frolicked. Inside the determined politico lurked the good time girl who forever liked to "get down and party."

During Eleanor's last spring on campus, she spent long days on the large front lawn where dappled sunlight played. "Spring in Yellow Springs was glorious," she reminisces, evoking the beautiful campus full of trees. On warm afternoons students emerged with books and blankets onto the grass, studying and socializing, doing cartwheels, taking the sun and air. In the idyllic setting Eleanor joined in "playing, like the part-children we still were. We were very grown and yet in some ways very childlike. A state much to be valued: the carefree innocence, the refusal to believe or face the worst, the inherent idealism that could flourish at Antioch, where you could dress like a child and folk dance like a child and refuse to wear makeup like a child. I didn't wear any lipstick or any of those things that would have made me more attractive, and attractive I was surely not. I remember seeing myself as an ugly duckling and saying, 'So what?' "

As Eleanor studied and played, off-campus determination stiffened on both sides of "the Negro question." White Americans saw their carefully constructed "system of caste and insult," as scholar W.E.B. DuBois called it, begin to fall. Negroes, in the minds of some, became linked with subversive Communists. An Alabama billboard displayed a photo of Reverend King and Mrs. Rosa Parks at Highlander Folk School, a Tennessee civil rights center, with the headline "MARTIN LUTHER KING AT COMMUNIST TRAINING SCHOOL." As the threat of change grew, Southern legislatures enacted new laws, from prohibitions against intermarriage to denying same-cemetery burials of whites and blacks. Alabama outlawed the NAACP.

Part of the wall of defense was to create a new face for the old order. In the mid-fifties White Citizens' Councils formed, "pursuing the agenda of the Klan with the demeanor of the Rotary," writes historian Charles Payne.

Segregationists made last-ditch stands. In 1957, Governor Orval Faubus ordered the Arkansas National Guard to block nine teens from Little Rock's Central High School. Day after day television showed howling whites spitting and lunging, until President Eisenhower called in a thousand Airborne Division soldiers to quell the insurrection against federal law. His intervention and the Civil Rights Act that year showed, however slowly and painfully, change was coming.

On Monday, February 1, 1960, four college students in Greensboro, North Carolina, lit the match that finally ignited a sustained civil rights movement. Just as Montgomery's bus boycott four years earlier had challenged segregated transportation, now activists disputed exclusion from stores and lunch counters. Franklin McCain, David Richmond, Joseph McNeil and Izell Blair Jr., all freshmen at North Carolina A & T College, went downtown to the local Woolworth's and asked for coffee and doughnuts at the lunch counter.

A Negro waitress rebuffed them. "You are stupid, ignorant! You're dumb! That's why we can't get anywhere today! You know you are supposed to eat at the other end!"

The students remained sitting at the counter until closing time. McCain later wrote, "If it's possible to know what it means to have your soul cleansed . . . I probably felt better on that day than I've ever felt in my life."

"What made them go into that restaurant?" asks Eleanor. "They decided they were going to take that abuse; it was obviously concerted revolutionary action. By that time, events were beginning to gallop. Events trigger what was always there. I sat in with my grandmother when I was a little girl! I distinctly remember taking the bus, getting off at 14th Street, going into the Woolworth's with my grandmother and sitting with her. Her asking and them saying, 'You have to stand at the other end.' "

" 'Not today!'

"I think my grandmother must have known they were not going to serve her, yet she wanted to try them out. But in 1960, those students, who had to know they could be mutilated, started a civil disobedience movement."

The next day nineteen students joined the original four. By Wednesday there were eighty; soon more students wanted to sit-in than there were places to sit. By Saturday, when bystanders threw eggs, the sit-in had over 400 students, including a vice president of the mostly white National Student Association. In two weeks the blaze spread to fifteen cities; by month's end, thirty-one.

Well-dressed students by the hundreds marched from churches or schools to lunch counters. While black America cheered, white America watched, dazed, as long lines of dressed-up black students filed into downtown stores in city after city, singing, "Ain't gonna let nobody turn us around, marching up to freedom land." Requesting service, the polite, resolute students carried textbooks to study while awaiting attack.

The movement begun in Montgomery four years before replayed, this time on a national scale. On Easter weekend, 1960—the twenty-first anniversary of Marian Anderson's historic Lincoln Memorial concert—Southern students gathered to form a militant new civil rights organization: the Student Nonviolent Coordinating Committee (SNCC). This group, mentored by skilled organizer Ella Baker, would play a major role in catapulting segregation into the national consciousness. A Fisk University veteran of the Nashville sit-ins, Marion Barry, was elected SNCC's first chair.

"I felt myself a part of the civil rights movement before there was a movement," reflects Eleanor. "I was always frustrated that we got our race consciousness so late. When these things broke out finally in fifty-seven and sixty, all I could think was, 'What took us so long?'

"Here I am sitting up at Antioch, gathering myself some people together." Eleanor remembers looking for actions that might match the Deep South students. In early March, several students from Central State began a sit-in at Geyer's, a restaurant in nearby Xenia. Refused service one Saturday, they sat in a booth; the restaurant dimmed its lights and announced, "Closing." The students remained seated until one of the Geyer brothers came into the restaurant, threatening to shoot them with his shotgun, and called the police.

"You have two choices: close or serve the students," the chief said.

Geyer closed. The following day, after contacting Eleanor and another Antioch student, Central State students arrived with two hundred pickets. That night students rallied in Antioch's café, pushing back tables and erecting a microphone in the center of the dining room.

"We will never give up! Never, never never!" Eleanor exhorted before others joined her at the microphone.

The next day, on a freezing early March Monday at 7 A.M., cars began to leave Antioch every hour and a half until nightfall, ferrying students to march in front of the shuttered restaurant. The ever-chilled Eleanor recalls, "I have been on a lot of winter picket lines but none colder than that."

That evening a dramatic announcement startled everyone: the Geyer brothers would reopen their restaurant, serving all. The movement from the South had successfully made its way to the marshlands of southern Ohio.

Eleanor and students from Central State, Wilberforce and Earlham quickly chose another target: a bowling alley in Xenia that only let Negroes bowl two afternoons a week. Carloads of students descended and picketed for several hours until the horrified manager ran out.

"We'll open up," he whispered. "Anybody can come at any hour to bowl."

With this victory under their belts, they triumphantly returned to Antioch, remembers student Steve Schwerner. "We thought we could picket for a few hours in the sunshine and change the world." Soon they learned it was not always so easy.

All but one of the barbershops in tiny Yellow Springs refused to cut "Negro hair," necessitating use of the one welcoming barber—a black man—or a long trip to Xenia. The issue had smoldered for years; Antiochians had debated a boycott in endless community government meetings and passed resolutions deploring the discrimination.

Emboldened by the sit-ins, Eleanor, as chair of the NAACP, planned a protest march downtown and wrote to the mayor announcing her group's intention. "That was as close as we could get to a Movement target in Yellow Springs, a Quaker town."

In response, the mayor met with local business leaders to resolve peacefully the "segregation situation." Women from two beauty shops testified they were "not familiar with the treatment of Negro women's hair," but would do their best. One proprietor, however, refused.

"It was then decided by Ellie Holmes," the *Antioch Record* reported, to organize test case groups. Small integrated groups attempted to get haircuts at every local barbershop. One cut the hair of David Crippens, "the first Negro ever served by Squires." Forty years later Crippens laughs, "I must have been crazy to do that. The guy had a razor in his hand."

But Peter Hambright, also recruited by Eleanor, recalls sitting in Gegner's barbershop for twenty minutes, "and poor Mr. Gegner told me he didn't know how to cut Negro hair. If he did, he'd do it." Student Offie Wortham, likewise refused at Gegner's, filed suit.

"Gegner was a hard nut to crack," Eleanor recalls. Taken to trial in Dayton, he testified he didn't know how to cut Negro hair. But Antioch testers showed that a Negro student with straight hair was turned away, while a white professor with frizzy hair ("a Jewish Afro") was served. Gegner would continue to flout the law until his case became a sixties cause célèbre. Eleanor's last weeks at college confirmed her ability to organize and win. From Gegner, the holdout, she learned the need for perseverance.

On the "wonderful, sunny morning" of June 18, 1960, five days after her twenty-third birthday, Eleanor K. Holmes participated in an outdoor ceremony conferring Bachelor of Arts degrees on 165 graduates. The celebration opened with a Mendelssohn sonata, the class marched in and it was, smiles Eleanor, "a glorious graduation.

"My father bought me a wonderful dress, willowy and with blue flowers, that was perfect for a young girl getting out of college. I remember just loving it. I kept it for the longest time." Wrapped again by Coleman, this time in a flowing dress topped by a little blue jacket, Eleanor stepped up for her degree while her beaming parents watched from folding chairs set up on the wide green lawn.

Quite different from her previous graduations, this commencement without religious ritual was "extraordinary, it was deep, moving, yet intellectual." She smiles again at the memory and says with uncharacteristic quiet, "I appreciated it very much, especially the wonderfully analytical commencement address."

The determined schoolgirl who had flown alone cross-country to the exhilarating world of the radical counterculture graduated as a maturing young woman, twentieth in her class, and a budding civil rights leader.

Like the characters with whom Eleanor had interacted so dramatically in *The Crucible* during her first spring at Antioch, in these five years she had come through her own crucible. She tested her mettle in a larger world, expanded her intellectual vision and confirmed her values. In those years, from 1955 to 1960, the country also came through a crucible, emerging from the fear days of McCarthyism into the light of an inspired civil rights movement that would, like an earthquake, release tremendous energies.

Hours after graduation the jubilant young woman packed her bags, threw them into her parents' car and drove off, staring silently out the back window at the world she was leaving behind. But before she set out to penetrate the ivy-covered walls of Yale University Law School, she would join a Washington, D.C., action group replete with luminaries of the new sit-ins. The Sixties Movement was in its infancy, and Eleanor Holmes was ready to jump into its center.

Part Two

"FULL OF THE HOPE THAT THE PRESENT HAS BROUGHT US"

CHAPTER 4

Ballots, Bullets, and Books

I know now that I would rather be a Negro in America than a white man any-where else on the face of the earth. So then, to live in harmony with men, to bring about a closer union between my people and the other people of the world—these are life aims that I as a Negro cannot escape.
ELEANOR HOLMES, LIFE AIMS ESSAY, ANTIOCH COLLEGE

When I came home that summer from Antioch on my way to law school, the Non-violent Action Group, NAG, had formed here out of Howard University. That's how I first met Stokely Carmichael, Courtland Cox and a whole set of Movement people." Eleanor evokes 1960, when zealous students looked for places to desegregate.

"What I really loved about what we did is we went to churches first, to involve the local people. It was a real basic SNCC philosophy. Because we were outsiders in the community, we didn't want to just go and sit-in.

"One weekend I was arrested sitting on a stool in a little restaurant in Rockville, Maryland," ten miles from downtown Washington. "The townspeople were arrested right along with us. These were people completely uninitiated in the Movement. We said, 'Leave this church and go sit-in with us.'

"We were all arrested, but ultimately the prosecutor never moved forward, perhaps because the townspeople had the courage to come out right along with us. It took real courage for them, but not for young folks like us."

The fire spread. Groups of students sat-in all over the area, triumphantly clapping and singing affirmation: "If you can't find me at the back of the bus, come on over to the front of the bus. I'll be riding up there!"

Eleanor, by day working to compile a Health, Education and Welfare summary of laws on the education of exceptional children, labored after-hours to demolish segregation. Separation permeated everything, from amusement parks to construction jobs. Local government was run by Southern white senators and congressmen. This was the implacable face of power these college students took on, all that hot, humid summer.

Eleanor often risked arrest with the others, but she was also on a quest for a device that would decisively destroy apartheid. Hating to waste time on "one-by-one" strategies of resistance, she wanted to discover sweeping mechanisms that would fracture segregation forever.

When August light faded and September days sparkled with a tinge of fall in the air, Eleanor once again left Washington. But this time, instead of flying off to the intimate, bohemian world of the white counterculture, she moved directly through the stone arches of white male power into Yale University. Founded in 1701, the school was chartered with the mission of educating youth "for publick employment both in Church and Civil State." Yale graduates led the country. Its medieval skyline of turrets and towers would become a familiar second home to generations of America's wealthiest scions.

The young woman setting out for the New England citadel—its leafy courtyards enclosed by wooden doors modeled on the English inns of court—was quite different from the eighteen-year-old who had left home for Antioch's small campus five years before. Now she knew she could be an academic star in the white world as well as the black.

Still, Yale was formidable.

The law school's stone buildings were "a bunch of churches, almost," Eleanor laughs. "They were built during the Depression when nobody had any money except Yale." The cloistered inner courtyard and legal library were beautiful examples of Gothic architecture, reproduced in stunning detail. Decorated Romanesque arches and oriel windows graced the buildings.

Women were relative newcomers to this sanctum; School applications reflected the assumption that its students were male. Financial forms requested data for "Income from wife's property, securities, and other investments," "Income from wife's earnings" and "Withdrawal from wife's savings," with no comparable husband categories. Male students dwelled in law school suites; females lived in old-fashioned dorm rooms, "cells really, in a gruesome place with mass bathrooms," recalls one hapless former resident. And Eleanor remembers, regarding the handful of women students, "Men would say, 'It's a whole lot of women when you consider that you all are not going to use these law degrees.' "

The expectation that men rightfully occupied the seats of higher education was displayed even in reference letters from liberal Antioch. One professor's recommendation was the mate to Yale's application forms. "There is always, of course, a certain risk in taking a woman student on for any kind of graduate work," he wrote. "I cannot say what would happen to her program if she were confronted by the possibility of marriage."

The very clothing at Yale bespoke the understanding that these students would shortly occupy the highest posts of government and business. At Antioch the Dunbar debutante had switched to dungarees, but Yale students dressed every day as if going to work at a law firm. Exchanging sandals and shorts for high heels and business dresses, Eleanor discovered, as she sat with men in jackets and ties, that many students also wore a different mental outfit.

"Students argued that late, in 1960, over dinner, over breakfast, about *Brown*, with many thinking it was the wrong decision. The arguments were pretty primitive, judged by today."

Dining-room meals, mandatory for first-year law students ("Otherwise they couldn't have gotten anybody to eat there") were eaten in splendor. Heavy red drapes shut out natural light; chandeliers lit high-domed ceilings. Waiters in uniform stood at the side of the paneled rooms, hands folded in readiness to meet diners' needs at polished mahogany tables.

Virtually all the students were white. "There was only Marian Wright [Edelman] and me." Eleanor remembers the black women in her class. Students of color were often mistaken for secretaries or janitors, recalls Dunbar friend Inez Smith, also at Yale. Eleanor, even in memory, resolutely glides over such slights, fulfilling her friend Barbara Babcock's description of her as a woman who "forgets the past even as it's happening," especially if it was unpleasant.

Eleanor had rather remarkably adapted to Antioch, just as she had earlier fit in at a white summer camp. Despite little cross-cultural experience, she learned early to encompass, rather than fracture, when faced with the unfamiliar. At Yale she did it again. Having already mastered black middle-class Washington and the iconoclastic milieu of Antioch, now her task was to incorporate the rigorous thinking of Yale Law School, fine-tuning a stance consonant with the environment, and yet her own.

"I was neither shocked nor traumatized" by Yale's sea of suited white males, claims Eleanor. "It was very different, but through Antioch I was ready for whatever world would come forward. The sophistication of Antioch was critical for Yale."

Eleanor softened the white-shoe, Ivy League environment of Yale by immediately contacting the local civil rights movement, and finding classmate Neil Herring, a Yale College graduate. "Neil and I made fun of it all and were in constant radical dialogue about Yale and all of its pretensions, the class-based society, the campus in which we found ourselves. I may have been at Yale but I was challenging Yale all the time."

Not one to dwell on the conservatism of the institution or her peers, or even the inconvenience of formal dressing, Eleanor took what was offered: extraordinary intellectual stimulation and a ticket to just about anywhere she would choose to go, though prestigious clerkships were still generally unavailable to women. Even liberals had excuses, says law professor Barbara Babcock, such as, "I like to tell dirty jokes," "I take off my coat in chambers," or "I work late and it wouldn't look good."

In hindsight, Eleanor is oblivious to difficulties. As Barbara further explains Eleanor's habit of forgetting, "She is a true intellectual. Her mind is occupied with ideas rather than being troubled by her own personal past. She doesn't dwell, and she doesn't hold grudges—probably because she doesn't remember!" Barbara, who loves Eleanor deeply, laughs with affection. "She not only glosses over the past, she glosses over the present. Her life has been one of struggle and hard work."

"I really have a hard time seeing life in terms of obstacles," Eleanor insists, forever casting her challenges as chances. "I don't think I've had any, I really don't. I've looked at my life as a life of opportunity, not obstacles. I never thought that 'Poor me, being black and female.' I just think what it did do is make me a fighter."

At Yale, in a more conservative environment than either Antioch or her home community in Washington, Eleanor chose the post of resident militant.

"It was a place of real intellectual ferment then, with civil rights and

Kennedy. The fifties atmosphere was passing. On the other hand," she grimaces, "I was anything but a Kennedy devotee."

One unlucky fellow, Clarence Laing, "a black friend, walked around with a Kennedy button. I'd just come out of the South where Kennedy, because he was a Democrat trying to get the nomination, hardly ran as a civil rights candidate."

Eleanor walked up to Laing, whom she called by his last name the way professors did.

"Laing, why the hell are you wearing that button? I understand why you have to vote for Kennedy, but does somebody as black as you have to wear a button? We don't have to be advertisements! We want Kennedy to win, but it's important for us to be harder to get than that!"

Even during her first months at Yale, she never let an opportunity pass for a political quarrel. Her blistering tongue would become as much a trademark as her reputation for integrity and sharp analysis.

"I've been fortunate to make transitions from very different environments. But my values were already formed. That's at my core. At Yale the radical in me didn't die. I didn't think, 'Now I'm at Yale, I'm an establishment lawyer.' I knew I couldn't change Yale like those who followed me in the seventies, a much larger group that came into white universities and tried to make a revolution."

No, she asserts, "I wanted to change something bigger than Yale: the world!"

First-year law classrooms were large. Even though Yale pioneered teaching students in small sections, the atmosphere was formal. Fixed chairs on risers anchored the formality of the pedagogical content. In 1960 law schools gave little attention to practical implementation; clinics to help the underserved and to train students in real-life law were yet to come.

"Classes then were very intimidating. Basically professors would look down the roll and call on people."

In this Socratic atmosphere, where the pedagogy required aggressive questioning of students in an almost hostile manner, Eleanor's "best buddy" Neil provided one of her fondest law school moments. The two rebels sat together in a class.

"Nothing could be more Yale Law professor-like but to ask the very first day of class, 'What is property?' "

Eleanor chuckles with delight. "That's the kind of question he meant to get volunteers on. There were people wagging their hands, nobody more than Neil."

"Property is theft," Neil answered, with a definition straight from the anarchist Proudhon.

"I just fell out laughing," Eleanor remembers. "That lasted me a long time."

As first-year students she and Neil also took Federal Practice with Professor Moore, "a character, who wrote the leading seven-volume treatise on the subject," remembers Neil. The professor had a rapier Montana wit, and Eleanor met him on every point. "She was not easily intimidated," declares Neil. "She could stand up to some high-powered law professor, but not somebody she had heart feelings for. Then she was a great softie."

One of the few problems that vexed the confident activist was money. By November she'd applied for the following year's funding, but was skeptical because, as she wrote in a letter then, "there is a girl in my class who has [the same coveted Whitney grant] for this year. Generally, I don't think they'd like giving money to two Negroes in the same class."

In spite of her fear that there was only room for "one"—and that one was Marian Wright—she did find out the following spring that she would be a John Hay Whitney Fellow, with a $2,400 stipend.

But Eleanor continued to worry. She worked part-time, as she had at Antioch, and scrimped. As her mother wrote on Eleanor's financial aid application, the family had to depend for support almost entirely upon her own salary, since "Mr. Holmes provides only food." And "Mr. Holmes refuses to give any information about his salary because, for the most part, it does not come into the home and, in any case, it will not be available for Eleanor's education or living expenses." In succeeding years she would complain that "Mr. Holmes refuses to sign this blank" and express regret that she could not "provide Eleanor with the funds my salary would allow if I were receiving adequate and fair cooperation from my husband." Coleman himself appeared curiously unaware of the impact of his actions on Eleanor. In New Haven to pick up his daughter, he took her roommate aside to ask, "Why is Eleanor so tight? We're not poverty-stricken, you know."

Eleanor was openly resentful at her working father's lack of financial support but appreciated the fierce pride he took in her. As time passed she made allowances, as she had long learned to do, for his failings, saying philosophically today, "You're more forgiving of faults the older you get, seeing your own faults or problems."

In signature fashion the student crammed, excelled, and trumpeted her accomplishments, just as her father had taught her. By spring she wrote an Antioch administrator, "I am one of four students in my class to make it through to the Moot Court finals." Moot Court, a mandatory first-year competition based on a real courtroom case, was arguably the most important moment of a student's three-year career. The Alumni Day competition was held in the law school auditorium, where the formal bas relief replicated an appellate courtroom and three prominent judges sat on a proscenium.

Eleanor was ranked top member of one finalist three-person team; her opponent was Barbara Babcock. Assigned sides by lot, Eleanor's team drew the defense in *Braden* v. *House Un-American Activities Committee*. Carl Braden, who had refused to answer questions from HUAC, had lost his case and was serving a year in jail. Coleman and Vela drove up to watch their daughter argue her First Amendment case, the forerunner to a real-life free speech case she would later plead before the U.S. Supreme Court.

On the big day Eleanor was even more tightly stretched than usual. "I remember being very tense because, my God, you had to climb your way to the top here!" Dressed in a brown and cream dress with matching jacket, Eleanor stood at a podium facing the judges, with her back to the audience. She and Neil had role-played the rapid questioning that would occur, but she couldn't think as fast as usual. After the argument, awaiting the decision, Eleanor debriefed herself. "I approach everything self-critically, thinking what I should have done."

Though Eleanor wanted to win—"always do"—she was bested by her friend. "Such a generous person," Eleanor invokes Barbara's relaxed style of advocacy that just seemed to flow. "Loving, but tough, and the fact is: she beat me!"

After the decision, Eleanor remembered her mother's admonitions to notice how high she'd risen rather than the peak she didn't scale, and told herself she was "pleased to get that far."

By the end of her first year, when Eleanor had fashioned a place for herself amidst the carved wood and leaded glass, she wrote back to an

Antioch mentor. "I do miss Antioch, but not in the way that one feels when he wants to return for some time to a place he loves. Rather I regret that a period in my life that had come to an end did so so quickly . . . Antioch was not just a great place to me but a place where events that turned the way of my life took place."

Influenced by Antioch's probing milieu, she'd been drawn to Yale Law's pedagogy that explored underlying social policy. She also selected the small school for its unusual joint program, where she could get a master's and law degree simultaneously, adding only one year of school. "Here I was going to law school, which was like going to a craft or professional school. To feed the part of me that was in love with ideas for their own sake, I also went to graduate school." For her second and third law school years she would simultaneously be in Yale's eminent American Studies Program; her final year she would return full-time to law.

Juggling many spheres, by spring Eleanor applied to Operation-Crossroads Africa, a New York–based group sending students to work projects in West Africa. She received a grant for the demanding two-month summer trip. In June 1961 the adventurous twenty-four-year-old flew off to Africa, first stop Nigeria, then the Republic of Gabon—formerly part of French Equatorial Africa—where Nobel Peace Prize winner Dr. Albert Schweitzer had his hospital, and on to the newly independent Congo Republic. The young militant's customary lack of sentimentality extended even to her African heritage, a newly hallowed subject in the politics of 1961, when black Americans en masse were on the cusp of proudly claiming African roots.

"An indelible memory is of a woman half my size carrying what was surely a tree on her head. The log was so long and big it could only be called a tree. I joked with my black and my white friends, 'Where can I find the man to thank for throwing me off these shores, because I surely don't want to be carrying these things!' I didn't see any men carrying them."

In newly independent, tropical Gabon, Eleanor's group visited Schweitzer. Accompanied by several African youth, the meeting startlingly revealed to Eleanor how much her perspective was shaped by her American, rather than African, roots.

"I had to understand why the Africans didn't regard him as I did, as a great man. They saw Schweitzer correctly as, however benign, a figment of nineteenth-century Europe. And that is what he was. The very best of it." What some Africans resented was that Schweitzer didn't use his celebrity to build the modern hospitals they desired. Instead, he conformed to the setting: a tropical rain forest.

"The place was nothing we'd call a hospital." Eleanor remembers her trek into humid Lambaréné and her shock upon arrival. "Goats and animals were all right there mingling in the open air with the hospital tents; it was a conglomeration of tents, conditions one associates with the bush rather than the sanitary conditions of a hospital." The young Africans found this abominable. When Dr. Schweitzer was about to address their group, they rose and left. But Eleanor remained.

"I had to face it. I did want to hear what he had to say, and then hear what they had to say." Fact-based to the end, she wanted to get the evidence, weigh it, and draw her own conclusions.

"That frankly is a very Western approach and revealed me to be the American I surely was. I completely associated myself with the Africans as brothers and sisters throughout the trip, but for me to leave the room as they did when he spoke would have been fake." Even her strong politics didn't allow her to rise in solidarity. She really wanted both perspectives. This significant encounter, where her ideological impulse was overtaken by her empirical desire to understand Schweitzer's point of view, inoculated her against the romanticism of the coming Afrocentric years. Eleanor now understood "the me that had the genes of Africa, but none of their experiences. You don't become an instant African," she concludes. "That was before the dashiki. There was no outer garment to pretend with."

On August 17, Gabon's first anniversary of independence, Eleanor wrote Neil her excuses for not writing sooner. "Among them has been an affair with a Frenchman," she scrawled. "And I know what you're thinking—believe me it's not my fault that I ended up with a white man even on the blackman's continent." Although she would always acknowledge her special bond with "colored folks," her social life was never exclusive.

Equally unsentimentally, Eleanor rendered a hardheaded political judgment: "All of the talk about independence is pretty farcical when you consider how much control the French still exercise here. But the other side of the coin is pretty damned cynical because one gets the distinct impression that all would fall apart if the French really did pull out. This of course, speaks to the poor preparation the French gave these people. Indeed, in every area of life and work, some Frenchman is really running the show. On the road gangs, there is always a Frenchman who is directing the operation, in the banks, in the shops— everywhere." She closed, "Rather than proceed with my developed political tirade at this point, I shall save this choice bit for times when we should be doing law but feel like doing anything else."

When Eleanor returned that fall, New Haven 1961 was a hot spot. The new mayor, Richard Lee, piloted a "model city" program, soon to appear as New Frontier and Great Society legislation. Whole sections of the city were slated for demolition, with the first a black ghetto, the Dixwell Avenue neighborhood just to the north of Yale. The slum clearance project generated broad support—and passionate opposition from residents who called it "bulldozer redevelopment." Eleanor lived at 60 Dixwell Avenue, "in the heart of where the African-American community began in earnest, and there was a church next door because we could hear 'em on Sunday!"

Evoking the apartment, she recalls the small furnished lodging, "neat and quite livable for a student, a little dark," with a bedroom and bath off a central living/dining area, and kitchen in back. The small apartment, shared with Inez Smith from Dunbar, soon became a center for civil rights activity. While some Yale students still debated *Brown,* Eleanor recalls "a whole country alive with the civil rights movement."

As part of that pulsating energy, Eleanor, Neil and others started a chapter of the Congress on Racial Equality (CORE), "the logical vehicle, because it was the closest thing to an activist organization in the North."

The group, uniting black and white academics with working-class blacks, mostly men from the town, often met at Neil's apartment. Afterward, Eleanor and Neil sometimes noticed that phonograph records were missing and discussed this in the context of the Movement. Eleanor's position—"Let's face it, they're expropriating us. You've gotta expect it"—reflected radical sentiment of the time. Relieved to have the cross-class mix of people working together, these revolutionary Yalies were loath to criticize "the broad masses" for their behavior. Nor would they be so elitist as to complain about their "personal stuff" being taken.

Today Eleanor says, "The last laugh was on us. Of course, we didn't know who did it. At that point you couldn't do anything about it. Many of the meetings were also held in my house; of course I didn't have anything to steal."

The simmering class tensions surfaced in debates over tactics. "This was the age of Malcolm X, so it was quite relevant to discuss whether nonviolence was the appropriate strategy." The working-class black men threatened that if provoked they would retaliate with violence; the white intellectuals worried because they knew some of the men had guns. CORE codes, derived from its World War II pacifist origins, were clear that its reputation for principled action was its greatest asset.

"All I can say about that," says Eleanor, "is if you were in the South and you preached nonviolence, that was the most manly thing you could do because you were thrusting yourself in extreme danger. That's why it was Rosa Parks who put her body out there, not a man.

"In the North, where the backdrop was entirely different, how do you show that same sense of manliness? You don't say the same to white people, who don't have any Ku Klux Klan or White Citizens' Council, who aren't looking to gun you down. You say, 'If you don't change this society, I'm going to get some guns.'

"In the North, you could get away with that! Look at where the Black Panthers started: in the North, not the South! That was the Northern way to show manliness, to say, 'Eye for eye.'"

Male rhetoric notwithstanding, in practice there was strict adherence to nonviolence. The group picketed Woolworth's to protest the chain's Southern discrimination, and demonstrated against urban renewal. In October 1961, Eleanor reported for the Socialist Party newspaper, *New America,* on a New Haven CORE "sit-out" where 125 people staged a sidewalk action to protest the creation of "an army of displaced persons." The young advocate explained in a letter to the Yale *News*: "To Negroes in this city, the central fact about New Haven's redevelopment program is that it has made them move—sometimes two and three times, but rarely to better quarters . . . There comes a time when even the most patient among us can't take it anymore."

Constantly the word went out: "We gotta picket City Hall," the imposing Church Street building on the New Haven Green. Eleanor shivers decades later, remembering the penetrating, icy New England wind as she joined her comrades. Torn from her studies, the militant always heeded the call. And, adopting the discipline of the Southern sit-in movement, people dressed up.

"We did not go down there with baggy pants and stuff. Look, they're not going to put that on us. If they're going to get us, it's not going to be for that."

The CORE chapter was led by a twenty-four-year-old city man, Blyden Jackson. A radical ex-marine, one of the first black drill sergeants, Blyden was "a charismatic figure straight from central casting," Eleanor describes his appeal. "In his speeches and his capacity to bring people to the chapter, he was The Man." In Blyden Eleanor saw every quality she admired: political commitment, brilliance, a hard-hitting style and good looks. In addition, in 1962, there was romance and cachet in his status: he was a local.

"I'm reasonably sure Blyden was her first working-class lover," Neil ventures. "He presented all kinds of problems for her: he wouldn't give her any prestige as a black middle-class woman; he teased her for talking funny. But Eleanor can get down, could talk his talk, she knew more about black radicals and history than he did, so she was his match. Blyden was such a magnetic, terrific speaker, with enormous native intelligence. I think she really cared for him a lot."

Blyden, a born leader, was a lot like Eleanor: articulate, impatient and talented. The two forceful leaders each represented a constituency—Eleanor the left-wing university intellectuals, Blyden the workers in the community—and together they led New Haven CORE. It was a powerful combination.

Often together, picketing, planning demonstrations and partying, Eleanor and Blyden sometimes traveled to New York to meet her political friends from Antioch. Characteristically egalitarian, Eleanor emphatically denies their speculation that the educational and social gap between Blyden and herself was problematic.

"He wasn't as well educated as I—how many were in America?—but he was extraordinarily intelligent and articulate. Blyden quickly pierced any class differences." Laid off from "some working-class job, he was getting unemployment insurance. He was always writing, and a leader in any talk about race."

But the idyll was soon punctured. One spring evening in April 1962, Blyden's wife, from whom he had claimed estrangement though he often stayed with her and the children, shot him in the chest with his own gun. It was a tremendous shock. Eleanor and Inez were questioned by police, along with other CORE associates. Seeking to protect his wife, Blyden had invented a story of attack on the street by a stranger. But the fabrication quickly unraveled.

The shooting abruptly dispelled Eleanor's illusions about Blyden and the affair deflated. His ability to act as her equal—a partner in politics and romance—was a compelling aphrodisiac. But even when gripped by strong feelings, head triumphed over heart. The violent incident seared her consciousness with the danger Blyden represented to her civil rights career; once she saw him for what he was, "a charming liar," she told a friend, she resolutely turned her attention elsewhere and avoided him, eventually urging Movement colleagues to do the same.

By June 1962, Eleanor was in New York on a summer job at Brennan, London and Buttenwieser, a law firm known for pro bono civil liberties cases. The law partners handled the famous Soblen case and Eleanor excitedly wrote an Antioch friend, "I was right there when the sensational news of his jumping bail broke."

Robert Soblen, a U.S. citizen convicted of spying for the USSR, sought asylum in Israel under its Law of Return for Jews. Eleanor, with a knack for finding herself in the midst of breaking events, had "a thrilling time. My office was the most exciting place to be in New York for the past three days." Every newspaper, radio and TV reporter converged for a spectacular press conference.

"Cameras, lights—everywhere," she typed a letter to Neil. "My employers handled themselves with the greatest aplomb. Mr. London, considered by many to be the best appellate lawyer in America and conceded by all to be in the top five," said Soblen was improperly convicted but "his running away was an indecent, contemptible act, as it left those who had aided him in untenable positions." As for law partner Mrs. Helen Lehman Buttenwieser, who put up $30,000 bail, "she, in a beautifully feminine terribly sharp performance, said she was not discouraged from helping people because of this and took the opportunity to criticize the bail system as one which favored the rich over the poor." Eleanor lauded her employer, "despite the fact that her husband is a banker and that she is from a quite moneyed securities family (niece of Governor Lehman)." Mrs. Buttenwieser, a longtime New York Civil Liberties Union Board member, would befriend her young associate, becoming, Eleanor says with affection, "the role model to end all role models."

The explosive Soblen case made international headlines, especially when Israel deported him. On the U.S.-bound plane, Soblen slashed his wrists and was hospitalized in London before he fatally poisoned himself, plunging Israel into a climax of painful soul-searching. Eleanor, disillusioned that it had come to suicide, dashed a note to Neil, "Off with Ben Gurion's head. The 1st political refugee in Israel's history ever to be refused . . . A Jewish homeland without guts."

Over the summer Eleanor was ever on the go, attending political meetings and rallies. Like the few other Negroes involved in left-wing parties, her politics were practical and urgent; she was impatient with interminable discussions about agriculture yields in Kazakhstan. "We dissipate too much energy discussing and formulating tactics of little use to us," she wrote Neil. In contrast, she described a picket line at Bethel Hospital that was "a real union line—lots of yelling at scabs and people who cross it, none of the non-violent overtones of CORE lines."

Eleanor's job and civic commitments didn't preclude a night life. "Last weekend was superb," she wrote. "Did they tell you how we capped it off—homemade (by Vicki) blintzes at 2 am Monday, preceded by a ride thru Harlem in a topped-down Chevy to the groans and screams of a Negro minister rapidly approaching orgasm in his zest for God."

Or "Tonite am going to Small's Paradise, a niteclub in Harlem, with an Antioch friend. Went once before. It swings." In a replay of the 1920s, the club was once again frequented by whites. "But the niggers still hold fort. There is a wild floor show . . . The chicks," she wrote unself-consciously before her feminist awakening, "all quite Negroid go from lighter than me to black as DP. They do a great twist, with the blackest chick coming on in the wildest way, which all goes to confirm the ancient myth. And I luv it!!!" At twenty-five Eleanor was so at ease with her black self—just as she had been at eighteen, when she wrote "Thank God I'm a Negro"—that she could joke about the stereotype to her best Yale friend, a white man, and simultaneously appreciate the truth behind the myth.

On another Monday morning she wrote, "This week-end was fantastic. Parties Fri., Sat., & Sun. nite. I twist myself to death at these functions & the practice I've had here has left me the current champ. If this dance to end all dances ever goes out of style, I'll die."

Weekends held their political quota as well. "Rally Sat in Harlem at 125th and 7th Avenue called by Malcolm, challenging the other civil rights leaders to come. . . . yesterday an even more fantastic unity at the Hospital Workers Rally . . . militantly calling for legislation telling the MAN that we're watching to see what he's going to do." At the rally a new mentor—an imperious, sophisticated, bohemian intellectual, the organizer Bayard Rustin—dragged her on stage with others to sing "We Shall Overcome."

Eleanor's life in New York City the summer of 1962 was organized much as it would ever be. Decades later, as responsibilities increased, proportions would change but her heart would remain anchored in all three places: laughter, hard work and the watershed events of the day, where she liked to keep the political waters roiling.

When Eleanor returned for her third fall at Yale, she moved into a second-floor flat at 106 Park Street with Moot Court opponent Barbara Babcock and American Studies student Judith Stein. The apartment, decorated with masks and baskets Eleanor bought in Africa, would be home for the next two years, one remembered by all three roommates as a haven of "warmth and laughter." This home extended to include Neil and Ethel—whose father owned the building—living just below with their baby girl.

Eleanor and Barbara shared a bedroom. One night as Barbara typed a paper in bed while her roommate slept, Eleanor jumped up screaming.

"Rats, rats, rats in the room!"

Sleep was typically a refuge for Eleanor, but the clinking of typewriter keys had mimicked rats—one of the few creatures Eleanor feared—running through the walls of her Cleveland room.

As might be expected, the cooking was all in-house. "We certainly didn't have money to eat out!" The other two quickly learned that Eleanor only cooked chicken. Ever one to find a rationale for her actions, Eleanor defended herself by insisting there were three basic foods: chicken, onions and rice, which could be combined in numerous ways to make different dishes.

The apartment was soon full of the vigorous debate that was oxygen for Eleanor's brain and soul. The three roommates argued politics constantly, with the two law students cross-examining Judith, bantering that this American Studies student didn't have the evidence to back her points.

"Eleanor especially could be very forceful in arguing against you," Judith remembers. "She'd ask, 'Why did you do this?' 'Who told you that? Well, who told *them?*' "

These nightly conversations never took a personal turn. Not the confiding type, according to all who knew her, Eleanor didn't respond to even direct inquiries with any response but her standard one.

"Everything is fine."

And in truth, she was not deceptive in this stock response. In her world, everything *had* to be fine. Eleanor had observed her mother maintain the "It's fine" façade about her marriage even when it wasn't—and thus preserve a satisfactory, respectable life.

And it wasn't just her family values that Eleanor exhibited. Given the priorities she had established, her life really *was* fine. She simply did not allow herself to be distracted by what were, to her, the essentially irrelevant complaints that occupied many peoples' attention.

Her refusal to confide in typical "girl"-style talk did not preclude close bonds: she would remain devoted to her two roommates and, in the busy years to come, find at least occasional time for other old friends. Eleanor might not divulge her own concerns, but would be loyal when others were in need.

The polemical roommates often argued with houseguests late into the night. Debate was constant, with "everyone always being attacked from the left," Barbara laughs. Brigadier General Telford Taylor, the handsome former chief prosecutor at Nuremberg, commuted from Columbia University on Thursdays to teach a constitutional law class. Barbara, Judith and Eleanor were fascinated by his famous post–World War II cases that highlighted the conflict between personal responsibility and immoral Nazi demands. Sometimes he dined with the young women.

"Before there were public intellectuals, Telford was one," Eleanor rhapsodizes, remembering this "real man of the world" who practiced law, conducted internationally renowned cases—and an orchestra—yet contributed as a scholar. A true Renaissance figure, this law teacher became one of a handful of Eleanor's notable mentors.

There were other visitors. Civil rights workers like SNCC's Bob Moses stopped on trips to the North, fund-raising and recruiting students for Mississippi. Eleanor invited such colleagues over, but after meals often disappeared when her habit of after-dinner drowsiness took over. Barbara Babcock laughs years later, "That's how I saw the Movement: the great leaders came through our apartment but I washed the dishes."

Many young activists criticized the NAACP for what they saw as its staid, court-oriented ways. They were also critical of Reverend King and his SCLC for rushing into Southern towns under duress and following what soon became a familiar scenario: march, get arrested, attract media, post bail, and scoot out, leaving behind local folks who, though galvanized and publicized, had to stay and live with the consequences of weekend actions. Students in SNCC and CORE pursued grassroots strategies, encouraging local autonomy and anchoring what they perceived as Dr. King's more "glamorous" glide-in-and-out role. SNCC staffers often ridiculed King as "De Lawd."

"Because we were young, we made fun of the style," Eleanor acknowledges. "SNCC people made fun of King for not being like us, that's what young people do. But that doesn't make them right! What would we have done without King? Or the NAACP?

"SNCC was organizers. That's not what King was! He was the conscience and the consciousness-raiser of the community; he was there to bring out the community so it could form a revolutionary cadre. We in SNCC were there to find Fanny Lou Hamer, to organize people to vote, not to raise consciousness." With her historian's analysis she adds, "The minister's job was to organize other ministers to lead their community.

"Everybody had their role and function: CORE, the NAACP, SCLC, SNCC. I think it's brilliant that our African-American community, instead of redundantly imitating one another and competing with one another, each found the niche that was needed. For all the difference and some of the tensions, I don't think there's ever been a movement that divided off as rationally and worked as well together."

Supplementing the stimulation of the movers and shakers who passed through her apartment, Eleanor also found mentors at Yale. One was the irrepressible Fred Rodell. An iconoclastic law professor, his infamous 1962 *Virginia Law Review* article, "Good-bye to Law Reviews" was a vivid example of his heretical views: "There are two things wrong with almost all legal writing. One is its style. The other is its content."

"Law has a job to do in the world," he wrote. "[It is] not just the slinging together of neat legalistic arguments." Rodell's course in legal writing was about how not to write lawyers' gibberish, for part of law school was teaching "lawyer-speak, a language that allows its practitioners to take with a straight face discussions that would cause most people to break out in laughter," says Eleanor's classmate Armand Derfner. "It was an indirect, elliptical, oblique style you pick up." But blunt-talking Eleanor, he observes, "picked it up and put it down." Fred Rodell helped her pop the balloon of obfuscation. But even this rule-breaker perpetuated one old bias: he held some of his seminars at the famous York Street Mory's Tavern, which barred women.

Helping buffer some of the women was another Yale mentor, Pauli Murray, the noted feminist lawyer then studying for an advanced legal degree. Marian Wright, Inez Smith, Eleanor and others often sat at the feet of this pioneer. Wright remembers the network that formed around Murray. "We had a world within a world. We had our own network and purpose, so one lived within two worlds."

"A much underappreciated figure," says Eleanor. "[Murray was] an eccentric woman who was not married, kept impeccable records that she moved everywhere she went, and had a beloved miniature dog. Yet her feminism seemed way out to us then. Although we thought she was right, we thought that she was a bit much. But I always admired her, believed I had to catch up with her, wanted to do so without all of her eccentricities. She seemed perfectly happy as a single woman and early feminist, alone in the world of her ideas and work."

In the early 1960s a new wave of feminists was just beginning to stir; President Kennedy had recently laid part of the groundwork by creating a Commission on the Status of Women. Chaired by Eleanor Roosevelt, it was a harbinger of a revolution on its way, in which the younger Eleanor would soon be a figure.

Eleanor studied both law and American history, while teaching English and Speech at New Haven College. Neil, who also taught, drove her back and forth on his motorcycle. Eleanor was in perpetual motion. And she loved it.

"Most law school material is inherently dry, reading property or corporate law, but this was the height of Warren Court decisions. I was learning law at a time when law was going through the most revolutionary change that any court has ever been a part of. Courts don't *do* revolution, but you're learning the law as it is changing beneath your feet.

"There hadn't been any constitutional law to speak of before the 1940s! Much of First Amendment law was developed out of the civil rights movement. That law didn't exist. People think the First Amendment was created in the writing of the Constitution. Only on paper. The whole civil rights movement was predicated on free speech." Coming of age during this heightened awareness, the student watched mass arrests for marching and protesting. Later she would work full-time to protect the free speech right that sheltered her movement.

The social intensity of the sixties led to a focus on real-world concerns, even in term papers. "I went to law school to be a civil rights lawyer. Like a laser beam I'd go toward a justice subject. A lot of the justice that we take for granted now was nonexistent, like the right to counsel, even in felonies! This was the time of the Warren Court when basic rights were being put in place."

Eleanor's 1962 Criminal Procedure paper critiqued the bail system as discriminatory, subjective and irrational. She offered as alternative a then experimental program—the Manhattan Bail Project—that selectively eliminated bail as a condition of pretrial parole.

Her American Studies work under renowned historians John Morton Brown and C. Vann Woodward also turned toward justice. A final paper, "World War II and the Beginning of Non-Violent Action in Civil Rights," described black anger at segregated armed services and the launching of an innovative World War II protest tactic: nonviolent resistance. The pacifist Fellowship of Reconciliation created CORE to pioneer the new approach. Tracing its evolution, Eleanor was "thrilled to have a real-live original source" in Pauli Murray, who wrote in 1945: "I do not intend to destroy segregation by physical force . . . I hope to see it destroyed by a power greater than all the robot bombs and explosives of human creation—by a power of the spirit . . . and by inviting violence upon my own body."

The status of blacks and other excluded Americans was a constant theme in Eleanor's time at Yale, where she used papers as virtual practicums on issues she would later confront. During her third year, in 1963, the lawyer-in-training researched President Kennedy's new Committee on Equal Employment Opportunity; she would later chair this committee's successor, making an impact she could not then imagine.

Eleanor was conducting research essential to her entire life, but she often left papers until the last possible moment. Able to easily fall asleep, she napped after dinner no matter what needed doing. Hours before a paper was due, Eleanor announced her plan.

"First thing I'll do is get rested. Wake me up, somebody wake me in a half hour."

She'd fall into a deep sleep, awaken, write it and hurry off. "I was famous for that." Anxiety, roused to fever pitch in the hours before a deadline, motivated production. As she admitted in her Antioch application, even as a child she put everything off until the last minute. "I sure was a procrastinator." But she simultaneously defends and criticizes her habit.

"I am at my creative best when I have to get it done. It's more intense. And it introduces sometimes necessary anxiety into the picture."

Coleman, also a perfectionist, had a similar tendency toward this "bad habit." Relentlessly self-critical, she says, "while I never missed a deadline, and I never turned in something that was bad work, I can't help feeling that if I had more time to be more reflective, I could've done better. Even when I got an A."

Last minute frenzy was to become a lifetime method, but in later years she would labor over each last minute draft that left her office. The child expected to produce stellar work grew into an adult still endeavoring to fulfill her family and community ideals.

Eleanor worked hard, but she also played. In preparation for one house party, she tried to teach her housemates the twist. They just couldn't get it. So, with a Chubby Checker record playing, all three ended up taking off their clothes so the two white women could see exactly how Eleanor was doing it and she could critique their moves. Eleanor "gyrated in sort of a frantic way, like a hula hoop, in a really cool colored way," laughs Barbara years later, slipping into the words of an earlier time, adopting the language Eleanor used.

In an era of segregation, Eleanor was the first black friend of virtually all her white companions at Antioch and Yale; she seemed impervious to barriers cultural differences might present to social intimacy. Her generous sense of friendship fostered fellowship across racial lines; personal remarks that might insult others did not offend—or even penetrate—the political militant's consciousness. "The whole notion that when there is inadvertent personal insult . . . given the history of race in this country, to pounce on some white person who is *trying* and makes a mistake is like being a bully, taking advantage!" Eleanor says today.

The trio held their dancing party, served the requisite onion soup dip and potato chips with gin and orange juice or a jug of Chianti, and danced the night away.

Another freezing New England December evening, Barbara and Eleanor arrived home from studying to find a man passed out on the street. Rushing inside they called an ambulance, then dashed back out to see about the man, who soon woke up mumbling. The ambulance crew arrived and realized they had a drunk on their hands.

"You shouldn't have called an ambulance, you should have called the police," they fumed. "Now you'll have to pay us fifty dollars!"

"Are you crazy?" Eleanor screamed. "This is your job. This man could have died. Get away from me with your fifty dollars!"

Barbara, brought up as a white Southern woman to accommodate the demands of others, was ready to run inside and get a check. Eleanor had learned well from Coleman, who allowed no indignity to go unremarked. The men backed off.

By midstream at Yale, Eleanor cut a figure. Lawyer Christine Philpot's vivid first image of Eleanor is emblazoned in her memory. The Law School Library, a grand stone edifice garnished by a series of spires, with thirty-foot leaded windows highlighted by intricate stained-glass medallions, was a formidable structure. Even the graceful wooden study carrels intimated history, reverence and silence. When fellow student Jerry Brown (later governor of California) showed Christine the sanctified library on her initial visit, there was Eleanor piercing the quiet.

"The hell with you, Goldstein!" she stormed, arguing with another student.

"I was just knocked out by her knowing what she was talking about and her fierceness and preparation," remembers Christine. "She was so very political and focused and strong and verbal that it was love at first sight. This world needed Eleanors, and there she was."

That spring Eleanor showed just how quick her wit could be. When classmate Armand Derfner planned a move to Washington, Eleanor offered her parents' home as temporary lodgings and went with

Armand and his wife to look for an apartment. One prospective land-lord looked incredulously at the threesome: two whites and a Negro.

"I can clean this, I can keep it clean," Eleanor smiled at Armand.

On that note the three laughed, turned on their heels and left.

During these years Eleanor indulged in every bit of the political exhil-aration of the time. But the summer of 1963 she did it all. "I went as an SNCC worker to Mississippi, I went to Europe to represent United States students, and then I worked with the March on Washington. A whirlwind time it was."

Opposition to new federal rulings had exploded all over the South. Crowds of whites screaming, "Two four six eight, we don't want to inte-grate!" became a familiar sight on the six o'clock news. Many whites developed a siege mentality. Civil rights bills, some claimed, gave Negroes "special privileges and more rights than us white people." In South Carolina, the legislature raised the Confederate battle flag as a gesture of defiance; it would be up for the next forty years.

But even in this climate of hostility, Mississippi was understood to be a place apart. "Mississippi is a magic word of universal significance," Eleanor wrote then, "In New York and Paris, in Peiping and Poland, Mississippi is one of the evil wonders of the world." Its open violence was incited by its legendary senator, Theodore Bilbo.

"The best way to keep a nigrah from the polls on election day is to pay him a visit at home the evening before."

Young SNCC workers had penetrated the sweltering Delta, encour-aging voting in an area blanketed by fear. The Delta, formed by rich silt washed from the banks of the Mississippi and Yazoo Rivers, was known as a vicious area. The fate of farmer Herbert Lee—who, wrote activist Chuck McDew, "attempts to vote on Tuesday and is dead on Saturday"—was but one example of how dangerous it was in the flat, Klan-dominated lands. The struggle was fierce. Less than 2 percent of Mississippi's half-million black adults were registered to vote.

Segregation, written into the very bylaws of the state Democratic Party, was enforced by an alliance of lawmakers, police forces, judges and White Citizens' Councils. The whole state—called by SNCC's Bob Moses "a South African enclave within the United States"—was orga-nized to keep black people from power, and the federal government provided no protection to those demanding change.

"My mother was trepidatious about me going to Mississippi," Eleanor shudders. "Everyone knew you took your life in your hands to run an operation of young people known for their militance in the part of Mississippi where a man's life wasn't worth the paper his birth certificate was written on."

Voting—a lever of power—was the focal point in 1963. Bob Moses, a Harvard-trained SNCC staffer famous for his courage in going to the fearsome Delta, encouraged Eleanor and her classmate Marian Wright to come: they had few black lawyers, and fewer still who would take their cases. Even law students could help.

Eleanor describes her June arrival in Jackson. The first sit-in had occurred just a week before. "We're talking about the raw atmosphere of Mississippi without any protection. That's why Medgar Evers [the first NAACP field secretary in the state] and everybody who went to the sit-in had their heads beat so bad. They beat the hell out of them on the stool."

Evers drove Eleanor around town to meet key civil rights workers. "He took me home. I met Myrlie [his wife], talked with them for some time and then he took me to the bus station." Just hours later that night, Evers was shot in the back, assassinated in his own driveway when he came home from a meeting.

Eleanor found out the next day. "When I came into Greenwood they took me to the home of a tenant farmer on the corner. 'Here's another person to put up.'

"That is the only time I've ever had a bath where you heated the water on the stove and then poured it in. Talk about primitive. And I did it." A mouse ran through the room as she heated water. She froze. But she forced herself to step in, and "I'm sitting in this washer tub, washing, when one of the young kids ran in, 'Medgar Evers was shot last night. You got to come.'"

Bob Moses was north raising money; the SNCC office was temporarily run by local student Lawrence Guyot, who had rushed to get Mrs. Fannie Lou Hamer out of jail in nearby Winona.

"Ms. Hamer had done what Fannie Lou was born in this world to do. She used the bathroom in the bus station, because it was an interstate commerce facility." Arrested with Greenwood teenager June Johnson and several others, "they proceeded to beat her." Eleanor spells it out sadly. "When Larry went over to get her in Winona, they proceeded to beat *him* and arrest *him*."

Less than twenty hours after Eleanor reached Mississippi, the senior Movement leader was dead. Others were out of state or in jail, threatened with murder. A law student was suddenly the most senior person around, even though she had just arrived the night before.

The students, "a bunch of SNCC kids" dressed in faded blue overalls like Delta farmers, asked Eleanor, "What are we going to do now?"

On her first morning in this dangerous territory, Eleanor's oftnoted, puzzling lack of visible emotion allowed her the mental space to do what she did best: think.

"Here's where figuring out what to do is important. Two had been beaten. So do you simply like a fool walk in as number three?"

Eleanor interrogated the young people, searching for clues, acting like the lawyer she was on her way to becoming.

"Tell me about what's been happening. I want to know more. Because we've certainly got to go get him now."

She learned that White Citizens' Councils regularly drove by the SNCC office to intimidate the civil rights workers.

"Of course," Eleanor laughs grimly, "SNCC would then call Bobby Kennedy's office and be told that under federal law they could do nothing. Which is why you never see me a big Kennedy type."

When Citizens' Council members circled civil rights offices in other towns, she heard, they frequently had law enforcement officers with them. However, the Greenwood police chief was known for not accompanying harassers. He didn't protect SNCC workers nor actively seek to arrest Klan or Citizens' Council members.

"But he was considered a man apart because he was never, like so many others, involved in lawless activity against blacks." Such relatively benign behavior was rare. "This was the unbroken Delta! I mean the terrorist Delta!"

On the basis of this information about the chief, Eleanor walked over to his office.

"I'm Eleanor Katherine Holmes. I've been told that you've been fair and decent. I'm going to ask you to do me a favor. I want you to call the police chief in Winona and tell him I'm coming to get the folks out of prison. And let me tell you something! I go to Yale Law School"—she outranked him—"and I have called everybody to tell them where I will be going. I have done that to protect myself. I do not intend to be the third person to enter your jails."

He made the call.

"I went over the next morning. It was so hot and nasty. If you had said, 'Create a scene of blacks held captive, in violation of every conceivable right under the worst circumstances in the most notoriously racist state and set of circumstance in America,' you couldn't have come up with a setting like that jail. Guyot had to get some clothes on because they had beat him so bad he was virtually naked. They had let him out at night to be beat by the White Citizens' Council. These people meant business. It was hotter than hell in there, with Ms. Hamer and some others in a segregated cell.

Ms. Hamer had barely survived a beating by black trustees, inmates instructed, "I want you to make that bitch wish she was dead." They were threatened that if they didn't use the blackjack on her, "You know what I'll use on you."

"That's how you humiliated people," Eleanor says somberly. "Make them beat their own people."

Ms. Hamer would later testify that, facedown, "I was beat by the first Negro until he was exhausted . . . After the first Negro had beat until he was exhausted, the State Highway Patrolman ordered the second Negro to take the blackjack. . . . I began to scream and one white man got up and began to beat me in my head and tell me to hush."

Two days later, after national news media were alerted and SNCC workers visited to let jailers know someone was watching, Dr. King's aide Andrew Young arrived and was allowed to post bail.

"The long and short of it is, our strategy worked," says Eleanor. "I claim no special courage. I do claim some brains . . . and Guyot never forgot it."

Attesting to his ordeal years later, Guyot's large body leans back in his office chair as he says, "They threatened to burn my genitals. I knew that I had to stay conscious, otherwise I was dead. [Eleanor's] involvement in building a bridge between political activism, academia, and her ability to deal with anyone she met on her terms is what ties me to Eleanor."

This capacity to travel across ethnic and class lines would be a lifelong trait. SNCC's mix was similar to CORE's. The Northern version combined intellectuals with working-class black urbanites; here it was students and poor farmers. Mississippi college students who had rarely left the state had not met someone like Eleanor before. Many were in awe of this woman going to "a big-time college, for *two* degrees," says one. Yet Eleanor plunged right in "and started talking to local people, as we were referred to," Dorie Ladner laughs. "When people like Eleanor and others came, thank God, they helped open this beast up."

At the end of June, Eleanor sent a postcard to Neil: "Greetings from Hell—the Delta, that is. . . . Have seen everything—from Negroes throwing rocks to Negroes being beaten . . . the fight is a revolution down here. The Northern movement looks puny beside this. Just being a freedom fighter down here is risking death—& I've been scared ever since I got here. Also found me the most fearless Nigger in the world to call my very own—just to round things out."

Looking back, Eleanor leans forward over her massive congressional desk, intently summarizing her Mississippi summer, "That's how you seal a lifetime commitment, when you've had a life-changing experience.

"I was a half-Southern, half-Northern Negro, from a sophisticated Northern father and a country girl Southern mother. I was real half-and-half, for whom the stark oppression of the South was a matter of current and past oral history and all there was to read. But I certainly had not experienced it myself. And now I saw it up close. This time my nose was not up against the glass. I had cracked the glass, I was inside.

"When you're down there and you're black it doesn't matter where you're from or how sassy you were up North, how many white people you had told, 'Better get out of my way,' or how much dignity you had—and I'm telling you I had a lot!" Her voice is grim.

"I'm telling you my father sent me back to the grocery store when I was a child and told me what to say: 'We don't accept bread that's not in a bag!' " She moves her head forward, jabbing her finger, punching her words across the desk. "In Greenwood it didn't matter that was the way I believed I could speak to white people in Washington. What mattered was that that culture," her voice rises, "was capable of *killing* black people for a simple misstep. They knew it and I knew it. Therefore it paid to be calculating if you wanted to prevail. And we had to prevail."

After a month in the terror of the Delta, Eleanor dashed off to Europe, "an amazing contrast to Mississippi," she scrawled on a postcard to a friend. The young woman cloistered by segregation took no time to decompress, but piled another extraordinary experience on top of her searing Southern encounter. One of five representatives chosen by the United States Youth Council, a group formed like others in the 1960s to represent "the American way of life" abroad, she flew off to meet her counterparts in eight European countries.

"Saw *Julius Caesar* at Stratford last nite," she dashed off in another postcard. "From here we go to Germany and ultimately to France, Yugoslavia, Italy, Austria, Finland and Holland. A free trip thru Europe is still something of a dream, even now that I'm in it!"

At the end of July the whirlwind rushed back to New York to organize for the 1963 March on Washington, a coalition of rights groups, churches and white-led labor unions. She was pulled into the historic event by friends like Michael Harrington, Bayard Rustin and Rachelle Horowitz, later political director of the American Federation of Teachers. Socialist leader Harrington was known, and sometimes debunked, for practicing "the left-wing of the possible," which in practical terms meant working within the Democratic Party or coalitions like this one. Eleanor would adopt this philosophy—to push and stretch, but in the end, to adapt—as a lifelong principle.

Rustin, the principal March organizer, "was probably the first openly gay person I was close to. It never occurred to me to have questions about his being gay. Nobody thought anything about it, even though that was unusual in those days." (Actually it had caused Rustin's expulsion in the mid-fifties from Montgomery by leaders who feared he'd taint the Movement; the label would haunt Rustin's public life for the rest of his organizing career.)

"He'd been arrested once. His gayness did come up during the March but was put away. It was raised by the racists, Strom Thurmond or some such, as a way to smear the Movement, which was the best way to get it raised because it pointed up the prejudice that was really at its root." On August 13, two weeks before the March, Thurmond denounced the pacifist Rustin in the Senate as a "draft dodger, a homosexual and a Communist." He inserted a copy of Rustin's ten-year-old Pasadena police booking slip for sodomy into the *Congressional Record,* making sure details reached news media.

"The big Six or the big Ten [as major civil rights leaders were variously called] rejected the attack," says Eleanor. "I'm sure everybody was nervous that the March could be attacked on any ground because it was such an unprecedented event." The powerful Roy Wilkins had opposed

Rustin's leadership because of his pacifism, his socialism, and the sex charge. "Do you think we ought to bring all that into the March on Washington?" he'd asked. A "compromise" utilized Rustin as behind-the-scenes deputy director, with A. Philip Randolph as titular head.

In New York Eleanor bunked in Rachelle Horowitz's one bedroom union co-op on 24th Street and 8th Avenue, with Dorie Ladner, up from Mississippi to work in SNCC's 5th Avenue office, her sister Joyce Ladner, a SNCC staffer on the March, and Rachelle. The space was jammed. Eleanor thrived in the lively environment, laughing and enjoying long, deep conversations about politics with the worldly Rachelle, as the two talked into the early morning hours.

The small apartment was a hangout where SNCC staffers, socialists, students and Movement people of all kinds went to relax and talk. One frequent visitor was Bob Dylan, who'd been in Mississippi and found an acolyte in Dorie. He'd pluck his guitar late into the evenings, while Joyce wished he'd go home so she could go to bed on the sofa. The three who worked at the March office on 130th Street—Eleanor, Joyce and Rachelle—had to dash out early every morning for the subway ride to work; they staggered home exhausted around ten each night, only to hear Bob's voice before they opened the door.

"Oh God," they'd whisper to each other, "that guy is here again." The twenty-four-year-old Rachelle was especially annoyed because Bob had complained that the apartment—her first grown-up one, painstakingly decorated with bat wing chairs, foam rubber couches and African art—was too bourgeois.

Like Eleanor's apartment at Yale, this one hummed. Eleanor's boyfriend from Mississippi, Frank Smith (later a Washington D.C. council member), arrived for an extended visit, squeezing into the jammed space. And a few days before the March, SNCC's chair John Lewis spent an entire night in the living room rehearsing, bellowing out his speech in what he remembers as the "very homey, warm, lived-in apartment." "We all slept in the bedroom that night," Rachelle sighs many decades later.

Eleanor was always in the social mix, dancing and having a good time, a trait much appreciated by the younger Mississippians. "She never made me feel as though I was a kid, though she was six years older than I," Dr. Joyce Ladner reminisces from the vantage of her own middle age. She sums up, "I saw Eleanor as a bohemian black person, very thin, with a razor sharp mind, and outspoken. She wasn't diplomatic then, and still today rather speaks truth."

Eleanor worked at March headquarters with Rachelle, the transportation director. The Harlem office, in an old building owned by Friendship Baptist Church, hung a giant banner from the third-story window: MARCH ON WASHINGTON FOR JOBS AND FREEDOM—AUGUST 28.

"Bayard was an intellectual and an organizer, the likes of which I had not seen before and have not seen since. He brought to bear a set of talents that usually don't come in one person." Not unlike Eleanor, with the aura of an intellectual but the hard-nosed determination of a strategist, he applied his theories to concrete problems. She was fascinated to watch her mentor operate.

"I was well aware of his analytical dimension," she says describing this man so like her in his ability to span worlds. "But the notion of pulling together something for which there is no formula, no precedent, no network; having to construct it from the ground up!" Eleanor speaks almost reverently. "Nobody who organized a march afterwards has ever, will ever get the kind of credit from me that Bayard got for breaking ground and showing that you could bring 250,000 people, for the first time. No one thought it would be that big. If it was that big, everybody thought it couldn't work.

"There was no experience . . . The '57 march [the Prayer Pilgrimage] was not in any league with this. That was simply a caravan, a drop in the ocean compared to what we were doing: organizing a national March on Washington, of the kind no one had seen before!"

The prospect unnerved the Kennedy administration. "They said this could not be done, had not been done and should not be done. They used every argument in the book, including 'Where will all those people go to the bathroom?' " She chortles. "Bayard was really ready for them, as a labor guy who knew where construction workers went!"

In preparation, Eleanor zipped around New York encouraging people to participate and hustling buses to get them there. On Tuesday, August 27, the last day before the March, Rustin passed out final duties. One person would have to remain to close the office, flying in to Washington just as the March began. Years later Eleanor still smiles her joy in a rare look of innocent girlishness.

"He gave it to me."

All the long night before the March, after the rest of the staff had departed by car, train and bus for Washington, Eleanor alone answered telephones. In the morning she turned out the lights, hurried to LaGuardia and boarded an airplane.

"As this plane flew over the Washington Monument, I saw the handiwork of our effort." She leans back in her congressional armchair and spreads her arms, beaming. "I looked out of the window and as far as I could see there were people. Voilà! I'm just so sorry that nobody from our office got to see this but me. I was ecstatic by the time I got off the plane." Eleanor's mood was mirrored by the crowd. The gathering sea of faces radiated joy. They had done it!

At the Lincoln monument SNCC staffers—the shock troops of the Movement—were embroiled in controversy over John Lewis's speech. All the previous evening March leaders had pressured him to tone it down, remembers Gloria Steinem. Eleanor adds, "Cardinal Patrick O'Boyle thought John's threat to 'march through the South' had too much of a military ring to it." Behind Lincoln's statue a fragile coalition of civil rights leaders met until they reached a formulation agreeable to all. With the help of SNCC's James Forman and Courtland Cox, Lewis furiously rewrote his speech on a portable typewriter while the crowd was warmed by freedom songs. The legendary Marian Anderson sang once again at the Lincoln Memorial and Mahalia Jackson delivered a husky "I Been 'Buked and I Been Scorned."

After an invocation by the soothed cardinal, veteran organizer A. Philip Randolph reminded the nation, "We are the advance guard of a massive moral revolution for jobs and freedom." The moral revolution, however, was decidedly male; all the speakers were men. This exclusion would smolder and ignite before the civil rights decade concluded. But as yet Eleanor, like most other activists, was oblivious to the gender disparity between staff and leaders.

John Lewis's revised words still criticized the government and both political parties. "For the party of Kennedy is also the party of Eastland," he said, describing well-known adversaries. "The party of Javits is also the party of Goldwater! Where," he asked, repeating a question asked by many young civil rights workers, "is *our* party?" The Democratic Party—and its appropriateness as a vehicle for change—would be a matter of contention between Eleanor and many friends for decades to come.

Finally, the last speaker of the day, Dr. King, opened to waves of applause. He counterposed current deprivations with the hypnotic, hopeful refrain, "I have a dream!" The huge throng, deeply affected, roared a response each time he intoned it, and thundered when he stressed, in his deep rich voice, that "we cannot be satisfied as long as the Negro in Mississippi cannot vote, and a Negro in New York believes he has nothing for which to vote. No! No!"

President Kennedy did not attend the momentous event but reluctantly endorsed it. His primary objection had been that whites would be too threatened by a gigantic black presence to ever pass the Civil Rights Bill. But the peaceful protest allayed more fears than it roused. As Rustin later wrote, it was "important to get thousands of white people into the streets in Washington," to signal new, broad-based support.

The day after the March a young people's socialist conference was held in Washington that Eleanor and many friends attended. She would soon leave any formal socialist connections, but her early radical roots, nourished in the soil of passionate commitment and rigorous analysis of injustice, would inform her actions for the rest of her life.

Fully engaged North and South, on September 9 Eleanor reluctantly left her March follow-up work in its Harlem offices and returned for her final year at Yale. A week later black Americans and their allies were further galvanized when dynamite exploded, killing four young girls in their Baptist Sunday School room. As a horrified nation grieved, Eleanor wrote a defiant poem, "For the Birmingham Children," that continually reprised the line, "We shall endure."

By midwinter, Eleanor wrote Antioch administrator Jessie Treichler, "I'm busy going ten ways at once here, teaching at New Haven College, tutoring a junior high school child, marking themes for another instructor at the college, and doing research for one of my professors who is revising a book on political and civil rights."

Running between the courtyards of Yale and the more pedestrian classrooms of New Haven College, she maintained her webs of contact: the black world of Dunbar classmates, neighbors and family back in Washington; white Antioch administrators and friends; a national group of socialist leaders; new colleagues from Yale; a legal network of scholars and civil libertarians; local CORE activists and SNCC revolutionaries spread all over the country; and national figures from the March. Her senior year flew by.

On a bright sunny day in June, Eleanor Katherine Holmes, capping the master's honors she won in American Studies the previous year, graduated from Yale Law School in a magnificent courtyard ceremony her proud mother called "inspiring."

In assessing her Yale experience, Eleanor muses, "I now understand, only in looking back, why schools like Yale are great. It drew students of such intellectual curiosity that everyone got pushed to a higher level than she might otherwise have attained." Essentially, Eleanor concludes, the community of peers more than the community of scholars drove the law school's quality.

"You analyzed everybody from Marx to Kennedy," she recalls, remembering her time at Antioch and Yale, "*why* this was wrong and that was right, not *that* this was wrong or right." She pauses. "After that kind of education, pure ideology never sufficed."

In the nine years since Eleanor had left Dunbar High School, the earth had cracked open. And Eleanor had discovered the world, just as she set out to do. Her application to Yale had contained her credo:

"Change is not something to be worked for simply because we can see it coming. The desire for a better life—or a better world—is a peculiarly human desire that does not depend for its vitality upon the possibility of success."

Her passion coincided with the country's, for the decade spanning her years in higher education was the one that dismantled the legal foundations of segregation.

"I grew up black and female at the moment in time in America when barriers would fall if you'd push them. I pushed . . . and then just walked on through."

Philosophically, when Eleanor entered Yale, she was already headed for the spot where she would land for life: "I need a reason for what I believe and I need to be able to think that through." Her commitment to "the evidence" was only strengthened by her legal training. In these four years she had evolved from a student risking arrest to a lawyer defending those arrested. Having mastered her craft, she was now primed to put it into service. Polished by Dunbar, Antioch and Yale, and sharpened by Mississippi, Eleanor was ready for battle.

CHAPTER 5

A Pivotal Year

"Eleanor could talk God out of a twenty-four-hour cycle in the day."
CHRISTINE PHILPOT, YALE LAW STUDENT

Shortly after graduation from Yale in 1964, Eleanor called Christine Philpot, the Bryn Mawr graduate who was "just the kind of colored girl I grew up with in Washington, and fancied herself a matchmaker." Eleanor opened the conversation.

"I hear you know all the men in the world."

"Yes," replied Christine, adding that she had little interest in them herself.

"Well, I'd like to meet some of them."

"You're too smart. Why would you need a man?" Christine discouraged her idol.

"Shut up, girl."

Right after law school Eleanor had spent a month at Christine's Philadelphia home while she took the bar review course, and knew the Philpots to be a family that "shared the values of my own parents. Wonderfully generous, attentive folks, a perfect proxy for my own home.

"There was no translation needed. Mrs. Philpot's values, the things she laughed at, were the things I'd laughed at all my life. There was very little distance between Philadelphia and Washington when it came to the shared experience, the culture." Christine's grandfather was a distinguished "Lincoln Republican" leader and minister, a man who gave the speeches of Cicero at the dinner table, and whose impeccable standards were reflected throughout the family.

Almost instantly, Christine thought of just the person for her friend: someone as argumentative as Eleanor. The tall and debonair Edward Worthington Norton seemed the perfect choice. Only the timing was a little off. He was currently involved; Eleanor would have to wait.

Besides, Eleanor had other things to do: fulfill a political commitment and begin a job.

After graduation Eleanor expected to return to Mississippi for another summer.

"I'm ready," she told Bob Moses in June of 1964.

But he had another task in mind. The new Mississippi Freedom Democratic Party (MFDP) planned to challenge the all-white Mississippi delegation to the Democratic Convention that summer. The MFDP, an outgrowth of the voting rights work she'd done the previous summer, attempted to offer black Mississippians a political voice after their exclusion from established channels.

Joseph L. Rauh Jr., a well-known white civil rights and labor attorney based in Washington, was in charge of writing the brief to the Democratic Party credentials committee, arguing that the MFDP should be considered Mississippi's legitimate delegation.

"We need one of our SNCC folks up there," Bob told Eleanor.

"And I was the lawyer," she says. "This was still a time when they were graduating two cents' worth of blacks from law school, so I was a very unusual commodity." Thus, the new graduate, radiating self-confidence, went for one last student summer to her parents' home. There she slid easily into her familiar round of politics, parties and work while she prepared the legal challenge.

Eleanor knew Joe Rauh by reputation. "Joe was who young lawyers wanted to grow up to be. One of the great lawyers in the McCarthy period who protected people, an extraordinary Washingtonian in our home rule fight. He lived a wonderful life."

Working with this man who "gave law a good name," Eleanor, delighted, went to work helping write the historic challenge. She and Miles Jaffe, a Harvard law student wrote the brief "as if we were partners to Joe Rauh." The junior partners drove in Miles's convertible back and forth to the law library. Then, remembers Eleanor, "we'd come in with what we'd done and Joe would sit and talk to us, looking at our work. That's how Joe treated us—though he was our mentor and teacher!"

The brief made the case that MFDP delegates should be seated at the Democratic Convention, rather than the fifty-eight white "regular" Mississippi delegates, because blacks had been systematically kept from voting and barred—sometimes at gunpoint—from every state precinct meeting. The powerful argument opened with a challenge, asking "whether the National Democratic Party takes its place with the oppressed Negroes of Mississippi or their white oppressors?" The brief, supported by the Democratic Committees of nine states and the District of Columbia, documented party disloyalty by the regular delegates, who supported Republican Barry Goldwater for president, and their methodical exclusion of blacks. Governor Paul Johnson, the leader of the Mississippi Democratic Party, was quoted ridiculing the NAACP acronym as "niggers, alligators, apes, coons and possums."

Eleanor and her colleagues left nothing out. They cited instance after instance of harassment: the names and addresses of Negroes who tried to vote were printed in newspapers, subjecting them to instant reprisal; would-be voters routinely suffered long waits in the blazing sun—six or seven hours, with no food or water. Homes were bombed. The list went on.

Yet within this pattern of terror, an extraordinary incubator of political participation was created. In response to bigotry, the seventy-page brief explained, the Freedom Democratic Party formed to give *all* Mississippians opportunity to participate; and despite harassment, it registered over 50,000 voters in its parallel process, held precinct meetings, conducted county and state conventions, and elected fifty-eight delegates who expected to represent their state at the National Convention. The legal summary compellingly argued that this delegation represented the legitimate party, the only one in the state run in accordance with the Constitution and the national Democratic Party.

The events of the summer bestowed a terrible added weight to the argument. On June 21, three civil rights workers, James Chaney, Andrew Goodman and Mickey Schwerner, were missing in Mississippi. "I shall never forget the hours and days of vigil amidst my work on the MFDP brief as we waited to hear word," Eleanor later told a *Jewish Currents* dinner. Soon the burned car of the three young men was found; on August 4 their charred, battered bodies were dug up on a farm near Philadelphia, Mississippi. Three weeks later MFDP delegates would bring the car hulk to the Atlantic City 1964 Democratic Convention and mount it on the boardwalk; a vivid, grisly illustration of the apartheid that existed a thousand miles south of the convention site.

Once she got to Atlantic City, Eleanor, operating out of a fleabag motel, directed the MFDP lobbying. She'd been appointed by a worn-out Miss Ella Baker, head of the MFDP office in Washington and "one of the great undervalued women. The civil rights movement was not open to women leaders."

Eleanor plunged into the nonstop work, determined that her lobbyists—Mississippians, many on their first trip out of state—would move every member of the 110-person credentials committee to the cause. Since other state delegations met at various times around the clock, the Mississippi lobbyists had to be ready to tell their dramatic stories "all day, all night. It was one of the most exhausting things I've ever done."

Directing the shabby office, she educated her lobbyists in the intricacies of a complex, pressure-cooker national process while she figured it out herself, using information gleaned from, among others, Christine Philpot's grandfather, a Taft delegate in the 1950s. In odd moments she dashed out to shore up wavering credentials committee members with vehement arguments; sometimes she ran by crowds of rambunctious sympathizers on the boardwalk outside.

"Ain't gonna let no beatings turn us around . . . marching up to Freedom land," demonstrators shouted with spirit. During the long sunny day they often sang Ms. Hamer's favorite hymn, "This little light of mine, I'm gonna let it shine. All over Atlantic City, I'm gonna let it shine. All over the Democrats, I'm gonna let it shine!" They encouraged each other and MFDP delegates inside the hall by singing the songs that had held their movement together. "Hold your eyes on the prize, hold on!"

"I remember dragging home to some dumpy rooming house at four o'clock every morning." Eleanor shakes her head. "And then getting up at seven o'clock to start all over again. No wonder Miss Baker gave it over to someone young enough to be her daughter!"

The work paid off. Delegates from other states were visibly shocked by Mississippians' horrific stories and swayed by their dedication to voting; the majority of the committee was ready to seat the Freedom Democrats. Sealing the commitment, the eloquent MFDP vice president, Ms. Fannie Lou Hamer, testified live to the nation. With tears welling, she reported eviction from her eighteen-year plantation job the day she tried to register and told of her savage beating in Winona's jail.

"Is this America, the land of the free and the home of the brave, where we have to sleep with our telephones off the hooks because our lives are threatened daily, because we want to live as decent human beings, in America?" As she closed, many of the seasoned politicians in her audience had moist eyes.

"When she appeared before the committee," says Eleanor, "the clock stopped in America."

But President Lyndon Johnson, terrified of alienating white Southerners, many of whom chaired congressional committees, called a hasty press conference midway through Hamer's speech. He successfully cut her off the air, then furiously pressed credentials committee members. Sixteen years before, Dixiecrats had walked out to protest a civil rights plank. He feared a replay.

"Actually," laughs Eleanor, "when you consider the party was running against Goldwater, it wouldn't have been much of a risk."

President Johnson dispatched his liberals—Hubert Humphrey and Walter Mondale—to arm-twist, dangling judgeships and threats. His tactics flipped the committee and prepared the ground for a paltry offer that included two nonvoting "honorary" seats for the MFDP and a promise to never again seat a segregated delegation.

Most of the group's senior advisors urged acceptance of the "compromise" as a first-step recognition. Rustin said rejection would mean turning their backs on their allies; he argued they were now in the world of politics, not protest, and that politics was the art of compromise. Dr. King reported that Humphrey had promised him "there will be a new day in Mississippi if you accept this proposal." Eleanor's mentors, including Harrington and Rauh, all recommended acceptance. They believed the Democratic Party was the vehicle to move the country: an emphasis on civil rights would drive racists from the party and create a liberal base, with a coalition of Negroes, labor, Jews, liberals and intellectuals. Southern Democrats would bolt, leaving powerful congressional positions open to the liberals.

Eleanor, not yet entwined in the Democratic Party, felt the compromise should not be accepted. But today she generously defends the position of those who supported it.

"They saw the breakthrough that was genuinely represented; on the other hand, they had alliances within the Democratic Party. They were engagé, men of their times, not simply radicals like us."

Supplying the key to her own politics, she explains, "They were people who wanted to accomplish something for working people in their lifetime! For people who had no jobs. In their lifetime! For black people. In their lifetime!"

But in 1964 Eleanor supported the MFDP rejection of two token honorary seats.

"We regarded the regular delegates as totally illegitimate. We believed we'd made the case that they had kept blacks out. It may have been naive to think that something as radical as throwing out the regular delegation would be done, but, given the facts of the situation, it didn't seem to us to be radical at all."

Ms. Hamer, near tears, told her people they had come with nothing and would go home with nothing. "We've worked too hard, we didn't come all this way for no two seats in the balcony." After several stormy sessions, she and several other women swayed the group to reject the Democratic proposal.

Although the loss was bitter, the outcome of the MFDP was far-reaching. "Never again would either of the parties have white-only exclusionary delegations. It changed both parties, broke open the notion that you could just have delegations sent from the party hierarchy." The birth of a genuine grassroots party had taken place. Before 1962, less than 2 percent of black voters in Mississippi were registered to vote. Six years later it was 62 percent. "In some countries," note historians Darlene Clark Hine and Kathleen Thompson, "armed revolutions have taken place that made less difference than that."

Yet in August 1964 the insurgents left Atlantic City with a profound sense of betrayal. They had mobilized a terrorized population with the firm faith that their party, with right on its side, would be seated. The rejection was a pivotal moment that set the stage for a great fragmentation of the Movement.

Until that moment the terms of the struggle, in the eyes of civil rights activists, were simple: right versus wrong. But Atlantic City showed that exposing inequity and playing by the rules was not enough. Power, not moral legitimacy, was the name of this game.

People responded differently to this understanding. Some turned their focus to local politics. "The Mississippi Freedom Democratic Party went home and took care of business and ultimately became the Democratic Party," says Eleanor. When she returned to the state fifteen years later, the MFDP's Aaron Henry, whom she had first met in 1963 in the Delta, would head the Mississippi Democratic Party. Looking back on that visit, Eleanor still seems stunned. "I was met by the state police who escorted me to the governor's mansion—a place I wouldn't have even dared to picket—for a reception in my honor." Twenty years later, Mississippi would lead the nation in the number of black elected officials. And Eleanor, says Guyot, "earned her place in the honor roll of those who forced the sea change."

But in 1964, crushed with disappointment at their party's rebuff, many gave up trying to build a base within the Democratic Party. Some of those who turned away, like SNCC leaders Stokely Carmichael, Courtland Cox and Bob Moses, became Pan-Africanists, attempting to build a global power base with African support now that homegrown allies proved so unreliable. SNCC, in the grip of disillusionment, soon expelled its white members and began to fracture. "Atlantic City was the beginning of the end for SNCC," believes Eleanor. "Black power destroyed SNCC. Ultimately Stokely ended up in Africa, with lots of work still to be done here."

Searching for self-reliance, some created the ideological rationale for Black Power and soon, the Black Panthers, Black Muslims and, eventually, black military separatism. But Eleanor saw no future in pulling apart.

"Once Black Power became black racism, hey, they left me too. And I think you've seen, like all inheritors of a revolution who carry it too far, they've had to fade away. I mean, where are they now? Those that lasted have been people like John Lewis, Julian Bond. The great unifying philosophies are what keep hold."

Other disenchanted activists of 1964, black and white, retreated. Some branched out to community self-sufficiency. Ms. Hamer herself was emblematic of those who turned to self-help projects; she created a pig farm for poor whites and blacks.

Some few—Eleanor, Andrew Young, Marion Barry, John Lewis and Julian Bond—decided to step further into the corridors of white power, attempting to broker justice from the inside. Over the next five years, as the Movement grew ever more angry and desperate, Eleanor's choices would sometimes be criticized. Especially when, in the midst of a black revolution, she would appear in court as an ACLU lawyer defending the segregationists trying to thwart her movement. Yet while those on the outside continued the essential work of pushing and pressing, she maintained a link to the power at the heart of the country.

The seductions of that power, and the human tendency to self-delusion—imagining that one can still broker access to those denied, for instance, long after that has ceased to be true—have always been snares for "freedom fighters" who move inside. Eleanor would have to navigate the traps, maintaining contact with a wide variety of people, seeking to keep her mind flexible and open. Yet the conflict between her desire for upward mobility within the political structure—even to gain power for her cause—and her ability to challenge that structure would always be a balancing act.

In 1964, Eleanor's whole life had prepared her for this move into the world of realpolitik. Family expectations and an upper-class education, combined with the national ties she'd built, all vaulted her to a position where she could do more than protest: she believed she'd be able to make decisions. To Eleanor, having ideas without a mechanism to implement them was a waste of time. And discussing whether to support the electoral process wouldn't change it. What other strategy was feasible?

"If the system failed you, work it better!" And so she chose to "work the system," maintaining outside ties while pursuing power in the inner corridors.

"It's very difficult to describe 'inside' and 'outside,' " says her friend Vernon Jordan. "When we went across the Edmund Pettus Bridge [in Selma, Alabama, where marchers were beaten in 1965] it was about being wherever the power is . . . If you look at the civil rights movement of the sixties, Martin was in the streets, Roy and Thurgood were in the courts and Whitney Young was in the boardroom. Each having distinct functions, all supplementing one clear goal. Martin got criticized for being in the streets, Thurgood for being in the courts, Whitney for being in the boardroom. But when it added up, something happened."

After Atlantic City, Eleanor stepped firmly onto the track she had chosen six years before: one of the main lines of white power, the justice system. In October 1964, the twenty-seven-year-old headed for Philadelphia to clerk for Judge A. Leon Higginbotham Jr., another graduate of Antioch and Yale, just named the first black district court judge. The timing was perfect; most federal judges had never had either a female or a Negro clerk. His appointment opened the door.

When Eleanor jumped at the opportunity to join an elite club of new law school graduates who clerked for federal judges, she remained within the privileged mainstream. But at the same time she stretched tradition: she would work for a pioneering black judge, one whose appointment made the history books. As always, she would straddle worlds.

"As it turns out," Eleanor wrote an Antioch friend just after her interview with Judge Higgenbotham, "his career and mine have not been dissimilar. Besides the Antioch-Yale combination, I have won some of the oratorical honors that he took away from Yale. He was most kind to me and obviously proud to see me trudging in his illustrious footsteps."

Eleanor's first sight of Judge Higginbotham at work was almost rapturous. She remembers him sitting in his office with the sun at his back, illuminated, radiant. "Immediately we had wonderful rapport."

The thirty-six-year-old judge, telling his new clerk he was not in touch with the mentality of the black student movement, immediately quizzed her.

"Tell me what happened in Atlantic City, tell me about SNCC. Blacks like you and Martin Luther King were raised middle-class. It was easier for you to embrace the Movement than for people like me, just up from poverty."

"Of course I didn't agree with that at all! But I didn't argue. It made me think about the advantages I'd had, that they had freed my mind, had made it possible for me to be a full participant in the civil rights movement, which did not come from the streets. It came from middle-class students who managed to get to college.

"He tested me, trying to use the fact that I had come from this milieu very far from where he was, to find out more, to test where he stood." Higginbotham was hardly an elder statesman, but the ten-year difference in age and class background put him light-years from the Movement.

"That experience was like being dipped in water and pulled out," says Eleanor. "And he knew it." Judge Higginbotham had challenged the racial status quo his entire life, but the Movement was a departure from traditional tools of change: suits, petitions, education. In the 1960s, students used dramatic new forms of direct defiance.

"We were saying, after *Brown*, 'Where is the integration?' 'What about black income?' 'Show us the real difference between the North and the South.'"

That was not the way a man who had come up through the NAACP and the court system looked at civil rights. That generation did the groundwork, filing cases like *Brown*. "In their time hard questions had to be asked. Later, even harder questions had to be asked."

Having just missed the civil rights generation, Higginbotham "was just nonplussed by me." Eleanor smiles at memories of their mutual fascination.

"One of my all-time great teases to him," she recalls, visibly cherishing her twenty-seven-year-old bodacious self, "was 'I would trade every black like you for a tiny increment in the standard of living for black people.' "

"Now, how much would that be?" he would ask with a glint.

The tall, striking judge and his clerk had exactly the kind of contentious relationship she treasured. A decade after her tenure Judge Higginbotham described Eleanor to an interviewer, "She had three basic qualities: first, extraordinarily bright; second, very tenacious; and third, compassion for people . . . Though I've had a galaxy of stars, Eleanor was one of the most talented."

It was an extraordinary apprenticeship. "We'd sit down together and write. He treated me as a peer." Even the fast pace of a district court suited her. The trial court atmosphere—with frequent witnesses, rapid rulings, and instant research—produced just the sort of deadline-driven adrenaline rush that invigorated Eleanor. And his work style matched hers. The two ordered in lunch and toiled late. "He was a workaholic from the get-go."

After she'd been in Philadelphia eight months the busy procrastinator wrote to Yale's Law School dean, enclosing her bar admission forms for his signature and requesting a special delivery return, "to keep me from missing being sworn in again. The last time the Supreme Court of Pennsylvania sat here, I was so busy at the court that admission day passed me by."

The job gave Eleanor lifelong habits; even researching data to confirm the judge's rhetoric for speeches was good practice. Her own lectures would evermore be laced with statistics, the more remarkable the better. "You're conclusionary if you just say it. You have to prove it."

And Eleanor learned to hire sharp staffers who could do for her what she had done for him. Her staff would one day be the kind of foil she was for the judge: bright, unafraid to argue a point or criticize the boss' writing. "Everybody in this world needs to be edited, and needs a sounding board."

Judge Higginbotham also inspired her with his multiple roles. A sitting judge, he moonlighted as an historian, earning scholarly accolades for research on slavery and the law, with landmark writings to his credit before he died in 1998.

In Philadelphia, Eleanor rented a large, furnished second-floor apartment at 432 North 33rd Street, near the University of Pennsylvania in a bohemian part of town "where you'd expect somebody from Antioch to live." Finally, during the spring of 1965, after she'd worked for the judge for nine months, Eleanor met Edward Norton. Christine Philpot hosted a party at her parents' home. Her intimation had been correct. The two were immediately attracted.

"It was a very quick attachment," reminisces Eleanor, recalling how they sat and talked intensely. Edward was so impressed by her "extraordinary energy and intelligence," he later told reporter Charlayne Hunter-Gault, that he began to call Eleanor "La Pasionaria," after the fiery leader who inspired Spanish republicans in their fight against Franco. This was just the kind of left-wing pet name that would appeal to Eleanor. It was also, Charlayne says, "the most loving tribute, because she has a passion that is more than most people can take, and people don't always know how to read that." But Edward did, and respected it.

He had grown up on Sugar Hill in Harlem, in a family as aspirationally middle-class as Eleanor's. His father, like many black men banned from other jobs, worked for the post office; his mother was a seamstress.

"They were extraordinary," Eleanor describes the great migration north, "bringing up family from Florida during World War II who lived in that little apartment with them. Brilliant people, the Nortons raised two sons, a doctor and a lawyer."

The day after her first date, Eleanor uncharacteristically called Barbara Babcock to report ecstatically, "I've just met this incredible man!"

On the rebound from Blyden, Eleanor had dated "these little intellectual wimps, little tugboats in her wake," says Barbara, so she was overjoyed by the news. Eleanor had despaired of ever finding a black man who was her educated equal, sharing values and tastes. Yet here he was. Just a year younger than she, Edward was a math whiz. He'd gone into the Navy after winning a Yale scholarship at sixteen; now he was a Columbia law student.

Handsome, smart and well-educated, Edward was a worthy verbal adversary. He also had qualities that Eleanor had not developed, like an introspective and psychologically questing nature. They seemed perfect complements.

His similarities to her father were striking. "My attraction to dark-skinned men may come naturally," she says. Like her tall, "gorgeous, dark-skinned" father, Edward was a lawyer who loved to banter, kept his head straight up, and would work as a government housing special-ist. Politically, Edward was more conservative, but her friends agreed: Eleanor had found the perfect mate.

Within four months they married.

The wedding, like Eleanor's choice of husbands, was traditional in form, though the couple modified its content. By the mid-sixties, some radical contemporaries flouted convention with avant-garde rituals in lofts or hand-holding circles in daisy-strewn fields. Not Eleanor.

"I wanted a traditional wedding for my family, I wanted it for myself, and I wanted that beautiful dress."

Displaying her usual blend of respect for heritage spiced by princi-pled irreverence, Eleanor stretched custom to fit her beliefs. The bride and groom wrote their own vows ("I took God and all the 'obeys' out of it"), two of Eleanor's three bridesmaids were white and she refused to have the wedding in a church. Eleanor selected a Unitarian minister from Howard rather than an Episcopalian from her upbringing or a Baptist from her grandparents' faith. And she and Edward went to Greenwich Village to buy a gold wedding ring.

"The last thing I wanted was any diamonds. Imagine somebody com-ing out of the Movement with some diamonds!"

On the morning of October 9, 1965, Eleanor left her parents' home in a splendid white gown, borrowed because "I wasn't going to spend any money on a one-time-only wedding dress!" The wedding party made its way to the large Silver Spring backyard of her grandfather, retired firefighter Richard Holmes. Her bridesmaids—Christine

Philpot, Barbara Babcock and Judy Stein—wore matching gold dresses; her sister Portia was maid of honor.

Coleman directed the wedding "so it was appropriate and elegant." Though afraid the overcast day would give way to rain, the radiant bride and groom bellowed their home-written vows with the confidence of the young and those newly in love. Then Coleman shepherded people indoors to the reception. There Edward placed his hand over Eleanor's as they cut the tiered wedding cake together.

The glittering wedding was full of excited people, good food, drink and high spirits. Eleanor and Edward glowed, sporting ear-to-ear smiles. "They looked so happy, it stood out," remembers one guest. At the end, Eleanor tried to throw her bouquet off the back porch to her friend Rachelle Horowitz who ducked, turning to a friend to complain, "That's way too bourgie for me."

After the wedding Mrs. Eleanor Holmes Norton told all her friends, "Edward is not threatened by my status or activities because he is totally secure, the most secure man I've ever met." He seemed as besotted as she. After the turbulence of dating, the to-and-fro of Antioch jobs and a decade's Movement work, Eleanor thought she had found her life-mate and stability.

CHAPTER 6

Free Speech—for All

You can't win what you don't fight for.
ELEANOR HOLMES NORTON

The groom was in his last year at Columbia Law School and Eleanor had left her clerkship, so the couple moved immediately to Manhattan.

"Of course, I came from the least democratic part of the country," says Eleanor. And at twenty-seven, she regarded 1965 Washington "as a two-horse racist, Southern, unsophisticated town." New York City was *It.* Sophisticated heaven.

"That was where I belonged. But I didn't know what I was talking about when I said I was going to law school to practice civil liberties and civil rights law. There were no jobs! There wasn't any poverty program, legal services for the poor, none of that existed." Even the NAACP Legal Defense Fund hired few lawyers. Yet Eleanor's life continued to be blessed with extraordinary timing. Long a free speech advocate, she inquired at the American Civil Liberties Union. In the tiny legal staff of two, one place was open.

"I thought I was the luckiest person in the world. It was nirvana."

The ACLU, cofounded in 1920 by suffragist Jane Addams, socialist Norman Thomas and civil libertarian Roger Baldwin, protected the Bill of Rights' guarantees of "free speech, free press, free assemblage and other civil rights." The nonprofit agency took an unwavering stand: these freedoms were never to be abridged. Baldwin was adamant.

"Unless we defend the rights of the sonsofbitches, we'll lose our own."

The agency lobbied state legislatures, filed friend-of-court briefs and took occasional clients to establish principles. Most court cases were handled by volunteer ("cooperating") lawyers who received no pay.

Eleanor's commitment had several sources. At Antioch, a critical value was the ability to discuss forbidden topics and express unpopular views. As she broke out of 1950s conformity, her appreciation grew for this freedom to explore all options. Devotion to the Constitution was intensified by her Movement experience.

"When black people had nothing else, they often had free speech. After all, civil rights was basically a propaganda movement. What was Martin Luther King? Not a military or political leader, but a great orator." Such an outpouring could not have taken place in a closed society. However circumscribed and dangerous the position of black Americans, the right to openly protest had been essential to change.

And this was the height of the Warren Court, with "its great civil liberties decisions, an ascendancy unique in the history of the Supreme Court. The ACLU got a tremendous boost, because it kept winning cases."

In defending the Constitution, Eleanor also lived out childhood values. Coleman had outlined his commitment in a college paper on the Constitution. "Under its rule the destiny of the great and the small, the high and the low, the rich and the poor, is provided for with equal assurance." Because it provided such assurance—like a parent—the people should reciprocate. Thirty-five years later, Eleanor followed her father's injunction.

Eleanor and Edward moved to the liberal Upper West Side just south of Harlem, near Columbia University, where Edward had a law school research job.

"I thought it was silly for him to work, while I worked for the ACLU making $8,500 dollars a year. But he insisted. He wouldn't think of living off of a woman. So he said, 'No, no, no.' "

The streets of the multiethnic Upper West Side were the heart of the Democratic Party's left wing, a perfect place for Eleanor to jump into the progressive mainstream. The couple found a small one-bedroom apartment in a virtually all-white building on 102nd Street. Furnishing their "beginner's apartment" with art and books, they dove into the life of the bustling neighborhood.

"There can be no more political community in the United States," Eleanor remembers fondly.

Several years later the two looked at a larger apartment nearby, a charming two-bedroom. They'd seen an ad and called a landlord about what sounded like the perfect rent-controlled apartment at 245 West 104th Street, two blocks away.

"We told him we were both lawyers and had no children. The man was delighted and told us to come immediately and leave a deposit. It was available; the apartment was ours."

When Eleanor and Edward showed up for their appointment, "they saw we were black and all of a sudden it wasn't available." The owner called hours later to lament that actually there'd been a mix-up: someone else had gotten the apartment.

"The next time you hear from us will be through the Commission on Human Rights!" Edward told him.

"We went right at them and filed with the Human Rights Commission to get the apartment. We caught them red-handed," Eleanor says with satisfaction. "We had a very direct case because they had said it was available. And then we showed up and it wasn't. The landlord didn't want to have trouble with the Commission, so we got it."

Soon they enjoyed the luxury of a second bedroom, and a dining room instead of an alcove. Painting the apartment yellow, they furnished it with light-colored fabrics, creating a pleasant and sunny home. "Earth tones, lots of books," recalls one Mississippian. "Comfortable for young middle-class marrieds, not a SNCC freedom house."

Eleanor and Edward frequented nearby clubs on Broadway and Amsterdam Avenue. There Eleanor played catch-up, for she had essentially missed the popular music of the last ten years. At Antioch and Yale she heard little except folk music and freedom songs; her white friends didn't listen to popular music.

"That was a big gap after high school. I lost track. When I hear some songs today I say, 'How did I miss that?' The music is part of the culture of the African-American community. You can't stay away from it for too long. You lose the rhythm of your life that way." Now Eleanor absorbed the music that filled the airwaves. "The Jackson Five, Fifth Dimension—they were a little smooth, not funky enough. The Four Tops absolutely, Barry White, Aretha—oh my God yes! Stevie Wonder!" Eleanor and Edward went out, listening to the jazz that filled the clubs. A new musical militancy echoed the era's dynamic politics.

Or sometimes the two heard poetry. But Eleanor, always a morning person, often returned home before Edward. One night he came home with a surprise. "You should have stayed, because this extraordinary woman came and engaged the whole bar."

"And guess who it was," Eleanor says. "This tall, statuesque woman he described, before she became famous? The poet, Maya Angelou."

If the cultural nightlife of the Upper West Side was rich, evenings at home were also full. Edward's parents lived just a few subway stops north, and "we went there all the time. They were wonderfully warm and became a real family to me." Edward's childhood buddies and Eleanor's friends from her many spheres often stopped by.

"We'd fix dinner and sit around; Edward loved to talk with people. Edward liked to take that provocateur role, liked to bait me and my friends, because he was more conservative. Of course, I'd be sitting right there on the couch after dinner and I'd go to sleep. But Edward kept right on talking with folks."

In addition to the fascinating mix of their mutual networks—"people from the Harlem streets to politicos like Rachelle"—there were new people. Lots of them. Eleanor became vice president of the Riverside Democrats, a large, active neighborhood club of mostly white liberals and radicals.

With typical energy Eleanor joined a group of white and black artists and art lovers "who believed Harlem deserved a first-class museum. The point was to show that New York was full of extraordinary black artists, who, because they didn't have connections to the downtown art houses and museums, found it difficult to show." In the heady days of the mid-sixties, Eleanor was a founder and vice president of what became the influential Studio Museum of Harlem. "It had a kind of sleek, modern look to it, a beautifully done loft," Eleanor says, remembering the gala opening of a cultural institution that would become a gateway for generations of unheralded artists. Deeply involved in the cause, one by-product was a further extension of her connections: several fellow trustees would become influential New York politicians.

And Eleanor maintained contact with Movement friends. A board member of Rustin's A. Philip Randolph Institute, full of left-labor unionists, she also joined the board of the Workers Defense League and was still busy with SNCC's New York office.

"All these folks rarely interfaced. The fact is, our friends were high society, plus Movement people, plus union folks, plus Harlem, bourgie blacks and artists associated with the Studio Museum. But that's New York. The circles spun in all directions."

Eleanor reveled in the stimulation of the "un-Washington." She spoke at every possible venue. Appearing once on a *Jewish Currents* panel with Antiochian Steve Schwerner, the brother of murdered activist Michael Schwerner, she honored his family, "the only one in America where I've worked with two different generations [Steve and his parents] on ending segregation."

Eleanor was so active that soon after she moved to New York she heard that local black politicians like Charles Rangel, who had just been elected to Congress, wondered if she planned to run against him.

"It never crossed my mind," swears Eleanor today. "I was not interested in electoral politics. The kind of bedrock principles that the civil rights movement stood for, few political leaders could stand for . . . you could not always do what you wanted to do."

In the ferment of New York, Eleanor thrived. Ever in motion, she wore her hair—still an issue—pulled firmly back on both sides and swept off her face.

"I wanted an Afro more than I could taste it. Among my friends, nobody had one. But I wanted one. I was then representing somebody before the Court of Military Appeals and I didn't want to hurt him. Afros were so rare I wanted to make sure I didn't send any signal. I kept holding on. Finally, one day when I went to have my hair done in Harlem I said, 'Take it.' "

It had a straightener perm, so the hairdresser had to cut it very close. Her head was almost shaved. "I was going right after that to Mrs. Norton's and Edward was going to be there for dinner. Boy, could she cook." Eleanor smiles.

"I walked in the house with no warning. They took it well. But hair is still important in the black community.

"Hair was a very confining, debilitating thing. I look at what white women do: nothing! Nappy hair was associated not just with 'bad hair days.' You were unpresentable if your hair wasn't straight! Now there are so many ways to wear black hair, but then there was only one way: straight. If it got nappy around the edges you were in trouble.

"It was always difficult to find a place to have it done. It kept you from doing what you had to do; it kept me from being interested in swimming or exercise because my hair would get nappy. That's why getting the Afro was one of the great liberating moments of my life."

In one bold moment Eleanor solved the vexing expense, inconvenience and restriction of straightened hair. Yet her belief in her own "ugliness" would persist until finally, today she says, "I may be one of these rare women who look better as a middle-aged or older woman. And my look may have improved because of the Afro, which fits the features of black people."

On January 10, 1966, two months after Eleanor started her ACLU job, Julian Bond, an SNCC veteran she knew, was refused his elected seat in Georgia's House of Representatives. A special committee, voting to bar him, quoted a taped media interview: "I like to think of myself as a pacifist and one who opposes that [Vietnam] war and any other war, and [am] eager and anxious to encourage people not to participate in it for any reason if they choose."

The ACLU signed on and Eleanor helped write a successful friend-of-court brief asking the U.S. Supreme Court to overrule the Georgia House. Dr. King, who lived in Bond's district, joined as a plaintiff.

"It seems astounding from any point of view that they would deny his seat. That's what I'm talking about: how First Amendment law in the 1960s and early 1970s got made. People think it was created in the Constitution. But that was only on paper. Nobody protected First Amendment rights until after I was born, and then only gradually until it really picked up acceleration in the 1960s." It took a year to seat Bond.

As the unpopular war heated up and the politics of protest raged, Eleanor was deluged by scores of handwritten pleas from soldiers court-martialed for demonstrating in uniform, or refusing what seemed like racially biased orders. With only two lawyers on staff, few could be helped. Unsentimental as always, Eleanor was curt in her brief responses.

"We cannot help," she simply replied to most. Sometimes she recommended that the soldier or his family contact "your influential congressman."

With limited resources, the ACLU selected only the occasional appellate case that could establish constitutional principles in the ever-changing armed services. Then, Eleanor had to learn the law as she went, for the army constantly created new rules to quash the burgeoning militants, deserters, resisters, conscientious objectors and free speech advocates. Hurricane-force political winds began to blow about the once obscure combat.

"The Vietnam War was the seminal event of the period. Most of us had been children in World War II and the Korean War. It was our first real war and it turned out to be a war we could not embrace, a civil war where we intervened, a war without a cause, a war with the wrong cause, a war that was on automatic pilot where you keep going because you're American and you are supposed to win! In Vietnam we picked up where the French left off and amazingly got our head handed to us, something that no one ever expected would happen to our country."

With her instinct for putting herself at the center of defining events, Eleanor handled Vietnam resistance as well as First Amendment cases. In 1967, Muhammad Ali was stripped of his championship by the World Boxing Association and the New York State Athletic Commission for draft refusal, and convicted in Houston of violating the Selective Service Act. Fined $10,000, he received a five-year prison sentence, though his objection was based on his Muslim ministry, plus opposition to this war. Eleanor worked on the amicus brief. Ali's stature, and the emotionally charged issue of his newly proclaimed Muslim faith, guaranteed that his resistance would be front-page news. His defiance motivated thousands of conscientious objectors and Ali became a cause célèbre. Four years later, on June 28, 1971, the U.S. Supreme Court unanimously overturned his conviction.

Eleanor didn't stop with antiwar and civil rights protesters. In March 1967, she was one of nine lawyers on a friend-of-court brief to a Select Committee of the House of Representatives, "In the Matter of the Right of Adam Clayton Powell Jr. to a Seat as the Representative from the 18th Congressional District, New York, New York." Powell was the powerful Harlem congressman who, though duly elected, was expelled from Congress by his colleagues. His alleged abuses were public expense junkets, income tax evasion and a Harlem slander judgment.

The venerable chair of the House Education and Labor Committee, skilled at steering his bills through, had in five years passed sixty major reforms: an increased minimum wage, fair employment practices, a manpower development training act and a ban on sex discrimination in pay. Legislation from his committee formed the basis of President Kennedy's "New Frontier" and President Johnson's "Great Society."

The friend-of-court brief stuck to a simple principle: since Powell was elected (and reelected by Harlem voters six weeks after his expulsion) his district had the right to be represented by the person of its choice. Almost two years later, the defiant Powell was seated; shortly thereafter, the Supreme Court ruled his suspension unconstitutional. Yet Powell could never regain his stature at home or in Congress "because of drinking and flamboyant abuses," says Eleanor. Still, he was widely viewed by blacks at the time as a man destroyed for having too much power in a white world.

Honoring constitutional principles, Eleanor also found what some considered a puzzling delight in representing right-wing militants, once writing an amicus brief defending an Ohio Ku Klux Klan leader convicted of criminal syndicalism, "a statute most often used against left-wingers." The man charged had spoken at a Klan rally featuring the burning of a huge wooden cross; he had yelled, "Bury the niggers!" and "Send the Jews back to Israel!"

Yet Eleanor believed that for speech to be truly free it must have "a perfect score," permitting even such statements as these. The ACLU successfully filed a brief to the Supreme Court, which ruled that Ohio's conviction violated the First and Fourteenth Amendments.

Confirming her point, her next high-profile client was segregationist George Wallace. As part of his 1968 presidential campaign, he tried to use New York City's Shea Stadium, a public facility, for a rally. Mayor Lindsay flatly refused. The New York Civil Liberties lawyer, Aryeh Neier, approached his African-American colleague.

"Eleanor, how would you like to go out and represent George Wallace in court on Monday?" he asked facetiously.

"Great," she said.

"I was only joking!"

"I'm not."

Today, Eleanor explains, "This was the middle of the civil rights movement when many of the great First Amendment cases were filed by black people trying to demonstrate. And here was the most liberal city in the United States, denying the other side the right to speak. I thought it was a wonderful opportunity."

Over the weekend she prepared her argument. On Monday morning Ira Glasser, the city chapter's associate director (later ACLU president), drove her through snowy streets out to Queens Supreme Court. Walking into court, "Wallace's campaign manager gulped at the sight of this black woman but Eleanor never stumbled," ACLU executive director Aryeh Neier said. Eleanor herself typically recalls, "Wallace's very Southern lawyers did not flinch when I said, 'I'm Eleanor Holmes Norton. I'm here to argue the constitutional issues in the case.'"

She was out to prove her point, and she did. It was an open-and-shut case; George Wallace did appear in Shea Stadium.

"I regarded civil liberties as far broader than my own predicament as a black woman, because I thought, and still do, that it was a way to secure freedom across the board: for working people, black people, for women, as they try to press their causes. I thought it was the umbrella under which I could do the things I had gone to law school for in the first place."

Still deeply involved with SNCC's New York office, Eleanor frequently made trips south. Although some activists lauded her civil liberties stance, introducing her at meetings as "the sister George Wallace needed to represent him, in order for him to get some constitutional rights," others did not.

Eleanor, with her habit of erasing disturbing memory, today recalls, "SNCC people loved it; I didn't get any criticism. They understood the irony. Remember the situation our people were in: you started to march down the street, you'd get arrested. You'd sit-in, you'd get arrested."

But not everyone understood or agreed with the principle. Some believed that troublemakers like Wallace didn't deserve free speech; they were confused by her defense of a man who would just as soon see her dead. To them, the free speech argument was bogus liberalism, not acknowledging the power of offensive language to lead to action. Dr. Joyce Ladner from Mississippi, a Movement activist who would move to Africa in the late sixties, was representative.

"How in the world can you defend George Wallace!" she asked Eleanor.

"If I don't defend his rights today someone will come along and abrogate yours tomorrow."

"Eleanor, as an activist, how can you support this man?" Dr. Ladner repeated, in disbelief.

"I couldn't focus on the First Amendment," Ladner acknowledges now. "All I knew was that this man had called us racist names, stood in the schoolhouse door, did everything he could to keep blacks from any power whatsoever. He and [Mississippi Governor] Ross Barnett were just absolutely horrible people, confrontational forerunners of the far right political movement." Thirty years later, Ladner reflects, "Eleanor had studied constitutional law; that was her specialty. She understood and was mature enough to focus on the principle."

For some whose visceral response was dismay thirty years ago, the symbolism of a civil rights militant defending a famous racist still does not sit well. By now, however, most former critics appreciate the necessity of one standard for all; they just want it to be uniformly applied.

Eleanor truly did not take in the criticism and gloried in her ACLU job. She understood there had never before been a moment like that provided by the extraordinary Warren Court. Having missed the landmark fifties civil rights cases like *Brown*, she was in an equally significant legal arena, when opponents sought to quell the Movement by shutting off its weapons: marches, speeches and written protests. And her side was winning.

In the 1960s, First Amendment cases were wending their way up to the Supreme Court in greater numbers than ever before. When defending the right to speak became a linchpin of the Movement, Eleanor became a First Amendment specialist. Her training in law and history, joined to her political acumen, allowed her to see beneath the surface of a George Wallace to this deeper forward thrust. In a twist of history, he could be put to the service of her principles.

"Today," she says, "if you're a constitutional lawyer, you spend your time trying to *keep* cases from going to the Supreme Court, because once the Court speaks, you don't have another chance, and the Court is likely to speak against you." But in the sixties it moved civil rights and liberties forward, and those decisions remain.

"Today, even the most conservative justices say the First Amendment can't keep you from burning the flag. This law is now well grounded. But it wasn't then. So in a real sense it was even more exciting than being at a civil rights organization."

A case Eleanor personally argued before the Supreme Court brought the young civil libertarian her greatest notoriety. The National States Rights Party, a white supremacist group, held a 1966 rally in Princess

Anne County, Maryland. Its speakers used constant racial epithets, announcing a repeat performance the following night.

"You white folks bring your friends, come on back tomorrow . . . Let's raise a little bit of hell for the white race!"

The city, alarmed at the aggressive provocation in the tense racial atmosphere of the time, convinced a judge to bar the coming protest as "prior restraint" of possible danger.

"That is the most dangerous thing to do to speech! You can't stop people from speaking before they speak. That's the essence of a totalitarian state. I jumped at the opportunity because if there is a constitutional or civil liberties point to be made, you make it most convincingly when you stand up for the right of somebody who disagrees with you to speak. You must obviously be serving a higher cause. And I love that idea. My George Wallace case and my National States Rights Party case were high points."

In October 1969, barely meeting the Supreme Court's requirement to have passed the bar three years before, Eleanor represented the States Rights Party in that august chamber, with William Zinman from Baltimore as her cocounsel.

After incessant preparation ("I'm very capable of asking myself the hard questions, but I want to make sure I know the answers"), there was the delicate question of what to wear. In this formal, tradition-bound atmosphere, where a young black woman, especially one with an Afro, was a rarity, she determined not to even try blending with the dark-suited white men around her. She told an interviewer then, "I resisted wearing a black suit below the knees and wore a pretty blue dress with short sleeves and a high neck." Miniskirts were in style, so the dress was short.

The day of the argument Eleanor nervously entered the high-chambered room with red drapes and walked alone to the podium facing nine black-robed justices. They sat high above her.

"The United States Supreme Court is now in session! Oyez, Oyez, Oyez." The gavel rang down.

Standing before the justices, the thirty-one-year-old dressed in blue repeated the rally's slurs on Negroes and Jews, deliberate insults amplified by a public address system.

"They praised the spirit of the townsfolk who lynched a *nigger* there in 1933," Eleanor said loudly, jabbing a finger forward, repeating the slur. After puncturing the sanctity of the Court with such epithets, she stated her position: democracy had an absolute need to never prohibit even such speech as this *in advance*. Therefore, she asked the Court to overturn the "prior restraint" injunction on the second rally.

The justices peppered her with questions, though the one black justice, recently appointed by President Johnson, held back. "Justice Marshall all the time had this bemused look on his face," Eleanor told an interviewer. Not knowing the justices' thoughts, the fast-paced argument was nerve-racking.

After she closed and the gavel pounded once more, friends and family gathered around; Edward and her parents crowded in, with ACLU attorneys shaking her hand and Yale classmates ringing the family. Then the waiting began.

A month later, on November 19, the opinion was released. Although Justice Abe Fortas, who wrote it, acknowledged that the speech was "aggressively and militantly racist," such that "listeners might well have construed their words as both a provocation to the Negroes in the crowd and an incitement to the whites," the Supreme Court unanimously upheld Eleanor's objection to lack of notice or opportunity for the States Rights Party to participate in judicial discussion. Maryland authorities had violated free speech rights, violating a basic First Amendment freedom. Without both parties present, especially in a controversial situation, a court "does not have available the fundamental instrument for judicial judgment: an adversary proceeding in which both parties may participate." Due process was flawed and free speech abridged.

"When it comes to free expression, I suppose I am an extremist," Eleanor said then. "There is only one test of free speech: That is our tolerance for speech we do not want to hear.

"Surely the Warren Court had not seen such a spectacle before. A young thin animated black woman, fresh from the civil rights movement, arguing for the right of free expression of young members of the National States Rights Party . . . That I was their lawyer served them right, a fate they seemed ironically to embrace."

Eleanor's success in this front-page case, right on the heels of defending Wallace, brought her national attention. "The New York press had a field day, asking me if I would vote for Wallace." The anomaly of the

Afro-coifed militant arguing these segregationist cases was a puzzle to the public.

On the one hand she proclaimed, "I believe in Black Power . . . I support the rebellions that occur in the street, though violence tends to be counterproductive. Black people went into the streets to express their legitimate grievances." And less than a week before the November 1968 election, she'd told the *New York Post* she was having trouble deciding whether to vote for Eldridge Cleaver or Dick Gregory for president.

On the other hand, the civil libertarian explained her defense of right-wingers. "When I'm defending a racist's rights, the object lesson is dramatically clear." More speech, not less, she spelled out, was the remedy for repressive thought. When hate was out in the open, people could see it and act.

"I'm not afraid of Black Sambo and I'm not afraid of Tom Sawyer. The last thing I want is to have them suppressed. Black people and white people will never understand white racism so long as we suppress its expression." But if it was hard for some of her civil rights colleagues to understand, it was even more difficult for many newspaper readers to reconcile the two disparate images of Eleanor's public face: the fierce civil rights advocate and the equally fierce constitutional defender of racists.

Soon a powerful third image was superimposed. While Eleanor was at the ACLU, a women's rights project began under the direction of the reigning expert on women's rights law, Ruth Bader Ginsberg, "the Thurgood Marshall of the women's movement. She handled most of the groundbreaking cases and did it for the ACLU while I was still there. I don't think anyone thought a person like Ruth would ever get seated on the Supreme Court . . . She argued six or seven cases in front of the Court for women's rights."

Eleanor's own feminist consciousness was "underdeveloped," she concedes. When she first applied to law schools in 1959, she had included New York University because it had the largest scholarship. Rejected, she had simply walked away, saying, "Oh, I didn't realize the scholarship was for men only."

"I let it go, instead of being outraged," she says. "Betty Friedan's book hadn't been written. There was no NOW. There was the National Council of Negro Women, but that seemed just another bourgeois organization at the time. I thought, 'Ladies in hats.' "

(top, left) Grandfather,
Richard John Lewis Holmes,
early 1900s
Courtesy of Eleanor Holmes Norton

(top, right) Father,
Coleman Sterling Holmes,
circa 1915
Courtesy of Eleanor Holmes Norton

(left) Aunt Selena King,
Coleman's sister,
early 1900s
Courtesy of Eleanor Holmes Norton

(above) Engine Company No. 4,
Washington D.C., early 1940s.
Lieut. Richard Holmes (center)
Courtesy of Eleanor Holmes Norton

(left) Grandmother Lucinda
Fitts Lynch, circa 1910
Courtesy of Eleanor Holmes Norton

Mother Vela Elizabeth Lynch,
Central High School graduation,
Syracuse, 1930
Courtesy of Eleanor Holmes Norton

Parents Coleman and Vela Holmes,
late 1930s
Courtesy of Eleanor Holmes Norton

With grandmother Nellie Holmes
and father Coleman Holmes,
circa 1939
Courtesy of Eleanor Holmes Norton

Vela Holmes with (left to right)
Portia, Nellie and Eleanor,
circa 1943
Courtesy of Eleanor Holmes Norton

(left) In grammar school,
circa 1948.
Goldcraft Portraits

(below) Surrounded by Dunbar
High School friends
Courtesy of Eleanor Holmes Norton

(top, left) As a high school
debutante, 1955
Photo courtesy of Pease Photograph

(below) On graduation day,
Antioch College, 1960
Courtesy of Eleanor Holmes Norton

(lower, left) In New Haven,
early 1960s
Courtesy of Eleanor Holmes Norton

(opposite, top) With Barbara Babcock,
teammates and judges,
Yale Law School, 1961
Photo courtesy of Barbara Babcock

(opposite, bottom) Eleanor and Edward
Holmes Norton
Courtesy of Eleanor Holmes Norton

(above) Sworn in by Mayor Lindsay, 1970 *Dick de Marsico*

(below) Rep. Shirley Chisolm, Mrs. Coretta Scott King at Eleanor's swearing in for 2nd term as NYC Commissioner, 1974 *Courtesy of Eleanor Holmes Norton*

Ten years later, much had changed. In 1963, the President's Commission on the Status of Women had documented discrimination. In 1964, when President Johnson signed the Civil Rights Act prohibiting employment discrimination on the basis of race, creed, or national origin, he signed a bill to which sex had been added as a joke, in hopes it would defeat the entire bill. But, led by Representative Martha Griffiths of Michigan, Congress had passed it. The result was Title VII and an enforcement arm, the Equal Employment Opportunity Commission (EEOC). Its first director, Herman Edelsberg, treated the gender provision as a fluke. In the liberation-conscious atmosphere such ridicule was a catalyst for the National Organization for Women to form in 1966.

By the mid-sixties, Simone de Beauvoir's feminist manifesto, *The Second Sex,* was circulating. Eleanor passed it out to friends. Soon SNCC women wrote statements about unequal treatment within the Movement, though Eleanor was not among them.

"Not me. I never felt any of that. I was going to law school, while they treated the other girls as clericals." Though she was protected, her politics led her to understand.

"If you were associated with civil rights, with labor rights, the analogies are intellectually compelled. The transition to feminism is easy. What I *don't* understand is why the transition doesn't happen to everybody who was in the civil rights movement."

Suddenly she saw with a new eye the "help wanted" columns: one for men, one for women. "These were the basics. Once you looked at it, *everything* was separate and unequal! The deep stuff that's really searing today, like domestic violence and abortion, you couldn't get to, because you hadn't even established that equal protection of the laws applied to women."

Obvious as the analogies may have appeared to Eleanor, not every black American agreed. In fact, many opposed "women's lib," as it was derisively called, afraid that a female focus would detract from "the main struggle." Roy Wilkins, executive director of the NAACP, told the *New York Times* in 1969, "Biologically, women ought to have children and stay home. I can't help it if God made them that way, and not to run General Motors." SNCC's Stokely Carmichael was famously quoted, "The position of women in the Movement is prone."

"As the black movement was fracturing and splitting all over the place," Eleanor says, "many black men and women were getting angry about the women's movement. . . . Black people were very confused." Eleanor's long history of operating simultaneously in several worlds helped her in this complex environment where numerous groups claimed discrimination, setting off a competition for the small amount of justice perceived available.

"The women's movement was considered so white, and there was such hostility to it, that at the first women's rights march in New York [September 1970] I did something I never do. I wasn't into dashikis, but I found myself an African turban to wrap on my head, just to make the point that black women belonged in this damned march on Fifth Avenue with the rest of them." At the rally Eleanor bellowed, "Sex, like color, is a meaningless criterion and an oppressive criterion when it is made a condition for a job!"

Visible black feminists were few. Shirley Chisholm, a Brooklyn club-house politician who had fought off male contenders and ridicule to become the first African-American congresswoman, was one who "understood she was black *and* a woman." Dorothy Height, one of the "women in hats," was another, as were outspoken lawyers Flo Kennedy and Aileen Hernandez, soon to be NOW president, and SNCC veteran Frances Beal of the Third World Women's Alliance. But among her civil rights colleagues, Eleanor was often in a minority.

"I argued strenuously. We needed alliances! White women had been kept out of jobs for different reasons, but just as much. Blacks find it hard to accept that, perhaps for good reason. But they had to learn to and they have. There was confusion in the general community, though not with the black men in Congress at the time."

Many were skeptical of the women's movement; they perceived it as white, middle-class and racist. Eleanor was never one to let any of those features keep her out of a school, a job or a movement. Not mincing words, she said, sometimes pounding her desk for emphasis, "Black women had better find the women's movement!"

Yet she was aware they approached from a different vantage point.

"Do black women want to enter suburban split levels just as white women are fleeing them?" she asked a 1969 Connecticut College Conference on Black Womanhood, proposing a unique role: black women could "pioneer in establishing new male-female relationships around two careers."

Eleanor not only urged others to trailblaze; going back to her own legal base, she developed one of the first Women and the Law courses in 1970, teaching at the very NYU Law School that had turned her down for a scholarship on the basis of gender just eleven years before. As with her draft resister cases, she had to learn as she went, relying on the few women then developing curricula. Barbara Babcock suggested to Eleanor, Ann Freedman and Susan Deller Ross that they write a text, helping women use the law.

The four lawyers split up tasks: Eleanor wrote the first draft of equal rights and public accommodation portions and codrafted an abortion section. "It's hard to pin Eleanor down," remembers one coauthor, who, frustrated, tried to "focus" Eleanor by catching her at home. In 1975 they published one of the first case books, *Sex Discrimination and the Law: Causes and Remedies.* An updated edition of the interdisciplinary breakthrough text is still in use.

Eleanor also took a landmark ACLU case, representing women researchers at *Newsweek* who accused the magazine of discrimination. "For employers it has become a bit unrespectable not to hire minorities," she said then. "But most remain primitive in the woman market."

Newsweek researchers included a significant number of Fulbright and Phi Beta Kappa scholars, "pristine female brilliance, deliberately kept at ground level." These middle- and upper-class white women, products of the best education available in the United States, were relegated to background research rather than the reporter jobs reserved for men.

Eleanor met with the women "to bond them together, to make them understand what an extraordinary violation of law it was for them to be systematically kept where they were. *Newsweek* did what every employer did: found a ready pool of workers who would accept jobs for which they were overqualified and underpaid."

Outraged, she filed a class action suit and, in an unusual tactic, called a press conference. In the boardroom of the ACLU, all twenty women standing with her, Eleanor announced the suit. "Hadn't been done before. If there had been a women's class action suit, I hadn't heard of it."

Newsweek executives responded by asking Eleanor to negotiate alone. She insisted that plaintiffs be in the room, "because part of it was educating them about what I was doing." And she required Kay Graham,

who owned *Newsweek,* to attend. "I'm not going to have a woman pub-
lisher in charge and she not be there!" (Graham would later acknowledge, "The suits were right. We [women] made a lot of progress.")

The victorious class action precedent broke new ground for the
growing women's movement, and women entered reporter jobs formerly reserved for men.

At the same time a vanguard of Movement veterans led women to
feminism, the cry for Black Power got louder. "The expectations of
blacks were soaring out of the civil rights movement and society
couldn't keep up."

Yet Black Power posed huge problems for the coalition the
Movement represented. Dr. King felt it threatened his entire multira-
cial alliance. But, Eleanor asked in 1968, "When have blacks ever been
more than supplicants in the 'Negro-white alliance'?"

She believed the self-affirming revolution Black Power represented
was essential. "Should the black man emerge whole and should the
white man discover his role, then Americans may at last be able to face
one another as psychological equals." Today she adds, "Malcolm [X],
our other great leader, even with his gibberish about 'blue-eyed devils'
that came from how he had found himself," contributed to that sense
of wholeness.

"He seared the consciousness of black America in ways that nobody
before or since has done. He made black become what black always
should have been, but could never have been before he revealed it." Dr.
King, whose philosophy of love "swept over and miraculously transformed people," did not make the conceptual leap that Malcolm did:
the critical shift away from white norms that led directly to "Black is
beautiful."

Eleanor's own belief in the need for black people to "unite, to recognize their heritage," was shortly put to the test when she became a
youthful trustee of Antioch College, where students wanted to create
black dorms. "The all-black dorms presented a problem for me," recalls
the civil libertarian. "I didn't think you could keep people out. I
believed that you could have a black dorm, so long as you didn't keep
other people out."

This kind of dilemma, in which principle jostled principle, became
alarmingly frequent by the end of the 1960s. Everything had shifted

from a decade before, when public accommodations and the vote were clear-cut issues.

"Before, it was them against us." But in 1965 President Johnson had ordered federal agencies and contractors to take "affirmative action" in overcoming employment discrimination. This clashed with hard-won rules of seniority. "Once you got into jobs, you conflicted with people on your own side. The labor movement had to fight for seniority. Yet that was a problem for us who'd been kept out of jobs, and out of unions, for that matter."

And affirmative action split another loyal coalition constituency: Jews, historically opposed to quotas, since such measures had often been applied to *them* as a tool of exclusion. "Jews are not monolithic in that. But there was a break, though I never regarded Jews as the enemy. Quite the contrary! They were the exact opposite, far and away the best whites."

The great liberal coalition nurtured by Bayard Rustin at the 1963 March on Washington was coming apart at the seams. The "tidy melo-drama," as Eleanor called it then, was over. It was no longer a time when "those of us with dark skins, or Northern accents, or clerical collars were easily recognized as heroes; and those in white sheets were, of course, villains." Labor, people of color, Jews, white workers, liberals and intellectuals no longer saw eye-to-eye.

Many movements had grown out of one; bitter confusion reigned. The Vietnam War was protested by students and supported by labor. The women's movement, itself fragmenting, split men from women. Many blacks felt abandoned by whites, who were often baffled and angered by "Black Power" and the flames engulfing city after city, from Boston to Detroit, and Cincinnati to Memphis.

"People thought so little of the communities in which they felt con-fined they just tore them up." Rebellious violence increased after Malcolm X's assassination at Harlem's Audubon Ballroom in 1965 and, three year's later, Reverend King's murder in Memphis, Tennessee. "King's death became the watershed moment when the poorest blacks knew change just wasn't going to happen."

Despite Eleanor's own deep resonance to the call for Black Power, she, like Bayard Rustin, remained an integrationist. Politically she agreed with Rustin when he explained the need for black people to have alliances.

"One-tenth of the population," he wrote, "cannot go to Congress for the billions which are needed for jobs, for new transportation facilities, new roads, new hospitals, new libraries. To get these things, we must go with other like-minded people."

But liberals were wary and white fear rose, calibrated to rising black fury. The burning ghettos had their counterpart in black students who seized college buildings, demanding an Afro-centered curriculum. And the new poster boys of the Movement—the gun-toting Black Panthers in Oakland, California—completed the fearsome image for many liberals, splitting them from the Movement and from radical whites.

Blacks also fractured into myriad positions. Rustin critiqued cultural nationalists in words that thirty years later could be echoed by his protégé. "The alternative to politics is to cop out and talk about hair, about what name you want to be called, and about soul food. Wearing my hair Afro-style, calling myself an Afro-American, and eating all the chitterlings I can find are not going to affect Congress."

The great coalition of the early 1960s finally and fully blew up in the 1968 Ocean Hill–Brownsville school storm: an emotional battle between a Jewish-led teachers' union on one side, black parents and educators (with a few white allies) on the other. The parents, bent on community control, fired nineteen teachers from an experimental, decentralized school district in Brooklyn. This infuriated the union which, claiming jurisdiction over personnel, held to its principle of job sovereignty. Now labor, a former civil rights ally, opposed black demands.

Eleanor supported community control. But while she understood the deep emotion of black confrontation—laughing to an interviewer about the "new-type black students" at Antioch, "The brothers there have a touch football team that calls themselves 'The Niggers.' Can't you just see the well-meaning whites on the campus shudder?"—she refused to become isolated. The ardent advocate of alliances never gave up on whites and tried to help them understand the need for black control of local institutions. "To liberals who are fond of advocating redistribution of the wealth," she told a conference, "I can only say that surely they must also favor the corollary redistribution of power as well."

Yet, as Eleanor lectured then, "Ads in the *New York Times* criticizing community control are embarrassingly replete with friends, fellow activists from the old days, progressive labor leaders, social democrat pals o' mine, yes, and even men I regarded and, in some ways, still regard as my political mentors." Bayard Rustin was one who opposed it, believing local authority would not solve ghetto problems.

The conflict spiraled until it reached every school in New York: teachers struck citywide to preserve job rights; some parents throughout the city occupied their local schools and sat in all day and night to keep them open, demanding the right of neighborhood control.

"Each side," Eleanor would say publicly two years later, "thought itself completely rational and the other side completely irrational." The passionate clash left lasting bitterness. Schools were a charged battleground when every other institution was in white hands and the vibrant Brownsville community was already falling to urban renewal. This seemed like a last-ditch stand. Local people and teachers each marched in the streets, marshaling support for their respective causes. It seemed easy to reduce complex issues to a simple conflict between Jews and blacks—who, in the militant spirit of the times, now capitalized "Black."

By early 1970, the split widened further when a teacher, Les Campbell, publicly read some of his students' poetry on WBAI radio; it opened, "Jew-boy" and sounded pro-Holocaust. Bitter accusations flew: the terror of anti-Semitism collided with pent-up fury against whites, who once again seemed to be trying to limit black self-expression, this time in poetry. Even "fighting Shirley Chisholm" from Brooklyn got caught in the cross fire: residents in her district were furious after she signed a statement favoring Israel, at a time, they said, "when Jews are trying to close down Ocean Hill–Brownsville."

"The anti-Semitism was irrational," Eleanor says. "Strike out against the people who had been most in your corner, like liberals and Jews, the only whites that had any sustained history of opposing discrimination, that had ever been on your side. People were deeply into a negative reaction against 400 years of white racism, asking, 'Why hasn't it moved faster?' It always happens that way. Trouble in the family: go after the family members, leave the enemies out of it. It was totally irrational, but not as irrational as racism had been.

"The Ocean Hill–Brownsville debacle almost turned Mayor Lindsay out of office. And his Human Rights commissioner was seen as too much on the side of the community folks. So the administration believed Bill Booth had to go."

With the multiple fragmentations, by early 1970 the city had an urgent need for a leader with a rare combination of qualities: someone with stellar civil rights credentials who was also acceptable to unions and whites, and wouldn't intensify the polarization splitting the city. At a time when new cries for "Empowerment" constantly appeared from group after group, a leader of the city's Human Rights Commission would have to weave together strands of the tattered liberal coalition.

The thirty-two-year-old Eleanor heard rumors that her name had been put forward for the job, one that would require the confirmed outsider to finally go "inside." And in this volatile climate, the tough bridge-builder had another major endeavor in the works: she was seven months pregnant.

Part Three

"LET US MARCH ON"

CHAPTER 7

An Unexpected Motherhood

The child who raises its arms will be embraced.
YORUBA PROVERB

The New York City whose cross-ethnic relationships Eleanor was tapped to manage in 1970 was, like the nation, in a state of turbulence. Against a background of urban riots, Richard Nixon had just entered the White House. He immediately modeled an anti–civil rights posture by refusing to meet with Afro-American politicians, prompting all twelve black members of the House of Representatives to boycott the president's State of the Union address. The boycott eventually forced a meeting, though not a turnaround in Nixon's indifference to enforcing antidiscrimination statutes.

During the spring of 1970, ghetto rebellions continued to explode. Within one week in May, police killed five Afro-Americans in Augusta, Georgia, and two students at Mississippi's Jackson State University. The National Guard mobilized at Ohio State. "On no single issue has America been given so much time to effect change, and on no single issue has it failed so badly," Eleanor declared about the country's racial misery.

In New York, media visibility propelled Eleanor forward.

"The press was fascinated by a black woman representing George Wallace, because the stereotype is that black people don't have the sophistication to understand the relationship between the First Amendment and civil rights . . . I think Lindsay understood that somebody who could represent George Wallace could help bring Jews and blacks back together again."

The patrician Republican mayor's choice was bold. An outspoken militant, Eleanor was a Democrat who had sued his administration for Wallace and won. With no prior administrative experience, she was used to protesting laws, not making and enforcing regulations.

At first, Eleanor had no idea she was in consideration.

"One day a woman in the city government called me up and said she was going to propose my name for commissioner of Human Rights," the skeptic remembers. "I laughed at her."

During late winter and early spring, Eleanor began to hear from more and more people. "Finally I began to hear it from important people in the administration."

All her training had oriented her to work for people opposed to repressive government rules. What political trade-offs would she have to make to join government? But the commission was a unique administrative branch set up to represent complainants, prosecuting their grievances. Eleanor's own experience with apartment-hunting had encouraged her belief in its necessity. And now additional needs were surfacing.

"A very different challenge confronted civil rights activists. Hispanic Americans, Asian Americans, American Indians were invisible minorities. Women's unequal status went virtually unnoted," she would write at the end of her tenure. A Human Rights Commission could give voice to all.

Equally significant was a new concern: now that laws mandating equality had been passed, what mechanism would assure their fulfillment?

"Could we who were activists build a strategy for this decade as we had for the last one? What would 'Freedom now' and 'We shall overcome' mean in the years after civil rights laws were passed? Were we prepared for the years of sheer technical toil, bureaucratic innovation, and system-changing that were now needed?"

The commission appeared to be the venue to answer all these needs. And she trusted Mayor John Lindsay to support her in the byzantine universe of New York City politics, where ancient enmities and loyalties held sway.

As Eleanor told the press then, she had misgivings about trading the independence of a private citizen for the power of a government official.

"It's only possible in a bureaucracy that seems to offer hope for those on the outside. I couldn't be Human Rights Commissioner in just any administration that comes along."

Eleanor had signed a full-page *Times* ad with Lindsay the previous

July under the banner headline, "New York Spends More on War than on New York." In the ad he said: "The taxpayers of New York City send $3 billion every year into the war in Vietnam. They send $6 billion every year into the military-industrial empire. That kind of priority is insane."

Lindsay's record wooed the rebel. "He was a white mayor as the city was becoming blacker and browner. It was very difficult to do. He walked the streets of New York and kept the city from blowing up when there were riots in most big cities. Many of the white people detested him because the black people loved him. He was fabulous."

But no more would she be on the outside. If she took the job, she would be one of the most visible city officials, using government machinery, rather than protests or friend-of-court briefs, to create equality. Most of her friends were thrilled at the opportunity the post represented for a black woman to rise in an arena dominated by white men; a few were also critical. "Nothing progressive would happen within the context of the Democratic Party," Antiochian Judy Mage says. "And Eleanor was getting more integrated into it."

Indeed she was. She would finally join the bureaucracy of power and set in motion a lifelong career in Democratic Party and government politics. Eleanor believed she could hold her principles against the pressures that would surely be brought to bear. But the tension would never leave her professional life.

"I had on a navy blue dress—I loved that dress—for my first interview. Because it was a senior political appointment, I believed I had to tell that I was pregnant as a courtesy. I knew I didn't have to, and he couldn't tell with that dress on."

"How nice," the deputy mayor responded.

"He didn't know what to say!" Eleanor laughs. "But I regarded pregnancy as a completely natural condition. This has been a world in which women stooped down in the fields, had babies and kept on going. I didn't understand the notion that if you're pregnant you're sick, and can't do a job. I started my career in government trying to make the opposite point, that discrimination based on pregnancy is absurd."

Pregnancy had been a conscious choice. "I had to really think it through, given all the other things I wanted to do and what mothers owe their children. Would I give them enough attention? Did I want all that was involved? You don't have any right to have children, creating a life that's totally dependent on you, without being thoughtful. That's one of the reasons I'm so much for birth control and abortion."

Edward wanted children. Once, when she'd had ileitis, a painful inflammation of the small intestine triggered by stress, he had taken her to Mt. Sinai. "Edward said all he could think of was that I could lose my female organs before I had any children." But she didn't, and now she was pregnant.

On Monday, March 23, 1970, Mayor Lindsay announced Eleanor's appointment as New York City's next chair of the Commission on Human Rights. Three weeks later, on April 15, flanked by family and the city's black leaders, the pregnant thirty-two-year-old with the huge Afro was sworn in to the $30,000 job, the highest-ranking black woman in city government. Dressed in a green silk maternity dress, the combative commissioner quickly announced plans to create a powerful, activist agency.

Notwithstanding the morning sickness that caused her to vomit through half of every day, Eleanor dove into her high-profile job, eager to implement the "often excellent laws already on the books." Munching on grapes, a craving during her pregnancy, when she also coveted raw onions, liver and cheese, she was determined to create a first-order priority commission. During her final days of pregnancy, Mayor Lindsay was anxious during top-level meetings, hoping she wouldn't go into labor on the spot. But on July 8, 1970, she did. Her water broke and Eleanor was rushed to the hospital.

"Edward was fascinated by natural childbirth. I would wake up sometimes and find him practicing breathing." But when the moment came, "it didn't work particularly well for me. Edward had pushed me hard to be strong. But when he saw the blood run down my leg as we climbed the steps to Mt. Sinai, he softened and understood this took more than strength! He blanched. 'My goodness,' he said."

Eleanor was quoted in city newspapers saying she dictated memos from bed between contractions and worked until wheeled into the delivery room next day. There, she gave birth to a six and a half–pound girl.

"I trust you will be back at work presently," the mayor joked in a congratulatory letter. "How about tomorrow? Actually, the Cabinet was convinced that you would give birth in the Blue Room. Someone even went so far as to suggest that I have an ambulance standing by those last few meetings. These kinds of crises I can do without!!!"

When it came to naming the baby, Eleanor's strong sense of tradition meshed with Edward's. "We had the *exact* same sense. You name the child after something that has true meaning for you, and most often that's a name for a person in the family. Our ancestors who suffered and built this country had nothing to show for it. Nothing! At least let their children honor them." Their daughter would be Katherine—Eleanor's middle name—and Edward's mother would be honored with their child's middle name, Felicia.

Shortly after delivery, "Edward and the doctor came in," Eleanor recalls, looking dazed all over again.

"We think there may be something wrong with your baby."

Suspecting from the physical characteristics what it was, the anxious new parents awaited test results.

"We hoped and prayed it wasn't, and it was. Here I had this beautiful little purple baby," says Eleanor, who in 1970 knew little about Down's syndrome. The news was "a huge shock. They gave us genetic tests to see if we were carrying the gene, and we weren't. It's an accident of the x and y chromosomes."

A pediatrician soon visited the stunned parents in the hospital room; they were further astonished by his words.

"Now, of course, if you want to give this baby up, I could arrange for the child to be taken away."

"Are you out of your mind?" Eleanor blurted. "Over my dead body!"

"Why would we want to give up our child because she was born with a defect?" she says. "We were the last people who should give up a child! I wouldn't judge somebody who really couldn't raise a child, somebody poor or who had been psychologically devastated. But for people who have had the advantages Edward and I had . . . wow!" She shakes her head. "That would have been a profoundly immoral act.

"Katherine is more limited than I thought she would be, and it doesn't matter," Eleanor emphasizes. "She doesn't have heart ailments or some of the other problems. Parents used to hide these children away in the basement.

"The only regrets I have are for Katherine. There are certainly no regrets for me. If chances went around, it should have been somebody like Edward and me, because we could raise such a child. In a sense of perfect justice, for us it made sense. For her it's a terrible roll of the dice.

"The greatest trauma I've ever had was having a child with Down's syndrome. That was a great shock. But instinctively I knew what I was going to do: raise her and love her. It's just that it was the most unexpected thing that ever happened to me."

Typically, Eleanor did not confide in family or friends during the weeks she waited for test results to confirm the doctor's suspicions.

"After it sunk in, how do you survive that? You become dispassionate by explaining to yourself why it makes any sense at all." She forced herself to intellectually accept her fate, reminding herself that "if this had to happen to someone, it was best it was us.

"This child was accepted and loved. Katherine was a healthy child with a sunny disposition." Emphasizing Katherine's loving disposition, Eleanor made her peace with becoming the mother of a disabled child, while for once acknowledging the pain that even a rational explanation could not avert.

"Every once in a while," she says, "it hits where it's supposed to hit."

Katherine was one week old when Eleanor took her home to Washington to meet the family. Taking a look at Katherine, Portia was stunned. Stopping dead in her tracks, she blurted out, "She's . . ." and could go no further.

"She's what, what?!" Eleanor fired back.

"Aren't you talking about it?" Portia asked, hardly able to talk.

"Talking about what?"

"The baby!"

Today Portia says, "My heart was just breaking for her, but she was showing absolutely no sadness. Maybe she cried before she got there, but I cried all the way home. She didn't tell me, and the baby's about a week old!"

Eleanor, says Portia, never discussed Katherine's disability. But shortly thereafter when Portia's second child was born, Eleanor called her at the hospital.

"Is the baby all right?"

"Yes."

"Well, all right." Eleanor sighed. "If this had to happen to somebody in the family, I'm glad it was me."

Portia is still confounded by her older sister: "That takes a kind of strength, a kind of love that's so deep it's hard to come by. But we never had a real discussion about it. Eleanor has never demonstrated vulnerability. My mother was like that."

When Barbara Babcock visited she pondered Katherine, lying in her crib while Eleanor ironed. Puzzled by Katherine's appearance, Barbara mused aloud, "There's something unusual about this child."

Eleanor was silent.

"Is it that she's unusually beautiful?" Barbara asked.

"You can't ask the mother that. Of course the mother would think so."

Today Barbara exclaims, "Eleanor never told me. Here she and Edward, these two smart people, were supposed to have a brilliant baby, and they didn't. This wasn't supposed to happen. Edward told me a few months later that the baby was a Mongoloid and that Eleanor couldn't tell anybody. She just couldn't deal with it, and she couldn't bring herself to say the word."

Others confirm that, as law professor Susan Deller Ross says, "Eleanor was a closed person. She never talked about it." Yet over the next three decades Eleanor would demonstrate her tremendous capacity for love by caring for Katherine at home while simultaneously handling work demands that, taken alone, would overwhelm most people. And she never complained.

"Eleanor may have grieved that this wasn't a perfect child, but who knew?" says her friend Charlayne Hunter-Gault. "You would think God created this most perfect instrument. To hear her talk about Katherine is to talk about a perfect creature. 'Did you see her?' 'Did you see how pretty she looks when she has on this?' 'Did you see how she smiled?' Eleanor never missed a step."

Whenever Eleanor spoke of her daughter, her face perceptibly softened. "Oh, Katherine's fine," she invariably replied, just as she responded to queries about herself. Her capacity to transcend difficulties by looking over and beyond them served her well with this extraordinary new challenge. "Katherine's wonderful."

And, like any doting mother, she glowed.

Eleanor returned to work days after the birth and handled Katherine's introduction to the commission just as she had at home, with no advertisement that this child was "special." She simply brought

her baby in to meet staff. Gradually the news spread. But Eleanor, wanting to make sure no one thought she expected special consideration, or sympathy, rarely mentioned her daughter.

Edward, the psychologist in the family, talked to friends. But Eleanor, the true granddaughter of Nellie Holmes, who always said, "Keep the shades down so people won't get in your personal business," kept to her private ways. Even when holding a commission hearing on handicapped accommodation, she never opened the window to her own family's intimate knowledge.

When friends came over to celebrate Katherine's birth, "Eleanor wasn't saying anything and I didn't ask," recalls Judy Mage, "though I thought the baby in her cradle looked a little strange. She had a little red face and seemed kind of wizened. Maybe it was her cry. I knew there was something different, so I wasn't surprised later to hear."

Eleanor's staff went to her house that year for her first office Christmas party, "with two hors d'oeuvres and two bottles of soda, bring your own booze," laughs one loyal assistant, commenting on Eleanor's legendary reluctance to spend money. Katherine was at home. Again, no special notice.

"She's a good mother and did what she could to not institutionalize Katherine," comments Charlayne. "What does that say to you about Eleanor as a person? Because Katherine is no day at the beach. But she treated her like a normal child."

Eleanor and Edward presented their marriage to the world as a union of two smart people who understood each other perfectly: a modern professional couple in sync, supporting each other's careers. In one of the few personal conversations Eleanor ever had with a staff member, she told a woman about to marry, "If you share nothing else with a partner, you must share a sense of humor."

This comment didn't mean simply laughing together, but implied a generous, even wry view of life, one that could accommodate a child with a disability and still find everyday enjoyment. Eleanor and Edward seemed well able to adapt to the bumps that life presented.

Edward, working as general counsel for the New York City Housing Authority, was a frequent visitor at Eleanor's office. There, he visibly both supported and contended with her, setting a tone that allowed those staff members so inclined to argue vociferously with their boss

and walk away on good terms. He shared Eleanor's comfort with a kind of public "thrust-and-parry debating relationship," as one friend calls it.

Equally supportive to Eleanor's staff, Edward made himself a well-liked, friendly presence. A few found him irritatingly facile, but most discovered a perceptive and charming man, especially with the ladies. Several of Eleanor's associates believed he was having affairs, but Eleanor says she did not know, so, following her lead, not much was made of them. Eleanor and Edward seemed to be the consummate couple.

"It wasn't even just a case of people with the same education. It was sophistication—a worldview that it would have been difficult for black people to get living in the cocoon of racism. Both he and I got the opportunity to see well beyond that. Therefore at many levels the match made a lot of sense." Friends concurred. Impressed with their similar styles ("he liked to debate and she liked to debate"), they watched him support her bursting career.

Soon Eleanor, at thirty-four, was pregnant again.

During this second pregnancy—"which I had as soon as possible because, if you want children, by that age you should have them"—Eleanor had amniocentesis, though the chance of having a second child with Down's syndrome was remote, since neither she nor Edward carried the extra gene.

Nonetheless, even this rationalist was relieved when, twenty months after Katherine's birth, again "working until the water broke," she rushed to Mt. Sinai. The following day, on March 17, 1972, Eleanor and Edward were thrilled by a healthy five-pound four-ounce boy. Eleanor sent a birth announcement to Grandfather Richard and his second wife, Miss Olivia, with a photo and note: "Here is your great-grandson! He is a very robust boy, although he insisted upon coming into the world 3 1/2 weeks early instead of staying in there to get a little fatter. He seems to have lots of Holmes in him, judging by his profile and long feet. We hope you get to see him soon. Love, Eleanor."

When it came to this child's name, "We had no question. John was Edward's father, who had also named Edward's brother John." Eleanor rhapsodizes about Edward's family, especially the eager father who helped send his boys through college.

"When one was going to Columbia, the other was at Yale. You get an idea what kind of parents these wonderful people were. Edward sent his laundry home from Yale to be done by his mother," Eleanor says admiringly. "John Norton was an exemplary father. John was absolutely what our son's name was going to be. I didn't care if the whole world was named John. And Holmes for my given name. Portia also has a son with Holmes as a middle name. So our son became John Holmes Norton."

Eleanor was once asked by a journalist if she ever felt cheated of spending time with her children. "I sure never felt cheated of spending time with John," she laughed. "He didn't sleep straight through the night for six months, and I always got up with him when he woke up at three or four A.M. He and I had plenty of time together.

"He wasn't a particularly good student and we trace it back to his ear infections. We think that had a lot to do with his late talking, late blooming. He caught up though and when he catches up, he really catches up!"

Eleanor and Edward took him to a speech therapist to ask, "Why is this child not talking?"

"Actually he was talking up a blue streak," says Eleanor. "He was talking about what he heard but he didn't hear it right. Shoshana, the therapist, got him talking intelligibly in no time flat. And when he started, it was as if you turned something and it gushed forward. Somebody called him 'motor mouth,' which really captured him."

The little boy loved to be read to, especially Greek myths and dragon stories, which fed his imagination. "We bought him wooden blocks; he would make the most extraordinary things. We always thought he was going to be an architect because he seemed to have an eye. He does have this strong, creative streak."

As Johnny grew, "He didn't know anything about Katherine except she was somebody to play with. Just help her a little bit, and she'd go right along with him. They were very close. The best thing I ever saw him do was to try on some old clothes. He'd dress Katherine up too and then walk in with her. He didn't know any difference for the longest time."

The city provided its commissioner with a car and a white male driver, an irony Eleanor especially enjoyed. In the mornings, "I'd simply take the driver past Mrs. Norton's house, leave Katherine and Johnny, and come down to the office, until they were too big and Mrs. Norton's husband needed care.

"It's tradition to call the mother-in-law *Mrs.* Black people, that's how we did it in our community. What was I supposed to call her, Blanche? You revere your elders!" Some of Eleanor's friends became concerned about the strain Katherine's needs placed on Eleanor's marriage and career. Over the years, when they saw how low-functioning Katherine was, several tried raising the idea of a community residence.

"Maybe you need to think about another home for Katherine," Judy Mage once began. "There are nice community residences."

"No, Katherine is staying with me!"

"Sometimes the child is happier in a group home," Judy pushed. "And this is such a terrible strain on you, and the marriage."

"NO! I'd never consider that for Katherine. She's staying with me." Eleanor had no interest in discussing options.

Friends and family often commented to each other with alarm or admiration on the weight that Eleanor seemed to carry. "It's a huge imposition on her personal life," says one. "Extraordinary caregiving needs," says another.

But Eleanor vehemently denies any burden. "God made these children," she says, defending her daughter and herself. "He knew we would take care of them because they're so easy. Katherine is easy!" Her love revealed a side of Eleanor the public rarely saw, as she attended to her daughter's needs.

"Because of Katherine's limited vocabulary we have to learn that she uses proxies for what she can't say. If she really doesn't want to do something, she'll say, 'My stomach hurts.'

"Well, her stomach doesn't hurt. It just means, 'I don't want to do that' or 'I'm feeling uncomfortable.' It's a little scary because you don't have any way to know when she really is hurting." Yet Eleanor sailed on, smiling at Katherine—"That's mommy's girl"—while attending to business in a different voice.

At three, Katherine began school. "They had these tiny children who were supposed to be retarded, and I never will forget seeing them walk from room to room in a line. We had wonderful facilities in New York at the time."

When the two children were finally too much for their grandmother, Eleanor hired her next-door neighbor for after-school care. But to get Johnny home from Riverside Nursery in the afternoon, Edward's mother still rode a crowded city bus to pick him up. When

Mrs. Norton delivered her grandson at home, she stayed until Katherine arrived by van hours later and the neighbor took over. Like women the world around, even this high-powered professional had to patch her long day together with a group support system to make sure her children were tended while she worked. "And what would the average woman do?"

Edward, asserts Eleanor, was "excellent" as a father, trading off nighttime bottle-feeding and diapering, but, like many city-bred people, he didn't drive, and like most New Yorkers the couple did not have a car. His mother filled the gap. "Mrs. Norton, such a wonderful grandmother, if you could make a saint in the Methodist Church, that's where she would have been."

Later, after Mr. Norton died, Edward's mother lived with them. "And I'm telling you, as far as I was concerned, Mrs. Norton could have lived with me as long as she wanted. That woman did so much for me and my family.

"When Mrs. Norton fell out of bed one morning just before she went to the hospital, Johnny was the first one to get to her. This little boy had gotten a pillow to put under her head. We were just so moved by it. He loved Mrs. Norton."

"And that was the last time I saw her alive," mourns Johnny today.

When Mrs. Norton died in January 1981, Eleanor eulogized her mother-in-law at St. Mark's Church, invoking "the full, stately frame, the luminous black skin framed in bright colors . . . defined by a lifetime of love and generosity. I count it as a bonus of my marriage to have been in the same family with Blanche Norton and to have had her live with us much of the past several years."

Eleanor took the children to the funeral services. Later, Katherine would sometimes go to the living room mantel, look at a statue that Eleanor had brought back from Africa and say, "Grandma dead."

"That's one of the few workings of her mind I really got to understand. 'Grandma Blanche is dead' evoked the stillness of a statue."

Years later, Eleanor delivered the brief commencement address for Katherine's graduation from the National Children's Center in Washington.

"Each bird learns to fly in its own way. Some, like Katherine Felicia Norton, will fly close to the ground. . . . Our country is discovering that it needs us all—the birds who fly high and those like Katherine who fly closer to the ground . . . Katherine has changed my life. Every day she makes me strive to be worthy of her tolerance of my faults. Every day she teaches me the many meanings of unconditional love."

During the spring of 1971 Eleanor and Edward bought a beautiful old Harlem brownstone, at a time when most black professionals did not live that far "uptown." White people had sold these homes a generation before, often to West Indians who were now retiring and returning home. Eleanor and Edward, part of the new wave of move-ins, found their 466 West 144th Street house just five blocks from Edward's childhood apartment.

"It was pristine," says Eleanor. "We were only the third family to live in it in a hundred years. It was grand. There was a giant living room, a great middle room, and a big dining room, all with working fireplaces. We had huge New Year's Eve parties in there, dancing on the hardwood floors."

Edward loved to cook and the couple often hosted smaller parties. "Barbecue chicken," Charlayne Hunter-Gualt happily remembers. "Ribs. There'd be music, in this spectacular house with all original marble and mahogany. They pushed the furniture back, we'd have dancing, eating, talking—lots of talking. Uninhibited great parties with lots of interesting people." Eleanor, intense about virtually everything she did, included fun—especially dancing—in her short list of life's needs.

"Eleanor would have people swing by on Sunday afternoons," Christine Philpot recalls, "and do steak tartar. That was a quickie she could put together: raw meat ground up, mix with capers, mustard, soy sauce, onions, and dip your cracker into it. Gordon and Peggy Davis and a few others. I remember the scintillating wit of those evenings. We would be just knocked down with laughter. Sparks leapt from mouth to mouth."

"Nobody enjoyed parties more than Eleanor," agrees Charlayne, "though her work was paramount. But that stemmed from this sense of justice and commitment that was in her bones, and you don't relax too much if justice is paramount in your life."

With a group of friends, black women who all had baby boys born within six months of each other—Christine, Charlayne and several others—she chatted in the slivers of time between work and parenting tasks. But Eleanor rarely unbent beyond a certain level. Though she was passionate about work, intense emotion did not penetrate friendships: a personal zone of privacy remained even with intimates. Charlayne, then working for the *New York Times* and living in a brownstone around the corner, explains, "Some strong women like that have to close off parts of themselves. Otherwise it's too much energy to let people in and out of those parts of you. You wouldn't have the energy to do what you have to do."

"Charlayne and I became cut buddies when we had children the same age and realized we had everything in common," says Eleanor. "Her son Chuma and Johnny were born within months. I realized how Southern I was when I got to talking to Charlayne. She was more Southern than I, but all you had to do was be with somebody with your essential upbringing," Eleanor laughs uproariously, "to realize we were raised as Southern black girls. Here was a black woman, real black, real Southern, and real sophisticated."

Whenever the two talked, sometimes giggling in a way few saw Eleanor do, Johnny, a master mimic, teased his mother. "We would be on the phone for hours, so one of Johnny's favorite imitations was: 'Girl!' 'Chile!'

"Charlayne was such a fast friend, one of my best friends in this world. You know we're two writers together. Two people for whom the word, the English language, is it. Both of us are also oldest children, children of whom much was expected.

"Charlayne shares my sense of self. Both of us have never felt inferior. Her grandfather was a minister. And she was deeply involved with black things. We'd be on the phone about *Times* stories all the time."

Charlayne concurs. "There were not many dynamic women who were major players in the politics of the city. But Eleanor was smart, dynamic and, for a journalist, very quotable. It wasn't so much the children. I bonded with Eleanor's mind and her sensitivity to people. And if I ever needed a complicated legal concept explained, she could make it crystal clear when I called."

"It was both professional and personal," agrees Eleanor. "We had similar values—although on religion she tended to be far more unquestioning than I.

"But her sense of fashion, sense of what's important in this world . . . I was occasionally more skeptical of some things that were black than she was. You had to be more than black to get me! But after all, she came out of the belly of racism. Had one of the most searing experiences of the civil rights movement as a young girl, a lonely pioneer trying to break segregation."

In 1962 Charlayne had been the first African-American woman to graduate from the University of Georgia, where angry crowds threw a brick and glass bottles through her dormitory window after other students turned off their lights, making her lit windows an easy target. She and fellow student Hamilton Holmes had to be escorted by federal marshals.

"This was the girl who was *chosen* to open the University of Georgia. They didn't just say, 'Hey, we need somebody smart to do this.' They found them somebody who could do it!"

Eleanor would become lifetime friends with Christine and Charlayne, the companions of her early mothering years in Harlem. But in the early 1970s, the ills of New York City took most of her time.

CHAPTER 8

Madame Commissioner

"My view on all this business about race is never to get angry, no, but to get even. You don't take it out in anger; you take it out in achievement."
VERNON JORDAN

Eleanor understood that her job was to build consensus for a civil rights agenda that included many constituencies, at a time when it was unusual to interpret nondiscrimination so broadly.

"People just said: 'Not for them, but for me.' That can be very troubling, because you don't know what would happen in a pinch in a society. I know what happened in Germany in a pinch. It strikes me indelibly."

As a black woman, Eleanor had an unusual relationship with the Jewish community and was one of the few who could span the tension heightened by school decentralization. Her fifteen years of close ties to Jews—ever since her days at Antioch, continuing through Yale, the Movement and the ACLU—helped her understand anti-Semitism with an insight shared by few black leaders then. She often drew parallels, "because it does seem as if blacks historically have performed that same function [as Jews did in Europe] in the U.S."

Black-Jewish relations took much of her time. But she loved the tangle that New York ethnic politics engendered. "When I look back now I was an absolute natural to it. Because all the analogies were perfectly clear to me. Lindsay was right to choose me, even though I was a black militant—that's how I was known and who I was. However, he understood that I could maneuver my way with Jews and Italian Americans and the rest of them."

One of her first acts, seeking to fight bias against Orthodox Jews, was to announce Sabbath employment guidelines that directed employers to accommodate religious needs of employees. And in that heated time, Eleanor began to talk to Jews and blacks about their complicated relationship.

"Two peoples, each of whom know better than most the real meaning of oppression and bigotry," began one speech. "It was no accident that . . . although many of the finest young people of every background joined the civil rights movement, the two young white men who were murdered along with a young black man in Mississippi in 1964—Michael Schwerner and Andrew Goodman, who met their appalling deaths with James Chaney—were Jewish." She called the current breach "a falling out between friends who need each other."

Though the school strike had ended by the time Eleanor took up her job, Ocean Hill–Brownsville was widely regarded as a nail in the coffin of the black-Jewish alliance. However she refused to let the relationship die.

"All of us who value that friendship—and the positive social good that can continue to come from it—must be concerned enough to face squarely the damage that has been done to it. When are blacks and Jews in this town going to talk to each other *frankly?* The special interest Jewish and black organizations are quick to lead partisan fights against each other. But where is black and Jewish leadership in structuring a situation for honest and friendly exchange to work out differences?"

Facing the problem meant acknowledging the bigotry within each group. "A black anti-Semite finds in me an ardent foe," Eleanor firmly declared. "It is time we all looked back on those [Ocean Hill] incidents and examine this circular growth of misunderstanding—and vow to make sure it will never happen again. That means developing an affirmative strategy for black-Jewish cooperation instead of constantly hoping there will be no flare-up . . . The future for two great groups of New Yorkers can be bright indeed. It is up to us—to you and to me."

But there was a fresh issue dividing the two groups. "Jews opposed affirmative action," Eleanor says. Along with other whites, they feared being pushed aside. And historically, quotas had excluded Jews.

Eleanor repeatedly approached leading Jewish organizations and found they would generally support affirmative action so long as it contained *goals and timetables, not quotas.* But, doing the consuming work of building relationships, ultimately the commission led "a city in the forefront of affirmative action. And Jews were my allies throughout, because I demonstrated you could use goals without displacing people. We were pioneers."

From her modest office on the seventh floor of 80 Lafayette Street, near Manhattan's judiciary area, Eleanor fought for every human rights issue. "My own black people already knew me and understood who I was. The Hispanic community was not nearly as up and coming, though it seemed to me very important. And I pressed for and got a sexual orientation statute, when the Catholic church and many others were against it." The commission was at the forefront of emerging gay rights.

"I might go into a black church and say: 'What happens to a gay man, grabbed in the street because of what people think is his sexual orientation, is the precise same thing as grabbing a black man and lynching him because he's black.'

"I didn't think political capital was worth a dime if you just hoarded it and didn't use it. If you're a black your obligation is especially strong. Because white people, even the best, can't teach black people many things. They lack credibility. So who's going to do it then?"

One of Eleanor's strengths as commissioner lay in her continued insistence on equality for *all*. "They didn't know what to make of me, child!" This out-of-towner from an Ivy League, civil rights background, had a puzzling approach. Soon her overstretched staff grumbled about charges from Italian Americans and Jews. "We got complaints about individual cases of discrimination on religion and national origin," remembers staff member Charlotte Frank. "We were quite concerned that the basic mission of the commission—to take care of discrimination against blacks, Hispanics and women—was compromised by having to pay attention to complaints from white ethnic groups." Many staff openly rebelled.

Eleanor hastily called a meeting in her large conference room. As staff sat skeptically around the table, one remembers, "She went through a lecture that only Eleanor could, as the intellectual she is, on America's melting pot."

"The legacy of the past fifteen years of protest is that no group is any longer willing to accept 'second-class citizenship' in any form!" she told her staff. "There is only one city in the world with large numbers of every national group in the world living together. You and I are fortunate to be living in that city."

Explaining the brutal history of assimilation for white immigrants— where, for instance, a job applicant with an Italian last name had to pass the usual standards *and* be found clean of "suspect" associations— she characterized the current era as one in which these second- or third-generation immigrants could finally claim their heritage. It was "a flowering of ethnic diversity, a spring garden," and the commission would do all it could to help pride bloom.

"We walked away more comfortable about broadening the agency, understanding that we could and should preserve peoples' rights to preserve their national heritage and not have it undermined, but recognized as a good thing. And to help them file complaints if prejudice was keeping them from their proper place. That was Eleanor's unique ability, to help people understand issues and work together," says Charlotte Frank.

To build a citywide consensus, the new commissioner frequently spoke, utilizing any venue she could find. One was a weekly NBC-TV program, *Open Circuit,* she hosted, seeking to assure all her constituencies she would address their needs.

On one of her first shows, Eleanor, naming ethnic groups, used the term "Polacks."

A furor erupted. The *Daily News* had a field day ridiculing the woman who was supposed to be protecting people, not deriding them. All the papers carried the story.

"I hope people will forgive my stupidity and ignorance," Eleanor publicly apologized. "I didn't know it was a slur, and I should have."

Her forthright expression of regret disarmed most critics, but Eleanor still berates herself thirty years later.

"I shouldn't have made an unconscious slur. There is no excuse, except it shows you the closed world of segregation I had come from. I didn't know any better."

That slip was the beginning of a steep learning curve. Several weeks later her white TV producer said, "I'd like you to come in and look at some tapes of yourself on air."

When she sat in the control room and began to watch, he pointed out, "See, instead of looking directly at the camera, you often stare off to the side. Try to look right at the camera so you'll appear to be speaking face-on to the viewers."

Appreciative, Eleanor thanked him warmly. Later that evening as she rode home in the car of a black announcer, he ranted, "That was terrible, what the producer did!"

"What do you mean?"

"Calling you in like that."

"What he did was wonderful!" Eleanor shot back.

"He had no business cutting you down like that."

Today Eleanor reflects, "I was amazed that, even though he was a professional, he didn't see how helpful that was. And I can't help but believe it has something to do with color, that black people don't know how to accept criticism from whites."

Just a year after Eleanor's appointment Mayor Lindsay tapped her to also act as his executive assistant. In an era of "Power to the People!" she would decentralize city government. "If humongous city agencies operated at neighborhood level, services could be delivered quickly, without people having to travel all the way up the bureaucracy."

Offered the promotion, Eleanor discussed it with Edward.

"We finally decided it would be the right thing for me to do," she told the *New York Post*. "My husband is the answer to a woman's dream—a strong, completely secure male, unthreatened by women who want to improve themselves outside the home." Her salary remained at $35,000, somewhat more than Edward's.

"And it doesn't bother him in the least!" she gloated. "All our money goes into a common coffer. And he takes care of all the financial matters because he has a mind like a computer."

Historically anxious about money to get through school but indifferent once she began to earn plenty of it, one of the few times Eleanor's eyes rolled back in her head at commission staff meetings was during budget discussions. She thought conceptually and programmatically, and was uninterested in dollars. This legendary lack of attention to finances would, years later, prove an almost fatal neglect.

Every month brought fresh crises. School protests, strikes, antiwar rallies and ethnic battles dominated the news. Crime and welfare skyrocketed; emotions kept pace. Jumping into rough-and-tumble New York politics, Eleanor wanted "to clear up everything immediately," one colleague laughs, "from the past three or four centuries."

In the early 1970s women also were beginning to revolt; Eleanor stirred them up more. "I spoke to groups of feminists, asking, 'Where are you? Why aren't you filing complaints!' " Almost half worked outside the home for pay, a leap of 10 percent in a single decade. But their pay averaged only fifty-nine cents for every dollar a man earned. Inequality cut across the board.

"If you broke your leg, then your Blue Cross or whatever paid for the entire amount. But if you had your baby you might have gotten a few hundred dollars rather than the thousands it cost. All of that was just routinely accepted."

Eleanor had told reporters before her swearing-in, "I mean to do all I can to see that the principle of nondiscrimination becomes a reality for women as well." When the male reporters mentioned a recent demonstration at City Hall to demand more top-level jobs for women, she quickly retorted, "You might consider my appointment as an answer to their demand, mightn't you?"

Yet like other constituencies, women were not monolithic. The deep mistrust in the black community, for instance, included black women. Reasoning that it took 400 years to get the attention they were now receiving, some saw white women "jumping on the bandwagon." They didn't want to associate with irrelevancies like highly publicized bra burnings.

Many poor women of all colors had difficulty even feeding their children; they laughed when middle-class women protested having to wash supper dishes or suffer a male partner's emotional detachment. To add to the intramural bitterness, groups like NOW were roiled by straight women–lesbian conflicts. In this rancorous atmosphere, the notion of multiple movements was perceived by most activists as a source of competition and division, not strength.

Yet Eleanor steered a path here as she had between blacks and Jews. Following her mentor Pauli Murray's exhortation to terminate Jane Crow with Jim Crow, she focused on women's collective burdens and initiated a week-long public hearing, the first of its kind ever held on women's rights in the United States. The historic proceedings opened just five months after Eleanor began her job.

"It was my attempt to let people see in some kind of rigorous form, what is this thing called women's rights?"

Eleanor's personal stamp on this pioneering event was evident in the breadth of speakers. Flo Kennedy and Dorothy Height talked eloquently about being black and female; Faith Ringgold spoke as a black artist; Betty Friedan, Gloria Steinem, Margaret Meade and Kate Millett testified; Beulah Sanders of the National Welfare Rights Movement; unionists, business people and academics all illustrated discrimination, from jobs to housing and credit. Testimony was often personal and poignant. A young household worker, Patricia Jones, told of an unscrupulous employment agency buying her a ticket from her native North Carolina to New York; she ended up a virtual serf, working eighty-hour weeks for seventy-five dollars.

The groundbreaking testimony soon emerged as a mass-market paperback, *Women's Role in Contemporary Society*. Eleanor's introduction prophetically affirmed, "The growth of a grassroots women's movement cannot be stopped."

The new movement was often accused of involving only middle-class, white feminists. But Eleanor insisted on broadening the definition, asking women "to take on *as a women's issue* the cause of the most exploited women in America: household workers." Sixty percent did not even earn minimum wage.

Eleanor opened a first-time conference on the issue with her standard no-nonsense approach.

"It is easy enough to get an emotional response from people concerning household workers. Blacks respond out of the anguish that comes from knowing that so many generations of black women—our mothers, our aunts, our grandmothers—have had no alternative to this low-paid and often dignity-stripping occupation. Whites respond out of either frustration or guilt or both."

Instead, she recommended viewing this as a *women workers'* fight, focusing on practical solutions like unionization or cooperatives. The conference would "discourage the rap-session approach to discussion," she promised, "because the plight of household workers is too serious." Four months later, after intense lobbying, the New York State Legislature placed all household workers under minimum wage protection.

Including all sectors of women, the commission also investigated discrimination at major law firms. Eleanor and her staff reasoned that if they could negotiate affirmative action agreements for female lawyers there, the firms wouldn't be able to tell female clients they couldn't secure the same kinds of legal agreements for them. As part of the inquiry, Eleanor's team examined résumés of applicants for legal jobs.

"What we found was so blatant," recalls one investigator. "Scribbled across the tops of résumés at leading firms were things like, 'Her makeup makes her look like Dracula' or 'This woman is not strong enough for our first woman.' Or 'Her husband works for another law firm so might be a conflict sometime in the future.' " In another major breakthrough, most of New York's top firms negotiated hiring agreements.

But despite these successes—with their national impact—the commission was dragged down by its long-standing backlog and low rate of proving discrimination. Worker expectations were often raised only to be disappointed. Staff was demoralized. And newspapers complained that nothing was happening.

Eleanor dove in.

"We examined old cases and saw: 'Here, it looks like there was somebody willing to say they heard a manager indicate he preferred a white person for the job.' But by the time the case came up two years later, no witnesses could be found. So the commission had to close the case."

Eleanor wondered what would happen if, immediately after a case were filed, the commission called the supervisor in and said, "You don't have any blacks at that level and here was a black person that looked qualified."

The employer might be willing to say, "Tell you what, assuming this person continues to perform, she can have the next available promotion." If the case were settled before the trail got cold, the complainant could get a remedy or a promise in writing, even if not the promotion this time.

Taking a leap, Eleanor experimented. She converted her investigators into fact-finders who quickly got each side's version; then she settled cases *before* they got to court, where everything bogged down. "Basically the law teaches you how to stop things up. Due process is about slowing things down." By settling, an employee had a good chance of gaining the sought-after job, money or letter of recommendation. And an employer didn't have to expose records, plus the agreement remained confidential.

In a year, Eleanor had a rapid response system in place that mediated complaints within three months, resolving 60 percent.

Critics initially denounced the new approach. Businesses complained the commission strong-armed employers into settling. Without rigorous evidence, they charged, some people got remedies who didn't deserve them.

"We said that was nonsense!" Eleanor snaps. "People frequently settle to reduce their risk of losing. That's what the legal system does in this country. It's a risk-based system!"

Despite early complaints that the commission relied on flimsy evidence to award damages, or, conversely, that it wasn't getting *enough* for people, Eleanor's triumph at quick settlements was a significant pilot. Before the end of the decade she would revamp case processing on a national scale.

Eleanor also wanted to move beyond settling cases one by one. Her training led her to examine discriminatory *patterns* and take on entire industries: banks that refused mortgage loans in poor neighborhoods, industries, even city departments with questionable personnel practices.

On a humid day in August 1970, just five months into the job, Eleanor's executive director Preston David watched her Sunday morning TV show. An apparently well-qualified Puerto Rican told her he couldn't get hired as a school principal. Appalled, Eleanor announced on-air, "I want to say here and now that I'm going to do an investigation of discrimination in the New York City Public School System!"

"I fell off my chair," David says. Nothing was planned.

But as promised, Eleanor initiated a major public hearing into the entire city's school hiring practices. Many were furious at this encroachment on a sacred fiefdom, David remembers—"How *dare* she?"—but they came: Albert Shanker, president of the embattled teachers union; parents and community leaders; officials of the Board of Education; teachers; and national educational experts. "In order to keep anybody from getting out of hand, I had members of the community as marshals," Eleanor laughs.

She opened by acknowledging the deep feelings in the air.

"All over America school issues stir people of all origins and backgrounds as no other issues do. Whether it is school desegregation in Mississippi, school busing in Michigan, sex education in Iowa or hiring practices in New York, school issues are joined on all sides with unmatched fervor."

She laid out the problem: The one-third of New York City's population that was black and Puerto Rican was barely represented among teachers and principles, though over half the children were from these groups. Under the commission's mandate, "we must find the reasons

why. It is time to let the facts speak for themselves, for facts have an elo-
quence rhetorical statements most often lack.

"We must spend this week in trying to understand the intricacies and
origins of a system which—no doubt without malicious intent—has
taken on the trappings of exclusiveness." Thus lifting blame, she encouraged genuine problem-solving. The result was the sharing of detailed,
sometimes shocking information about current hiring practices.

"If you had an accent, you couldn't be a teacher," says Eleanor. "This
was a very elitist job then. New York City had these standards that were
not job-related."

After 140 experts testified, Eleanor concluded, "While we have criticized the efforts of many, we have nowhere found evil intent or lack of
concern for improvement." Yet with words that could describe many
U.S. businesses, she said, "The poor minority showing was not due to
conscious and deliberate discrimination, but to a de facto exclusion . . .
a reflection of the rigidities that infect the entire personnel system."
The Board of Education's hiring method excluded "anyone who
thought differently from those who designed and conducted the licens-
ing examinations." The hiring procedure, described by one expert as "so
inbred as to be sociological incest," embodied "cultural and geographic
bias."

The overwhelming weight of the 2,000 pages of testimony "compels
the following conclusion," Eleanor told the *Times*. "The current process
of selection of teachers and supervisors is outmoded, overly rigid,
unnecessarily costly, of questionable validity, discriminatory in its
effect, and inconsistent with the objectives of the school decentralization plan."

New York's Southern District Court soon found the supervisory
tests discriminatory; the Board of Education wrote guidelines for hiring and performance reviews and allowed decentralized school districts
to fill acting posts. This broadening of eligibility, with objective job criteria, finally put professionals of color into city schools and killed the
old testing system forever. New York's public school staffing would
never again be a virtually all-white domain.

Eleanor moved on. She attacked housing bills "segregationist in intent
and effect," cited advertising agencies for inadequate hiring of minorities, and ruled that the Biltmore Hotel could no longer exclude women
from the Men's Bar. When some blacks complained she devoted too

much energy to women's rights, she countered, "The myth that somehow black women are not a part of the struggle for women's rights, but belong only to the movement for black liberation, cannot be."

Eleanor's ambition was to change the face of the entire workforce in the world's most concentrated job arena, as she described her jurisdiction. Her investigation of twenty-seven major companies in the city resulted, over nine months, in a 50 percent increase in minority group employees. "Private business made these gains as a direct result of our investigation," she vowed in 1972, "even before the completion of signed agreements between themselves and the commission."

Yet as backdrop to these victories, New York teetered toward collapse. The near-bankrupt city cut services: branch libraries closed or reduced hours, garbage pickup became infrequent and streets in many neighborhoods were filthy. Poor neighborhoods were ravaged. As the city got dirtier and more dangerous, the quality of life deteriorated. Giant potholes ruined cars; graffiti-covered subways screeched and wheezed. The new highway system ringing the city—itself a contentious part of the deterioration—made the idea of moving feasible for many middle-class New Yorkers, who stepped up their rush to the suburbs.

In May 1975, the looming financial crisis exploded. New York could not meet its payroll. With no money in its "rainy day" fund, banks refused to issue bonds to the insolvent city. Panic hit. Urban colleges cut whole departments. Services already reduced had to be slashed. The chaotic city was rescued by the state, which became its fiscal overseer. The model of state takeover, though politically unpopular, became one Eleanor would remember twenty years later when her hometown of Washington D.C. faced a similar bankruptcy.

Rapid white flight, a national theme, threatened to change the city. In love with an endangered multicultural New York, "before changed immigration laws again brought in huge numbers of people and saved the city," Eleanor first took a tough law enforcement approach against discriminatory real estate and banking practices. She held explosive hearings, revealing lending bias, and enforced laws against panic-driven home-selling.

But she understood that a more positive approach was also needed ("You had to do more than stop scaring people") and devised a popular program to which neighborhoods could apply.

"It's hard for me to find any work in my entire life that more excited me than neighborhood stabilization. There's a liberal notion that integration works automatically," she scoffs. "That's false because the effect of racial polarization means anything racial left on its own can be manipulated by somebody, especially when economics are involved." Analyzing the resegregation of countless communities after Open Housing Laws, Eleanor and her staff realized that instead of simply saying, "Don't move, you racist whites," they needed to provide specific support. Otherwise, integrated blocks were merely a phase in the transition from all-white to all-minority.

The commission created block associations to resist panic rumors, did outreach to potential move-in whites who'd been steered away from "changing" neighborhoods, and contacted banks to discourage redlining. Then they established a direct line to City Hall, ensuring city services were delivered to these blocks.

"Lower middle-class neighborhoods in the Bronx and in Queens joined! It was one of the great and unusual stories of how to make integration work." Eleanor's heart, still in this program, relishes the memory. An Italian-American community in Rosedale, Queens, applied, after a home with a black move-in family was fire-bombed. To kick off the neighborhood program, Eleanor attended an evening meeting in a Rosedale living room, at the invitation of a white homeowner.

"It is hard to render the warmth I felt, from the moment a man raised his hand and said, 'Commissioner, could we just keep them out until your program comes in?' "

Eleanor shakes her head in disbelief. "It was naive, it was honest, and I knew he was moving toward us."

"It was a moment where you want to make sure people understand what they're doing, but to be personally insulted is to engage in a form of 'Gotcha!' To take advantage when he was showing the unabashed pure racism he was trying to overcome, would be like being a bully. Race is too serious.

"That was a magic moment. It was wonderful. We talked about what he had said, we ate Italian food, we all but danced . . . This was New York as I loved it."

The pilot program, including eight Reform temples in Brooklyn, did slow flight but in the end could not stem the tide of white urban dissatisfaction and fear. Eleanor's hopes that the program would be introduced nationally did not come to pass, in spite of her testimony to Congress detailing its accomplishments. But she took a problem plaguing American cities and created a successful blueprint, modeling a comprehensive approach still available to communities seeking ethnic integration and stability.

The city's fiscal crisis had numerous harmful equity effects. In addition to encouraging urban blight, it forced layoffs. "That presented a real challenge. Our commission had been getting women and minorities hired and promoted. Layoffs are a huge threat because they can undo affirmative action. There's a conflict between two important values: seniority and affirmative action. How to reconcile that?

"I proposed work-sharing, so everybody temporarily would work fewer hours. It was controversial. Some people believed there should be layoffs. The unions didn't like it either. They called it 'Sharing the pain.' They wanted to lay off and let those remaining get full pay. But I was trying to maintain affirmative action when it was just getting started." Indeed organized labor, long Eleanor's friend, strongly opposed her initiative; their hostility would later surface in a national arena.

While Eleanor was creating innovative programs responsive to her times, she also had to manage a hundred-person agency. Despite her lack of experience, one senior staffer says, "Eleanor was the best manager I've ever had. She recognized the need to have specific goals and management plans behind them, with milestones related to goals. It bored her to death, so she got the right staff to carry it out and did what she did best: speechmaking and grand ideas."

"Not all of managing is scintillating," acknowledges Eleanor. "But it was frustrating, knowing that a woman on the job, pregnant, was discriminated against, and you get the case a year after the baby was born. Or a black person was wrongfully fired and entitled to action—two years ago! That's heartbreaking. So you've got a real interest in management when you see that kind of result."

Eleanor thought large, but she also thought small. With her trademark zest for detail, she rewrote every document that came near her hands. Whenever the commissioner saw a piece of writing she picked up her pen. Once, preparing for a congressional meeting, she seized the draft of a speech written for her by a lawyer, a man with a national reputation. He sat nearby.

"This paragraph is just ass-backward!" she exploded.

The man was dumbfounded, though later grudgingly acknowledged her revision had helped his prose.

Eleanor's candid response was typical of many interactions with her staff. "When she has a goal in mind she will knock anybody down," says Preston David, "but always for a positive purpose. It's never self-serving, it's for the public good. She was not easy to get along with." Yet, like others, he would remain by her side for eleven years.

Other peoples' personal responses were often the last thing on Eleanor's goal-driven mind. Her blunt manner enraged some staffers and left others in tears, though Eleanor was generally unaware when she had wounded feelings. "Lots of people didn't like her personality or style," was a frequent comment about Eleanor's management.

Yet many saw beyond the sometimes hard words and admired her tremendous heart and compassion—once her attention was snagged. They respected her drive, and, seeing what her bold initiatives accomplished, were eager to work with a brilliant trailblazer hacking away at encrusted, exclusive traditions. They understood that to do what she did, a hard demeanor was needed. A cadre of professionals—Preston David, Brooke Trent, Charlotte Frank, Electra Yourke and others—would stick with her through seven years at the commission and later follow her to Washington. Having the ability to come back when she lashed out, they didn't take her fury personally. "Most passionate people tend to get somewhat emotional," was a standard defense from admirers who learned to focus on their tasks—daunting enough—and slough off their blistering boss. This ability to attract loyal, enduring staff, would be lifelong.

Still, sometimes it was tough.

When her team had prepared 200 letters inviting people to testify at a hearing, and Eleanor had seen each of the many drafts—then, after the letter was all set to go, decided one sentence was ungrammatical and stormed, "How could you let this pass!" while demanding complete revision, people shouted back.

The perfectionist commissioner, "smarter, meaner and nastier than the rest of us," according to one admiring staff member, was no more satisfied with her own work than with her staff's. As she told a legal publication, "The mistake people in public life make is measuring results by what they have accomplished as opposed to what there is to be done. There's so much to be accomplished in antidiscrimination in New York that I've only scratched the surface."

Eleanor was as oblivious to others' needs as her own. Staff members joked, "Maybe we can get cancer so Eleanor will pay attention to us!" For when startled to attention by crisis, her generosity of spirit came to the fore. Otherwise she poured that compassion into work, intending to make life better for masses of people.

The charged office, full of excitement about the agency's activist role, was driven by Eleanor to constantly operate at high speed; tension was relieved on all sides by screaming fights, complete with slamming doors. Those who had the temperament for it participated, respecting their boss' high standards and her strength in imposing them. She also chose a mild-mannered, sturdy buffer, Executive Director Preston David, a mediator with "a better brain than any ten men put together, completely unintimidated by me." He allowed staff to complain just so long, then sent them off with a metaphoric pat on the head.

The insistence on quality work paid off. When the city set stiff new management standards five years into Eleanor's tenure, the commission became the first agency to earn management-by-objective status. This greater authority sped up formerly interminable processes in their trek through the city bureaucracy. While blacks and Jews struggled, the school system battled and neighborhoods collapsed, Eleanor kept fighting on. The wave of promise Mayor Lindsay had ridden into office was one she continued to ride, even as the city began to sink.

Eleanor was so successful that when Mayor Abraham Beame took office in 1974 she was reappointed commissioner, though it was unusual to remain in a new administration. On March 8, 1974, International Women's Day, Eleanor, standing in a flowing flowered dress, was sworn in for a second term. Her glowing parents showered her with roses as a beaming Shirley Chisholm and Coretta Scott King looked on.

"Coretta had gone to Antioch several years earlier and we bonded immediately. I knew her through the Movement. Just on the colored girl level, she was somebody I always warmed to personally, quite aside from her role as the wife of a truly great man.

"I've always admired the fact that she understood equality beyond race. She instinctively understands Jews, gays, women—people who don't fit the racial paradigm." The photo of the three radiant women would grace Eleanor's office walls for the remainder of her term and follow her to future office suites.

By the mid-seventies, Eleanor had a strong national presence. She spoke at National Women's Week programs in Washington, attended luncheons in her honor and regularly showed up at civic events. Fine-tuning her ability to connect to a crowd, she helped audiences grasp concepts that explained their lives. In 1975, Urban League Executive Director Vernon Jordan invited Eleanor to keynote the national conference in Atlanta.

A decade before, New York's Senator Daniel Moynihan, then Assistant Secretary of Labor, had issued a controversial report, "The Negro Family: The Case for National Action." He described the 25 percent of black families headed by women—compared to 9 percent of white families—as a major source of poverty and welfare needs. A storm of criticism erupted: blame for families in trouble seemed pointed at these "matriarchs" who "reversed roles" rather than at discrimination or lack of jobs. Critics denounced his emphasis on instability instead of black family strengths: the strong kinship bonds, work ethic, religious faith and adaptability of roles in perilous times. Some worried that in a backlash atmosphere, a white researcher had presented a family pattern as pathological; regressive social policy was sure to follow. Dr. King, who agreed that "the Negro family condition is a social catastrophe," openly feared that "problems will be attributed to innate Negro weaknesses and used to justify neglect and rationalize oppression." The furor was so great that even a White House Conference on Civil Rights called by President Johnson was forced to strike "family stability" from the agenda, after sixty church and rights groups objected.

Eleanor recalls that when the 1965 report came out, she was "confused and disconcerted, because a part of me knew he was absolutely right, though I didn't know the statistics. I thought the problem was that a white person simply could not say that and expect black people to embrace him." In a country mired in racism, whites didn't have the credibility to name an internal black problem. Especially one about "my mama."

Ten years later, "I could see the handwriting on the wall. It affirmed what Moynihan said. But what did I do? Get up and say to black people, 'See, Moynihan was right!' No, that's no way to bring people to an understanding."

Instead, she crafted her Urban League speech as a love letter from a black woman to a black man. She opened with an affectionate rebuke. "I am told I am the first woman to have the privilege of being a featured speaker at a National Urban League conference banquet. To hear him tell it, my friend and brother in the struggle, Vernon Jordan, has spent these years in search of one who was qualified. However much he may have had to settle this time, International Women's Year at least has moved him to affirmative action."

Then, in her speech, Eleanor made a plea.

"Dear Brother: When is the last time you heard an honest discussion about black male/female relationships? . . . The repair of the black condition in America disproportionately depends upon the succor of strong families . . . Particularly in the nation's ghettos, where blacks are increasingly concentrated, it is simply too much to ask what amounts to an increasing number of black women to raise the children of the black nation alone.

"We cannot avoid personal responsibility," though government "bears the major responsibility for centuries of stunted black progress in America . . . In this bountiful environment. . . . If you were white, it was almost impossible to be in the same position as your father or grandfather; if you were black it was almost impossible to do otherwise."

She reminded listeners they had made it through the horrors of slavery, racism and migration from the South by staying together. Nothing had sundered "our families," needed now as ever.

"As always, your sister in struggle and in love, Eleanor."

"The response was so thunderous that they virtually carried me out of the room on their shoulders. It was as if, thank God, somebody who we can listen to has said it." Among others surging toward her was a mild-mannered white man, Governor Jimmy Carter, who thanked her warmly for "such an informative and moving presentation."

After Eleanor's talk it would take another decade for black leaders en masse to pull the shroud from the taboo topic, one Eleanor would call "an altogether different species of problem than the others that have absorbed our energies as a people."

Senator Moynihan would later become "a good friend." Upon his retirement from the Senate in 2000, she told Congress: "As an African-American woman, I think I ought to say right here this afternoon that the senator was prescient in his work on the black family." Eleanor explains, "I thought he deserved to know, when he was leaving the Senate as its reigning intellectual, that he was right. He deserved to hear it from me."

Black feminists were hardly in unity. In December 1973, Shirley Chisholm told the National Black Feminist Organization's first convention, "One of the cruelest labels has been that the black woman is a matriarch. First society forces her into that condition, then it criticizes her for it." Thirty-five years after Moynihan's 1965 report it would still be contested, with leading scholars like Francis Fox Piven, professor of political science at the Graduate Center of the City University of New York, calling Moynihan's research "academically invalid," "shoddy" and paving the way for conservative attacks on welfare.

Yet Eleanor was unafraid to open discussion of what she saw as a real-life disaster. "That speech was an example of leadership," Vernon Jordan says. "Leadership means you take on very tough issues. And the context of the Urban League Conference was a good place; she understood that. It's important to pick time and place. Eleanor's always had real conviction about what she felt and has never relented in the expression of that. Even when she's been wrong—and she is capable of that; she, like me, sometimes has difficulty admitting it. But one can never question the integrity of her views."

To those who disagreed with her framing of the dialogue in primarily family terms rather than discrimination, she rebuts: "a tired old excuse" that will never lift the race. With her ethic of personal responsibility and talent for identifying gut issues, Eleanor anticipated the national anger about welfare. Her position sometimes put her at odds with former colleagues, but she stormed ahead. "There is an inner voice that, when I hear stuff going against my principles, even though it seems left, keeps me from going there."

In the midst of her tumultuous life, Eleanor maintained connections to Movement colleagues. Whenever Ms. Hamer, for instance, came to New York, Eleanor saw her.

"We talked about what she was doing, and what I could do to help. Ms. Hamer had started a pig farm because people were hungry; she gave

food away to white and black folks alike. Her instincts were always away
from separatism. And she lived to see those poor white folks in
Sunflower County celebrate a Fannie Lou Hamer Day," says Eleanor,
shaking her head.

After Ms. Hamer had cancer and a mastectomy she told Eleanor, "I'm
fine, but them socks I got here in my breasts, got to do something about
that."

"Ms. Hamer, you don't have a prosthesis?"

"Not unless you call these socks a prosthesis." When she perspired,
she said, the rags, soaking up moisture, were an added weight.

Horrified, Eleanor took her shopping. "We made great fun of the
socks that she was carrying around."

When Eleanor waxes about this mentor, her face takes on a youthful
glow. "I saw what she could do before audiences. She could make people understand what they needed to know in order to move on. It's a
great gift to summon up what needs to be said to rally people at a time
when they need leadership, when they're confused or depressed, or
going off in the wrong direction.

"You look at a Fannie Lou Hamer and say, 'How much talent like
that is dust in the grave, never discovered. At least hers was. Late in life,
but discovered by somebody. Because America heard her."

When Ms. Hamer died in March 1977, Eleanor published a tribute in
Ms. magazine. Ms. Hamer would be remembered "for some of the very
best moments of public speaking anyone has heard in this century . . .
She will be remembered for her sober and principled ideology that was
never waylaid by the faddish and sometimes parochial philosophies
that inevitably attach themselves to great movements."

While Eleanor's career in the mid-1970s was, as she puts it, "on over-
drive," the perfect marriage began to fray. Edward wanted to talk psychologically, in a way that Eleanor didn't think, and she was always on
the go. Yet while their personalities sometimes grated and they experienced the challenges of any ten-year-old marriage, plus care of a disabled child, the couple nonetheless created a satisfying cosmopolitan
life. In her "keep-your-eyes-on-the-prize" fashion, Eleanor continued
to believe all was well.

Ensconced in their magnificent three-story Harlem brownstone, the
two created the kind of sophisticated circle Eleanor had always desired.

While "we're not romanticizing Harlem," the hard-headed commissioner said at the time, preferring their "marvelous Upper West Side neighborhood where you have blacks and whites, Puerto Ricans and Chinese, young and old," they had sought out "the only reasonably priced brownstone neighborhood in Manhattan." And she loved living in the capital of Black America.

Inheriting her father's love of antiques, Eleanor gradually furnished her new home, planted bright red petunias and socialized with the city's black elite and intellectuals of all colors. She served on several boards, started a Task Force on Minority Law Practice and advised the short-lived National Black Feminist Organization, founded in August 1973. "What the women's movement as a whole badly needs is a black nuance and nuances from Spanish-speaking women. The movement will only be truly sensitive to them when they join up."

All this Eleanor accomplished with the energy of ten—and the help of a live-in baby-sitter, the first in a series. (One would sue in 1980, claiming underpayment and verbal abuse. Eleanor contested but, to minimize time and publicity, settled out of court. Years later the former employee would call to apologize.) Admitting she sometimes tired, Eleanor told a reporter, "But you do what you have to do." Seeking even greater stamina, she added athletic activities to her schedule "the way boys do from the time they are little." Eleanor began regular morning exercise, occasionally supplemented by tennis later in the day with Edward, a serious player, when he had no other partner.

On summer weekends they got away. Eleanor's early mentor, the civil liberties lawyer Helen Buttenweiser, loaned Eleanor weekend use of her beach house. "She invited us to occupy one of the most luxurious and modern houses you've ever seen, right on Long Island Sound, in Mamaroneck," Eleanor said, delighting in the free extravagance. "It had been photographed for a magazine. They weren't using it, so we went there every week. It was our summer place, less than an hour from Harlem on the Westchester railroad."

But on July 20, 1976, the man who gave Eleanor the blueprint for the elegant life passed away. Coleman Sterling Holmes, to all appearances a healthy sixty-four-year-old, entered a hospital one evening complaining of pain.

"My mother got a phone call in the middle of the night and my father was dead. She never wanted a phone by her bed ever again.

"My father died from lung cancer that had not been diagnosed. He obviously had long-living genes but he smoked cigarettes, whereas his father Richard, from that old Baptist school of righteous living, neither smoked nor drank and lived to ninety-six."

Eleanor went home, organized a cremation and filled the sanctuary with "sophisticated yellow spider-mums, in keeping with the elegance of the man." The obituary she wrote noted her father's "entertaining and original wit" and mourned his passing just three years after the death of his own father. Coleman had recently retired as assistant chief of the D.C. government's Housing Inspection Branch and worked for a private firm on civil rights compliance.

Eleanor took the blow chin up—"Nobody takes time off when their father dies. What is that?! One doesn't go into mourning for a month!"—and was absent from work only for the time required to make arrangements. She never mentioned her grief. As with all her difficult emotions, she sublimated pain into work.

That fall, a peanut farmer from Georgia rode solid black support to a narrow victory as the first Deep South president in 128 years. Promising a fresh breeze after the scandals of the Nixon years, President Carter, once installed, appointed an unprecedented 150 African Americans to high-level positions: federal judges, ambassadors, and solicitor general.

The self-proclaimed "outsider president" had first seen Eleanor during her "Letter to a Black Man" speech two years before. He remembered the fiery woman with the giant Afro whose hair extended so high she couldn't even wear academic caps for commencement addresses. (As she carried her mortarboard in hand to the stage, the lack of fit always gave her an opportunity to note, "The fellows who invented these things had neither women nor Afros in mind.") During the spring of 1977 President Carter began to consider her for leadership of a national antidiscrimination agency.

But first, to get the job, there was a political battle to be won.

CHAPTER 9

Brand-New Law

We're caught in a moment of history not of our own making, called upon to
unsnarl a racist past. Someone's got to do it and, like it or not, it's now fallen to us.
ELEANOR HOLMES NORTON, 1977

I t was a very competitive contest between Ron Brown and me as to
who would get it," Eleanor says, recalling the struggle to chair the fal-
tering Equal Employment Opportunity Commission (EEOC). Brown,
an old friend who headed the National Urban League's Washington
office, had strong support from many black political leaders. He was
one of the boys, whereas Eleanor, in every sense, was not.

Sexism—mixed with racism—took a bizarre twist, remembers Gloria
Steinem, who was lobbying for Eleanor. "The argument made by white
administration representatives," she says, "was that the black male ego
was fragile, and it would not be good to choose a black woman over a
black man." This was especially ridiculous, Steinem points out, in light
of the fact that numerous African-American men—most visibly, Vernon
Jordan—supported Eleanor.

Key unions, a strong component of the Democratic coalition, also
backed Brown. Some in the AFL-CIO pushed especially hard. Officials
didn't forget that during the mid-1970s she had proposed worksharing, instead of job cuts that disproportionately hit "last hired, first
fired" African Americans. Her proposal to trump seniority had been
anathema to labor.

Eleanor's well-known temper also exacted a price. The very quality
that so many admired—the sense that she was a straight shooter who
didn't play games—had a flip side: she could let her fury fly, then forget
it. But for others the sting often lingered. Once, at a union luncheon in
New York, she'd gotten into a heated argument with the AFL-CIO civil
rights director. Afterward, her old labor friend Rachelle Horowitz
brought her together with George Meany's assistant, Tom Donahue,

thinking they could work it out. But instead, Eleanor angrily dressed *him* down in front of his peers. Now that Carter's people wanted Eleanor for EEOC, Donahue exploded.

"That screaming harlot? Never."

But Eleanor lobbied in the way she went after every goal. Endorsements flowed from feminists and some black coalitions. Vernon Jordan strongly backed Eleanor, whom he considered the superior candidate, despite Brown being his Urban League protégé. Ultimately, Eleanor's experience as the successful manager of a small-scale EEOC carried her. On March 24, 1977, administration sources confirmed that Eleanor would be the first female chair of the EEOC. The National Women's Political Caucus issued a statement ("We're elated") and two months later President Carter announced the appointment. Her old friend Ron Brown graciously called to congratulate his rival, "You are one tough mama."

In June 1977, the young girl who grew up outside the federal gates returned, after an absence of twenty-two years, with a mandate to open all discriminatory workplace doors. She would have the title to do it, and the backing of the president.

Unlike her New York appointment, now she was not an "only." Then she'd feared a token role that didn't open doors for others. "I don't mind being women's pioneer," she'd said. "I just don't want to always be up here alone."

This time, Eleanor came accompanied by a group: One in six presidential appointees at the cabinet and subcabinet level was female. Her Yale friend Barbara Babcock was a new assistant attorney general at the Justice Department.

Her civil rights colleague Andrew Young was ambassador to the United Nations, Clifford Alexander was the army's first black secretary, seventeen black congressmen were reelected and Thurgood Marshall remained a Supreme Court justice. *Jet* and *Ebony* magazines began appearing in executive offices all over town.

Not only were appointments different, so was the city. "It was really like coming into a different country," marvels Eleanor. "It was night and day politically."

District governance by an appointed three-member commission had fallen; the Home Rule Act of 1973 had given Washingtonians back the right, denied since 1874, to elect local officials. "The civil rights movement should probably take the credit. The notion of having home rule began to seem possible when the civil rights movement penetrated the consciousness of people in this town." People like SNCC's Marion Barry had led the fight.

But home rule was limited. Congress retained control over the city's budget and courts, with the right to override district legislation. It prohibited one potential source of revenue, a commuter tax. And it refused to allow congressional voting representation.

There were other changes. The city Eleanor had left twenty-two years before was mostly white; now it was mostly black. And it looked different; rioters had demolished fifty-seven blocks in the wake of Reverend King's assassination.

"Rebuilding made D.C. quite prosperous for a while, with developers building federal offices, pouring tax money into district coffers. And it was a more sophisticated city. There were splendid restaurants." For the first time the city—with its new opera house, theater and concert halls at the Kennedy Center for the Performing Arts—was touted as a cultural capital.

Eleanor and Edward bought a three-story whitestone, the closest she could find to her palatial Harlem home. "New York had a merchant class. To have homes like the kind that are now broken up into apartments, you had to have a corporate class." The historian, warming to her subject, leans forward, "Washington has no industry, and this has been both a blessing and a curse. The blessing is little pollution, no smokestacks and few labor problems. The federal government has been a steady employer. The downside is that federal buildings and land, not taxable, make up more than 50 percent of the capital; and federal workers didn't have money for grand homes."

It wasn't only houses that disappointed. "The first thing I noticed when I returned was black and white faces. New York was a city of ethnic faces. I could tell if somebody was from Italy or Ireland or which country in Asia. I missed the pulsating ethnicity of New York, the ultimate cosmopolitan city."

Her love was reciprocated. New York's *Amsterdam News* was the first to urge her appointment; in late 1977 Eleanor was voted a Top 10 Favorite New Yorker in a *New York Post* poll. And the paper congratulated the "well-merited advance for a conscientious, imaginative public official [though] . . . The agency [EEOC] has not fulfilled either its potential or its responsibilities—in part because of inadequate support from the White House." Now prospects were different; the president proclaimed 1977 the year for international human rights.

The glory days of the early civil rights movement were over. Affirmative action had opened whole sectors of business and education but now, in the trauma of recession, black "newcomers" were seen as rivals in a stiffening competition for jobs and college slots. The last thing many anxious job seekers wanted was for people of color—or white women—to be given extra consideration. Thus the cry, "Reverse discrimination!"

With this battle call, the late 1970s opened a transition period that would shape domestic politics for the next two decades. The complexities Eleanor had faced at the New York Commission were magnified as more complicated issues emerged: the rights of pregnant workers and those with other "disabilities," as pregnancy was categorized; different (and differently paid) job slots for men and women; wage gaps between people of color and whites. The intensifying challenges called for a leader who would protect "new" workers while not dislodging others. There were few ready answers.

"The liberalism of the fifties and sixties utterly failed to build in the flexibility and tools for dealing with the more complex maze of problems it should have seen lay ahead," Eleanor said then.

She faced the daunting task of moving affirmative action forward when already there was a backlash. How was she to overcome a history of discriminatory tradition—in which, she told an audience of managers, "Your kind of plant might be the kind that a black man's father would never have gone in"—to make sure new people walked in the door? Once they got there, how could she ensure they were treated fairly? And as a black woman, how could she fulfill the sky-high expectations of her numerous unofficial constituencies?

"If you're black and you're appointed, black people look to you for a special kind of leadership."

Eleanor was about to inherit an agency in no position to take on these or any other dilemmas. The EEOC, established under the 1964 Civil Rights Act to enforce its employment discrimination provisions, had

had a merry-go-round of leaders. Eleanor was its seventh chair in thirteen years. Her predecessor had been fired years earlier, leaving a vacuum of power. And her familiar nemesis, a backlog—130,000 cases—had spiraled out of control. The EEOC was a laughingstock, so ineffective even its natural constituents wrote it off. Civil rights and women's organizations often advised those needing help not to go the EEOC but to state agencies, not much better off. The agency's repute had sunk so low that during Eleanor's confirmation hearing one senator was moved to ask an extraordinary question.

"What's a nice lady like you want to go to a place like that for?"

But on June 17, 1977, clothed in the type of light flowing dress she often chose for ceremonial occasions, Eleanor was sworn in at the White House Rose Garden. Standing on the green grass, she took her oath of office as Katherine looked on.

Eleanor's first actions signified change: she immediately ordered the suffix "man" erased from the double glass doors that led to her office on Columbia Plaza. Her new title simply read "Chair." And Eleanor showed the agency was serious about eliminating bias, even in its own language. All correspondence reflected the new designation, inspiring frequent quips. Reporters dubbed Eleanor "her furnitureship" and routinely labeled assistants "the couch" or "the desk."

"She had public opinion against her on that," says Maudine Cooper, president of Greater Washington's Urban League. "The newspapers made fun of her: 'Do we call her or do we sit on her?' But Eleanor doesn't care what your opinion is. She was adamant and it took hold."

At the same time elated feminists all over the country echoed the words of one city official, "I just love tough women. I can't be like her but I sure can take a lot of lessons out of her page." Despite ridicule, Eleanor persisted and today trumpets the lasting effect of her sex-neutral title. "Now we no longer have Chairmen in this society, we have Chairs."

Nonetheless, name change or not, the EEOC barely functioned. "Every week there was a bomb scare and they let the people out while dogs sniffed. My first week they tried that."

Eleanor followed procedure by calling police and having dogs brought in to sniff for bombs. But she did not evacuate the building.

"Everybody is going to sit here! We're not going to get run out of here every week!"

Staff remained with racing hearts. "I never had a bomb scare after that," Eleanor chortles. "That's how out of control it was."

Eleanor also called a mammoth staff meeting—"I was told there had never been one before"—and held another for district directors in her giant conference room. With this cynical group of bureaucrats who had seen chairs come and go, who sat back with the attitude, "We were here when you came, we'll be here when you're gone," Eleanor was both decisive and inclusive. She let those who'd jumped into the power vacuum know who was in charge.

"You are going to see speed some might view as unfair," she warned. "We're going to go so fast you're going to say, 'Lady, can't you slow down?' "

"She did a blood transfusion on everybody in the room," says one long-term staffer. "She turned it upside down, laid the challenge down and said, 'If you don't cut it, you're out.' They weren't used to hearing that." Preparing to create an effective, potent agency, the new chair urged, "Take my hand."

Eleanor's style—try to negotiate; failing that, blast ahead—would soon permeate the EEOC as it had the New York Commission. If mutual agreement could not be reached, adversarial proceedings took over. "One of the reasons people did reach a settlement" at the EEOC or elsewhere, "is they well know I'm going to make you work for a victory. How much time, effort, sweat and tears are you willing to put into this?"

Eleanor drove others as she did herself, to ten-plus hour workdays. "You've got to create a balance whereby people feel sufficiently rewarded, but also feel under pressure—the pressure you are under."

"It meant working late, working hard, and working smart," says senior staffer Alvin Golub. "She ratcheted the level of work up. I'm an old bureaucrat, and she got through to me."

Acknowledging no fear ("I felt no trepidation at taking over this job"), Eleanor charged double time into a male-run arena hostile to an outsider, who came with what some derided as her "New York Jews." She never admitted anxiety, though her hands sometimes shook so hard when she entered press conferences her papers rattled. "We all deal with fear with different mechanisms. Mine is to grapple with a problem before it grapples me," she told a reporter. "I always take the offensive."

Eleanor's curt interactions with staff could seem harsh. Disciplining herself to a morning jog as often as she could, by the time she entered

the office, Eleanor was ready for work. An assistant distributed "SEE ME
TODAY" and "SEE ME NOW" memos she had written at home. Staff dutifully lined up outside her door. If someone entered without paper and
pencil, she abruptly joked, "Where are your tools?" made assignments
and asked about tasks previously dispensed. Though given to great
belly laughs in the right context, there were few personal chats at office
meetings with Eleanor. This was work. She never entered a meeting, nor
allowed staff to enter one, ill prepared. "If you came in with a draft or
portion of a draft and it wasn't right on target, she'd do open-heart
surgery on you," says Golub.

Sometimes issuing instructions while she lay on the floor of her
giant office exercising, Eleanor might respond to objections with colorful language. Her method, she spells out today, "was to actually pro-
voke staff to come to the other side [of an issue]. Sometimes I had to
watch out because if people weren't used to it, they could be intimidated by the fact that I said, 'Oh God, that's bull.' And I expected some
body to say, 'What *you* just said is bull, and let me tell you why.' "

Eleanor was often surprised when others didn't understand that her
salty language and rough treatment meant she regarded them as peers.
She had discovered that for herself, when angered, "the adrenaline flows
to my brain." It was a style she didn't always like, but found effective.

Some staff objected; most capitulated; and those who lasted the
longest were invigorated by this hold-nothing-back style of debate.
Inspired by her rapid-fire intelligence and unshakable commitment,
these staffers recall their years with Eleanor as the high point of their
working lives. "She always took that bold step," says one loyalist who
followed her from New York. "That's what made her so exciting to work
for. She made an impact, and spoiled me forever after."

A handful of New York staff had moved with her. This group of
whites, "crackerjack, brilliant New Yorkers," swept in to adapt, on a
larger scale, the commission's work and methods. "These were people
who rarely made a mistake, who knew how to make things happen, who
had all my vision about what society ought to look like, who had tough
New York minds of the kind I most admired." And they'd been successful. By the time they left the New York Commission, 60 percent of cases
were completed within three months of filing and 80 percent within
ten months.

But the workplace culture in Washington was different. After the intimacy and informality of the Human Rights Commission, with barely a hundred people, the lumbering, headless bureaucracy of nearly 3,000 EEOC employees was a shock. It took months, if not years, to get anything done, everything was leaked to the press, and receiving information requested from district offices was almost impossible. The sense of fighting upstream was overwhelming.

"Look, before I came to the commission, it was a place were people battled each other." Rivalry between old-timers and Eleanor's new staff was intense. "Of course, here comes this woman trudging in from New York. They look for something they can get you on." Her team was also hampered by isolation. The large-scale environment, where the rabbit warren of offices seemed miles apart, meant they couldn't dash into each other's rooms—especially Eleanor's—to brainstorm. Before, Eleanor could yell to David through her doorway; now he wasn't even on the same floor. Each of her New York team now ran their own huge operation; they rarely had time to make their way through the serpentine hallways to each others' offices. And at night they hardly dared, for the building was full of rodents scampering up the walls.

Nothing, however, could turn aside the change Eleanor was determined to make. The New Yorkers had arrived with a plan.

"I knew how to run a much smaller agency that I needed to transplant. I knew how to get rid of backlogs," Eleanor says with satisfaction. "I knew I had the basics there." In night after night of late night sessions her team hammered out a federal version.

Six weeks later Eleanor stunned the House subcommittee to which she proposed her ambitious plan. Presenting clear concepts, backed by charts and cost estimates that normally took a year to develop, she presented a long-range vision for total overhaul. Her clarity and poise created a markedly positive impression in Congress, where the agency had often been criticized as a circus.

Still, sparks flew over everything. Some rights advocates believed Eleanor's rush to settlement, with rapid charge processing, left claimants vulnerable. Pressured by the far greater power of employers, aggrieved parties might accept too little. Feminist lawyer Wendy Williams says, "We got mad. We thought, 'There won't be enough attention paid to claims.' "

While such criticism hurt, Eleanor's response was sharp: as in New York, the old method of formal charging and lengthy data collection was so unwieldy that complaints bogged down for years. Then, with stale evidence, potentially meritorious cases had to be thrown out.

The backlog literally overflowed everywhere. Eleanor's team found file folders tucked away in the ceiling under loose tiles. They were stunned to discover locked rooms stacked, floor to ceiling, with five-year-old musty cartons full of unopened documents of evidence about the large systemic cases.

"They were in no position to protest," Eleanor says, "because the agency was on its knees. And I came with some folks that knew what they were doing." Her management team started by opening three model offices: in Dallas, Baltimore and Chicago. They separated out the backlog so new cases didn't go to the back of the interminable line, and formed a separate unit to clear them up. Eleanor initiated rapid charge processing and integrated EEOC lawyers—some kicking and screaming into the revamped regional offices, rather than retaining separate litigation centers.

Early model office returns produced dramatic results: Within a year, average settlement time was only thirty-one days. Dollar benefits for complainants were raised and the backlog in those offices was reduced by 88 percent.

On the Hill, Eleanor turned around the troubled agency's reputation. Widely viewed as confident and dynamic, she generated the feeling that if anybody could do the job, she could. Many former advocacy critics also changed their views. "Eleanor had the guts to stand up to some in the civil rights community and say, 'Justice delayed is justice denied,' " says Williams. "I ended up thinking, in an imperfect world, getting an imperfect resolution is better than never getting to their claims at all!"

But EEOC employees were not uniformly happy. Staffing shifts for newly formed district offices resulted in massive personnel disruptions. Some were furious when restructuring affected grade level and pay; they brought the union in to take up their cause. Others were miffed when their opinions were not sought by the new "efficiency train" that seemed to run them over. "The woman with the mouth" had her hands full. Staff members, says one, "either loved her or hated her." While Eleanor's fans inside and outside the agency saw the makeover as necessary, staff resentment grew so great that the American Federation of

Government Employees picketed Eleanor's headquarters and seven district offices. Employees marched and chanted, embarrassing her with their signs:

EEOC WORKERS CARE ABOUT CIVIL RIGHTS—EVEN OURS!

Furious at what she saw as lack of trust in her humane motives, Eleanor fumed over desk-place lunches of tuna-packed-in-water and lemonade. (Only on Fridays did she allow herself fried fish, drenched with the spiciest hot sauce she kept in her top desk drawer.) But she signed an agreement protecting employee rights during reorganization; a decade later, the union would be the first to endorse her run for Congress.

Staff themselves generated frequent discrimination and sexual harassment complaints. With the highest proportion of people of color in any federal agency, many were suspicious of their workplace treatment. Hispanics were especially angry about their lack of representation.

"Hispanics were experiencing racial discrimination, but they have had a very different experience, not nearly as harsh an experience as blacks, because many were newly arrived immigrants. The blacks thought they were taking over. And the Hispanics had a natural reaction to want their piece of the pie."

Eleanor's solution was to state a zero tolerance policy for intra-agency ethnic strife, taking "a harder stand on polarization than I did on anything else." She sponsored events like National Hispanic Heritage Week, similar to other groups' commemorations, and just as she urged employers to do, set herself hiring goals, in this case 10 percent Hispanics. Her comprehensive approach modeled her understanding that this was not "just one more minority group," but had its own concerns. Instituting affirmative action recruitment, her office issued complaints to companies that discriminated, monitored immigration legislation and created bilingual materials. Her new district directors included nine blacks, eight women, and six Hispanics.

Problem after problem arrived on the desk of the gum-chewing chair, who sat with one foot propped in a drawer while doing the massive paper preparation that tagged her. She not only faced staff revolts, she had to contend with a different breed of commissioner. Unlike New York, these were paid, full-time presidential appointees whose oversight roles were unclear. In the absence of strong leadership they'd expanded power. People who knew Eleanor predicted she would clash, for, as one former aide told a reporter, "In New York, she was very much a one-woman show . . . She is the kind of person who can walk into a meeting, speak for three minutes and everyone else is eclipsed. She is used to having things done her way."

Eleanor collided with one commissioner, who, says a staff member, "dared raise his eyebrows over her budget figures and grumble, 'Well, I don't really think you've solved it.' " He was fired by the president, his office lock changed, and the other commissioners learned their proper role: policy, not operations.

"There could only be one person running the place," Eleanor says. "I was able to do that, in part, because everybody believed I had the confidence of the president." Utilizing her inclusive model, the twin to her tough side, she adds primly, "I dealt with them very deferentially in their policy-making role, bringing my commissioners in on the ground floor to devise new policy in a way they had never been involved before. I simply took charge of my administrative responsibilities."

Six months after she took office, the EEOC saw a 35 percent budget increase, while the FBI was correspondingly cut. "I said to the White House, 'I'm going to take this agency apart, step by step, and put it together again. In order to do it, I need a one-time increase in budget to put in place systems that will keep backlogs from forming in the future.' " She got it.

And Eleanor told her staff, who gulped, that the EEOC would expand its jurisdiction. The following year Carter collected the forty job bias statutes scattered over eighteen agencies—who often issued contradictory orders—and, over Republican objections, gave all the policy functions to the EEOC.

"Eleanor and her magic wand. It would leave those of us who worked closely with her reeling," says Alvin Golub. On May 5, 1978, when the new plan became law, Eleanor took key functions from Labor, Justice, Treasury and the Civil Service Commission, absorbing, for instance, enforcement of the Equal Pay and Age Discrimination Acts. "She has a wide wingspan, and a lot of people were carried on those wings," adds Golub.

This merger, urged by black leaders and the National Women's

Political Caucus, was fought by business, happy to have enforcement done "out of fifty-eleven places," says Eleanor. They'd been able to play agencies against each other. "When Carter gave me the authority, he consolidated enforcement, which gave us great credibility. And we needed that to deal with agencies like the Justice Department, which were used to running the show. They did not run the show while I was there. We worked together."

Eleanor boasted to members of the Washington Press Club that her agency, reborn, would be the government's civil rights "single-stop operation." She told the *New York Times* the plan fulfilled "one of the oldest goals of the civil rights movement: to get a strong, single-purpose equal employment agency." Within a year, Eleanor had shown she was a force to be reckoned with. She had moved the EEOC from its nether status in the federal establishment to the president's choice as the nation's premier civil rights agency.

Twenty years later she explains how she fostered interagency cooperation, after she had just taken others' power. "You bring people together and sit them around a table, and you make them all part of the decision-making process. Look, I'm a very strong personality, but I am not an authoritarian personality that says, 'Don't want to hear from the rest of you.' " Instead, Eleanor presented goals—"Okay everybody, this is where we have to get"—and asked for help figuring out how to get there. And her commissioners were involved in her new Office of Inter-Agency Coordination, creating one set of consistent government-wide regulations. "That involved policy," says Eleanor smiling, "So they were involved from the ground level."

Within a year, Eleanor had transformed the creaky EEOC. Some district offices, like Dallas and Seattle, even ran out of old cases. The advocacy community would come to regard Eleanor's tenure as a golden age for national antidiscrimination efforts. But still she pressed forward.

"One of the things that's most fun about public policy is not grappling with the events of the day, but saying, 'How can we push this beyond what anybody's thinking yet?' "

Stepping back to view problems systemically, Eleanor's goal was lasting change in business practices, and she had the confidence to put her ideas into action. "Self-esteem has never been a problem," says everyone who has ever known Eleanor.

One strategy was to throw substantial EEOC resources into large-scale cases. During the hearings to confirm her appointment before the Senate Human Resources Committee, she'd told members they could "process individual cases to the end of time without in fact substantially affecting the patterns and practices that bar minorities and women from the corporations and industries of America." During Eleanor's first year she closed a landmark AT&T case that had dragged on for a decade while the company struggled over employment goals, including hiring black operators. When AT&T complied, becoming the first company to sign an EEOC consent decree, it took flak from the business community for "caving." But Eleanor had made her mark. In 1980, Ford Motor Company would sign a commission agreement providing women and people of color 23 million dollars for refusing to hire or promote them.

Eleanor targeted "worst first" companies and filed charges. " 'Worst first' meant looking at a particular metropolitan area, for businesses with the worst practices relative to the statistical norms of available minorities and women.

"We will choose targets on highly rational criteria which will be public," she announced then. "We will be tough in enforcing the law, but intelligent and fair. When you have this much power though, you want to be bold."

Millions of American businesses and schools still violated laws requiring equal opportunity for jobs, excusing themselves with the well-worn defense, "Only white men applied." Eleanor put employers on notice.

"I am not one of those who believe that in a single generation we can in fact get rid of the consequences of 200 years of racial discrimination, but the lighter the remedies, the more guarantee that the period of rectification will be drawn out. Putting an ad in the paper and taking what comes in the door is not legally sufficient."

Another proactive change technique was to issue guidelines. "That's an example of where you push to the next step. I knew we could shape the law, because the EEOC's guidelines tended to guide the way the courts ruled on cases. It's very important that courts have something to go by. They'll look at what the expert agency says. That was where EEOC did its best work since it began in 1965."

Eleanor was set on writing voluntary affirmative action guidelines.

"We felt this stuff might go away, unless the courts understood the basis and why it was so important." The controversial program of goals and timetables was a temporary remedy for past as well as present discrimination, "a debt to history, which like all debts, must be paid." With increasing threats of "reverse discrimination" lawsuits from whites, Eleanor decided to strike preemptively, to protect both plaintiffs and newly vulnerable employers. "On one hand the law said, 'Correct your [discrimination] violations.' On the other hand, you might get sued [for reverse discrimination] if you corrected them.

"Writing guidelines is a Herculean process," Eleanor almost moans, remembering it. "You don't just sit down with a piece of paper and write." A consultant she'd brought from New York, Al Blumrosen, first proposed guidelines in June 1977. Eleanor sent back his proposal, scribbled, he remembers, in every margin with the "eight zillion errors." He responded; five times their memos flew back and forth before she grudgingly allowed, "We'll let senior staff look at it."

"It involved lawyers, investigators, policy makers, the commissioners," Eleanor recalls. "We sat down and figured it out, based on the case law, examination of the statute, and analogies from other discrimination law." By December she published draft guidelines, giving three months for comment. Amid extensive press, she told employers to put a spectrum of remedies in place, including goals and timetables, and guaranteed that if her process were followed the EEOC would never find in favor of reverse discrimination.

"We insisted on formal Notice and Comment. The more comment you had the fewer mistakes you made. The business community and the civil rights community each had an opportunity to weigh in as much as possible."

Her strategy worked. In the end her guidelines did carry greater weight with the courts. And the procedure was compatible with Eleanor's style: reach out and bring opponents in. If they chose not to come they lost their opportunity. Then she never shrank from mustering her forces to demolish their position.

By 1979 Eleanor decided to "grab hold of sexual harassment law and shape it, because women were so reluctant to come forward.

"You've got to decide in this world whether you're going to let things happen to you or whether you make things happen. Being a black child growing up in this town may have helped me believe that. And stopping sexual harassment was similar: can you make it happen?" At the time there were few cases; the very phrase "sexual harassment" was just coming into vogue. Conceptually, it wasn't clear that federal courts would embrace it.

The EEOC had issued guidelines on labor topics, from job selection tests to accommodating religious beliefs. But none on sexual harassment.

"There were a few cases here and there, not even court of appeals, no cases with any precedent value. I was concerned that the courts would be all over the map, because there wasn't anything to tell them about where the EEOC stood or about where anybody else stood. There were no Supreme Court decisions."

This was uncharted territory; women were on their own. "They had to come forward, testify against some man, against a corporation, and allege this terrible thing. This was a topic embarrassing to even talk about in 1978 and 1979, when a lot of folks thought you must have done something to deserve it. I'm not sure we even had rape shield laws. So I said to myself, 'This isn't fair. I want guidelines to protect women, and to put employers and courts on notice about what sexual harassment is.' "

Black women, subject to harassment since slavery days, played a significant role in developing legal redress. Several brought early landmark cases; Eleanor—with at least two great-grandmothers the targets of slavery rape—took on the historic problem. Later another black woman, Anita Hill, would electrify the nation with her momentous assertions.

The concept of sexual harassment was not even mentioned in the Title VII statute Eleanor administered. "Employers could fairly ask, 'What in the hell is it? How do I know what sexual harassment is?' "

Businesses were embarrassed and confused by it, "so it seemed to me the guidelines ought to be welcome. If they knew what it was then they could issue their own set of rules and keep this from happening. Or at least cut down on it.

"I could clarify it, and give the courts an offer that would be hard for them to refuse. And that was one of the most satisfying parts of being an administrator under a federal statute.

"My staff and I worked long hours, writing over and over, thinking it through." The result was language unlike that in any other EEOC guidelines. It encouraged employers to issue their own directives, laying out what specific behavior they expected or prohibited. This would protect employers, while encouraging women to proceed.

However, employers, who traditionally shied from government rules, were not happy with this attempt to cohere an unformed branch of law.

"But there was nothing they could do. I had the authority to do it," Eleanor declares, explaining her power without hesitation. "They liked rapid charge processing because it was quick . . . Yet they were afraid of guidelines. They just thought, 'Oh my God, how can you put in writing everything somebody thinks is sexual harassment? How will you ever catalog it all?'

"I issued the guidelines in such a way that not only outlined the prohibited conduct; they made it clear if employers took action they would have defenses." By the time the guidelines were finalized in 1980, the *Wall Street Journal* had dubbed the EEOC "guideline happy." But employers began sending in copies of their own workplace rules, trying to demonstrate to the EEOC what they were doing to cut down on sexual harassment. "Once you put people on notice, a lot of folks will say, 'I'm not going to risk my job, pension or whatever.' So, the very people who had protested that it was impossible to write guidelines took ours and wrote their own."

The guidelines had lasting force. "There was nothing close to the Supreme Court yet. By the time the first case got there, the court looked dead at our guidelines and followed them."

She had taken a human rights violation with little legal standing and created law that would impact the American workplace for generations. Indeed, the very concept of sexual harassment was only four years old. Gloria Steinem remembers when it was first named, "in 1975," she says, "in a speak-out at Cornell." Eleanor fundamentally altered the legal landscape when she lifted the responsibility that had been on women to complain and reversed it, saying to employers, "This is your burden. Chase it from the workplaces. If you don't, these guidelines will help a woman prove sexual harassment." Rejecting a passive posture—waiting for a woman to be harassed and then come forward—was quintessentially Eleanor's own character, transferred to a federal blueprint. And her ability to do it by providing an incentive for employers as well, if they issued their own sexual harassment policy, was also emblematic Eleanor, who liked nothing so much as a win-win.

"Eleanor," says one colleague, "approached every problem as if it had a solution; you only needed to spend a moment searching for it. There was always a way."

When a legislative battle brewed over language on an affirmative action proposal—with Jewish groups protesting it as quotas—Eleanor stepped in to mediate. "Very few people had credibility with civil rights leadership *and* the Jewish community," says Barbara Williams-Skinner, then congressional Black Caucus executive director. Eleanor acted as liaison between Williams-Skinner and Rabbi David Saperstein, a leading public policy advocate in Washington.

"What about this word?" the wordsmith asked the two repeatedly, working to expand the thin line of agreement. Carefully crafting language acceptable to both, she kept everyone at the table and adroitly negotiated a document that became the basis for one set of affirmative action legislation.

"Eleanor was always trying to find the common ground," says Williams-Skinner. " 'What is the human issue here? What is the core?' That's the lawyer in her, she sees both sides. She is very passionate but backs away from demonizing. 'What would others want?' 'At what level can we bring them in?' "

Yet even the bridge builder would write several years later about the problematic role of "Blacks appointed [by the president] to high positions. . . . a hybrid who often functions in a mixed role with dual allegiances." The situation was complex, because the appointee, "responsible to the appointing officer, lacks the unfettered freedom of the elected official to respond." If the black appointee was not perceived as responsive to her constituency, the appointing executive might find the appointee no longer useful. Thus was the position fraught with "anomalous disabilities."

Though Eleanor was usually backed by the president, "perhaps my greatest test as an EEOC appointee" came in 1978 when the Justice Department prepared its draft brief to the Supreme Court for Allan Bakke, a thirty-nine-year-old white male who claimed "reverse discrimination" after being turned down at a University of California Medical School with racial admissions quotas.

"We were astounded at the initial draft [opposing affirmative action]. I was horrified." Eleanor contacted advocacy groups and raced over to meet Drew Days, the black assistant attorney general for civil rights, and the solicitor general, Wade McCree. "He was also black, and that's why we were so taken aback," she acknowledges. The administration's concern was to eliminate any sanction of quotas.

"One of the things I had to make them understand," Eleanor says doggedly, "was that we didn't have to embrace quotas to write a brief that retained affirmative action." Although the *Bakke* case was not about employment, "the real question, was, 'Would they take us all down with them?' "

The president found himself caught between opposing currents. HEW Secretary Joseph Califano and HUD Secretary Patricia Harris, agreeing with Eleanor, opposed their own Justice Department. "Presidential appointees were central in reversing the government position. We got some changes in the Justice draft that made it palatable. But that was really something. And I was sitting right there in the middle of it."

Civil rights organizations were also split: the American Jewish Congress and the Anti-Defamation League filed briefs opposing quotas, while the NAACP filed in favor. Eleanor said publicly the split was needless since quotas were unnecessary. Other approaches could be used.

The 1978 *Bakke* decision did strike down fixed quotas in education, but left the basis for affirmative action intact by permitting admissions committees to consider race as *one* factor, thus leaving an opening wedge for another generation seeking middle-class entry.

"That was a real high point of my professional life, to be in government when *Bakke* came down, to have to think it through, when the president had already come out against quotas. Not that we were ever for quotas, but at that time it was difficult for many people to make the distinction."

Speaking four days later on NBC's *Meet the Press*, Eleanor defended affirmative action: "There is simply no way to move from a period of racism to a period where racism is no longer a part of American life without some dislocation to the society, at least for a limited period of time." She encouraged people not to lose heart at the "imperfect victory" *Bakke* represented, warning employers they "proceed at great risk if they use *Bakke* as a retreat from their obligations."

She reminded an NAACP convention later that week, "It is incomplete victories that have nourished our will to struggle against any and all obstacles . . . I say, let me at it! We must take affirmative action to save affirmative action. Sing no dirges at this convention. The *Bakke* decision is not a call to lay down your arms. It is a challenge to choose your weapons."

Her framing of the decision as an "incomplete victory" put her at odds with much of the advocacy community, who regarded this pivotal case as the beginning of the end. A day after the conference, the NAACP and the Institute for the Study of Educational Policy, publicly critical of Eleanor's remarks, described *Bakke* as an "insidious threat" to progress and disputed her contention that *Bakke* and court-imposed quotas were not central to affirmative action. But she would continue to maintain that quotas were unnecessary and that *Bakke* required no substantial changes. Since the Supreme Court had ruled that race could still be used to fashion remedies, she accepted the challenge of creating cures both strong and constitutional. People simply had to innovate.

"Life is about struggle," Eleanor once told a reporter. "The struggle for equality is a very motivating one." That "it lumbers on, always beyond" only spurred her on. Fortunately, battle energized the warrior, for her private life was as challenging as her public one.

"I was chair of the EEOC, the first woman to chair an agency that was on its knees! I had two babies. One had Down's syndrome, one was a spunky little boy. And my husband was also in the government." Eleanor juggled so many balls at once that it was a challenge just to get home evenings to "two very young children, who had a mother in charge of one of the most troubled agencies, that had been in all the newspapers, yet these were the formative years of their brains. One of them was retarded.

"You want to know what I did?!" Eleanor fires. "I *tried* to get home every night by seven. I brought my work; I read to them. I tried to make sure that I wasn't so overpowered by my career that I lost my children."

"There you were at seven P.M. trying to finish," one staffer recalls, evoking the memory, "and she'd want a ride." Other times Eleanor offered rides in her little Volkswagen. A daring driver, she amazed long-term staffers in flashier cars with her unprepossessing 'bug' and unorthodox driving. "When I get behind something slow moving," she says, "I generally find a way around it."

At home, Eleanor pored over dimly lit paperwork in her upstairs study long after the children went to bed. The couple now rarely entertained. Every minute was precious.

"Considering when that job required me to leave in the morning, when it required me to get home in the evening, how many hours a child has to sleep and that Saturday and Sunday were also not entirely mine, I had to plan my time real carefully." The experience was so rough that Eleanor has concluded, "I have never accepted the notion, 'You can have it all.' If you work to the bone, you can *perhaps* have it. But it comes at a price.

"I am a feminist who tries to be realistic. Mothers who think about whether they should take some time off from work are thinking right. I believe that my generation of feminists may have made some mistakes in underestimating what children require. But it was perfectly understandable because we were in reaction." Of course her own views also formed in reaction to a life with unusual burdens: heading a highly visible and troubled national agency while caring for two children, all in the context of a challenging marriage. And Edward was a typical husband of the time: he "helped" rather than shared the weight of home.

"Edward shared considerably in the care of the children but I did more of the grunt work. He cooked, I took the children to the doctor's, because I'm the one that drove a car. The whole time I was at the EEOC there was a school car pool. I drove in that."

They'd long had a live-in baby-sitter. In New York, she had a room on the third floor, where Katherine and Johnny had their rooms. "There was room for a whole flock of people to live in that house." In Washington they repeated the pattern of live-in help.

"The part of me that wants to save, that makes me a good environmentalist and makes me frugal, that part wanted to make sure all these rooms were filled." And they were full with the life of five.

Eleanor often had to rush Johnny to a pediatrician for ear infections. "The armchair rule of mothers on earaches is to deal with them right away," she told a reporter, echoing her rule of life. Once she tried vainly to review materials for an upcoming meeting while her driver rushed them from her office, reporter in tow, to an emergency appointment.

"Mommy, when are we going to get to the doctor's?" Johnny asked almost before they'd pulled away from the Capitol; the five-year-old peppered her with questions while Eleanor kept attempting to work, glancing at her children between scribbling notes on her papers.

Like most working mothers, she was pulled by guilt on those nights when she didn't arrive home for bedtime stories. Or when she did pull into the narrow driveway just in time, run up the three stone steps with heavy bags of paperwork, and moments after hanging her coat on the rack, got an urgent phone call.

Besides, her marriage was fracturing.

"It happened over a period of time," she struggles to explain. "Obviously cracks were developing over the entire marriage. Those are nuances that are very difficult to detect. They don't happen in big fell swoops."

Edward's job, as deputy general counsel at HUD, didn't work out; he got a position at the Small Business Administration. With more free time than she, Edward was a voracious reader, watched TV and was often eager to have dinner with friends, hers as well as his. Eleanor was consumed with work and children; virtually all discretionary time was allotted.

In the beginning Eleanor had cooked. "Edward lost twenty pounds when we were married. Not because the cooking was so bad, but because he moved from his mother's house and delicious soul food. I did only steak and salad." Later Edward began to cook on weekends, "and it became clear that he had a real knack. I mean a knack that's better than my knack ever was. He said it may have been that he was also good in chemistry." Edward started cooking fairly routine dishes, then graduated to more complicated meats and fish.

"Edward could buy a chop, stuff it with crabs," Eleanor relates admiringly. "That's the kind of thing I couldn't begin to do. All this good cooking occurred on the weekends. During the week we ate leftovers."

Edward complained to friends that Eleanor was cold, didn't cook, and didn't pay attention to him. Eleanor, he said with considerable acumen, was Marx to his Freud. On the topic of their difficulties, she has little to say. "The cracks that came were those that come in many marriages over time," she simply repeats. "I never sat down and analyzed them. Remember, as Edward said, I'm Marx."

Not one for small talk, Eleanor was invariably engagé, determined to move the politics of her day. She occasionally went out partying with

Edward to friends' homes. Once, getting wind of a shindig thrown by her press director, Eleanor invited herself.

"I understand you're having a party. Well, the chair would like to come to that." She did, and danced late into the night, amazing those at the EEOC who had never seen their boss unwind this way.

Eleanor had several friends who occasionally lightened her evenings, when she'd laugh late into the night by telephone. "Charlayne and I kept up when I went to Washington. She was on *MacNeil-Lehrer:* 'Look, we're going on the show, tell me what you think about this.' Especially about legal issues. It's a rare kind of friendship when you have that many things in common, private and public."

No matter the topic or how long since they'd spoken, the two regaled each other, "Girl, you should have seen his face when . . ."

The chair's only regular respite came from jogging and television, where she escaped late each evening into news programs and crime dramas, simultaneously reading papers and writing "SEE ME" memos. Not happy with her own TV habit, Eleanor nonetheless found both stimulation and solace in the portrayals of worlds where people did not look to her to solve their problems.

As EEOC chair, Eleanor spoke to chambers of commerce, central labor councils and conferences across the country. Essentially she said, both poetically and with statistics, "There's a sensible way to deal with equal employment. If we do it this way, we'll all benefit. And here is how." Giving audiences a greater understanding of context, she told them they were not to blame for history. But they were accountable for today.

In 1979, Eleanor arrived at the Chicago Hilton for an unprecedented return invitation as an Urban League keynoter, just four years after her "Letter to a Black Man" speech. Wired with tension, Eleanor rejected the suite the league had arranged ("As a government official I don't want to take anything") and shoehorned herself, with Edward, into a small room.

"But I got the government rate!" she claimed over his protestations.

After breaking the cord off her travel iron and fervently directing her assistant to "Call Vernon! Call Vernon!" she borrowed an iron, frantically refining the speech she'd been writing for days.

Yet hours later the tall, composed woman ascended to the podium and opened, reminding the middle-class audience of their responsibility.

"We must march out of poverty as part of a great battalion, not as so many straggling troops. We must say to America, 'If you take me, you must take my brother and my sister too.' . . . We do not want to get out of the ghetto. We want to get rid of the ghetto!"

Because of America's "inhospitality to the black family" the country "has allowed many blacks to enter the middle class only after a long trek and often only one by one instead of family by family." Updating the theme of her previous Urban League remarks, she was determined to help families move up collectively, unit by unit and generation by generation, as was the American norm for other ethnic groups.

"America nurtured every other garden, but she left its darkest flowers to languish on a starved and struggling vine." The "perilously placed" new middle class, "topsoil not yet layered deep" and lacking stable anchors of its own, still needed to see kin through "the nation's ancient tragedy."

When Eleanor closed, the audience was in tears.

By 1980, Eleanor, rated by one opinion poll in the top ten of "favorite black leaders," was routinely considered "one of the twenty-five most influential women in America." Yet that same summer she was confronted with a turning point beyond even her control.

"We didn't know whether Reagan would win the presidential election. Carter had crises that were hard to overcome. The oil crisis, which didn't have anything to do with him, was worldwide. He had the right response: 'Turn down your damn heat. Put on a sweater.' That wasn't quick enough with people lining up for gas."

The hostage crisis also "wasn't anything he could get control of, and then the third crisis was double-digit inflation, in part a product of the oil crisis." The stage was set for a Republican.

After the Democratic Convention in New York, where Eleanor was a delegate, staying in Charlayne's "wonderful West Side home " and running in the park, everyone had to campaign. The Carter/Mondale Re-election Committee sent talking points: Support full employment, affirmative action, health, housing and the ERA. But Carter's tepid support for the ERA and other liberal planks made it difficult to mobilize the party base.

When Vice President Mondale called and asked Eleanor to go to California—a grueling trip with a quick turnaround—she looked at her press director and asked, "Why can't I, like Jesus Christ, say 'Pass this cup from my lip?' "

The answer—" 'Cause you're a girl, Eleanor"—brought howls. Eleanor often surrounded herself with black women who helped her open the deep reservoir of laughter ready to erupt, though busy stretches went by when it was rarely tapped.

During the campaign, Eleanor and her colleagues were alarmed by Reagan's support. He had made his opening "I believe in states' rights" campaign speech in Philadelphia, Mississippi, where the three young civil rights workers had been murdered in 1964. Chaney, Goodman and Schwerner's burned car had been an indelible part of Eleanor's—and the nation's—history at the Democratic Convention in Atlantic City that year. If Reagan won, it was not going to be an easy time.

At an Aspen Great Books Conference that fall, Eleanor shocked participants discussing Socrates.

"If Ronald Reagan becomes president, I will resign."

"Why would you do that before your term is up?" others argued. "You've whipped the EEOC into shape. And there are so few blacks in high places. If you stayed on, think what you could do. Why would you resign?"

"For the same reasons that Socrates drank the hemlock. A president should have somebody who can carry out his policies. I cannot. You don't hang on to a job simply because you have a term; you leave with dignity, when, by understanding who you are, you know your time has come."

"No, you have a year to continue!"

"I did essentially what I came to do. You have to know when to come and when to go."

The morning after the election was a strange one. Doors in the long endless EEOC corridors were closed. People didn't know what to say or do.

Though Eleanor had sat stunned the night before in the Sheraton Ballroom on Woodley Road, shocked by the size of Carter's loss and dismayed when he conceded even before California's polls closed, she called her staff together.

"Everything is going to be fine."

Her successor would surely retain the orderly process she'd initiated, and she was upbeat about staff finding jobs. Concerned for those who'd come to work for her, she made sure they followed job leads. SEE ME NOW memos appeared on office seats; people were summoned into her office, this time queried about job searches. She directed them to friends like Marian Wright Edelman, who led agencies outside of government.

But Eleanor had no idea where she would go.

On January 22, 1981, she submitted her resignation to the newly installed President Reagan, effective February 21, four months before the end of her four-year term. Her final days were spent trying to wrap up half-completed projects, like a paper about problems of the aged, groundwork for a program in one of the new EEOC areas of jurisdiction.

Finally the moment came when she had to clear out her office and depart, though for days she called in, directing staff working on the age project. But her time was over.

For eleven years Eleanor had been a government official, constantly in the public eye while she shaped two drifting agencies. Just as in New York, Eleanor had again taken a job that was hardly a plum and created real recourse for working people. Pledging at her confirmation hearing "to give the best that is in me," she'd done just that, and was going off-stage with a revitalized agency as her legacy. Now the chair would once again become a private citizen. How would she make her mark in the difficult days to come?

CHAPTER 10

Exile

A new administration, uncaring, took power.
ELEANOR HOLMES NORTON

Eleanor could see what was coming: within six months she and the handful of other prominent black women would be gone, turning their jobs over to Republicans set on undoing everything they'd accomplished. In fact, within six months *Ebony* would ask, "Whatever Happened to Carter's Top Blacks?" They seemed to vanish along with the peanut soup.

But even Eleanor, tough realist that she was, couldn't imagine any administration wanting to tear down her work at the EEOC, where she had all but eliminated the infamous backlog, spelled out discrimination law and created effective remedies. She'd made the agency an effective, high-profile organization. Why would anyone want to gut it? Yet within a year, they did.

Senator Orrin Hatch, the new chair of the Senate Labor and Human Resources Committee, directed an EEOC review and found "financial chaos," even "possible violations of the law." Despite years of glowing results, with case-processing time cut from two years to four months and a doubling of case resolutions, a series of GAO reports alleged millions of misspent dollars and unfounded settlements.

With her usual statistics, Eleanor detailed a twenty-two page rebuttal. But the ideological turn was complete. The dearth of black Republicans led the new administration to reach way down into the bureaucracy for a new EEOC chair: the young Clarence Thomas, a former legislative assistant to Senator John Danforth before his tenure as Department of Education assistant secretary for civil rights. Plucked from that brief position, by May 1982, he was in place.

Thomas abolished rapid charges, promising, "We will not be settling these cases. Everybody's entitled to a full review." He successfully reversed reforms that had, in the end, been hailed by business and interest groups alike. The new chairman so slowed the process that, after eight years of such leadership, President Clinton would open his 1992 presidency decrying the mounting backlog of 200,000 complaints. And Eleanor's fear—"Justice delayed is justice denied"—would come to pass.

As the first black women disappeared from Washington's top-level jobs and the EEOC slowed its work, job competition worsened "because, of course, the first thing Reagan wanted to do was bring down inflation, and he did it in the worst way, with huge unemployment in his first term." Many civil rights advocates were discouraged by *Bakke* "even though it didn't undermine affirmative action as much as it demoralized the atmosphere," Eleanor said then and affirms today.

For years Eleanor had done the government's work. Though it served her advocacy ends she had nonetheless been constrained by a role that even she could stretch only so far. Now, for the first time since leaving Yale almost two decades before, she could speak with the fullness of her own voice. A national stage awaited; the need was clear.

Job options were few. Several years before she'd been floated in print as a possible "daring" appointment for the Supreme Court; now, of course, any government work was out of the question.

Eleanor investigated private law firms while applying for Rockefeller research funds. The grant came first. With $100,000 in hand for a book on affirmative action, she made her way to a Washington think tank, the Urban Institute, as a senior fellow. "A lot of the most serious thinking then was by black intellectuals, not civil rights leaders. These were people who wrote about the underclass, poverty and social issues." Among them, Eleanor sought to investigate how "there would be anybody left out, given the kind of automatic way people advance in United States society from generation to generation."

But more oriented to action than scholarship, "I still haven't finished the book," she regretfully admits. Instead, retaining a speaker's agent, she began to travel the country, spreading a message of resilience in the face of adversity, urging people to creatively resolve new brands of old problems. As she set out to address the questions of the eighties, jetting from coast to coast for a quick turnaround conference was common. Striding through airports became a way of life. As part of the "government in exile," Eleanor took up virtually a full-time role as advocate for her demoralized movement. Evolving with the needs of the time, she became a public intellectual. No longer having an organization to use as her instrument, she used herself.

The issue that had created the civil rights movement was discrimination. Now that was illegal; the issues facing African Americans became far less high-profile.

"We were so demoralized as a people, and as Democrats. When we saw this extreme right-wing nemesis come to power, we were accused rightly of 'whining.' I saw too many of us simply defending the status quo. And I said, 'This ain't me.' I've been a change maker all my life. I'm not going to defend everything that we've done as if it should never change. I'm going to defend the principled core of what we've done. And be part of changing it to meet new times.

"I thought we should articulate new policy initiatives for the black community. But what we were doing was sitting back and saying, 'Save everything we've done and stop criticizing us' instead of offering our own policy initiatives.

"There had been no reason for black people or black leaders to change their agenda for a hundred years. For the first hundred years, your agenda had to be get rid of slavery, for the second hundred years it had to be: get antidiscrimination laws. What do you do for the third hundred years? Social problems, the legacy of discrimination, relate also to other levers in the society, far more complex to manipulate."

While Eleanor began to articulate the evolving politics required in a changing climate, she also interviewed for tenure track positions, simultaneously taking visiting appointments, like one in Berkeley, where she'd spent such carefree time twenty years before. In 1981, she returned for a month as Boalt Law School's distinguished lecturer, taking Edward and the children. It was a grand vacation for a woman who regarded working only a forty-hour week as "time off." Enjoying dinners with the university president and faculty, Eleanor taught, recuperated, and found this "a perfect scholarly existence."

The pleasurable month was prelude to a permanent position at home. When Eleanor had been at the EEOC, meeting with feminist law professors about guidelines for workplaces or pregnancy leave, she had said, laughing, "What an easy job you have, you professors!" She'd scorned

Barbara Babcock's first law-teaching job: "Why would you want to do that when you could be more activist and accomplish something?"

Now, in the terrible Reagan years, "she saw a law school as a good place to be, a good platform," says Babcock. Appointed professor at the then small Georgetown University Law Center, Eleanor moved into her modest, narrow office, unpacking boxes of books and her beloved black-and-white photograph collection: civil rights heroes mingled with personal African-American and feminist history. In spite of her senior status in the world, Eleanor was a junior colleague here. As she would soon bluntly note to another African-American woman, younger than she and new on campus: "You must really rate, you have an office with a window, girl!"

One of only three African-American faculty and one of the Law Center's first women, Eleanor slid easily into a familiar white male environment. Soon her office was piled high with books and papers; her high-energy profile became familiar as she hurried to class or raised her voice on issues affecting any of her many constituencies. Fueled by the peanut butter she stocked in a desk drawer, she ran off to meetings, sped to catch airplanes, wrote speeches and still squeezed out late-night hours to read student papers, prepare for class and write for tenure. Appearing "slim, healthy and vigorous" to colleagues, who remarked almost as often on her energy as her integrity or brilliance, she became a valued member of the academic community. People counted on her to bring her moral authority and negotiation skills to race-related tensions that arose. Unlike some faculty of color at law schools who felt their history of exclusion so keenly they couldn't become active community members, Eleanor, in trademark style, joined right in, though she was not a frequent presence. Known to never make small talk ("She can't," say colleagues), she reserved her famous stamina for higher-level discussion. Unless she was with a handful of close friends, Eleanor didn't waste time on trivia. And even then, she usually stuck to political topics.

Her major areas were labor law, employment law and negotiations. Ever since student days at Yale when she'd written about the differential impact of bail on people from different classes and races, Eleanor had sought to improve the justice system. Justice "is assumed to result from formal systems and suspected of falling short in informal systems," she wrote as a law professor. Yet she had seen at her commissions that the slow pace of traditional procedures often froze out equity. Now she asked, "Do methods of dispute resolution such as mediation and negotiation, that seek an accommodation rather than a formal zero-sum solution, render justice?"

She answered "Yes," believing her success with rapid charge-processing was replicable and measurable; she'd found the quality of justice was greater with "alternative methods" like fact-finding, mediation, arbitration or conciliation. Creating an innovative law curriculum, she used the Harvard Negotiating Project's guidebook, *Getting to Yes,* rather than a law text. There weren't any.

"[The book] was to take peoples' minds and cleanse them of the adversarial paradigm that every law school student learns from the day he walks in the door." She began to publish in law journals, increasingly focusing on how traditional hard bargaining and competitive approaches were giving way to cooperative methods.

In part, Eleanor's life in the 1980s was so hectic because—along with incessant speaking—she took her law teaching, like everything she did, so seriously. "It's not possible to just say, 'Oh well, I taught that last year.' You've got to sit down, read the cases again each year, do the same kind of underlining, writing in the margins, as you would do if you'd never seen the case before. You've got to look at the developing case law." She patiently takes her eyes off the television screen in her upstairs family room as she explains, though her hand remains on the remote control, itching to turn up the volume. But the topic takes her over. She leans forward.

"Then you engage the class in an exchange! You're trying to pull principles out, but in a very sophisticated way. It's very intellectually labor-intensive. But I like that kind of thing. Legal teaching gives my brain the exercise a lawyer needs."

Demanding as much of herself as of her students, a year after she started teaching Eleanor told one of the activist professors whose load she had earlier scorned, "This is the hardest job I've ever had!"

"I always thought I worked hard," she told an interviewer. "But I have become a workaholic in the true sense of that word and I am not proud of that. In crowding so many things into my life—this may be a lesson for women—what has been crowded *out* is pleasure."

Johnny concurs. "My mother worked all day and then worked up here in that middle room, with her nose in a book, until eleven P.M. every night."

In her first year at Georgetown, Eleanor met up with Yale classmate Eli Evans. "From the time I got out of the government, Eli, at the Charles Revson Foundation, had this notion of funding me for my own policy organization, as he had helped Marian [Wright Edelman]."

She asked her old friend, "How about bestowing foundation money for a women's clinic about to run out of money? We can redesign it for young lawyers who want to work on women's issues."

He agreed. "And he has funded it to this day."

With feminists she had met in her EEOC years, Eleanor set up a pioneering Women's Law and Public Policy Fellowship Program at the Law Center. Judy Lichtman of the Women's Legal Defense Fund, Wendy Williams from the Law Center and Marsha Greenberger, founder of the National Women's Law Center, served as the board, with Eleanor as chair. In later years, when her role was more titular, she would continue meeting with the fellows at least once a year over a meal, provoking them to enthusiastic argument. The innovative program would become the root for many other women's law efforts as fellows set up infrastructures elsewhere, profoundly influencing women and the law for the coming decades.

Eleanor, by now an icon of the civil rights and women's movements, was always just a jump ahead of deadlines. Once, arriving for a reception in her honor before a talk she was to give at nearby Smith College, she found herself in a familiar predicament.

"Do you have a room where I can work?"

After a brief "Hello" to those eager to meet her, she retreated to a spare office, kicked off her shoes, put up her feet and dug a stack of papers from a large leather bag. Her host, an old friend, inquired whether Eleanor was finalizing her speech.

"I better not be! I'd be in trouble if that were the case! I'm preparing an article for publication." Bending her head over her work, she signaled an end to the short conversation.

"I never don't use an hour that's free," she muttered. "I can't."

Carving out protected time for major scholarship like her affirmative action book, without "the hot breath of deadlines warming my neck," proved impossible. Instead, the advocate churned out speeches, law review articles and radio commentary, spending additional precious hours on boards, all while teaching.

Lecture requests and scholarly appointments frequently came her way. Airports became as familiar as her living room. Once Eleanor had been EEOC chair, she was "queen of the world," as one friend puts it. Colleagues from networks new and old sought her out. Marian Wright Edelman was typical, bringing Eleanor in for keynotes. Invited to roundtables, or lecturing, Eleanor was both dryly humorous and intense. Over the clinking glasses at conference dinners she enthralled audiences with her tight logic and concrete stories. But mostly, people wanted her to come because she kept the flame alive in a perilous time.

"Don't give up! We've endured worse. And look at our victories!" Audiences of all kinds listened because they knew she anticipated tomorrow's issues. To those trying to turn back the clock in America, Eleanor warned, "We are not going away. We will prevail."

She took on a breadth of topics, gathering honorary degrees by the fistful even after Judge Higginbotham told her: "Eleanor, after twenty you can stop!" But she didn't. She spoke everywhere, from prayer breakfasts to AFL-CIO conferences, covering drugs to displaced workers. Rallying women for the Equal Rights Amendment, she consoled after its 1984 defeat: "Yet the good news is that a remarkable consensus embracing continuing change in women's status continues to build in this country." To other audiences she explained the strong remedy of affirmative action, or assailed academic censorship codes. "Without free expression I do not see how women would have won the right to vote, how the trade union movement organized, the Vietnam War exposed . . . Let us not unwittingly fall on our own sword!"

Above all, Eleanor zeroed in on the black family, challenging African-American leaders to address the "national catastrophe" on its way: the rapid increase in teen pregnancy and poor single mothers. Attacking the problem from all sides, she urged attention to the changed nature of black economics. In a 1988 LIFE symposium discussing "where Blacks stand today," she told William Julius Wilson, Vernon Jordan, June Jordan, Charlayne Hunter-Gault and others, "The major problem for black people during this twenty-year period has been that all the legal equality in the world has not compensated for the international-ization of the American economy, which weakened the economy just when blacks were getting their chance for parity." The jobs that created a working class and a middle class for whites evaporated at the very moment blacks had their first chance at those jobs.

Today she ruefully acknowledges, "One of the great problems with black leadership since the 1960s—and I have a been a critic even as I have been part of it—is we did not quickly move on as the issues moved on. We had a hugely grand moment for an entire fifteen years, from the middle fifties until about 1970. And then the world changed.

"The pervasiveness of drugs that devastated whole neighborhoods— there were no easy answers. You couldn't have a meeting and decide to see the president on these. They are not something you pass a law against. People had difficulty making the transition to an entire new set of far more complicated problems. Discrimination was a lot of things, but it was not complicated."

When conservatism ascended, "blacks were confused and scattered. Their basic strategy was to respond with the same kinds of proposals. If you're change-makers, your response can't be the status quo.

"One response should have been more emphasis on affirmative action as a *temporary* remedy, that had to have time to do its work. Some blacks talked as if they were for quotas instead of goals and timetables, instead of saying, 'We're not dug in on this as a permanent way to organize society.'

"But the attacks from the right wing were so virulent, they almost forced defense of what was there. Defend what is there, but go forward with new strategies, so that you begin to change the conversation, instead of fighting on their turf."

Eleanor warned that African-American leaders were in reaction, not taking *her* trademark approach, the offensive. "What's always required, if you are behind, if you are the underdog, is to be proactive. So if you are responding to attacks from conservatives, when you're already behind, you're in real trouble."

Eleanor decided to change the conversation. During the 1980s she didn't stop talking, determined to at least "hold onto what we had, when conservative courts were kicking in, tearing up huge parts of Title VII. We had to fight or face a decade of defeat."

Wanting to address problems differently, she picked up the heretical topic she'd initiated with her 1975 Urban League "Letter to a Black Man" speech. Eleanor took on welfare.

"All that we have won, even the best of it, from affirmative action to food stamps, needs not only our protection but our critical scrutiny. If there needs to be reform in our reforms, let it come from us," she wrote, again diagnosing female-headed households as a root of intransigent black poverty.

"You go into ghetto areas, for blocks and blocks, and there are only women on welfare, no fathers, nobody going to work. The kids see none of the standard models. You don't bring children into the world without taking responsibility for them!"

Eleanor's rhetoric about unwed mothers sometimes sounded like moral judgments on people with little chance to escape their circumstances.

"Muddled liberal thinking!" she throws back. "The welfare system was a brilliant innovation, a completely necessary temporary solution for families. And then it became *the* way to take care of poor women with children. It became the way to deal with structural unemployment of black men. The system did not change with the times. Therefore, it needed to go."

"Welfare," she said then, "has become almost entirely identified with race; it has been savagely and grossly stereotyped. Our attempts to undo that stereotype have not met with success. I don't believe any people who subsist disproportionately on even increased welfare benefits are, in fact, equals or will ever be regarded as equals or on the road to anywhere . . . Providing work for women on welfare at a standard wage rate with professionally provided day care, with Medicaid, is the beginning of a route out of the terrible trap in which increasing numbers of black women and black children find themselves."

Putting forward a solution to what she saw as a tragedy, Eleanor wrote a 1985 *New York Times Magazine* feature, "Restoring the Traditional Black Family," the first on this sensitive subject in a popular journal.

"At the heart of the crisis lies the self-perpetuating culture of the ghetto. This destructive ethos began to surface forty years ago with the appearance of permanent joblessness and the devaluation of working-class black men. . . . Buried beneath the statistics is a world of complexity originating in the historic atrocity of slavery and linked to modern discrimination and its continuing effects . . . The black family has been an issue in search of leadership."

With one-third of black children born out of wedlock, Eleanor urged her peers to involve themselves in the multiplying problems of black family disintegration. Two years later she and historian John Hope

Franklin would spell out ethics they hoped to restore: "These values—among them, the primacy of family, the importance of education, and the necessity for individual enterprise and hard work—have been fundamental to black survival."

On the ethical deterioration undermining family, Eleanor's vision is apocalyptic. "It's going to collapse the Western world! And it's one of the reasons for the appeal of conservatism. People copulating on TV, cursing on TV, and some of the worst of it is black, accentuating problems we're trying to get rid of.

"If you let black boys call women bitches and hos then you have no principles. If a white man did that you'd be all over him.

"There's no question that these young people are being exploited by largely white CD and movie types, and they're spreading this garbage throughout the world. Adults are leading it. But they've made apologists of these young men, who say, 'This is our art, we're describing reality as we know it.' " She grows increasingly animated and her voice rises.

"Oh, really?! Reality, as you know it, is a black man talking about his mother and calling her a ho, saying you're going to rape her and kill her and cut her up! Is that the kind of reality you want to pass on? We've got to challenge that! *That's* where black leadership should be."

As Eleanor traveled the country reconceptualizing the black agenda, she was also an early voice for the Free South Africa Movement.

"It was precipitated by the [1984] arrest of fourteen South African trade union leaders, held incommunicado. Randall Robinson of TransAfrica really feared for their lives." Robinson asked Walter Fauntroy, Washington's congressional delegate, and Mary Frances Berry, the U.S. Civil Rights commissioner, with Eleanor, to accompany him to the South African Embassy. "He wanted people who were prominent enough to get in to see the ambassador."

On November 21 the four went to the large stone embassy at 3051 Massachusetts Avenue, NW. They had secured an appointment for the afternoon before Thanksgiving—a slow news day.

"Boy, come on down," Fauntroy remembers the South African ambassador acceding to their request.

They showed up at 3:30. Ambassador Bernardus Fourie received them politely. Responding to their inquiry about black progress, he spent an hour describing his version of how Africans accepted apartheid. Finally Robinson interrupted.

"Sir, you've not been persuasive. Unless you call Mr. Botha [South Africa's president] right now and tell him to release the labor leaders, we're not leaving your office."

"What? I'll have you arrested!"

"Good," Fauntroy replied. "Do it about six P.M.!"

"What we really wanted to do was to get in there," explains Eleanor. "The plan was that after an hour I was to come out and tell pickets outside that the other three would not leave until the trade unionists were freed."

The ambassador, as expected, ordered the sit-in protestors in his office hauled off to jail. Police put them in handcuffs and the evening news carried their photo around the world. As spokesperson, Eleanor interpreted the historic event, while pictures of the three prominent African Americans in fetters illustrated the story for the army of reporters. Eleanor had alerted Tom Brokaw and other journalists. "With her prestige and level of respect, we thought she would be the ideal person to contact key people at the networks," says Fauntroy.

The ambassador's response to the sit-in gave Thanksgiving newspapers not only a morning headline, but a plethora of photos to match. And Eleanor was spokesperson for a Free South Africa Movement that would ripple the world for another decade.

A ritual of daily arrests began. With high drama, senators and members of Congress, movie stars, sports figures and ordinary citizens marched every weekday afternoon at the South African Embassy, attracting intense media attention. Coretta Scott King, Jesse Jackson, Harry Belafonte, Arthur Ashe, and Tony Randall were a few of the celebrities who demonstrated. Coordinated by Randall Robinson, people picketed closer than the required 500 feet from the embassy, so that soon "every famous person was arrested," Eleanor says gleefully. On December 2, South African Bishop and Nobel Prize winner Desmond Tutu attended a special Washington Cathedral service and thanked embassy protestors.

Two months later, singer Stevie Wonder, saying he chose Valentine's Day to become "a conscientious criminal for world equality," was taken away in handcuffs singing "We Shall Overcome." Forty-seven arrests were made that day, including Washington Area Scholars Against Apartheid.

Soon, thousands were arrested. The sustained pressure was pivotal. Discussions ensued all over America about economic, cultural and political sanctions against the apartheid regime. The decade of resistance sparked by Soweto's uprising in 1976 urgently needed international endorsement. The AFL-CIO, NOW and the NAACP immediately backed the protests; soon Middle America joined in.

"Constructive engagement," the Reagan policy of maintaining ties to South Africa in hopes of influencing change, was widely discredited. Eleanor said then it meant little more than "letting the South African government go and do what it feels like doing." States, cities and universities began to call for divestment in companies doing business in South Africa. Within six months support rose for congressional legislation to ban all new business investment and bank loans in South Africa, as well as U.S. purchases of Krugerrands, South African gold coins.

The sanctions movement would build so much support that even the Republican-controlled Senate was forced to drop its constructive engagement response and, by a 78–21 vote, pass a 1986 limited-sanctions Anti-Apartheid Act over Reagan's veto. A critical segment of white South African businessmen, alarmed by their increasing global isolation as well as by the agitated masses at home, would ultimately conclude that apartheid was no longer in their own best interest.

Day after day, in all kinds of winter weather, Eleanor walked the picket line. "I left law school to picket." Spring passed and summer came; Edward, Katherine and Johnny joined her, and finally they were arrested.

"They put me in the jail over here. You could get arrested and be released; many people took a citation and went home. But I had been one of the original four to go in. I couldn't do a token arrest. Obviously, I had to stay overnight. Boy, that's something. They keep the lights on all night!"

At first, the guards put Eleanor in one set of cells. Then as her time got closer to go fully inside, they herded her into another.

"As we went from one set of cells to the other, I'm in line with women who had been locked up for drugging and whoring and stealing. I'm just by myself with all these women in jail for crack and so on."

On each move the women filed past the guards. Every time at least one would say, "How are you, Ms. Norton?"

"Fine, thank you," Eleanor invariably replied.

Finally, one young woman, "who looked like she had just come out of the crack house, it finally got her. She said, 'You must be in here all the time; they all seem to know your name!' I never did tell her."

Eleanor had been an Antioch College trustee for fifteen years and served on dozens of progressive boards. But in 1982 she was elected to the Yale Corporation, the governing body of the university. There she served with men like Cyrus Vance, Carter's former secretary of state, and Paul Moore, the Episcopal bishop of New York City.

"This was quintessential establishment," says Eleanor, laughing. "We flew up to New Haven on Friday nights." Edward often accompanied Eleanor, traveling on the small planes she didn't like.

"These were always close-knit dinners with board members, very social and very pleasant. The wives and husbands were invited too. Edward's a real old blue, he loved Yale . . . Just like Yale itself is a very close-knit school, at least at the undergraduate level, so was this board."

As contentious issues came up, "I was a progressive voice but basically boards are about supporting the president. Or else getting rid of him. Universities are run by, and should be run by, presidents. This one was one of the most elegant and eloquent men of the twentieth century: I loved Bart Giamatti! There just was no man I have ever met with a deeper mind. Or whose use of the English language was more eloquent." His fatal 1989 heart attack at only fifty-one still shocks her.

Eleanor served on several committees, including investor responsibility. "Of course I spoke up; I fought, but we never could get the Yale Corporation to divest from South Africa. The states and cities were the ones who divested."

While she struggled to have her voice heard behind closed doors, publicly Eleanor was part of a united Yale front. During a bitter, hard-fought unionization drive by Yale clerical and technical staff, "because they knew I was pro-union, I became a real target." When she spoke in Boston during negotiations, unions formed a huge picket line.

"Norton! Get Yale to do the right thing!" they chanted.

"Yale was in bargaining!" she says, grimacing at the uncomfortable memory. "I couldn't come out as if I were an independent agent. There was nothing I could do about that. They wanted me to be their voice, but the board doesn't negotiate. Obviously they knew I was with them, should be with them, would be with them. And I don't blame them for picketing me to publicize the issues."

Characteristically, Eleanor doesn't bewail the complexities of her position. "I was a part of the board. I understood my role and function. If you're going to be a part of the board, then be part of the board. Use your role *in* the board to press those issues. You can't have it both ways."

In 1986 she wrote her classmate Neil Herring, "My life is too complicated and multilayered to catch you up on in a letter. It still features Edward who has formed his own law firm here, Katherine (15) and Johnny (13). It features an unrelenting workaholic schedule for me—my full-time law teaching (including labor law), speeches all over the country, and all varieties of activities—from the Free South Africa Steering Committee to a corporate board. My most interesting board, from the perspective of our good old days, is the Yale Corporation. The place looks a little different from that side of the table. Politically I'm fighting in a dozen ways to do what I can to keep our issues from being kicked over a right-wing cliff. Our side is on the defensive in the worst way. We have lost the art of the fight to take the initiative."

Always poised to take an aggressive first step, Eleanor became increasingly frustrated. Soon she would write that only gays and lesbians were on the offensive in the 80s; by doing so, they'd created an historic shift in majority opinion during a conservative period.

In 1985 Pitney Bowes had a vacancy on their board; investment banker Julia Walsh suggested the former EEOC chair. After Pitney Bowes came Metropolitan Life Insurance and then Stanley Works, all Fortune 500 companies.

"You get paid. And of course that was one incentive." But she wanted the perspective she represented at the table. And it was important that these be progressive companies.

"I would have been like a fish out of water if I had been a hard-nosed defender of somebody who had been sued for massive discrimination. These were extraordinary companies: their general employment policies, their policies toward women and minorities, their social and corporate citizenship policies.

"Some regard corporate boards as a way to make a living. I regard that as awful! Even though I could have made a nice living off my corporate boards alone, it's not meant to be a job! . . . You have to have a larger life."

Eleanor sometimes used board meetings to catch up on rare personal correspondence. In May 1989, she began another letter to Neil. "Here I am during a Metropolitan Life Insurance trustees meeting, in a room with the highest ceilings I've seen outside of a castle, adorned with the pictures of white men from various ages who've built this company and, as it turns out, the American economy. Whether I 'belong' here or not, here I sit without the slightest sense that I don't." She trundled the letter to a Rockefeller Foundation meeting a month later, adding a page. Finally, six months after beginning it, Eleanor completed her letter at a Stanley Works trustees meeting in Farmington, Connecticut. In December, she mailed it.

While Eleanor was crisscrossing the country, so was her colleague Jesse Jackson. Though she was not involved in his 1988 presidential campaign, when Jackson had enough delegates to impact the Democratic platform, he asked Eleanor to negotiate his issues into the platform, while asking Ron Brown to be his convention leader.

"Now if I'm going to negotiate, I'm going to negotiate," Eleanor told Jackson.

He agreed.

"Jesse never once called me up and said, 'Eleanor, what are you doing? Make sure you . . .' Never once. He left it entirely to me. It was terrific the way we handled that."

But some Jackson loyalists, sitting around a large conference table, reminded her, "Remember, Jesse is for recognition of Cuba."

"That's great. But I ain't negotiating that into the Democratic platform. Y'all can go back and tell Jesse that for me."

Ever the realpolitik strategist—a trait some leftists would ever fault—she would not risk essential planks for one that couldn't survive a floor vote.

"We could not have gone to the American people with Cuba as the issue. The graviton of Jackson's campaign had been working people, people of color; it had been about poor people."

The final platform did incorporate several Jackson priorities: rule changes ending some "winner-take-all" primaries, voting rights, child poverty and health needs. And candidate Michael Dukakis agreed to declare South Africa a terrorist state.

But there was one issue where "Jesse was way out there, the Palestinians." Eleanor shakes her head. The divisive question of their homeland—bitterly debated between two prominent Democratic factions, blacks and Jews—was one of several issues Jackson took to the convention "because Madeleine Albright [Dukakis's foreign policy negotiator] would accept none of the formulations I offered." At the Atlanta Convention in July, that one lost.

As the country reversed many of its earlier commitments to equality, Eleanor pushed the barriers harder than ever. Once, after Jesse Jackson derisively threw "Miss Ann" into a speech "and people 'yepped,'" Eleanor followed him into the hotel elevator.

"Jesse, every time you make an antifeminist remark, think my black face!" she said, determined to reeducate this man who had shown such readiness to assimilate new ideas. On labor unions, which he first opposed because of their antiblack history, and on abortion, he had changed.

"I was in his face! White privileged women were seen as competition but they were also our allies. What was that going to do to affirmative action? Oh Lord. I spoke all over the country about feminism, and I wasn't about to let him say that in the middle of a black speech, unchallenged.

"I spoke about the greatest feminist of his time, Frederick Douglass. This was before the understanding that there was a whole wide world in which everybody was denied.

"And once Jesse gets it, he gets it," Eleanor adds. "This is the best advocate you could have."

Eleanor herself made a pretty good advocate. One stifling summer afternoon when heat enveloped the city, a young neighbor of Eleanor's discovered just how vigilant she could be. Steve Bumbaugh, a black teenager dating a girl on A Street just around the corner from Eleanor, was visiting his girlfriend's grandparents' elegant home, full of books and paintings. Her grandfather, Mr. Bond, heard a ruckus outside. A distinguished African-American community leader and a man used to taking charge, he went to investigate.

"What's going on?" he asked a knot of police.

They looked right through him.

"What is it?" he persisted.

Silence.

Steve ran out of the house just as police seized Mr. Bond.

"Hey, you're putting handcuffs on the old man!" the startled teenager shouted. "Hey wait, don't do that!"

In response they grabbed Steve and threw him against a patrol car, wrenching his arms behind his back.

At just that moment, Eleanor came jogging down the street.

"Leave that boy alone!" she screamed. And they released him.

"Everybody knew who she was," the young man, now thirty-two, gratefully remembers. "She saved me from a beating."

Since Mr. Bond had already been arrested and couldn't be released on the spot, Eleanor, "ugly and sweaty in my shorts," accompanied the refined, elderly gentleman to the "dank police station. Absolutely abandoned. The only light was the sunlight as we came in."

"I'm a lawyer," Eleanor told the desk worker.

"Really, you are?" was the disdainful reply.

Nonetheless, jogging shorts or not, she got him out.

Other than exercising, Eleanor used her brief discretionary time for family and a few old friends. But mostly she worked. "Generally, I don't take vacations," she told an interviewer. Johnny confirms that family vacations, which he remembers as an earlier childhood highlight, stopped in the 1980s.

Jet sometimes featured Eleanor and Edward in its "Washington Scene" column, at "gala receptions" and holiday parties. Or they'd turn up at dinner parties with friends like Marian Wright Edelman and her husband Peter, or Joyce Ladner and Chris Philpot with their husbands. Occasionally the gatherings featured newer friends, women's rights advocates or colleagues like Roger Wilkins Jr., and his wife, who taught at Georgetown. At sit-down dinners with eight or ten people they spent evenings talking politics, reminiscing and laughing.

"It was good conversation," remembers one participant, "tough rigorous debate, arguing all the difficult topics of the day. And Edward, one of the smartest, most engaging people in the room, loved to talk about old times at Yale." Eleanor more often focused on current events.

In a nod to the past, she rarely missed a SNCC party. She'd drop in for a fish fry, dipping into the crabs with delight. When Courtland Cox held the annual party in his yard, "everybody got to dancing and Eleanor got right out there and danced and danced," he says with a smile. Mississippian June Johnson recalls how relaxed Eleanor was, "just being a person" at Movement events. "You don't see that out of her every day; she's a busy bee." The emotional affinity group that SNCC became, for those who'd survived the crucible of the early sixties, was as significant to Eleanor as to other civil rights veterans. "We were part of a Movement and became part of a Movement family," says Congressman John Lewis. "There's no way to run away from those times." Later, when former SNCC member and chair of the City Council, Johnny Wilson, committed suicide, Eleanor was there with her SNCC buddies attending the wake.

Edward was more social and easygoing than his driven wife. Though her intellectual equal, he neither worked so hard nor was so passionate about world events. While she worked, he'd sometimes get together with mutual friends for drinks. His greatest compatibility with Eleanor, he often told them, was intellectual.

When Edward came out of the Small Business Administration, he had, according to friends, "a tough time," ending up in a small law partnership with an old Yale friend. The woman he'd met in 1965, so full of potential, had ripened into a public figure. And he hadn't.

"Edward was always a different kind of guy," Vernon Jordan tries to explain. "He was sort of to himself, and he had his own thing. I've thought about the extent to which he was intimidated, threatened or maybe felt insecure about her prominence."

While many of Eleanor's friends believe Edward was unhappy being married to a famous woman, he publicly concurred with her frequent comments about his comfort with a supersuccessful spouse.

"The great thing about our marriage," she says adamantly, "was that I married a man who wasn't the least bit intimidated by me or my role and that was unusual, especially for black men of the period."

Yet Eleanor's husband, like her father, didn't seem able to fulfill his sparkling potential. Friends suggest that Edward, part of the first generation of well-educated black men to emerge from the morass of racism, was handicapped in ways that comparably skilled black women were not. Eleanor characteristically dismisses such speculation ("I don't think that applies here") believing their personality differences—hers hard-driving, his less so—account for their differing success.

Featured as one of five husbands to famous wives, Edward had told an *Ebony* interviewer in the late 1970s, "The attention Eleanor gets is deserved, and for me to resent deserved attention would not reflect very favorably upon me. Also I am not an insecure person, which is to say, I think very highly of myself . . . Publicity is not a particular goal of mine and, indeed, I've said on more than one occasion that I want my epigraph to be, 'Who was that masked man?' "

Edward pointed out that two breadwinners eased financial problems. He claimed to be unintimidated by Eleanor's higher income, adding that a working wife had many pluses. "If they're working, they don't look to you to make life happen . . . I decided fairly early on that I would be better understood by an intelligent woman. It tended to follow that intelligent women or people are about their own agendas. To the extent that that included a career, you gotta pay for what you get."

But now he was paying. The tennis and biking they'd enjoyed together in New York was a thing of the past. They took one weeklong vacation in the mid-eighties, visiting historic spots in Virginia, but most years they didn't get away. Once Edward left the Small Business Administration, Eleanor tried to help jump-start his career. The law firm of Boesberg and Norton included on their letterhead: Eleanor Holmes Norton, 'of counsel.' She simply offers, by way of explanation, "I wasn't in the firm. I was a law professor, but my name might help."

Life at home grew increasingly tense. The two lawyers were chronic arguers. As friends say, "They would litigate 'Pass the butter.' " They had screaming fights, never a particularly unusual occasion for Eleanor; but, in the way of long-term couples rehashing painful ground, they flung increasingly bitter accusations.

Over this decade the children became teens, but Eleanor was on the road or preparing to go much of the time. Edward, while he may have cherished Eleanor and her brilliant career, did not pick up major care of the home. As Barbara Babcock says, "Eleanor was out doing good for the world, and Edward wasn't doing much." One bathroom ceiling sagged, threatening to fall; the home's neglect reflected the state of the uncared-for marriage. Yet Eleanor continued, as had her mother before her, to act the role of wife even as its reality became more hollow.

And the marriage still provided sustenance. "Their quarreling was simply part of both of their natures," Charlayne contends, asserting that Edward artfully supported his mate "by staying out of her way without diminishing himself." Eleanor depended on him to handle family bookkeeping while she brought home an increasing share of the income and focused on her ever-expanding world. Over a rare lunch with three other law professors—Wendy Williams, Patricia White and Susan Deller Ross—Eleanor compared notes and discovered that her family's financial division of labor was common: one partner typically paid the bills, balancing that with other chores. Eleanor told the little group how relieved she was to know she had someone as competent as Edward handling her finances.

Money was a subject Eleanor avoided whenever she could, and she'd constructed her life so that was possible to a remarkable degree. So little did Eleanor focus on finances that once when a Revson Foundation check for $200,000 was sent to her home for the Women and Public Policy Fellows Program at Georgetown, she lost it.

Eleanor also looked to Edward to read her speeches and publication drafts or to brainstorm ideas. Together they published an article in *Legal Times* on minority businesses. And Edward energized his famous wife. To a question once asked about what sustained her, Eleanor had earlier responded, "A kind of endless and unattainable search for excellence, and the encouragement of my husband and family to reach beyond the possible."

But his conflicted feelings found public outlets. At Georgetown faculty dinners Edward told unflattering "Eleanor stories," several times regaling uncomfortable groups with graphic descriptions of Eleanor working up to the last second before delivery, dictating memos while blood flowed down her leg. At another social occasion a new faculty member was startled to learn that Edward was Eleanor's husband, so hostile had his comments seemed. Mutual friends observed bitter fights. Charlayne, though, cautions again, "A lot of people might see that public quarreling as indication of some subliminal resentment. But he had this incredible respect for her. He used to call her 'La Pasionaria,' the most loving tribute. . . . Eleanor had a fight with just about everybody she knew, but I recognized what it was about her personality that made her overbearing. I knew it was a good thing: it was passion."

"The light of my life," as Eleanor describes Katherine, attended St. John's, an excellent all-day school. And Johnny was at Georgetown Day. Now that he was growing up, the child whom some called a "daddy's boy" answered the phone in a voice many thought was his father's. Eleanor elucidates the family dynamic, "Edward was excellent with him. But I was the taskmaster saying, 'Do your homework!' I was more the disciplinarian."

Johnny confirms, "When my mother came home from business trips, the first thing she said was, 'Have you done your homework?' " Though Johnny says he "tended to rebel against this stress," that was how Eleanor expressed her love.

Near the end of the decade, she wrote Neil, "Johnny is looking at colleges this year and will surely find some place that fits him and that he fits. He's big on California. We're not, but we're trying to play it cool so as not to court a backlash. What we do agree on is a smaller school that will allow Johnny, a late bloomer, to continue to grow." He would, in fact, select a "small, good, liberal arts" school, Occidental College—in southern California. And once far from home, he would proudly bring his "workaholic" mother out to speak.

Diligently crisscrossing the country, Eleanor maintained connections to an astonishing breadth of people. Her complexity was enduringly visible in a painting presented to Yale for permanent display. Overwhelmed (and amused) as she was by the public fanfare, she was pleased to have the array of formal white male portraits punctuated by her own and described the painting's October 1989 unveiling in a letter to Neil: ". . . my 25th reunion, to which I went only because some students used it as an occasion to give an oil portrait of me to the law school, if you can believe that. But no ordinary portrait this, it's done in bright greens and yellows instead of the usual fudge-like somber browns and dark blues and greens. And it's not a portrait at all but several sketches in oil, light and nearly transparent, with a somewhat larger transparent likeness and finally a portrait of sorts to the side. I have my favorites and not-so-favorites in this mosaic but I like the idea—which seems to me that I am becoming, rather than 'I am.' "

After seven years of full-time teaching, in 1989 Eleanor accepted a visiting scholar appointment at Boston College, where she had "a fabulous time" as the O'Neill Visiting Chair in American Politics, teaching "The Bargaining Society: Ethical Dilemmas of Deals, Disputes and Litigation."

"I took a semester off from Georgetown and flew up to Boston a couple of days a week. It was a rather prestigious fellowship with a stipend and I thought it would give me more time to write." But "other stuff piled on, wiping out any relief," she wrote Neil. "Not the least of it all was the editing and reediting of my article, which became something of a compulsion arising out of my perfectionism." Finally she finished the long *New York University Law Review* article on bargaining and the ethic of negotiation, part of her tenure package of publications.

In early 1990, Eleanor participated in a South African trip visiting grantees for Rockefeller, "one of the great foundations of the world." She had spoken to them in the early Reagan years about priorities. While others touted education, she said: "Single mothers." Partially as a result of that closed-door talk she was invited onto the board. And, with her knack for finding herself at ground zero of breaking news, there she was in Capetown on February 10, the day President de Klerk announced Mandela's release from prison.

"It was one of those golden moments. We heard it on the radio in the hotel." The government released a photograph of de Klerk and Nelson Mandela, his hands folded formally, taken after their historic meeting the previous evening. It was the first public picture of Mandela since the 1960s; people were delirious.

"We couldn't believe it. That struck the world like a bolt of lightning." With thousands of others, her group made their way toward Parliament. The grand capital buildings took Eleanor by surprise. "It was, after all, a completely illegitimate government." Yet it looked surprisingly, materially "real."

Standing in front of the majestic white building, Eleanor saw Africans dancing in lines, thronging the streets, shouting, "Our leader is coming!" The sound of freedom songs and car horns joined in the glorious din. People ran by holding newspapers high, with the headline: He's FREE! Bishop Desmond Tutu came by in shirtsleeves, literally dancing a jig of joy as his cross slapped his chest.

"I didn't know what kind of man Mandela really would be upon release," Eleanor reflected, regarding the seventy-one-year-old who would ride through the Victor Verster prison gates outside Capetown. "He had been fearless, a man of great intelligence, he had earned respect by suffering and his willingness to take risks at a time few would.

"When he became president he saved his country. It's what only great leaders are capable of doing. It's what Abraham Lincoln did. Lincoln understood what leaders do is bring people together after a civil war, not exacerbate it. That's what Mandela did.

"It's amazing that one man could have embodied so much of the hopes of a people and have lived up to that hope. Very seldom has that occurred. He is, for me, the quintessential hero, Christ-like, not doing unto others what they did to him. He had the notion to look at the other side and see if you can meet that, without losing what is essential to you."

Reflecting on why a "great" like Mandela, Malcolm X or King hasn't recently surfaced in the United States, she says, "There's not supposed to be anybody like that. You could use someone like that *then*. Now we're down to personal behavior and crime. There's no other person like them, because there's no other issue to compare with the racial issue in America. What would a person do now? In terms of somebody with the overarching effect that he changes his time and is a memorable figure of his century, the issues have to meet that. I don't see those issues. It's like Clinton can't be Roosevelt. Those kind of inspirational figures require a context."

As the 1980s closed, Eleanor made a fundamental shift in political strategy: no longer looking to the courts for social change, she began to say that only legislators could restore what the Supreme Court was taking away. "To counter revisionism by the court, supporters of equality now move on to the Congress," she wrote in the fall of 1989, a year she described as "the worst year in memory for blacks." When it came to equality, the Reagan administration "left no rock unthrown."

"Leadership for African Americans really passed to elected officials," she says. "The leadership of black people in the nineteenth century was ministers. They were the only free men. The leadership in the twentieth century was with civil rights figures, and leadership near the end of the twentieth century passed to the people chosen by the people. Those were first the mayors and state legislators, then more and more members of Congress."

For thirty years Eleanor had done everything she could to expand opportunities: she'd administered justice agencies, lectured, joined picket lines, sat on boards, written legal articles and popular columns. Wherever she'd seen a place for her hand, she had extended it. Now maybe it was time to throw her hat into the ring and stop appealing to legislators for relief. Maybe it was time to move directly into that locus of power herself.

Within a few months, events would conspire to create an opening. And Edward, arguing fiercely against a change, would finally throw up his hands in resignation.

Part Four

"TILL VICTORY IS WON"

(top) With Edward
and Baby Katherine
Courtesy of Eleanor Holmes Norton

(left) With Johnny and
Katherine in front of their
New York City home.
Courtesy of Eleanor Holmes Norton

(above) Senator Daniel Patrick Moynihan introducing Eleanor to the Senate for EEOC hearing, 1977 *Courtesy of Eleanor Holmes Norton*

(below) Judge Higginbotham swearing in federal appointees while President Carter looks on. Edward holds Bible for Eleanor. Rose Garden, June, 1977. *Courtesy of Eleanor Holmes Norton*

(above) With Gloria Steinem, July 13, 1981 *Courtesy of Eleanor Holmes Norton*

(below) Portrait of Eleanor by Robert Graham Carter, 1989,
hanging in Yale Law School. *Photo courtesy of Yale Law School.*

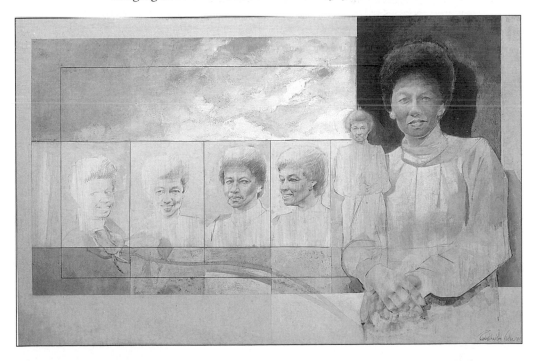

(above, left) With her sister Portia *Courtesy of Eleanor Holmes Norton*

(above, right) Sisters Portia and Nellie, early 1990s *Courtesy of Eleanor Holmes Norton*

(below) Celebration after additional ceremonial swearing in by Judge Thurgood Marshall (seated at center), 1991 *Courtesy of Eleanor Holmes Norton*

(above) With Rev. Jesse Jackson, (far left) and NOW President Pat Ireland on Women's Choice March, Washington D.C., 1992 *Courtesy of Eleanor Holmes Norton*

(below) With Johnny and Edward at Johnny's
Occidental College graduation, 1994.
Courtesy of Eleanor Holmes Norton

(above) With Congressman Ron Dellums, President Nelson Mandela (center) and Senator Carol Moseley-Braun, October, 1994. *Courtesy of Eleanor Holmes Norton*

(below) With President Bill Clinton in the Oval Office, March 19, 1996 *Official White House Photo*

(right) With Hillary Rodham Clinton
Official White House Photo

(below) With Vernon Jordan, President Clinton and Mayor Anthony Williams at birthday party for Eleanor at Jordan's home, June 13, 2000.
Beverly Orr

(left) With the author
and President Clinton.
Beverly Orr

(below) President Clinton
introducing Eleanor
at Equal Pay Event,
February 2, 2000
Official White House Photo

CHAPTER 11

An Election Explodes

If anybody causes waves, everybody goes.
OLD WASHINGTON SAYING

Eleanor—a woman known for being everywhere and never running down—lay exhausted on the bed, her thin frame curled in a ball. Her small suite at the Washington Plaza Hotel was filled with sweaty, tired campaign workers. Too weary to take them in, Eleanor, just minutes before, had walked right through the crowd and crawled into bed.

But through her fatigue she felt a flood of relief. It was over. After the bloodbath of the last four days, tonight she could stop. Soon she'd have to go down to her supporters and probably concede defeat, but for the moment she stretched out on the hotel bed to watch the numbers come in. People who came into her darkened suite remarked to themselves on how quiet she was. It was a side of this aggressive woman they'd never seen.

The morning boxes, always the predictor in D.C. elections, were in. And she was losing. Her campaign manager Donna Brazile kept saying, "You're gonna win, I know it in my bones." But the numbers just weren't there.

Eleanor's mind, that formidable instrument she'd depended on for fifty years, wouldn't completely let go of the shock, the betrayal that had derailed her front-runner status. She kept replaying the scene, trying to understand.

Four days ago, an anonymous fax to every media outlet in the city had opened her to ridicule and contempt. Or was it Edward who had demolished her reputation? And why? He was so meticulous about their finances. Too tired to think it all through, for the first time in her life her brain jammed. The circuits wouldn't connect. It just didn't make sense. She'd more than played by the rules: she'd exceeded them. Later she would recall the days following the "fax attack" as the most difficult of her life.

"My sense of loyalty is such that, at first, a marriage doesn't break apart because of even something as horrific as that. I wanted to come to grips with it, to understand it. But it became clear that it was not just that it happened, but Edward *knew* that it was happening. It really left me out there."

Four days before the primary the news had erupted: the front-runner in the race to represent the nation's capital in the United States Congress hadn't filed her city income taxes. For seven years. One of the most distinguished women in Washington, D.C., a professor of law known for integrity, suddenly found herself at the center of a grisly domestic and financial scandal in a town that thrived on just this blood.

In 1990, Washington was a traumatized city. The public problems of its mayor, Marion Barry, capped a series of scandals: mayoral aides charged with fraud, bribery and extortion, with eleven officials indicted and convicted and an equal number resigning under fire. Staggering under the barrage, the District was split between those who believed the Barry probes were yet another white attack on a "too powerful" African-American politician ("Mayor Barry had become a jewel for conservative interests," says Reverend Walter Fauntroy) and those who said they were tired of mismanagement. Meanwhile, the District was on the losing end of a credibility gap with Congress. Facing an unprecedented deficit, the city was in crisis.

In early spring, following his nationally televised arrest for cocaine possession, Barry underwent substance abuse treatment. With the city's population still in shock, Fauntroy, the District's only congressional delegate since the position was created in 1971, made a surprise March announcement: he would leave his post of nineteen years to run for mayor.

Public response to the twin openings—for mayor and delegate—revealed a yearning for new politicians untainted by the scandal-plagued Barry years. The setting, nationally and locally, was ripe for a candidate of unquestioned integrity, prestige and credibility to step forth. After the city's long nightmare, a person of Eleanor's stature might be able to compel Congress to return more home rule and increase federal funds to the bankrupt city.

But running for political office was not on Eleanor's mind that spring. Among other reasons, she'd had no role models: until she was thirty-two years old there were no African-American women in Congress (Shirley Chisholm finally broke the ban in 1969). And her hometown didn't have a congressional delegate during her youth. So Eleanor did not at first consider Fauntroy's seat.

"I had gone through the grueling process of getting tenure at a major law school. That's what you do for life—when you put that kind of effort in! Professionally it was difficult to simply say, 'Well, that's that.' In fact, I found the intellectual life very rewarding."

Even though Eleanor had gone "inside" in Mayor Lindsay's Human Rights Commission in New York and President Carter's EEOC, those were administrative positions. And she'd been out of that arena for a decade. Accustomed now to her public role as advocate and commentator during the difficult 1980s, she considered herself more than ever a political outsider. "I didn't respect how many politicians approach issues: without any depth and totally opportunistically, unanchored in principle."

Women were running in record numbers that year. Dianne Feinstein was mounting her first statewide California race and feminist icon Ann Richards was closing in on the Texas governor's mansion. Lady Bird Johnson's ex–press secretary Liz Carpenter spoke for a nation of passionate women when she said about Richards, "Ann is one of us, and we are part of her. We would have crawled to the polls on ground glass if necessary."

Women in politics still faced old double binds. "If you're married, you're neglecting him; if you're single, you couldn't get him; if you're divorced, you couldn't keep him; and if you're widowed, you killed him!" cracked Senator Barbara Mikulski. And a married woman might be injured by her husband's financial dealings. But Eleanor was safe on all fronts. Her twenty-four-year marriage was untarnished by any hint of financial impropriety. She was a woman above reproach.

When Fauntroy made the announcement on a Saturday that he would step down, campaign guru Donna Brazile ran around the corner to Eleanor's house to tell her about the opening and urge her to consider the seat.

"Donna's a true political expert," Eleanor says, describing this woman who would become central to her political life. "I met Donna when she directed several marches on Washington and knew her from campaigns. Her reputation as an organizer is legendary. When we started the National Black Women's Political Organization, she was executive director; I was on the board and did a lot of their legal work."

After Donna, others called with the same thought. Quickly, Donna gathered persuasive support. "I called Mary Frances Berry and she thought it was a great idea," Donna says. "I called Lawrence Guyot and he thought it was a good idea. I talked to Marion Barry, Judy Lichtman, Karen Mulhauser . . . I called all over the city. Everybody thought it was a great idea."

Eleanor was not convinced.

Donna began an intensive effort, offering to be campaign manager without pay, arguing that Eleanor would bring backbone and prestige to the needy city. The two began to meet regularly to discuss possibilities and soon the buzz was on the street.

"Edward opposed it for a long time," Eleanor says, still seeming puzzled. "It was very unusual for him to be against something like this because he had been just the opposite when it came to my career. He had been very much a booster."

"I'm local and you're national," he even told her, uncharacteristically. Edward was so upset about the prospect that when Eleanor conferred daily with Donna, the two talked upstairs in Eleanor's study at the top of the stairs, out of Edward's way. Or they met elsewhere.

All through the spring Eleanor pondered the decision but kept her thoughts from Edward, who believed her desire to run was dissipating. Convincing Eleanor was no easy job. "Knowing Eleanor the way I know Eleanor," Donna chuckles, "she would second-guess me and put me through the rigorous process of being in a trial, where she is judge and jury too. I went over to her house being fully prepared to argue my case to her. I had to convince her she could win, that it was worth it, how much money had to be raised, that she could do it."

"It was one of the most difficult decisions of my entire life," Eleanor says, evoking that momentous spring. "We did a poll and it showed I didn't have as much local name recognition as I should. But I'd been thinking about public policy since I was a child. People said, 'A seat comes open, you're a Washingtonian, you've been an administration official, you're nationally known. What are you going to do about this city?' "

For weeks she stewed. Georgetown colleague Wendy Williams

remembers, "We rode to a faculty retreat in her cheapo car; it could barely get up the hill. She said, 'People are saying I should run. I'm not sure I'm going to do it. It's not me.' "

"I came with great distrust for government," Eleanor confirms. "The civil rights movement was real distrustful of anybody who was an insider. 'They all were apologists,' we thought. There weren't any of us on the inside to begin with, so we figured that the inside wasn't a good place to be. [Yet] we were fighting to get people on the inside. But you had to find conditions under which you could go on the inside without selling out."

But she began to believe that "representing a city like the District, a very progressive town, far from putting me in conflict with my values, would probably allow me to carry out my values. It's a wonderful jurisdiction. The blacks and the whites have the same politics, unlike cities like New York or Chicago. Here there's not a dime's worth of difference across the eight wards on the major issues.

"One ingredient that was not in the decision, which may appear unusual, was money. My congressional salary would be maybe a third of what I was earning. So it meant a considerable draw-down in income. But money has never meant anything to me. In fact, the money I made I didn't even have time to spend. And I didn't live extravagantly, unlike people who live at the top of their income.

"Leaving the university was a real consideration. I also had to consider whether I'd win. Was this worth the kind of effort that you put in?"

The time approached when she had to decide: people were writing checks and petitions to get on the ballot were coming out soon. She believed that Edward ultimately would be with her. Despite his resistance she had good reason: her husband had not simply tolerated her public career; he'd encouraged it.

One evening Donna ran into WAMU political commentator Mark Plotkin on the street. He said he was going to leak Eleanor's candidacy, not as speculation but as fact.

"What's the truth?" he demanded. Donna had promised Eleanor that she wouldn't discuss the candidacy publicly until Eleanor got her husband on board.

"I can't confirm or deny," was all she could reply.

Shortly thereafter, Mark bumped into Edward at the airport. Edward was definitive.

"She ain't running."

Mark called Donna to get the truth, and Donna called Eleanor. Realizing the moment had come for decision, Eleanor resolved to go forward and go public. On April 20, she filed papers with the Federal Election Commission for the D.C. delegate seat.

"All hell broke out at home," Donna remembers. "Ed was livid . . . I tried my best to avoid Ed. I was the culprit, I was behind Eleanor 100 percent. If it meant Ed being upset, so be it. Get over it. It just didn't matter to me. The bigger good mattered. That's why Eleanor and I are so close; we both love public policy."

"Donna thought the campaign was a fabulous idea and took it over," Eleanor says. "I wouldn't have done it without her. I didn't know what I was doing. She took care of monies, she took care of every bill. She raised a lot herself because she had very deep roots in politics. She even raised money from members of Congress. She knew them all, she's been involved in national politics for so long. She could call up Gephardt and say, 'I need a thousand dollars.' She knew him better than I did.

"I might have been the mentor to her before, but I have to tell you, the mentor in this campaign became this girl who could have been my daughter! She is a rare combination of organizational smarts and pure unadulterated gray matter. That is to say, she's brilliant! Equipped even with a photographic memory."

People knew Eleanor through NPR, books or magazines and *MacNeil-Lehrer*. But they didn't know her personally. They did know Donna.

"I have always needed strong people around me because I am a strong person," Eleanor elaborates. "Donna has changed my mind on many a thing. I argue because I feel strongly. I need staff who can say, 'Nope, I really think that's wrong.' " With Donna she had a match.

A campaign volunteer describes them: "The congresswoman without Donna is like Abercrombie without Fitch, or Abbott without Costello. The congresswoman is the intellectual and Donna is the brass knuckles political. Neither is afraid to speak her mind, sometimes in short words. And Donna will tell you herself she put the 'B' in bitch. When they disagree they have very forthright debates, sometimes bordering on the obscene." Donna once bluntly explained to the

Washington Post the narrow range of options she saw for black women: "I had to decide if I'd be a bitch or a whore. I chose bitch. I'd have to be strong, tough, abrasive."

Eleanor's candidacy scared off much of the potential competition, but the race was still a six-person Democratic primary, tantamount in this Democratic city to the election. In addition to Betty Ann Kane, a white councilwoman, Eleanor had four rivals, all prominent African Americans: former D.C. Council chair Sterling Tucker, former school board member Barbara Lett Simmons, Joseph Yeldell, a Barry administration official, and congressional aide Donald Temple.

Some African Americans feared the crowded field would split the black vote and give Kane, the only white candidate, a plurality in the September primary. Kane, a neighbor of Eleanor's in racially mixed Ward Six, was the early front-runner. Money rolled into her campaign. Until Eleanor announced.

Kane was viewed—for better and worse—as the local politician. Some residents were afraid Eleanor would be too academic, more interested in theory than the brass tacks of politics. But despite her scant local experience, Eleanor's national prestige and long-standing relationships with Congress and key rights leaders cast her as the one to beat.

Joe Rauh, the lawyer she'd worked with in Mississippi Freedom Democratic Party days, hailed her as someone with "an entree on Capitol Hill that very few people in the District would have." The *Washington Post* enthused in an editorial, "Now that Mr. Fauntroy has decided to step aside, someone else will take over with a most critical mission: to show what more a new voice on Capitol Hill might do for a city whose well-being depends so heavily on congressional understanding . . . he has proposed someone of exceptional local and national standing as a candidate to succeed him: Eleanor Holmes Norton. Her entry into this contest would bring valuable attention to the campaign—as well as to the possibilities for important public service by a knowledgeable, respected envoy to Congress."

Eleanor's vulnerability was her lack of local experience. "When's the last time you've been to an ANC [Advisory Neighborhood Council] meeting?" she was taunted. Radio station WOL owner Cathy Hughes bluntly gave one of Eleanor's advance people, Philip Pannell, her advice.

"I want to see the sister, I want to meet her. She's got to stop looking

like a dowdy law professor. She needs to go shopping with me." Soon
Eleanor morphed from an academic to a candidate with a new haircut,
more makeup and accessories.

She also learned to work a room. As an intellectual, her inclination
was to discuss each topic in depth, giving the historical antecedents.

"Press the flesh and move on!" Pannell told her. "If someone wants
more details, tell them we'll send a position paper."

On May 5, the campaign, braving an oncoming thunderstorm,
kicked off at Eleanor's old elementary school in the heart of the black
community at Georgia and Irving Street, NW. Before a diverse crowd,
Eleanor invoked the escaped slave Richard Holmes as proof of deep
District roots, and cited her long congressional history: "I have been
unanimously confirmed by the Senate." The festive occasion was full of
music; Eleanor delightedly joined in the electric slide, her signature
song. People noticed Edward's absence; many in the crowd understood
this was an historic day. "I was proud to be there," remembers law professor Wendy Williams. "I took my son and I said to him, 'This is an
exciting thing.' "

Eleanor soon appeared at several alma maters, often calling up the
memory of her inspirational great-grandfather who walked over the
bridge from Virginia to Washington. "The Holmes family has been here
ever since," she told the crowds.

Eleanor also presented herself to the polarized city as a unifier.

"As I have spent my life building bridges and coalitions among people of all backgrounds, I can build a bridge between the hometown D.C.
and the Capitol." Winning endorsements and donations from every
major sector of the population, she had white feminists volunteering
alongside black community activists and civil rights veterans. Labor
unionists filled envelopes side-by-side with upper-class residents from
wealthy neighborhoods.

People knew Eleanor from her frequent commentaries on National
Public Radio and knew "this was an honest-to-goodness, dyed-in-the-
wool feminist running for Congress." Eleanor laughs. "Somebody who
had been keynote speaker at NOW conventions and National Women's
Political Caucus Conventions. They knew me from the EEOC, from the
sexual harassment guidelines."

Pro-choice organizations were so enthusiastic they broke their tradition of withholding support when there were several pro-choice women

candidates. The National Abortion Rights Action League contributed $5,000. Kate Michelman, the executive director, explained, "There are other impressive pro-choice candidates in this race, but the fact that D.C.'s representative cannot vote makes that person's ability to lead a compelling consideration. There, Eleanor Holmes Norton stands alone."

EMILY's List likewise asked its 3,000 members to support her with $100 contributions. "This is a difficult situation," acknowledged executive director Wendy Sherman, but "Eleanor Holmes Norton has been such an extraordinary leader that we felt it was our obligation to recommend her over other women."

The D.C. Coalition of Black Gay Men and Women released its first-time rating of candidates for delegate: Eleanor was their top choice. And the old civil rights coalition came to her aid. In July, Eleanor got backing from the influential American Federation of Government Employees, from autoworkers, steelworkers, nurses (while the doctors' PAC supported Kane), teachers and the Metropolitan Council AFL-CIO. The council also pledged a telephone bank and poll workers.

"Girl, I raised so much money. Oh God, was it hard! You work from dawn to dusk, not knowing if you were going to win or lose. All over D.C. I raised money because I had track to go back."

The campaign attracted scores of enthusiastic volunteers. Her kitchen cabinet included former SNCC staffer Lawrence Guyot, feminist fund-raiser Ellen Malcolm, Democratic pollster Celinda Lake and local activists like Betty King and Howard Croft from Ward Six, Eleanor's home base. People called from all over the city to say, "What do you need—money or people?"

The campaign occupied an entire building on Stanton Park, at 513 C Street, NE. Ten rooms painted green were jammed with sagging—and on humid days, soggy—cardboard desks, mismatched plastic and metal stacking chairs, cast-off office furniture, old pizza trays and chicken buckets. One room overflowed with stacks of posters and signs.

In the evenings the office came alive; twenty or thirty people moved into ward meetings or phone banks, and always a child or two waited downstairs. Upstairs the phone-bank table partitions—nondescript green, flecked with enamel—echoed the shabby color scheme, relieved only by posted sign-up sheets, homemade notices for events, and Eleanor's red, white and blue posters: "ELECT ELEANOR HOLMES NORTON, DEMOCRAT" (the city had 90 percent Democratic registration).

Fund-raiser Vic Basile's story is typical of the enthusiasm Eleanor generated. "I knew Eleanor by reputation and had been a fan, but never met her. Fauntroy had made this horribly homophobic reference to the gay community, comparing our rights to penguin rights ... Eleanor satisfied me that she was absolutely comfortable with our issues. I got very excited and decided I would do a fund-raiser for her at my house, and also that I would try to deliver as much of the gay vote as I could. I kept calling—I have a fairly big Rolodex—to say, 'We should publicly endorse her, and would you come to the fund-raiser?' "

Basile also led a fight at the Stein Club, the influential local gay Democratic club, to get an endorsement. More members turned out for the meeting than they had in years, and the vote was close: Eleanor lost by four votes to Kane, who, as a City Council member, had long ties to many gay activists. "Eleanor came away from it looking very good even without the endorsement," Basile believes. "I think lots of gay people voted for her."

As always, Eleanor attracted varied followers. Howard Croft, a respected Board of Parole member, statehood leader and scholar, coordinated what would become the close-knit Ward Six "palace guard." He recalls that Kane had asked him to work on *her* campaign.

"I said 'No.' On the council she had tried to get rid of rent control, so I'm certainly not going to work for her! Then Eleanor ran. I certainly couldn't think of anyone else who could have been better, or even her equal. When Eleanor ran, that said to me we had an opportunity to have a member in the House who would embody the kind of competency we have in the District of Columbia."

Eleanor's campaign drew experienced local organizers like Mary Preston. "I met her standing in the sun, getting signatures to put me on the ballot," remembers Eleanor. "She got so many signatures; she's one of these great local talents with organizational smarts that every campaign treasures. 'Y'all come and give Eleanor money.' "

Philip Pannell, another longtime activist already working two jobs, was from Ward Eight, the poorest, blackest part of Washington; he became its ward coordinator. He'd admired Eleanor since his teenage years in Harlem when she was commissioner of human rights. "When I got the call to go to her house it was an honor. I was calling her Ms. Norton. Within five minutes she said, 'Would you please call me Eleanor.' She is my 'shero.' "

Pannell crammed twenty-five people into his one-bedroom apartment for Eleanor's first Ward Eight meet-and-greet, and helped her navigate in what would prove to be a critical community.

The campaign treated its volunteers to barbecues at headquarters—chips, ribs and pep talk, with Eleanor personally thanking her crew, a gesture candidates didn't often make. But mostly the office saw little of her; she was constantly campaigning, though occasionally volunteers saw her walk by to an office in the back where she rested on the floor.

By mid-July Eleanor raised $117,250, considerably more than any rival. Contributors included Vernon Jordan, Senator Moynihan, Democratic lobbyist Anne Wexler, Bill and Camille Cosby, Gloria Steinem, and NBA head David Stern, a law school classmate of Edward's.

"We campaigned during the day in the black community and raised money in the white community at night," laughs Donna. "The whole city went up in temporary ecstasy . . . we worked it all, we exploited every part of Eleanor's past: the civil rights struggle, Georgetown, her New York years. It was a great campaign, with a wonderful precinct organization intact." In July, Eleanor turned in 8,000 petitions; she needed only 2,000 to get on the ballot.

Eleanor was everywhere, and she mesmerized crowds. "She's very good on her feet." Basile smiles admiringly. "I remember the way she described civil rights for gays and lesbians. It's a very thoughtful description that I had actually never quite heard anybody articulate as well before." Eleanor consistently called gay and lesbian rights part of the unfinished agenda of the civil rights movement.

"She doesn't suffer fools gladly," adds Basile, "and she did yell at me once. I was trying to get her $5,000 from the Human Rights Campaign. They had the money. And frankly, they were getting an enormous amount of pressure to either support Betty Ann Kane or to stay out of the race. At one point I just wanted to throw up my hands."

"Eleanor, you've got a lot of money!" Basile told her. "Do you really need the money? This is proving to be a little difficult. How badly do you want it?"

"Of course I need the money! And I want the endorsement!" Eleanor shot back.

"So we got it," Basile says. "She should have had it."

Eleanor and Kane went head-to-head in campaign appearance after appearance. Eleanor pledged to work for statehood, a strategy many regarded as the best solution to their fiscal and self-governance problems. She charged that Kane's statehood support "has been tepid and the people of Washington know it."

Kane depicted Eleanor as an outsider who stood on the sidelines during congressional battles over District voting rights, didn't back gay rights activists at Georgetown University and didn't vote in five of the past thirteen local elections. Kane contended that despite Eleanor's lofty national reputation, "Norton has done nothing of substance on local issues."

The attempt to portray Eleanor as an outsider, despite her family's four generations in Washington, actually backfired. Many wanted an outsider; local officials weren't doing their jobs. Sharon Pratt Dixon (who would marry and change her name to Kelly) ran for mayor as an outsider, and although Eleanor didn't campaign that way, she benefited from the label.

Eleanor fired back, refuting Kane's charges and attacking her record: opposition to tenants' rights and other progressive issues. "Kane has been shooting blanks ever since I got in this race. It is clear they are a cover for her voting record . . . Kane's political philosophy is not in keeping with the majority of the people of the District of Columbia."

As summer wore on, with its blistering, humid days, and the contest heated up, Eleanor seemed to have the perfect campaign in place. Volunteers poured in from every major District constituency and she was raising buckets of money.

During the summer the city was obsessed with Barry's trial. Voters relentlessly followed the media spectacle of drugs, crime and illicit sex, all featuring their mayor. But by late summer, the focus turned to the delegate's race.

On August 29, a *Post* poll showed Eleanor leading by a large margin: she had cut into Kane's support in the white community as the choice of 42 percent of white voters surveyed, compared with 27 percent for Kane. As Kane's base eroded, the prestigious *Post* was rumored to be on the verge of an endorsement.

A week later, on September 5, Eleanor became the first to launch an extensive television campaign. Her ads stressed her deep Washington roots, Carter administration service and civil rights advocacy. And the public forums continued. At one ("the thousandth one," Eleanor told the press) the week before the primary, the candidates addressed twenty-five students at Georgetown University Law Center. They reiterated their positions: All were for statehood and for the District to get more money—and autonomy—from Congress. The question was: Who could deliver?

On September 7, the Friday before the primary, Michael Abramowitz wrote in the *Post,* "The Democratic primary campaign to succeed Walter E. Fauntroy as the District's delegate to Congress has turned into a feisty referendum on Eleanor Holmes Norton, and whether she can use her credentials as a national civil rights leader to restore the city's tarnished image on Capitol Hill."

She was indisputably the front-runner. Until a few hours later that night when "all hell broke loose." The next morning, three days before the primary, Eleanor's reputation was so tarnished it seemed unlikely she had any prestige left over to lend her beleaguered city.

At 5:30 P.M. on Friday, September 7, someone anonymously faxed the *Post* and every other media outlet a Certificate of Delinquency disclosing that Eleanor and Edward had not filed city income taxes for seven years.

Abramowitz immediately called Donna, who put him off and raced to Eleanor's house. She was out campaigning. Donna breathlessly told Edward about the call.

"We have to call the paper, they're on deadline. It's going on seven P.M. Come on, I need to know the truth."

She asked repeatedly, while the *Post* called and paged. "I couldn't get it out of him, confirm or deny," she recalls that frantic moment. "I kept saying, 'I've got to call Eleanor.' "

"Relax, wait, I'll get some wine," Edward said.

"Ed never really came clean with me that night."

Eleanor, coming from a fund-raiser in Bethesda at a physician's house, was on her way to a meet-and-greet in Ward Three when the news hit. As she pulled up, television reporter Bob Strickland was there.

"Wow, we're getting TV coverage for a meet-and-greet!" Philip Pannell remembers thinking.

When Eleanor stepped out of the car, Strickland asked, "How are you doing, Ms. Norton?"

"Well, the sun is down but we're still working, we have one more place to go tonight," Eleanor replied and began to walk toward the house. But Strickland stopped her and jammed the mike in her face.

"Do you have any comment on the fact that you and your husband haven't paid taxes for a number of years?"

"What are you talking about?" Eleanor was blank.

Strickland produced the fax, showing the Certificate of Delinquency. "I just don't understand, what is this?" she stumbled.

Eleanor called home, with the TV camera still trained on her. Donna answered and Eleanor screamed, "Put Edward on the phone!"

Edward simply said, "Come home."

But the campaigner went off to one more house meeting.

"I don't understand," she repeated in the car, shaking, while she kept asking Pannell, "What is going on?"

In a fog, she whipped through the Georgetown meet-and-greet, where no one had heard the news yet. "I had come to talk to a group," she says. "People were raising money for me, and I had to go and talk to them."

Finally Eleanor got home. As she walked in the front door she yelled out, "How could you do this to me, Edward, how could you do this to me?"

"What do you mean?" he asked, before admitting that the story was true.

That night Cartwright Moore was out leafleting the bars on Pennsylvania Avenue for a campaign event the next day with Betty Shabazz, Malcolm X's widow, down from New York to campaign. "I got strange comments from people who were watching TV," he says. Bewildered, he joined other stunned volunteers at the campaign office. Most didn't believe the story. They knew their candidate. Shirking her tax obligation didn't seem credible or possible.

Donna called key supporters to inform them of the breaking news. Everyone was in shock. Rene Redwood, pollster Celinda Lake's associate, recalls, "When we took candidates as clients we asked these kinds of questions—'Have your taxes been paid?'—so we would know the secrets. There wasn't anything in Eleanor's closet. We were stunned because we'd asked this question."

In a series of meetings, some one-on-one, some in small groups

("None of us slept that night"), Donna, Celinda Lake and Rene Redwood and others discussed what to do, trying to assess whether the news was true and how feasible an ongoing candidacy could be.

"We thought Eleanor could still win," recalls Redwood, "because her numbers had been so strong, the fact that she didn't know was such a believable scenario, and there were so many candidates in the field."

When Howard Croft came into the office on Saturday morning and heard the news, Donna was on the telephone with Eleanor, who adamantly refused to get out of bed for the planned appearance with Betty Shabazz.

"I started talking to Eleanor on the phone," says Croft. "I remember getting angry, saying, 'You have to get up and go.' "

Eleanor didn't want to do it. Donna told her, "We're hemorrhaging badly in the white community; they don't believe you. We have to put out another statement today."

Still the devastated Eleanor wouldn't get up. Finally Donna went over to her house.

"You can't quit now."

"How can I face people?" this very private woman replied. "I'm so embarrassed."

But people like Alexis Herman, Ron Brown and Vernon Jordan came out, asking, "What can we do?"

"Just hold people together," Donna told them. "Meanwhile," she says, "I was trying to hold Eleanor together with Elmer's Glue. She was coming apart personally, her marriage was coming apart. I couldn't even tell her my private thoughts: 'If I could kill him for you I would.' I had to help her get out of bed and tell her supporters, 'I'm still running.'

"You had to prove every goddamn thing to her," Donna adds, "but it makes you a better person. I never go into an argument now without knowing all the facts."

Pushed by Howard Croft, Josh Williams, head of the Central Labor Council, Lake—"You've got the votes"—and others, Eleanor decided to stay in the race and to fight back hard, though observers noticed her visible pain. She seemed near tears in several public meetings that weekend and her hands were shaking. Everyone could see how distraught the drawn candidate was. Her usual rapid energy had fizzled.

But she made it to the rally featuring Shabazz and Ward Eight's

Councilwoman Wilhamena Rolark, back at Bruce Monroe Elementary School in Northwest. Eleanor stood in front of the microphone and explained what had happened: Edward kept the books, Edward had told her the taxes were filed, and he lied about it. "What I did every year was actually nothing except sign forms."

Some disbelieving volunteers left the campaign immediately, but in the midst of the mob scene, with reporters hounding her and other candidates booing and hissing, most stood by Eleanor. Taking a leap of faith, they said they believed her, she was neither a tax cheat nor an irresponsible person, and they still wanted her to represent the District.

"For me," one volunteer explains, "it was realizing she was the same person on Saturday as she was on Friday, I just knew a little bit more about her husband. My opinion of him had been confirmed. She hadn't changed."

After the rally, supporters showed their commitment in various ways. A woman in Ward Five did a motorcade; one volunteer brought flowers. Howard Croft laughs, "I had a sound truck. We were going to show the goddamn flag. Lou [Zapata] and I got in the sound truck, played Tracy Chapman "Talkin 'bout a Revolution," and played it all over the city. The way to deal with this was to take to the streets."

Most campaign workers were outraged at the anonymous, eleventh-hour attack and many were bitter about the way Edward had set Eleanor up. Invoking the television movie *The Burning Bed,* Rene Redwood says, "I would have done the Farrah Fawcett thing, set the bed on fire."

Most volunteers had inferred by Edward's absence from the campaign that he was not happy about Eleanor's candidacy. Philip Pannell had thought it odd that Edward wouldn't sign his wife's petition when the campaign first gathered signatures. ("I thought he would be the first to sign.") Edward had explained his objection: this would take time from their marriage and "Eleanor is more suited to be a professor."

Some of Eleanor's supporters surmised that Edward was having difficulty dealing with a celebrity spouse while his legal career appeared to have topped out. Several speculated that Eleanor's breadwinner role might be the basis of Edward's opposition. Her disclosure statement showed she earned $328,000 in 1989, while his earnings were negative: a business loss of $10,000. Congressional salary would be $120,000.

Years later, Eleanor sits in her kitchen at a white-tiled counter, struggling to understand.

"I still haven't quite figured out what happened." Her face creases with pain. "Especially since Edward was excellent at paying bills. He did math in his head. He paid them promptly. He would say, 'I'm going to pay this' because he considered it a real waste to—and he's absolutely right—not only to pay penalties, but to pay a little bit at a time. So not only did I leave it to him; leaving it to him worked. We had an excellent credit rating.

"It's hard to unravel what happened except that it becomes clear he contested an earlier bill." It was a $10,750 charge, which Edward would later explain he thought should have been $3,700. The bill kept coming and "That's when I got angry and crazy," he later told the *Post*.

"And it apparently grew for seven years," Eleanor continues. The city sent six notices of delinquency, which Eleanor's campaign discovered and later displayed to the press.

"It is certainly the case that he knew it was building, because he knew he hadn't paid it initially. And I ended up having to pay a huge amount of money from a little bit of money. Because you build up penalties, and you build up beyond penalties. What's the other thing called? Penalties and something else, so it's a huge amount of money."

It is totally unlike this razor-sharp brain not to be able to come up with the word "interest." It's clear a decade later that this is still excruciatingly painful. "He knew about the initial thing. He knew it had not been paid. And he did not tell me about it. He let me go out and run and he did not tell me."

"My heart went out to her," says Rene Redwood. "They had been married twenty-three, twenty-four years. You have that kind of implicit trust in your partner, you don't want to find out these things from a fax. But she is such a strong woman. She held her head up high, she was honest with the people, with reporters. At that point I knew she could win this. We've not seen that kind of integrity in this city. You take it, you admit it. She sought to make the remedies and then to move forward."

"And that was the awful night," says Cartwright Moore. "It hurt the congresswoman, well, very badly. Because her proudest possession is her reputation."

While some—her strong core—rallied around Eleanor with unconditional support, others were furious. Her rivals lost no time.

"The last thing we need is another person without personal integrity representing us in Congress. It really does smack of Marion Barry to me," Kane contended.

Rival Sterling Tucker was "flabbergasted. I don't possibly see how she can stay in the race. How can she be fighting with the federal government on the issue of its tax payment to us, when she paid not at all? . . . With all this talk about a new beginning and new credibility, how can we send someone to Congress who is the antithesis of that?"

Her numbers went shooting down and the campaign started to unravel.

"I was shunned by many white people," says Eleanor ruefully. "They were originally major support. It was heartbreaking to lose it. Many people couldn't believe that this very competent, educated woman would leave the finances entirely to her husband. But busy feminists should have been the first to understand the division of labor!

"Here I had two children, one of them disabled. Everybody knew because my life was an open book by the time I ran. I was on three corporate boards, I had become a tenured law professor. I couldn't have possibly handled it without some help. And the major help that Edward gave me—I did the carpooling to school, took them to the doctors—the major help really was in his caring for the children and financial matters. I didn't even look at an envelope. I left them on the sideboard. He did all the investing. It was a very rational division of labor." She knew Edward understood government regulations. He had chaired the D.C. Board of Elections and Ethics.

Once the campaign regrouped over the weekend and decided to go forward full blast, the two days before the primary were spent in a blitz of appearances. Everyone worked double-time. "Now we really had to hit the pavement, we were in sixth gear on a five-gear bike," says Redwood. "Now we had to reestablish her integrity."

They were back on track, but with a shift in strategy. This coalition campaign looked at the numbers and saw a gaping racial divide. Eleanor, accustomed to white support, attended anxiously to the sudden white drop-off; Donna and her strategists turned their attention to the black base. While most whites disbelieved Eleanor's tax story, most African Americans found it credible: she trusted her husband, he was supposed to do it, he didn't, that was it. Croft says, "In Ward Six my strategy became that if we could turn out a large vote east of the river and in Northeast [mostly black areas], we could withstand a major loss in Capitol Hill." A new focus emerged: concentrate on the black wards.

Now it was going to be a campaign the old-fashioned way: out late at night and up early in the morning, working for every single vote. As the city's white leadership started to denounce Eleanor, black support mushroomed overnight. That Sunday morning, church sermons all over town claimed Eleanor as a hometown girl. "She's one of us. We're proud of her, and we won't let them take her down."

"Everything we'd been preaching throughout the campaign began to catch fire," Donna exults. "For the first time, I saw that we could win the whole black community, and win with that. Almost overnight, Dick Gregory, Jesse Jackson . . . they all came out. Civil rights took over the campaign. It became a civil rights crusade."

And Eleanor "got her groove back." In an hour-long interview with the *Post* on Sunday, she was defiant. "I have a lifetime record of integrity that can withstand the storm." Despite appearing weary, the warrior was back on track and didn't allow herself any further collapse.

Edward left that morning for New York on business, so was unavailable for comment. But Eleanor told a group of neighborhood activists from the Wisconsin Avenue corridor that she lay in bed with Edward in their darkened bedroom Saturday night and discussed the crisis. "People were on the edge of their seats," Joel Odum told the *Post*. "I think she got converts because she spoke about it as a personal tragedy."

Still, while not concealing her pain, nor deviating from her insistence that she had signed blank returns each year for Edward to fill and file, she invariably concluded: ultimate accountability was hers alone.

"I accept responsibility," she told the public. "They were my taxes. I take full responsibility for this matter, which I should have monitored personally."

On Monday she held a rally at Freedom Plaza.

"No dirty tricks can drive Eleanor Holmes Norton out of this race! Those who thought they could chase this woman out of this race with some anonymous faxes after the close of business Friday don't know a fighter when they see one!"

By Monday, the day before the primary, the weekend bombshell hit the consciousness of people who had only watched the Redskins' game—the home opener—the day before. At a news conference outside the Stanton Park campaign headquarters just blocks from home, Edward acknowledged that he had realized the tax problem could jeopardize his wife's candidacy. But "it was a matter of, if I make this payment and I'm in some kind of communication with the District government, then somehow or another this becomes a public matter. It was my intention, as soon as this primary was over, whether she won or lost, to pay the taxes." He added, "I would ask those of you who are disposed toward Eleanor to not turn away from her because of who I am and what I did."

That same day Eleanor hired an accountant, filed taxes, severed her finances from Edward's, and began to pay off the debt, although confusion would continue for weeks, on the part of the city and her accountant, about how much was actually due. (Over the next two months she would pay almost $90,000, most for interest and penalties.) That day the *Post* endorsed Betty Ann Kane, saying Eleanor's failure to file D.C. income tax returns was "not just disabling, it is disqualifying."

As public criticism mounted, Eleanor and her supporters aggressively battled the tide. Energized by combat, Eleanor appeared on the WOL morning show of Cathy Hughes, who asserted there was a racially motivated effort underway to undermine the campaign. Eleanor contended that she didn't believe she was a victim of conspiracy, but acknowledged the concern within the black community about a strong black woman with impressive credentials being "subject to ridicule."

In the last hours before the crucial primary, Eleanor's people intensified their efforts. They worked the phone banks, leafleted and canvassed. By refocusing their get-out-the-vote efforts on black neighborhoods, they virtually conceded the white vote—about a third of the electorate—to Kane.

On election eve, Eleanor returned to headquarters to thank her volunteers and encourage them for the long, difficult day ahead although privately, she told Donna, she was afraid she would lose. But her campaigners were avid.

"That night we got up in the middle of the night, put up signs in all the wards, and got to polling places by 6:30 to hand out literature as people were going in to vote," recalls volunteer Rosemary Addy. "And it was cold."

*   *   *

As the chilly morning of Tuesday, September 11, dawned, volunteers working the polls in white neighborhoods heard angry cries as soon as voters saw their NORTON signs.

"Tell her to pay her taxes!"

"Tax cheat!" And worse. The taunts continued all day.

But on primary morning in black neighborhoods, "when we got in the streets," says Donna, "it went from a campaign to a crusade. Everybody from the civil rights movement got out that day and they stormed the city to elect Eleanor. Cathy Hughes stayed on the radio for almost twenty-four hours, reminding people they had an obligation. We campaigned like hell. On election day we went from pillar to post begging people to support us." The campaign pulled out all the stops to get people in Wards Seven and Eight to vote. Philip Pannell had been up all night; after returning home from work at midnight he'd gone directly out to post flyers.

In the morning hundreds of volunteers covered Washington's 140 polling stations. They called, drove voters, knocked on doors, and made sure seniors got to the polls. Donna got "the meanest, biggest vans she could find," says Croft. "We looked like an army."

But the tax revelation gave Kane new ground. By evening, when volunteers left the polls, "we thought we were probably going to lose," says Addy. The white wards, with more retired voters, had voted heavily in the morning. When their numbers came in late in the day, Kane was in the lead; news outlets started to report she was winning.

That night, as Eleanor's supporters trooped in to the Washington Plaza Hotel, most of them exhausted, dirty, and discouraged, Donna kept telling them, "We're gonna win, I know we are!"

White volunteers came in with war stories: they'd been vilified all day, with terrible slurs flung at their candidate. Eleanor, who had traveled to polling places throughout the city, had heard the anger directed at her personally. She knew she was unpopular.

But black poll workers reported an entirely different story: Barry, Jesse Jackson, Dick Gregory, and other leaders had been out working the polls. The support of voters in African-American wards was palpable.

"I am telling you," says Eleanor, "when we went around to the polls, the black people were standing in line." When polls closed those in line could vote.

"I'll never forget, I went to the hotel, I didn't know what to think. Got in the bed, I was so tired. Out in the suite, there were lots of people . . . There cannot have been a bigger battle in my life than that. There cannot have been. I was completely exhausted." Eleanor just crawled into bed.

"I'm cold. And we're going to lose," she told Donna. "Nobody ever beats the morning boxes." She'd just learned this electoral tidbit.

"We're going to win," Donna repeated.

At eight P.M. returns showed Eleanor losing. When Donna went down to the watch party in the ballroom network anchor Rene Poussant told her, "We're going live at nine from the headquarters."

"We're gonna win," Donna responded with a grin.

"No you're not, you can't. The morning boxes are in."

But when Donna went live on TV at nine o'clock, saying, "The tide is going to turn," the crowd behind her started to chant, "The tide is turning! The tide is turning!"

Donna raced back to Eleanor upstairs to reassure her again. The suite had filled with friends and supporters; now family flowed in. When Katherine arrived, Eleanor's face softened, even in this moment of anxiety. Campaign workers poured in, most coming directly from a day at the polls.

"I was still in my stinky T-shirt," Redwood says. "She was sitting up on the bed. She was so quiet, I'd never seen her that quiet."

At ten the tide did start to turn. Still Eleanor worried.

"What about the absentee ballots?"

"Those came in before the tax news came in," her manager chortled. "That closed at five P.M. Friday. They timed it wrong."

Meanwhile Eleanor was still in bed, Donna remembers, working on her concession speech.

"It's a victory speech, Eleanor! You've got to talk about what you're going to do!"

At 10:45 P.M., television news projected Eleanor the winner. She got out of bed. "By this time, Eleanor went from being quiet," Redwood recalls, "to being Ms. Norton. At that point I called her the congresswoman. Once you win the primary in the District, it's yours."

As Eleanor began to feel the elation of triumph, her energy returned. She got up, put on a dressy skirt and blouse, applied her makeup, and began to prepare a heartfelt victory speech.

Downstairs in the ballroom, hundreds of people sprawled around tables covered with white cloths. The mood, at first subdued, became electric as Eleanor started to pull ahead. When the giant TV screen first showed a victory projection, a colossal cheer erupted.

"It was frightening. The place went wild," says one volunteer. "It was a wonderful scene."

People started to hug, shout, cry and dance. They screamed and sobbed; relief, elation, and regret for Eleanor's public humiliation, with the wreckage it signified in her personal life, all mixed in the poignant moment.

When Eleanor came in "like a conquering hero," more cheers exploded. She pushed through the noisy crowd, shaking confetti from her hair and clasping hands as she moved through the mass of dancing supporters. At the podium Eleanor stood in front of her people with absolute poise, thanking those "who never lost their faith and confidence in me." Supporters hugged through their tears and the music broke in with the electric slide, Eleanor's signature campaign dance. ("The electric slide made people happy, gave them something to do besides listen to speeches. Everybody was doing it.")

When the music started up on this evening of triumph atop tragedy, Eleanor raised her arms, began to clap, and smoothly moved into the slide, just as she always did. Lean forward, step back, twirl and slide. Each person in the room, old folks, children, everyone slid, stamped, clapped and leaned in one gigantic, pulsating, radiant mass. After the tension of the last four days, it was a wonderful release. The Eleanor who had danced her way through junior high and Dunbar was in her element.

Later, after most people stumbled happily home, some of the intrepid Ward Six palace guard continued the celebration by going to the home of a virulent Kane supporter who had repeatedly made derogatory statements about Eleanor. Several volunteers gleefully remember their revenge. "That night we took one of the vans to her house around one A.M., turned the volume up as loud as we could and started singing, 'We survived the fax attack.' "

Intensive, old-fashioned campaigning, coupled with a revival of the civil rights spirit, had triumphed. Eleanor won six of the District's eight wards, losing only Wards Two and Three, the whitest sections of the city. Those losses, however, were painful. It was unusual that someone with her militant reputation and black sense of the world had developed strong white support; in 1990 there were few black public figures with such broad crossover credibility. Yet in the end, it was the black people of the city who put her in office.

Ward Six's Howard Croft explains the loyalty, after Barry's demise. "In the context of a people being demoralized, Eleanor was a form of redemption: 'We are better than what you say we are, what you think we are.'" He adds, with exactly the same words Liz Carpenter used to describe Ann Richards's support in Texas, "Eleanor comes out of us, she is one of us."

When all the votes were counted, Eleanor won 40 percent, with 33 percent for Kane. (Eleanor's vote—46,620—was almost 4,500 more than Sharon Pratt Dixon's winning total for the Democratic mayoral nomination.) Trailing far behind were the three others still running: Sterling Tucker, Joseph Yeldell and Donald Temple. Jesse Jackson also won the Democratic primary to become a "shadow senator," a D.C. funded lobbying position to encourage congressional support for statehood.

In the Republican primary, former Reagan administration official Harry Singleton won. That meant that in November, Eleanor would face Singleton and George X Cure, a member of the Nation of Islam running as an independent. Most assumed Eleanor would handily win the general election.

The day after the primary, Eleanor continued to campaign hard. She wanted to regain her lost support in vote-rich Ward Three. (Polls before the tax scandal showed her with over 40 percent of the Ward Three vote; on primary day, she received less than 15 percent.) She wanted to be the voice of all the District constituencies "to lead the city the way I want to from the Hill." The dogged campaigner was back on the streets amid cries of "Tax cheat!" and "Shame!" thanking voters at bus stops and appearing at a drizzly noontime rally against a proposed furlough of federal workers. Later, during rush hour, she shook hands at the Cleveland Park metro station; many whites noisily shunned her.

She was out on the streets because movement was simply Eleanor's style. This woman who power-walked every morning and hurried through fifteen-hour days had long-legged men racing to keep up when they walked her to her car.

"But also I was out there because the *Post* was out there, really stirring things up in the worst way." After the primary a week rarely went by without an anti-Norton commentary or editorial.

"Is someone who is so cavalier about her obligations as a taxpayer qualified to represent the nation's capital in Congress? It is particularly sad to see a woman who had risen to almost heroic stature within the civil rights and women's movements felled by her own misdeeds. But there are standards of conduct that must be upheld by those who aspire to public office, and to bend these to fit the sentimental favorite is a disservice to all."

The condemnation hurt. Croft calls the string of admonishments "one of the fiercest political attacks I've seen in this city. The *Post* attacked her in a worse way than Barry. What I've learned from this is don't be their darling. They will never forgive you for not being perfect. She went overnight from being the darling of liberal, progressive D.C. to unconscionable attacks, to the point that in the general election the *Post* endorsed a nobody Republican."

The relentless series of editorials backfired, just as Kane's attempt to paint Eleanor as an outsider had failed. The denunciations welded Eleanor's supporters even closer together. African Americans felt under siege, as this woman with whom they identified took a barrage that appeared disproportionate to the crime: trusting one's husband.

Eleanor became a symbol of resistance. Yet, like any icon under attack, she suffered. The taint followed her constantly. People in the streets called out, "Pay your taxes!" And whereas previously she had been described as a "distinguished law professor," "national civil rights activist," and "former Carter administration official," now her tax problem was her only identifier in news stories. A typical insult was *Post* columnist Mark Shields's wisecrack, "representation without taxation."

As September wore on, Republican opponent Harry Singleton sharpened his criticisms. "She refused to pay her taxes year after year, with an apparent arrogance that she was somehow better than the rest of us working stiffs. How could she get away with placing herself above the law?" he asked, beginning to call Eleanor the "Leona Helmsley" of Washington.

All spring and summer Eleanor had been looked to by a cross-section of Washingtonians as the redeemer who could bring stature to the District after the shame of Barry's arrest; now she was regarded by most whites as yet another corrupt (black) politician. While many African Americans still viewed Barry as he presented himself—a racially besieged victim—others were frustrated by Barry-style domination of local politics. Eleanor, the hometown girl made good, "could show the world what a black woman was really made of and could accomplish," says one volunteer.

Eleanor did show what she was made of. Her reaction to the facts when revealed "showed her true character," wrote Sam Smith, editor of *The Progressive Review*, in a *Post* commentary. "A brave individual facing squarely life's cruelest twists. Within days she moved to clear up any liability; she took far more responsibility for her husband's actions than some of us feel was necessary; and she took swift steps to ensure that the problem would not occur again. She repeatedly faced her critics in person—in large groups and small, and did so with dignity and integrity."

Earlier Eleanor had played on the need for prestige and clout, saying, "We need a delegate who can command respect for the people of the District." Following the tax revelation, she retained enough self-respect to make the same claim.

After the primary most Democrats closed ranks around Eleanor. But Ward Three's Democratic Committee refused to endorse her. Its executive committee declared her "unfit" for public office and voted five to zero (with two abstentions) to urge her to withdraw. The Ward Three Committee as a whole withheld party funds from her campaign. Some Democrats—who years later "would be crawling to be on the same platform with Eleanor," says Donna—worried she'd bring the whole ticket down.

Yet allies remained. The Democratic State Committee voted to support the entire ticket. Ministers came on board, labor remained enthusiastic and the coalition that elected her in the primary remained solid. Volunteers who had stepped away started coming back. Media attention, focused over the summer on the mayoral race and Barry's trial, returned full force.

The campaign continued in high gear. Eleanor gained the Sierra Club and other endorsements, and met for almost an hour with Speaker Thomas Foley. He reassured her his wife did their taxes, "and he would not know a thing about them."

After the tough primary, however, money became an issue. By mid-October, Eleanor retained only $7,000 of the $362,000 she had raised. At the end of October she made a $20,000 loan to her campaign, and labor again came to the rescue. During the election's final weeks the sense grew that Eleanor would win, though the *Post* continued its censorious editorials.

Eleanor's campaign kept up the effective precinct-by-precinct organization that had worked so well in the primary, taking block walks, ringing doorbells, passing out leaflets, holding small events in homes and talking to people one-on-one. Every Saturday volunteers stood in front of Safeway grocery stores, put brochures on cars and ran the sound truck. The feverish pace continued.

On October 31 the District Bar initiated an inquiry into Eleanor's tax nonpayment; she explained again her unawareness, her up-to-date payments, and her separation of finances from Edward's. The Bar took no action.

Like her mother before her, she had to detach her funds from her husband's while living under the same roof. But unlike many who devote their lives to overcoming injustice, Eleanor never presented herself as a victim. Vela and Coleman Holmes's daughter simply took life's hard knocks when they came, got up off the floor, accepted her share of responsibility and moved on.

A week before the November 6 election the *Post* endorsed Singleton, claiming again that Eleanor's tax imbroglio disqualified her. "It particularly irritated me when they endorsed Singleton," says Addy, "because the issues he stood for were not what the *Post* stood for . . . they chose to believe Eleanor's critics, not to believe her side of the story."

Singleton made nonstop attacks on the delinquency. Eleanor said publicly that she had discussed her taxes "ad nauseam" in the weeks since the disclosure; Singleton argued that the lapse was critical.

Days before the election, the two butted heads in back-to-back television debates, one live on the *Fox Morning News*. Singleton basked in the *Post* endorsement; Eleanor interrupted to say it didn't matter. He attacked her record on taxes and she snapped back that her fiduciary role on three Fortune 500 corporate boards and the Rockefeller Foundation was a better measure of her fitness for public office than her husband's handling of their joint bill-paying.

"Even though I didn't know, I was responsible," Eleanor reiterated days before the election. "They were my taxes. Passing the responsibility, or allowing the responsibility to gravitate to my husband, was a matter for me of absolute necessity because I may have been the world's busiest woman. But that does not absolve me of responsibility. That's why I had to take charge of my own finances."

The weekend before the election the weather was especially glorious; all the candidates staged rallies and fund-raisers. Washingtonians were out and the *Post*, conducting an informal survey, found the public still mixed on Eleanor. "The woman purports to be a legal scholar and professor, and to pull the old dumb blonde routine is beyond the pale," one fifty-year-old woman, an educator from Ward Six, told the paper. Another resident believed "the cloud she has over her head isn't of her own doing."

The day of the general election, Tuesday, November 6, turned cold. Donna sent Eleanor out all over the city, keeping upbeat people like Philip Pannell with her so she wouldn't be discouraged by the insults she'd hear all day. Late in the day, Eleanor worked the polls herself and thanked her volunteers.

On election evening, Channel 4's political reporter Tom Sherwood had the numbers shortly after 8 P.M. Eleanor led Singleton by a margin of two to one and Dixon won 86 percent of the mayoral vote. Once again feeling that strange mixture of elation, weariness, heartbreak and relief, Eleanor jumped into the electric slide at her victory party, crowded with cheering supporters.

The turnout of 165,466 voters surpassed the record for local elections set in 1986, when Barry was elected to his third term. Voter registration was at an all-time high, and nearly 59 percent were women. Eleanor was helped by being the Democratic nominee, "but she pulled it out," recalls Vic Basile. "It's one of the proudest campaigns I've ever worked on."

After November—and a rare three days at the nearby beach house of a friend—Eleanor moved out of her Stanton Park headquarters to a two-room office around the corner. Sustaining her headlong pace, she planned her first months in office, identified staff and made the rounds, thanking supporters and asking, "Tell me your concerns."

Even with Eleanor's tax imbroglio, most Washingtonians felt a fresh breeze blowing in the nation's capital. Two African-American women—

both long shots at various times in their campaigns—were suddenly the District's most powerful officials. Black women as a political force had arrived.

Key congressional Democrats signaled strong approval of the twin victories and a readiness to assist the financially distressed District. "I haven't talked to anybody here today who doesn't believe this is a new beginning," Rep. Julian Dixon of California, chair of the House D.C. appropriations subcommittee, had said after the September primary, assuming a Norton-Dixon win in November.

"Let's give the new leadership a chance," echoed Senator Barbara Mikulski. "I ask my colleagues who have used the District of Columbia appropriations [bill] as vehicles for other social agendas to really have a new attitude."

The show of support sharply contrasted with the testy relations between Congress and the Barry administration. Now even Minority Whip Newt Gingrich affirmed that "compared to Marion Barry, she will be a relief and a sign of virtue."

It was a new era. The old guard that had led the city since the 1970s was banished. At the same time, the family life that Eleanor had known for over two decades, with a husband and two children at home, was over. Johnny had just left for college in California and her marriage was close to collapse.

CHAPTER 12

Warrior on the Hill

Eleanor always speaks from the perspective of a black woman. She never seems to have forgotten who put her where she is, who helped her and how she got there. . . . and she never lets them forget who she is.

ELEANOR ELLIOTT, A CHILDHOOD NEIGHBOR

O n Thursday, January 3, 1991, the disparate parts of Eleanor's fifty-four years all came swirling together. Old friends from Dunbar and Antioch mingled with Yale Law School alumni; her family rubbed shoulders with campaign volunteers, ex-EEOC staff, labor unionists, feminists, civil rights and Free D.C. activists gathered together in the giant stone foyer of the Rayburn House Office Building for an evening of celebration.

At 5:30 P.M., Judge Leon Higginbotham administered the ceremonial oath of office, reciting again the official pledge given in the House by Speaker Tom Foley. The woman who had so ardently defended the Constitution as an ACLU lawyer held up her right hand and pledged, "I, Eleanor Holmes Norton, do solemnly swear that I will support and defend the Constitution of the United States against all enemies, foreign or domestic." She began to choke: "That I will bear true faith and allegiance to the same; that I take this obligation freely, without any mental reservation or purpose of evasion." Her voice rose proudly, "And that I will well and faithfully discharge the duties of the office on which I am about to enter. So help me God."

Her mother kissed her, and Eleanor took up what she would ever after call "the time of my life, the great joyous challenge."

"That was a very big number," she declares, happily recalling her swearing-in, where supporters jammed the high-ceilinged foyer. "We had it in the biggest place we could find in the House. Everybody in the world was there. It was a humbling show of confidence." The good feelings among the rustling crowd reflected the wave of hope that

Eleanor's election brought the city. Residual bitterness remained about the *Post*'s attempt to "take Eleanor out," but the prevailing emotion was one of joy.

Eleanor was made for the United States Congress. "The biggest show in the world," she delightedly describes this most exclusive club. When Pat Schroeder had entered the House in 1972, the atmosphere, she says, was "a cross between a plantation and a fraternity house." By 1990, Congress was down to just one other African-American female member—Cardiss Collins—until Eleanor, her friend Maxine Waters and Barbara Rose Collins joined her in the 102nd Congress. And only 5 percent of Congress was female.

Typically, Eleanor insists, "There were no male-female difficulties!" After Yale and her years in government, the U.S. Capitol was familiar, with its old wood, inlaid marble and aggressive, dark-suited men. "When I went to Congress it didn't occur to me I didn't belong there. Or that anybody would *dare* treat me any way but the way they treated me. There may have been a time when women were not treated equally in the Congress. That time had gone." She felt right at home with the culture: a bright group of self-important men doing verbal battle.

"There's an ocean, jump in. Splash, you're in there; you're big boys and girls now. You swim. You look and you see what happens, you ask questions, but essentially you learn by doing."

Old-timers like California's Ron Dellums, chair of the House Committee on the District, and Julian Dixon, another Californian, befriended her. John Lewis, the SNCC worker who had practiced his March on Washington speech in her apartment almost forty years before, was also in Congress. "I've known Eleanor longer than anyone else here," he says, sighing affably. "When certain things come up on the floor, we've been down this road before."

But representing Washington, D.C., whose delegate had the responsibilities and privileges of other members but no vote on the House floor, was a challenge her mentors had not faced. She had to figure out how to maximize what power she had. Her predecessor, who organized nationally to threaten seats of congresspeople voting against District and congressional Black Caucus interests, was criticized for giving priority to national over local affairs. Eleanor chose a different strategy.

"You learn how you go to the floor to speak during one-minute sessions." Talking powerfully for her "one minute" over the rustling papers and babble of other voices, during her first year Eleanor spoke more frequently than any other member. Most spent their days in dark-furnitured offices with televisions tuned to the House floor, the sound on low. While they worked at mammoth desks or met with aides, they kept one eye cocked on floor debate.

"When certain people are on," Eleanor explains, "you turn it up to hear. I was trying to make sure that people understood they should respect the city I represented. And one way to do that was to make them respect me."

She also wanted her constituents to know she regarded the institution as a place to get things done for them. By speaking, the *Congressional Record* showed how she *would have* voted.

The debating style of the House suited Eleanor perfectly. "We go at one another hard in negotiations and on the floor," she says happily. "But I don't have anyone I consider an enemy in the House. And some of my best friends have been on the completely opposite side of the planet from me politically. I've had to take them on harshly on the floor. And I love the way the House works: you shake hands afterward, you can eat, drink and be merry. That's what I love about the House of Representatives."

Eleanor opened her term with a negative 70 percent rating, "a very high disapproval going into office," says Donna, who became chief of staff. "We wanted to reverse that. The *Post,* after all, wrote eight editorials against her." Characteristically, Eleanor chose an aggressive strategy: she initiated a monthly column, "Notes from Eleanor" for *The Hill Rag* and other papers, and daily press releases to every outlet in town.

"Child, we went at it full throttle. These folks began to hear from their congresswoman like nothing you've ever seen before! I had not been in office any time before people came up and said, 'I didn't vote for you. BUT let me tell you, I support you now.' It had a lot to do with how Donna and I blanketed the town. I tried to be everywhere and into everything. But that's just me anyway."

"We decided that Eleanor's role depended on her being a good local lawmaker," explains Donna, "versus a national representative like Maxine Waters or John Lewis. She was on the short list of national speakers. We turned down every invitation." But she would attend all her congressional hearings and every community meeting. "Wherever two are gathered, Eleanor would be the third," laughs Donna, paraphrasing Scripture.

Eleanor, like the four other voteless delegates—Guam, Puerto Rico, the Virgin Islands and American Samoa—learned that without the large state delegations other representatives had to guide bills through, she had to rely more than most on alliances. Especially in President George H. W. Bush's early 1990s Republican administration.

"It's a terrible disadvantage not to have a senator," she does allow herself to protest. "Because of the clubby atmosphere there, a senator can really stop things from happening the way a House member can't. So if somebody messes over you here, you run over to your senator. She has leverage even if she is not in the majority, to put holds on things, to do trades." But Eleanor found out, "Trades don't work over here because there are too many folks. And they almost always vote as their constituents expect." Lacking a state delegation and thus having to work harder to bring her agendas to the floor, Eleanor negotiated her way onto bills. She joined subgroups, among them the Black, Women's and Progressive Caucuses, and built credibility by vigorous work in committees.

"What I didn't know early on was that it would have been impossible to get on Appropriations [crucial to the District] because I didn't have the vote. I tried to get on. Foolishly. Nobody even told me."

But Public Works and Transportation—with jurisdiction over public real estate, determining much of the economic landscape—"is to the District what the Agriculture Committee is to Kansas."

"On that committee she was able to retain her national prominence as a champion for women and minorities," says Donna, describing Eleanor's leadership on affirmative action for contractors' programs.

Once she got on committees, Eleanor had to figure out how to work them. "I had been elected to Congress not to further my own interests, but to bring resources and respect to the District of Columbia. The ethics of the bar require zealous representation. A lawyer is supposed to go to the mat—or the moon—for her client. That's how I understand my relationship to my folks."

Since her priorities were economic development and political independence, her D.C. subcommittee required a unique strategy. "The name of the game is putting them on the defensive. Put pressure on them the way they put pressure on D.C. I have something I want to have done. Apply pressure. If I were not willing to do that, I would get no r-e-s-p-e-c-t for the District of Columbia. And I get a lot that way."

She was also respected because, as even adversaries commented, "Eleanor comes prepared." Hard work, pragmatic committee choices, and an aggressive strategy helped Eleanor transform the unenviable nonvoting delegate role into a powerful generator of funds for Washington. The Ronald Reagan Trade Building, Southeast Federal Center and other projects, including rebuilding the Northeast corridor, shored up city finances. "Some people switch committees, but I won't do it. These are too important to the health of my district."

During these early successes, Eleanor had heartbreak at home. Six weeks after inauguration, on February 22, news leaked from the courthouse that Eleanor filed suit in D.C. Superior Court for separation from Edward. He told the *Post,* "I have not had any conversation with Eleanor about our marriage since before the election. It was a total surprise to me when she served me with papers seeking a legal separation."

Barely two weeks later, on March 7, her aunt Selena Mae Holmes King, the only daughter of Richard and Nellie Holmes, passed away at ninety-three. Eleanor mourned the musical woman so influential in her childhood, when Grandmother Nellie and Aunt Selena lived just a backyard away. And the man with whom she'd had a contest of wits for twenty-five years was no longer by her side.

"When the taxes first occurred, I didn't think of ending the marriage at all. I thought just the opposite. He was paralyzed. I'm sure he never intended what resulted, but that paralysis and whatever caused it destroyed the marriage. The marriage wasn't so strong that it could withstand that kind of blow. It was very painful to finally decide, after twenty-five years, that it was gone. Especially since this marriage would probably have held."

Edward lobbied Eleanor's friends, trying to make his case. He complained that Eleanor was cold, too busy, uninterested. He wanted his wife's "total responsive interest," says Barbara Babcock. "Eleanor is second to none in her love and loyalty, but the absorption in the beloved, she's just not that way. It's not withholding; it's not in her range."

For her part, Eleanor, clearly chastened, told friends that Edward's failure to file had humbled her. The calamitous publicity and personal suffering had made her see herself in a different light. Now, she said, she understood from bitter experience how even someone with a good reputation could be brought low.

The estranged couple stayed together in the house while trying to sell it; then, since prices were low and the kitchen needed renovation to successfully market, Eleanor bought Edward out. Finally he gathered his clothes, books, and some of the furniture for his move to an apartment across town. Over the days that Edward packed, Eleanor bustled off to work each day at the Capitol until there came a morning when his closet stood bare, mute testimony to the empty place in the home. Her main verbal sparring partner was gone. For the first time Eleanor lived alone with Katherine, now twenty-one, in the three-story townhouse.

"My God, I was married to somebody for twenty-five years! It was a very difficult period for me. I was in the middle of becoming a member of Congress. But for me to sit and brood about what happened in my marriage—damn, that's not me! I try to go on."

Yet even this woman, trained since childhood to focus and forget, found "That was very difficult to do. God, in the middle of being elected to Congress, my life blew up with this tax bomb. I had to somehow keep on going, somehow manage to do the impossible after that and get elected, and then figure out how to get my credibility back and be a congresswoman. Then I had the hardest job that any member has because I had no state delegation! I had no senators and my city was in trouble from the get-go." She jabs the air with her index finger.

"Look, we are all complicated human beings. I am the kind of person who, when I hear certain kinds of music or, on countless occasions, when I've looked at something on television—tears flow down my cheeks. A certain kind of music comes and I'm gone; I can't stop it. I just try to keep from embarrassing myself," this private woman says, gazing straight ahead. "So I don't pretend that this defense mechanism works: 'Marriage ends, betrayal, that's the end of it.' No!"

Her friends worried. "I just said to Eleanor that I was there if she needed me," Vernon Jordan says. "I worried about her pain and about what would happen to the daughter, but they seem to have worked that out and shared it. It was obviously a painfully, publicly embarrassing circumstance. Would that it could have been otherwise. Eleanor was obviously very hurt about it."

Yet even with the strain of her dissolving marriage and work pressures that would turn most people to frantic mush, Eleanor radiated energy and electric intelligence. Her capacity to concentrate in the face of difficulties—a capacity some would call denial and others would say was tied to the optimism that was one of her greatest strengths— showed at this traumatic moment. And the new mission fueled her.

Eleanor jumped into Congress and made service to the District her single-pointed focus. The woman who had crisscrossed the country and the globe for thirty years suddenly considered a trip to Maryland or Virginia "foreign travel."

"It put a lot of pressure on other local politicians." Donna smiles. "You go to an ANC [neighborhood] meeting and your congresswoman was there, but your mayor and your council members often were not." In Eleanor's first year she averaged over a hearing a day and attended almost 500 local events. No issue seemed too minor to attract her attention.

Katherine often accompanied her on weekends, when Eleanor cared for her without the help of an aide. Whereas previously Katherine had hesitated in crowds, now when Eleanor entered a gathering, turning from side to side and extending her arms to those around her, Katherine came behind and emulated her mother by also shaking hands.

The focus paid off. Within four months, the *Wall Street Journal* featured Eleanor under the headline, SURPRISING STAR. "The District's new Delegate gets high marks in the House despite the taint of nonpayment of taxes, which surfaced during her campaign. She is credited with quiet effectiveness in winning extra funds for her strapped city." Winning good reviews from committee chairs and Hill watchers, she soon got the satisfaction of a *Washington Post* editorial affirming that the woman who came into office under a cloud had impressed them. And her talents were recognized by colleagues. Early in her second term Speaker Foley appointed Eleanor to a small joint committee seeking to end congressional gridlock and improve relationships with the president.

Simultaneously, Eleanor retained tenure at Georgetown Law Center by teaching "Law Making and Statutory Construction." In the third-floor classroom where she held her seminar on alternate Mondays, when Congress was out, Eleanor sat at the head of the wooden table, chalkboard behind her.

"One of our great assets has now become one of our great problems," she lectured on opening day. "We have a separation-of-powers government. It requires a lot of costly litigation and travel through three branches in order to get anything done. Most of the world has parliamentary forms of government—Japan, Great Britain, France, South Africa and India—unified government. It's equally democratic. Zap, it's done. No going to court or to an agency once a law is passed." The country's founders, distrusting government, had created a process to slow things down.

"Can we keep the same system? I'm a conservative when it comes to changing the constitutional framework. But can we play the game the same way in the twenty-first century?"

After the first few classes where Eleanor described this uncharted space, students generated original research on interbranch communication. Sitting around the table like lawyers in a firm or law faculty, they critiqued each other's papers.

"Peer review is classic training for how a lawyer has to deal," Eleanor told them, giving out her home number and encouraging them to use it.

"She was one of the most challenging professors at Georgetown," former student and now legal staffer Jon Bouker says. "Once we submitted our outlines, we got back little essays, typed, talking about the strengths and weaknesses of our papers with suggestions of areas to explore. No other professor did that."

Having to wrestle with "the nth degree of legal reasoning," Eleanor found class the perfect complement to her day-to-day focus, especially when Congress got wild.

In the midst of her whirling activity, Eleanor was on an "adrenaline high. You don't want her to relax or she'll think of five more things for you to do," says one long-term staffer, describing a New Year's Eve when he worked with her for hours, laboring to get the exquisitely right words as she handwrote an op-ed piece for the *New York Times* in the penned script staff members call "slightly more legible than hieroglyphics."

Often scheduled to be in more than one hearing at a time, Eleanor mercilessly expected staff to keep pace.

"There is not enough time to do anything except say, 'I hope you all are on top of things,' because the pressure here is just abominable."

A few couldn't keep up.

"I'm burned out," one told a reporter. "She makes us feel guilty when we take a day off."

"Don't work for Eleanor unless you're ready to work your fingers to the bone," affirmed Donna. "She demands of us what she demands of herself."

Like her namesake, Eleanor both pushed and protected her staff. When gifts of food arrived, she shared. When an office intern hoped for a summer off to study for the bar, it was granted. And when constituents' needs demanded late-night work to fine-tune a strategy, staying was expected.

With her great ability to focus, Eleanor sometimes fixated on details. Yet for all her force, she was open to argument.

"You can convince me, but you can't simply slide around me," she often said. Her opponents—including staff members—learned that, were they to argue against her, they'd better be very well prepared. Her motto was, "I don't play checkers, I play chess." Her staff learned to generate carefully structured ideas, speculating what opponents might do; otherwise she scoffed, "Please. We are not playing checkers."

The constant work, perfectionism, long hours and few breaks made her office culture not a "family friendly" place for those with children. Yet it became family to many who would remain twelve years later. For all her brusque and demanding ways, Eleanor generated devotion unusual on the Hill, where staff turnover was notoriously high. Julia Hudson, who's been with Eleanor eleven years, says, "A lot of the staff are dedicated to the city, and they love her. She's implemented a team approach and a family vibe. We're an extremely close-knit group." Late Friday afternoons Eleanor occasionally took them all—Team Norton—out for a drink and hors d'oeuvres. Her office developed a "Movement" feel, with that same sense of urgency, drive, and dedication to a cause, crystallized in the persona of the leader.

Always in a hurry, Eleanor regularly race-walked the six flights of marble stairs up to her small Longworth office (a "dungeon," one staff member calls her first dingy suite), while twenty-year-olds accompanying her huffed and puffed. When she finally readied to leave—moments before she was due across town—Eleanor was out the door and at the elevator while others zipped briefcases. They ran to catch up, hoping she hadn't turned a corner or dashed into the elevator.

Her desire for perfection made Eleanor habitually late. Ramming her car through city traffic, whizzing by federal buildings and burned-out storefronts, she amazed constituents by pulling up alone, late in the evening, to honor their affair.

"Drivers are a waste of staff time," she said, rebuffing suggestions.

Driving herself to event after event, shivering in winter, she instructed staff on her car phone while constituents waved and honked. Most grinned when they recognized their fiery congress-woman; a few muttered, "Pay your taxes!" Even some admirers could never believe that this savvy lawyer hadn't been privy to her own tax dealings.

Philosophical about the challenge her impatient temperament pre-sents, Eleanor concedes the match of a hyperactive style to her job.

"It's twenty-four hours. People didn't put you here to keep you at home. They get encouraged by believing that someone with some kind of authority or power has cared enough to come out. It can run you ragged. That's why you have a schedule. At some point, they can only schedule you for so many things at the same time."

About her legendary stamina, she says, "I should get no credit for it because it just comes naturally." Yet she fortified it: morning workouts in her underwear to a workout video or long-distance race-walking. Personally self-denigrating—a style startlingly intermixed with her strong opinions—she parries compliments about exercise.

"I think it gives me an excuse to eat pieces of cake."

In October 1991, nine months after her term began, a cultural tidal wave hit the United States. Law professor Anita Hill charged that President Bush's nominee to the U.S. Supreme Court, D.C. Circuit Court Judge Clarence Thomas, had sexually harassed her. Eleanor, sit-ting in her office with her television on, heard the allegation along with the rest of the nation.

She scrutinized Hill. Everything in her conduct bespoke a woman reluctant to come forth with this story. In fact, she testified only when compelled by the Judiciary Committee. The architect of the 1980 sexual harassment guidelines, Eleanor knew how difficult it was for women to step forward. She also sensed history breaking.

"This woman is telling the truth!" she told herself.

Eleanor had been drawn into the fray over Thomas's nomination during the preceding months since she, like he, had headed the EEOC. Her office received more phone calls about the nomination than on any issue since she'd come to Congress; callers overwhelmingly opposed confirmation.

"This man was on the other side of the mountain from us," Eleanor says, contending that he embraced "none of the legal issues that have animated the black community for a hundred years. This man had taken the EEOC down to its knees. He had stopped enforcing the law; he didn't even follow Supreme Court decisions. It was a heartbreak for me to see what he had done."

Now, having seen Hill, Eleanor also felt a lawyer's responsibility to the Supreme Court. Hill's testimony had to be heard. Otherwise, she later wrote, it would "allow an unchallenged taint to be passed on to the high court itself. To do so would leave the Court tarnished."

Eleanor ran to the House floor to say the Senate had to hear Hill's charges, but Republicans kept interrupting to stop congresswomen from talking. "Then we realized we would have to walk over to the Senate or there would never be a hearing . . . If nothing happened and the whole thing went away, the guidelines weren't worth the paper they were written on." The guidelines that Thomas was to enforce as EEOC chair included prohibitions on unwelcome sexual advances and requests for sexual favors, both of which Hill alleged. In this larger-than-life contretemps Eleanor's multiple roles gave her unique authority.

Pat Schroeder, a twenty-year House veteran and dean of the women members, coordinated a two-part strategy to get Hill a hearing. While some women would stay on the House floor to win a vote ungagging Rosa DeLauro of Connecticut (who, trying to use a "one-minute" to speak about Hill, was stopped on a technicality: she had referred to the Senate by name instead of the "other body"), other congresswomen would walk over to the Senate, where the Democratic Caucus was meeting on this very subject. The women anticipated a welcome from their Democratic colleagues.

Eleanor, Pat Schroeder, Louise Slaughter, Jolene Unsold, Nita Lowey, Patsy Mink and Barbara Boxer took the famous walk, striding up the Senate steps in the shot flashed to the country.

"I walked for the guidelines, I walked for the EEOC, I walked for the Supreme Court, I walked for women, I walked for Anita Hill." But Eleanor said she particularly walked for "black women who have had their sexuality trivialized and scandalized; black women who have had their sexuality demeaned just as Clarence Thomas had done to Anita Hill.

"Because Thomas was a black man, it was important to wipe away any notion that this was about white women against a black man."

The seven marched swiftly up the steep Capitol steps. When they arrived at the Senate, the closest they got to their Senate counterparts was a set of large, closed, mahogany doors. Behind this fortification their colleagues sat at their usual Tuesday Democratic caucus lunch, discussing how to handle the Hill-Thomas embarrassment. Senator Barbara Mikulski, the lone woman in the room, was vainly requesting a hearing.

As the women approached the doors, they were asked by an aide who they were.

"We're seven congresswomen who want to meet with our colleagues for just a few minutes on a critical issue."

"No, you can't come in."

Refusing to accept the rebuff, the women knocked. The door opened a crack. "You can't come in," said a senior staffer. "We're meeting."

"For goodness' sake, we're members of Congress. Please ask."

The staffer returned. "You can't come in."

The group huddled in disbelief.

"Can we meet with the majority leader now?"

"No, you can meet with him later. When the caucus is over."

"That's ridiculous!" bellowed Eleanor. "There won't be any point after the caucus is over!"

"No."

Boxer, another warrior, threatened, "Listen, there are about a hundred cameras out there and they all took our picture going up the Senate steps. They know what we came over about and they'll want to know what happened. If we don't at least meet with the majority leader . . ."

"One moment. Wait here."

When the staffer returned to the door she said, "Okay. The majority leader will see you in the side room now."

Thus they were finally heard by Majority Leader George Mitchell. "They didn't want to expose it, have all this stuff come out," says Eleanor.

"Well, you'd better have it come out now rather than after Thomas gets on the bench," the women told him.

Mitchell reluctantly agreed. The hearing, flung together in just a few days, transfixed the nation in one illuminating week as the all-male Judiciary Committee tried to shake Hill's credibility and put *her* reputation on trial. Pictures of Strom Thurmond wagging his finger in Anita Hill's face roused women around the country. Hill herself sat with utter stillness and an unsullied, calm expression, even as she was belittled and degraded. The most dependable liberal, Ted Kennedy, was mute, bound to silence by his own recent headlines: a late-night Florida carousal with his nephew. Other committee members slumped in their chairs throwing out disbelieving questions.

"No one will believe you" was the refrain women had heard all too often; Hill's treatment resonated nationwide. The complete absence of women on the committee, which might have changed the outcome of Thomas's close confirmation, set the stage for the following season's election, and Eleanor became a visible spokesperson for the Year of the Woman. Those 1992 victories would swell women in Congress from twenty-nine to forty-eight, propel the first African-American woman, Carol Moseley-Braun, into the Senate, and the first Puerto Rican woman, New York's Nydia Velazquez, into the House.

By the time of the Thomas-Hill hearings Eleanor had already achieved congressional success. She and Sharon Pratt Kelly won a 40 percent increase in the federal payment to the District for services rendered, like fire and police protection, and revenues lost from tax-exempt federal land (67 percent of the city). In addition, the team obtained a hundred million dollars in no-strings-attached emergency supplemental money. After Barry, Congress embraced the female duo.

The first bill Eleanor tackled was local. D.C. Council member Frank Smith wanted a small parcel of federal land for a Civil War memorial at 10th and U, in the heart of the old black business community, the first memorial in the country that would commemorate African-American soldiers. Even such a noncontroversial matter took enormous work. "You've got to get the appropriate members to pay attention to your bill. It's difficult." Senator Mikulski agreed to move the bill; land was appropriated.

Eleanor also took on a "royal battle" to fight exploding District crime. She wanted the Capitol Police to patrol beyond the close Capitol perimeter. Her view was: we've got this huge force of well-trained, well-paid, underutilized officers, let's use them! But they'd never been shared. Eleanor got House agreement, yet her bill stalled in the Senate until an elderly woman was beaten almost to death near the Capitol. Then it moved. Cracking tradition, the Capitol Police would no longer be a virtually private force. Public Law 102-397 expanded their territory, freeing city police for neighborhoods that desperately needed them.

And, looking beyond D.C., Eleanor worked with old civil rights allies to strengthen the 1991 Civil Rights Act, restoring the right to sue for discrimination, an ability stripped by several Supreme Court decisions. In a *Wall Street Journal* editorial, she contended that the Bush administration "shamefully exploited" the racially polarizing issue of quotas, maintaining again that the "dangerously false issue" must not be used as a scare.

Although it was rare for a freshman member to have a major amendment accepted for floor debate, she offered one to a transportation bill, hoping to reduce conflict between people of color and white women. Both were squeezed into the same Disadvantaged Business Enterprise Program 10 percent hiring goal. To reduce friction, Eleanor proposed a separate 10 percent for each group. After it failed she said, "I'll try to find another way of reducing this harmful intergroup conflict. When federal legislation causes polarization among groups, a suitable remedy must be found."

However, the overriding issue was then and would continue to be self-rule, with a vote in Congress. "I don't simply represent another congressional district. I represent the city that is at the center of our democracy, and it doesn't even have full rights for its citizens! If you go to Paris, you certainly don't expect their citizens to have any fewer rights than anybody else."

Every topic led back to that. "Alone among democracies," Eleanor says, residents of the capital city enjoyed less than full rights. Day-to-day she worked around her lack of a vote on the floor. But the denial of fundamental rights grated on her and on her constituents. Eleanor might be able to intimidate some of her colleagues, logically convince others and devise strategies to strong-arm holdouts, but even this "force of nature" could not single-handedly tame Congress. It constantly meddled in District business.

During 1992, Eleanor came up with an ingenious strategy to get a floor vote, in the Committee of the Whole (as the entire House was called). Assisted by law professor Jamin Raskin, she reviewed relevant laws and the Constitution. Though no delegate had ever claimed a right to vote, they found nothing that *prohibits* it. Her conclusion: "Well, if it's not prohibited, then it ought to be permitted."

She submitted a legal memo to the House Democratic Caucus who, with outside legal opinion, could find no bar. When the 103rd Congress opened in 1993, the Democratic House leaders granted Eleanor and the other delegates a vote. Essentially, they decided, she could vote unless, in a rarity, her vote broke a tie. Because delegates had always been treated the same, the four delegates from U.S. territories were included, although significantly their residents, unlike the District's, did not pay federal income taxes.

For the first time in 200 years, when the House bell rang signaling a vote, the District delegate could rush to the floor along with her colleagues and not only debate the District budget, but vote on it. City residents savored their victory when both the U.S. District Court and the U.S. Court of Appeals upheld their vote, after Republicans filed a suit. And Eleanor's ingenuity—along with her determination—would be a hallmark of her congressional years.

The Democratic Party platform in 1992 called for District statehood. Standing at the July convention podium dressed in bright red Eleanor roared, "It's too late in the century for Americans to accept colonial rule at the very seat of government!" The *New York Times* concurred in a series of pro-statehood editorials: "The Federal Government treats Washington, D.C. like a plantation . . . The District has 608,000 people, more than Alaska, Wyoming or Vermont . . . They can't pass a budget or even reschedule garbage collection without groveling before Congress. . . . The citizens of Washington, D.C. deserve relief from this kind of imperial arrogance. Statehood is the way to provide it."

By January 1993, all the stars seemed aligned for statehood. There was the momentum of having won the vote on the floor. President Clinton had testified for statehood before his election and sentiment was strong. The previous May, when the theme for the annual Malcolm X Day celebration at Anacostia Park was self-determination, thousands of energized citizens had showed up. Stickers reading "Mend the crack in the Liberty Bell. D.C. Statehood Now!" began to surface all over town; a bumper sticker displayed the red New Columbia Star, with a 51 in its midst. The New Columbia flag flew its red and white colors. For the first time in a generation there was real hope: Democrats, traditionally supportive of this Democratic city, controlled both houses *and* the presidency.

In early 1993, Eleanor thought the nonelection year might enable members to vote "Yes" on a controversial bill. She, Mayor Kelly, the Leadership Conference on Civil Rights, Rainbow Coalition, ACLU, Stand Up for Democracy, labor unions, churches, synagogues and local activists met, all ready for a major push. The coalition planned a major campaign, mobilizing civil disobedience demonstrations outside Congress with anticipated mass arrests and publicity.

As excitement built, street demonstrations grew, the coalition lobbied and Eleanor persuaded the House leadership to put their own machinery behind her statehood bill, H.R. 51. The day when the District might be a state was at last in sight.

In July, the coalition began weekly demonstrations at the Capitol and, commemorating the country's founding tradition, had a tea party. Dramatically making their point—"Taxation without Representation"—citizens poured tea all over Independence Avenue in front of the House Longworth building.

"We want independence! Statehood now!" Eleanor and others cried at rallies. Residents closed down traffic in street sit-ins, chanting, "Sit down for D.C. statehood!" Hundreds, including the mayor, City Council members and national leaders like Jesse Jackson and Dick Gregory, went to jail.

The multilayered strategy ("From the suites to the streets") paid off.

But in early November 1993, Eleanor publicly worried about a House vote. In a letter to constituents she argued pro and con, saying the vote would rally supporters, but defeat might preclude further action for years. "The point of seeking a vote in the first place is to give momentum to statehood, not to damage it, as a very low vote might," she wrote. Statehood did not have a majority of the House. However a good vote on the floor *could* push the statehood cause to the next level of acceptance.

"If not now, when?" members of the coalition urged.

She went forward.

"Many who had wanted statehood talked about it and prayed about it," she says today. "I went at it like a legislator . . . I went to the Speaker and got him to say we could have a vote." Just before Thanksgiving Speaker Foley agreed to give Eleanor the floor debate she and other statehood supporters had so long sought.

President Clinton was first on Eleanor's list. She called the White House.

"Make sure the president does phone calls to support the bill."

He did, and distributed a letter asking House members to vote in favor of H.R. 51 "as a matter of principle."

Eleanor wrote her own series of "Dear Colleague" letters, knocking down myths about requirements for states by describing how others, often spurned, came into the Union.

On Thursday, November 18, advocates stepped up their civil disobedience. Twenty-four people blocked a door to the Cannon House office building and were arrested.

Friday, the day before debate was to begin, Eleanor, volunteers and statehood lobbyist Jesse Jackson walked the halls of Congress. Buttonholing Democratic allies, they beseeched, "Be there tomorrow for the vote. This is historic."

"We won't forget who voted with us!" Eleanor reminded. To back her up, the Leadership Conference on Civil Rights significantly notified every member that this would be counted as a civil rights vote. Many would not want this marked against their record.

Saturday, November 20, the first day of debate, Speaker Tom Foley personally gaveled the session. His presence dramatized the commitment the Democratic Party had made to this bill, with over a hundred cosponsors. The visitors' gallery was noisy, with clapping District residents. Eleanor stood.

"Mr. Chairman, the residents of the District of Columbia seek passage of H.R. 51 and admission to the Union as the State of New Columbia, the only full remedy for their untenable status . . . Opponents . . . will argue that the District is so small that it should not have two senators, even though the District is larger than three states which already have their two, and the District is the only jurisdiction that pays federal taxes but lacks representation of any kind in the Senate. . . .

"Opponents will argue that the Congress cannot change the size of the District even though it has done so twice, once to preserve slavery for the former Virginia portion of the District. Should we not then, Mr. Speaker, reduce the size once again, this time for freedom, not for slavery's sake? Should we not reduce the size so that the neighborhoods of the eight wards which have no relevance to the federal presence can be granted equal representation and full self-government?" Official Washington, the monuments and federal buildings, would remain a federal enclave. But hometown Washington would become New Columbia.

Others cited the injustice done to the District's largely black constituents, who abided by the rules, paid federal income taxes (third per capita in the land) and yet, alone among citizens, could not control their civic destiny. Instead, they suffered the indignity—and disruption—of having to submit every local law, and their locally raised budget, for presidential and congressional second-guessing.

"Mr. Chairman, I ask us to get above our biases, our prejudice, and do what is right for America," thundered New York's Charles Rangel. "We are not willing to deny people who love this country, who have fought for this country, who died for this country, to play according to a different set of rules."

Barney Frank from Massachusetts contended, "the principle is very simple. Should American citizens . . . be allowed to have representation?"

The District's neighbors were mixed. A Virginia Democrat, James Moran, feared that if the District became a state, it could levy income tax on federally employed commuters. Yet a Maryland Republican, Wayne Gilchrest, would become the lone member of his party to support the bill.

Representative Ballenger spoke in opposition, warning that New Columbia had insufficient resources to support a state government.

Eleanor shot back, "Mr. Chairman, I want to rebut the remarks of the gentleman who preceded me . . . Eleven states raise fewer local government revenues than the District of Columbia. I would like to call that roll, if I might, Mr. Chairman: Delaware, Idaho, Maine, Montana, Nevada, New Hampshire, North Carolina [Ballenger's state], Rhode Island, South Dakota, Vermont and Wyoming."

The heated debate raged over two days.

"Unfortunately, these statehood advocates won't accept equal rights.

They insist instead on having superior rights," California Republican Dana Rohrabacher angrily asserted. "They insist on having rights that residents of no other city in this country would dream of asking for. They want to be able to elect two U.S. senators, and a state government, all by themselves."

Representative John Lewis rose. "Almost thirty years ago on a Sunday afternoon just like today, in a little town called Selma in the heart of the Black Belt of Alabama, some of us were beaten with billy clubs and bullwhips, bloodied and trampled upon by horses. We wanted to march across the Edmund Pettus Bridge, the Alabama River, on our way to Montgomery. . . . We had one simple message: one man, one vote.

"What happened that bloody Sunday was shown on televisions all over the world. Our nation was shocked, embarrassed, moved. . . . What people all over this country are seeing on television today ought to embarrass us, ought to move us . . . It is not right that there are still Americans for whom one-man, one-vote is still a dream."

Michigan's John Dingell, chair of the Committee on Energy and Commerce and a Democrat who opposed the bill, railed in response, "There is no citizen in Washington who is chained to the pillars of the Capitol or the Washington Monument. They can leave any time they are so minded."

Representative Neil Abercrombie from Hawaii, the last state admitted to the Union (1959), detailed: "Alaska: the arguments against were the population was too small for statehood, resources of revenue uncertain, 99 percent of the land federally owned. Arizona: violence, territory lacks resources to sustain a state government . . . Florida: population too small . . ."

But Representative Tom DeLay of Texas opposed on social grounds. ". . . . The District's hug-a-thug attitude on violent crime and the continued misuse of the city's police department is one example that clearly demonstrates the fact the District is not a state and should not be considered for statehood . . . The District, a liberal bastion of corruption and crime. . . . Let us take it back and clean it up."

Eleanor jumped in again. "Mr. Chairman, I ask that in light of the remarks just made that this vote be decided on the basis of democratic principles and not District bashing."

The debate continued until Majority Leader Dick Gephardt

closed, an appearance reserved for the most important issues. Citing a city resident whose son died in Vietnam, he concluded, "Vote yes on H.R. 51 and end this travesty of justice in this capital of the United States . . . Grant statehood . . . It is the right thing to do."

On Sunday, November 21, the New Columbia Admission Act was defeated, but an emotional visitors gallery packed with supporters broke into applause when the House voting machines showed 150 pro votes. In a defining moment, Eleanor was forced to stand by vote-less.

"We got a majority of the Democrats," Eleanor rejoices, with 63 percent, and the lone Republican. "It was—oh boy." She shakes her head with pleasure.

Even though the bill lost 277–153, the vote on record, with well over half the full committee chairs voting "Aye," was a benchmark. Many pundits had expected one hundred votes; 120 was a "good vote" start for such a structural change. The Black Caucus, most in the Hispanic Caucus and the Democratic women had supported it. And most of all, it had now entered the national discussion.

"It had never even been debated here!" Eleanor rejoices. She had warned supporters they'd be knocked out on the first try. Creating the state of Hawaii had taken a number of votes; this one would "get us off the dime."

Yet even after the historic vote, the large block of Democrats who refused to go along with their leadership was troubling; possibilities for the country's only majority-black state did not seem bright.

Nonetheless, Eleanor planned to use the strong vote to press for more self-government. Within months, however, city newspapers reported a fiscal crisis that doomed claims of the city's ability to become a self-supporting state. At first, Mayor Kelly tried to keep a positive spin on the terrible financial news; but as it emerged, statehood came crashing down.

Eleanor describes Kelly's difficulties. "Congress was so glad to see her come after Barry that they rescued the city from what was then impending bankruptcy. A new mayor in place helped my first term be successful. There was such hope in the city; Congress regarded it as a new beginning."

Having gotten a $300 million congressional bailout, Kelly still had to reduce her budget. She tried to cut jobs "but got slaughtered." Eleanor shakes her head. "Workers put a picket line around an entire city block, in the dead of winter, during a mayoral event. She just didn't have the political strength to make the cuts." Not able to go back to Congress because she had been bailed out once, Kelly covered up the deficit. And the city went down.

By the end of the year Eleanor wrote, "The District has run out of choices. Only decisions are left." Totally engaged by the crisis, she put aside work with a Georgetown assistant cataloging her speeches as the basis for a book on equality, and another on affirmative action.

One high note countervailed the bad news that seemed to swamp the District. For the first time in the city's history, Eleanor got her friend Bill Clinton to grant her senatorial courtesy: the right to name appointees for U.S. attorney, federal district judgeships and the U.S. marshal, as senators do. This appointing power was significant.

"The U.S. attorney—my God!—gets to decide who's going to be prosecuted for everything from treason to petty theft. That's the most powerful U.S. attorney in the country."

With the help of a nominating commission chaired by Pauline Schneider, Eleanor broke tradition by choosing a diverse group—including Eric Holder Jr., the first black U.S. attorney in District history. Ultimately she appointed the first Hispanic judge on the District Court, the first woman in fourteen years, and the first black female U.S. attorney. For the first time the court was not a white male bastion.

"The U.S. attorney was always resented by the local population," explains Washington lawyer Arthur Finch, also an Antioch graduate. "They didn't investigate the issues of black people, so residents' points of view were not represented. Before, D.C. was basically a captive of white lawyers and judges . . . I don't think people in D.C. other than lawyers understand the profound difference. It may be her most major accomplishment. Marion blackened the executive branch of D.C. government; Eleanor did the judges."

And, in spite of the frightening financial news, residents had the satisfaction of knowing that come what may, they had a bulldog on the Hill, one who would move the heavens to advance District interests. When Congress wanted to divert federal agencies outside the District—to Virginia or Maryland—city residents had a fighter who would go to the mat to defend their jobs. When riders were attached to bills, they knew their delegate was vigilant. Representatives might "beat their chests and beat up on the District to score points back home," as Eleanor wrote in a *Post* editorial, but their warrior was there.

Her opponents might feel scorched by her biting tongue, but residents relished the spectacle of their delegate taking on the powerful men who sought to second-guess their every law. Many understood that her armor was necessary protection in the world of Congress, where, Eleanor laughs, "they throw bombs at the end of the day. In the morning they just throw grenades."

"She gives 'em fits!" was a typical sentiment. Most constituents felt well-represented, even, some add bitterly, "with the limited representation we have in Congress." Eleanor had taken what many considered a thankless job and made it shine.

On election night in 1994, Eleanor watched and waited in yet another election eve Democratic victory party ballroom. Even while she moved to her trademark dances, laughing and chatting, she wondered about the fate of her city. In four years she had reversed the negative polls, flipping her approval rating to an astonishing 80 percent positive mark. As the city's most popular politician, her seat was virtually guaranteed. But would the Democrats be able to hold Congress—and her limited vote on the floor of the House? If they did, perhaps her drive for greater home rule would have another chance.

CHAPTER 13

Under Attack

"I don't think political capital is worth a dime if you just hoard it and don't use it."

ELEANOR HOLMES NORTON

Eleanor's worst fears were realized. In 1994's November election, a rout reporters dubbed "an angry white male backlash" turned the House. "We had no idea the Democratic Party would be wiped out," mourns Donna, who watched results at party headquarters with Eleanor's son, Johnny. Fresh from college, he had worked a campaign season for the Democratic National Committee.

"We were going great guns for the District under the Democrats and here come the Republicans. So I had to shift gears. And here," explains Eleanor, who'd lived through so many civil rights ups and downs, "is where you've got to will things to happen."

For the first time in forty years Republicans gained majorities in both houses. When they rewrote the rules, they simply did away with the 1993 Democratic rule that gave the five delegates—all Democrats—voting power on the House floor.

"If it had only been D.C., there might have been less resentment," Eleanor speculates. "It was Sovietesque. Because they just left it out of the rules, although I campaigned hard and two Republicans went with me to the Rules Committee to ask for it back." In early 1995, Eleanor wrote Senate Majority Leader Bob Dole and House Speaker Newt Gingrich:

> The withdrawal of a vote, once granted, has not occurred since the Civil War. The precipitous withdrawal of the vote of delegates when a different political party became the major-ity party in the House raises serious questions under the International Covenant [on Civil and Political Rights, rati-

fied by the U.S. in 1992]. The apparent violation is made more serious by the fact that the leadership of that party had previously challenged delegate voting in the courts on legal and constitutional grounds and the courts had vindicated delegate voting.

But there was, it seemed, little else she could do. Every day brought fresh news of the city's economic disaster; District relations with Congress rapidly slid downhill. Kelly, running for reelection against a comeback Marion Barry, got only 12 percent of the vote, so Eleanor had to deal not only with a Republican Congress, but also with a mayor avidly disliked on Capitol Hill.

Now, with four years in Congress under her belt, Eleanor set to work building a bridge between the liberal city, where SNCC veterans like Barry, John Wilson and Frank Smith were key players, and the Republican House. First, she told the press, "We mustn't rush to pre-judgment."

"When they took over I had to decide how I was going to behave. I've been able to make alliances with all kinds of Republicans without los-ing my liberal virginity. Nobody in the Congress expects you to give up your own politics. *The question is how you carry yourself.*"

The woman "with no power and less authority," as many District res-idents describe the job of their delegate before Eleanor took it on, believed that her constituents were entitled to a seat at the table. And "you've got to work with what you've got."

Eleanor set out to make allies of key Republicans. "Brilliant at turn-ing enemies into friends," according to colleagues, she sought out the new speaker, Newt Gingrich, with whom she had had a superficial rela-tionship. Now, whenever there was a crisis, she went to see him.

"I did not become one of the Republican boys, by any means. No, I went and talked to him about my district. He was going to close down the government over an appropriations dispute with Clinton. 'Newt, don't do that to the District.' We developed a relationship; thereafter, through Newt's personal intervention, I was able to keep D.C. open.

"His fascination with the District and sense of history led to the unusual request that he participate in a town meeting. I took him."

That hot August evening in 1995, just nine months after the "Republican Revolution," people waited in the sun for hours to enter a town meeting featuring Speaker Newt Gingrich, the conservative who embodied every value antithetical to the liberal District. By eight P.M., the auditorium at Eastern High School in Ward Six overflowed. No Democratic speaker had ever appeared; the idea of a Republican was unprecedented. A thousand Washingtonians packed inside; another thousand were left outside in the heat, a few with "No Newt" banners.

"Newt was just absolutely intrigued. Newt is a very interesting and complicated guy. But as far as my people were concerned, Newt Gingrich was the stereotypical conservative."

"So how do I introduce him?" she asks, relishing as always her contrarian role. For Eleanor is as complicated as Newt, the liberal twin to his conservative mirror. She opened with the truth.

"I want you to know that the Speaker has helped me in many ways. When it looked like the District was about to lose $200 million dollars for these raggedy roads out here, I went to the Speaker and was able to save that money."

After giving her audience three other instances in which their nemesis had helped the District, she turned and said, with a grin, "But the Speaker knows I oppose his entire national agenda, from the Contract on America to the death penalty, and he knows I seek to replace him as Speaker of the House of Representatives."

This in-your-face style, where nothing was hidden, nothing said later in private that she hadn't said to his face, brought down the house. And to his credit, Gingrich, by then damp with perspiration, just laughed. Right on the heels of her public disavowal of his entire legislative program, Eleanor capped her introduction with her classic twist, "I'm very pleased to introduce to you my good friend, the Speaker of the House, Newt Gingrich."

Having made it clear to those in the District that her politics hadn't changed at all—while this "enemy of the people" had helped her do good things for them—she asked the raucous audience to listen to the man. Some boos mixed with the polite applause that greeted him.

The Speaker, joined onstage by Eleanor, Barry and a dozen local officials, pledged to support home rule: "The citizens of the city have to deal with the reality of everyday life, and those of us who visit do not have the knowledge and do not have the right to micromanage the daily lives of the people of this city."

During questioning, Gingrich listened intently, taking notes for several hours. Afterward, he told Eleanor that he wanted to visit every ward of the District, which could be a showcase city. She cooled his ardor but had made an ally whom reporters would call the city's "unexpected guardian angel." Today he says, "Without her courageously legitimizing the event, it couldn't have happened. She always walked a tightrope with incredible integrity."

But no matter how hard Eleanor fought for her city ("I'm known as a fighter. 'Eleanor will get you!' ") the District hemorrhaged money. Kelly had gone in with her broom but hadn't been able to create the smooth, professionally run city she imagined. On the contrary, by the end of her term the District was over $700 million dollars in the red, almost double the deficit she'd inherited. On November 10, 1994, Eleanor, calling the local government one "everybody admits is too big for its britches," urged Barry to make cuts immediately. If he didn't, "somebody else will be making those decisions for the city."

By January 1995, the District spiraled out of control. City payments to pension funds were deferred again and again. In February, the city's credit rating was downgraded to junk bond status. "It was a horrible situation," remembers Eleanor's first legislative director, Cedric Hendricks. "That was right after Republicans took over, and Tom Davis, a Virginia Republican, became chair of the D.C. Subcommittee."

Davis says he was warned by his predecessor Pete Stark about the confrontational District delegate. But Davis saw another side of Eleanor; she jumped to his rescue when, as a freshman, he described the District's sticky status to a reporter as "a real tar baby."

"Eleanor said, 'Give the guy a chance,' " Davis remembers appreciatively. "I never forgot that. She came more than halfway and told me she wanted to work with me. She will take shots—and land some punches—but she won't take a cheap shot. Once you get through all the bluster up front she's pretty easy to work with."

The particular set of circumstances to which the District was heir made it uniquely subject to financial trouble. Costs for prisons and Medicaid, for instance, which states absorbed for other cities, were borne solely by the District; Medicaid alone accounted for 40 percent of the deficit. The District's annual federal receipts (less than 20 percent of its revenues) were a smaller percentage than state aid to comparably sized cities like Boston, Memphis and Baltimore. And, along with other aging cities, Washington had a shrinking tax base, since middle-class whites—and later blacks—had fled. More than two-thirds of those who worked in the District by day went home to Virginia and Maryland suburbs at night, paying taxes there. Repeated requests for a commuter tax had been denied by Democrats and Republicans alike.

The District was going down. Running out of money, it needed operating funds and breathing room to improve its bond rating. New York, Philadelphia, and Cleveland had been bailed out by their states when they went bankrupt. Here, there was no state. Instead, there was the history of antagonism between the city and its federal overseers, now exacerbated by congressional distrust of Barry.

Realizing that the Republican Congress was about to take fiscal oversight, Eleanor stepped forward, determined to shape the inevitable future. On February 16, 1995, speaking before local policy makers, she initiated the unpopular call for a temporary control board. "Of all the options we looked at," says Donna, "Eleanor took that one, because she thought it left more of home rule intact than any other." From then on, Eleanor would play a critical role in who would run such a board and how it would operate.

"I called the chair of the City Council, I called Barry," she says. "Neither wanted it, though I told them what our choices were."

"I called Tom Davis and Jim Walsh. 'I want to do this myself, knowing this is going to happen.' If you can't borrow money, you can't live!"

A control board would allow the District to negotiate loans from the U.S. Treasury. Stretching its deficit over several years could avoid massive service cuts and layoffs.

"It was a threat to home rule, but the fact is that other cities didn't lose their home rule. I told my constituents, 'We must shape this board in keeping with home rule; we must not allow a structure to be simply imposed upon us, while we are voyeurs.' Then I engaged in the hardest negotiation of my life. It was me against the world. Because the bill, of course, had to be written by the Republicans.

"The District got so close to running out of money we had to do a bicameral, bipartisan negotiation with our Appropriations and District Committees, and Barry not even in the room."

Once again, two critical principles—this time, home rule and solvency—were at odds. Eleanor, trying to resolve them, told a packed February 22 House hearing on District finances, "Washingtonians have heard me speak about my great-grandfather Richard Holmes, the ancestor who laid down our family roots in Washington before the Civil War . . . [He] didn't walk here to freedom only to have his family surrender a century later to the bondage of insolvency. Richard figured out how to pick himself up and move on. We in the District must be ready to do no less."

For the next ten days she battled a hostile Congress. Forcefully wagging her finger into the lens of a television camera in late March, she promised: Only District taxpayers would be eligible for a federal oversight board.

"People have called and said, 'Eleanor ought to hide out from this issue.' My answer was people should hear it from the person they sent to Congress. It would be morally repugnant for me to hide out."

"She was a major player," says Tom Davis. "Gingrich and I saw she needed to be in the room. The Newt people understood her utility in this. Getting Eleanor in the room helped the city, helped the castor oil go down easy."

On April 7, Congress established a five-person oversight board; its members would be local. And ultimately, in a city deeply sensitive to matters of race, Eleanor saw to it that four of its five members would be black.

As a result of her negotiations, the original control board also left most powers of the elected mayor and City Council intact. Yet it would review financial plans to ensure a balanced budget for the next three years, and it could act if elected officials failed to take necessary action, such as renegotiating contracts. Though not as strong as New York City's controversial board (Big MAC) had been—that one could fire and issue binding orders on city officials—this Financial Responsibility and Management Assistance Authority, as it was officially called, was a political step back for a city seeking self-determination.

Some home rule advocates were furious at what felt like betrayal by their "Warrior on the Hill," as Barry had named her. Eleanor's old civil rights colleague Lawrence Guyot represented the activist response. "Everything that we fought for in Mississippi is being taken away." The Republicans, some felt, had thrown a rock and hidden their hand, showing hers instead.

To her critics Eleanor responds, "What would they have done? Gone down with the ship? Hey, it was the life or death of a city! They're real people here. You must borrow money because of people."

Having done what she could to ameliorate a terrible situation, Eleanor was caught in the classic position of activist-turned-legislator: she had to work with what was there. It wasn't much, and it wasn't enough for her critics. Activist June Johnson says, "She really overcompromised herself, or the people." But, adds Johnson, "I didn't hold it personally against her. I feel very sorry for Eleanor; she fights so hard, that must be a very lonely feeling to be up there battling all these racist white men."

"My greatest regret about the control board is not what we put in place," Eleanor says today. "Because with hard negotiations, we left in place the mayor's and city council's power. But Barry did not show his legendary acumen in his dealings with [control board chairman] Brimmer. Marion openly fought instead of negotiating behind the scenes." Congress retaliated by attaching riders to D.C. appropriations each year that progressively cut Barry's power.

"The D.C. government has an attitude," she said then. "Nothing will work unless it is reformed agency by agency, where the waste is . . . The control board's plan to cut 10,000 jobs [about a quarter of the city payroll] is a good one." Her no-nonsense approach brought acclaim as well as censure. A *Post* poll taken just weeks after her proposal for a board showed a 74 percent favorable rating, the highest for any local politician, with identical results from black and white residents. And she won support from influential local commentators like Mark Plotkin. "Norton is right in saying this is not a surrender but a temporary arrangement."

Eleanor had the primary responsibility to recommend control board members to President Clinton. Republican Connie Newman, who had held major positions in Republican administrations, was an early choice; Dr. Joyce Ladner, by then interim president of Howard University, was another. Characteristically, even those two battled.

"I thought she didn't have sufficient understanding and respect for how difficult it was for us to get things done on the control board," says Ladner. "She'd get on the phone and scream at me; I'd wait for her to cool down and call her. She doesn't carry grudges."

The tendency of this reflective woman to sometimes "just lose it" worried supporters who found her behavior "totally out of character." Prominent Washingtonians joked that they could hold the phone twelve inches away and still hear her raving.

Many friends describe her temper as born of impatience, "her brain going a hundred miles an hour faster than those around her, and not understanding why the rest of us can't keep up."

"It's a flash kind of anger," explains Vernon Jordan, "mostly instant, spontaneous; when expressed it cools off and she becomes a reasonable person. She is not an angry person. Some of that is passion for what she thinks and believes."

Newt Gingrich concurs. "I have seen her on the floor get very fiery. There are others who are angry all the time. You think, 'That's how they are.' But Eleanor is so pleasant 99 percent of the time that the transformation is startling."

"You don't want to get cussed out by this woman," confirms her old friend Christine Philpot. "But that's a source of her vitality. None of her energy goes into front."

"Eleanor doesn't have what I call that 'soft touch,' " says Donna, hardly known for that herself. "I used to go around and just smooth out all the ruffled feathers that Eleanor would ruffle up. I have seen Eleanor make grown people cry. . . . This is a woman who can eat and lick up the hottest hot sauce on the planet."

That same quality of energetic argument, however, impressed constituents. One says, admiringly, "Eleanor can take those jaws and pout with the best of them. When she stands up to the white people who head the D.C. committees, she says, 'Oh no, over my dead body. You will not disrespect the District of Columbia.' She makes her constituents think, 'Go Eleanor, we are going to get respect!' "

Applauding her work, even her predecessor concedes, "I would not know how to act in the minority on the Hill. In light of that, she's done a remarkably effective job, not only advocating against overwhelming odds but also addressing local concerns that I did not address as well. [The Republicans] don't play. I would hate to have been there in her shoes."

People on the street continued to approach her, beaming as they called out or hugged their delegate. Eleanor didn't turn away ("She never even sighs," says Connie Newman) but returned the warmth. At Eastern Market on Saturdays clerks excitedly shouted her name while passersby gave her a thumbs-up, smiling, "Great job!" And every two years, they continued to sweep her back into office with virtual unanimity.

* * *

Despite the control board's efforts, two years later the city was still down and out. By 1997, its drinking water was polluted and trash pickup was down to one day a week. A new congressional rescue package, written by Clinton budget director Franklin Raines and fiercely negotiated by Eleanor, finally lifted costly expenses from the District. The Revitalization Act—taking the city's prison and court costs plus its $5 billion pension liability and reducing its Medicaid contributions—together with significant home-buyer and business tax cuts, jump-started a rebirth. "I credit Eleanor with the city's success," says Tom Davis.

However, the new act, denounced by Barry as the "rape of democracy," had last-minute attachments that stripped much mayoral power. Many residents' worst fears were realized when, on August 5, after President Clinton signed the new control board powers into law, Andrew Brimmer announced nine city department head replacements. An unelected "dictator," according to home rule activists, now ruled. A group of protestors led by Mark Thompson, chanting "Free D.C.," charged a table at Luther Place Memorial Church where Brimmer and the control board met. Member Joyce Ladner acknowledged, "Of course the city is a colony. The question is who fixes the colony. Congress or us?"

Some accused Eleanor of selling out their hard-won right to elect a mayor and city council, achieved only twenty-three years before. One sign called her "Eleanor Benedict Arnold Norton." Her reply was that Senator Lauch Faircloth had forced in these terrible last-minute riders. In a poignant reminder of the tensions she faced, the *Post* headlined her, WOMAN IN THE MIDDLE. "In the end, Norton, the city's most popular and arguably most volcanic politician, found a deal she couldn't turn down."

She herself compounded her difficulties. Eleanor's usual ability to take a complicated issue and clearly articulate it failed her during these tension-filled days.

She initially hailed the legislation as a triumph, calling passage "a big win for the District." Defending its management reforms, she told D.C. officials, "If you want home rule, rule." But then, criticized by those like Jesse Jackson who described the newly empowered board as a "military junta," and faced with taunts from protestors, Eleanor seemed to waver on the legislation she had just coauthored.

"When the Revitalization Act came through, I said, 'This is a tremendous breakthrough, because we've gotten all these burdens taken off of us.'

"Then I was to give opening remarks at the Urban League Convention. I had fought the inroads into home rule, but the fact is they'd gotten in. When I went to greet the Urban League, a national audience, I emphasized the fights we have to make for our rights. In my three minutes' opening remarks to a civil rights audience, I talked about how Congress had used the bill to take down part of home rule in this package. The press, hearing that, reported, 'But yesterday she said it was a good thing!'

"It was difficult to explain why I had said one thing one place and another thing another place. And they were both true!

"If I had to do it over again, I would say, 'A good thing just happened in the District, and a terrible thing has also happened.' So I learned. I reject the notion that it was a flip-flop, but I accept that it looked like that. I selectively picked out a piece that was appropriate for the Urban League audience. I created the confusion; I paid the price."

Then there was a picket line with "Free D.C." signs where Eleanor went over to talk to protesters. "And what did I do that for? One of them had a sign saying, 'Eleanor sold us out.' But I went to talk to them because you don't run from your constituents. You explain yourself! I knew what had actually happened. And these were people who had supported me." Newspapers ran pictures; though she was not *in* the demonstration, some stories portrayed her seemingly picketing her own program, denouncing the legislation she had just coauthored.

"BUDGET DEAL CREATES HEAT FOR DISTRICT OF COLUMBIA'S DELEGATE," the *New York Times* headlined its story, while the *City Paper* charged, "Norton abandoned her message altogether. . . . Norton was shifting again like a barrier island in a hurricane."

Eleanor wrote an explanatory *Post* editorial. "The line I walk between democracy and efficiency may be thin. I may fall off sometimes. But I will always get right back up. I won't stop working for what this city needs to survive, and I can't stop fighting for full democracy."

In Congress Eleanor's combative style, her "sheer force of personality," Democrat James Moran of Virginia said, was both "her biggest asset. And her biggest problem." He implied that, since "her MO is to lash out," she may lack some influence she could have had. "The door is not necessarily open to someone who is so antagonistic as to question all your motives."

On the contrary, Newt Gingrich believes her style is her greatest asset. "Because the District is not part of a state she never has the power of bargaining her vote; she is always negotiating from weakness. If the District were part of Maryland . . . she would be a very powerful member, because her natural intelligence and charm and energy would carry her to a significant leadership role. But she's had to get up every morning and try to gain for the people of D.C., from an indifferent or critical Congress, the resources. So a bit of temper may be because she gets tired of working from a position of no power. I think more remarkable is her ability to get back up every day and go back into the fight."

In fact, Eleanor's go-to-the-mat style may have prevented a total city takeover. "She's up against a Congress which was intent on a coup against the District," said American University law professor Jamin Raskin. The District paid a stiff price, but her "slashing rhetoric," as the *Post* called it, probably achieved more than it lost. Eleanor negotiated a huge financial package with long-term benefits, rather than a simple emergency bailout, and significantly reformed the financial relationship between the District and the federal government. Many, including Congressman Davis, credit her for the city's successful turnaround. Even after the partial loss of home rule, with the mayor stripped of power and the school system in the hands of an appointed board, Eleanor was overwhelmingly reelected.

Despite a schedule that included every significant city event, several friends managed to lure Eleanor to occasional Friday night movies. Driving to a local multiplex, greeted warmly by constituents even as she parked, the congresswoman especially loved movies about courage. "She's very old-fashioned in her values," says Barbara Williams-Skinner. "In the best way. She gets teary-eyed and passionate when she sees someone uphold honor or valor." One of her favorites was *Bridge on the River Kwai,* the epic 1957 World War II film about duty and the fatal flaw of perfectionism. On these movie evenings, a quiet, thoughtful self sometimes emerged. "She isn't about to show the fact that she has this side, this Achilles heel," says Connie Williams.

In 1996, Charlayne Hunter-Gault, one of Eleanor's oldest and closest friends, called from New York to say *MacNeil-Lehrer* was consolidating operations. She was moving to Washington.

"I got this big old house, come and stay with me," urged Eleanor.

Charlayne did come, converted an unused study to a bedroom and remained for a year before moving on to South Africa; her investment banker husband had preceded her.

"Big fun," Eleanor remembers the long visit. "Katherine was in seventh heaven. Charlayne cooked! Katherine would run down the stairs because a master cook was in the house. We had several dinner parties together, with friends. Oh, it was great. I hated to see her go."

"I'd come home from work every night, make a little meal," concurs Charlayne. "You know Eleanor doesn't cook. What makes her happy is a good hot meal. You'd think she was seven years old the way she'd sit there and marvel over this food. The tough, aggressive, razor sharp–minded woman who most people see in combat—but she's an innocent! She's so pure; she's one of the world's great innocents. She was so grateful and complimentary you enjoyed doing it; you just love her so much."

Eleanor lived near the flowers of Capitol Hill's Eastern Market; on weekends Charlayne made huge arrangements so when Eleanor came in the door they were the first thing she would see.

"Oh my God!" she'd scream at the top of her voice.

"Anybody would think she'd been shot," says Charlayne. "Her level of appreciation of the smallest things was so intense."

"Charlayne taught me the importance of having flowers in the house all the time," Eleanor affirms, now regularly buying her own bunches every Saturday afternoon, one for an elegant copper vase on the sideboard near the front door, the other upstairs on a copper table in her large study–family room.

After Charlayne left, Donna frequently prepared meals: delicious chicken, potatoes, gravy and vegetables. Eleanor loved to have friends around the house, but only with one or two intimates did she breach her personal reticence, and then rarely. "Being the kind of high-energy person she is, to maintain that she compartmentalizes," says Charlayne. "When you sit down and emote with people, that's a lot of energy. She doesn't expend any more energy than she needs to. You have to peel back a lot to see that soft core. And she can't reveal it to everybody because people will abuse it and mistake it for weakness."

Her Movement colleague John Lewis agrees. "Eleanor is not a hugging person, not the type of politician of Bill Clinton. She maintains a distance, an invisible wall. She doesn't allow people to get too close. Even on the [House] floor or in a meeting, she's not primpy, but everything must be in line, every crease must be there, every ruffle, every hair in place. We don't like to be associated with things that look disorganized, that look raggy; they've got to be disciplined, have a little class. I have seen her laugh and carry on, but she's not that playful."

When momentarily freed from work, the teenager who loved to dance, read or show tender concern for a friend was occasionally visible. In the evenings she sometimes chuckled on the phone or sniffled over a sentimental movie at home.

But mostly the congresswoman focused on the interests she'd been elected to serve. Faced with constituents living around the corner and across town—unlike other members of Congress who worked far from home—she continued to drive herself, literally and metaphorically, attending local events almost daily. Showing up without an entourage or security, Eleanor remained unusually accessible. Residents became used to seeing her at neighborhood meetings or, on Saturdays, in her race-walking pants at the corner CVS drugstore.

Inside Congress Eleanor met weekly with the Congressional Black Caucus at its Wednesday lunch. "She has the sense that we have an obligation, that she's been blessed," says John Lewis. As chair of the CBC task force on nominations, she was a dependable watchdog for judicial appointments.

Eleanor never sought to chair the caucus, however, preferring not to embrace some of its "automatic positions." For example, despite good personal relations with Minister Farrakhan and many Black Muslims, she couldn't support a speaking invitation to Farrakhan. "My problems come largely from my view that our moral authority as black people stems from the universality of equality. Given the hell we've experienced, we should be especially vigilant against homophobia, anti-Semitism, sexism and the like." While the caucus often pressed these issues with great success, sometimes it took a more racialized view of the world than Eleanor did.

The bipartisan Women's Caucus was "a wholly different kettle of fish. If anything," Eleanor laughs, "they can't take positions on some of the things I feel strongly about, like abortion, because some are pro-life. But 95 percent of what we want to work on, you can get Democratic and Republican women to agree upon."

Since 1977, the handful of women had gathered for mutual support. In their twentieth anniversary year, when congressional women were at their all-time high of fifty-one, Eleanor was elected cochair with Republican Nancy Johnson. They initiated an annual dinner, getting the president and first lady to attend, with Secretary of State Madeleine Albright as keynote speaker. And Eleanor used a familiar structure—hearings—so women could gather "the facts" to back positions, whether on child care, contraceptive research or gender equality in education.

"One hearing was on breast cancer when this extraordinary new drug came out. They actually had to stop the trials because it worked so effectively. We flew in the surgeon general for that."

In another "first" they started the notion of "must-pass" bills, formed fourteen bipartisan legislative teams and began annual meetings with the majority and minority leaders to back up their demands. During Eleanor and her cochair's tenure, the caucus became a tougher, more effective legislative group, with over half its "must-pass" priorities enacted into law.

In January 1999, Eleanor had an unusual opportunity to underscore the lack of District democracy. Congress was set to vote on impeaching Clinton, for whom she felt a personal warmth, despite his actions. "You don't have to be a feminist to say that was no way to behave. But we would have become a very unstable democracy if that level of wrongdoing in your personal life could result in upsiding an election. That would have been a perilous precedent.

"Impeachment comes up. We have a right to vote for president. The District got that right [in 1961] under the Twenty-third Amendment. Now they're about to impeach him. Shall the District, which voted to elect him, now have no vote?

"Umpteen people are making speeches about what's wrong with this impeachment process. I can join, or I can think about how impeachment highlights the terrible injustice to the residents of the District.

"So two days before, I negotiated with the [Republican] majority. I gave notice that I would offer a privileged resolution. Very seldom done." This resolution, stopping action on the floor, was a dramatic moment. For the first vote of impeachment, every House seat was full.

"Henry Hyde was on his side ready at the mark. And John Conyers, the ranking member for our side, was just as ready. There is the Speaker. and America's poised: 'What is Henry Hyde going to say?' "

He recognized "the gentlelady from the District of Columbia," giving her the almost unprecedented privilege of speaking on the House floor without a time limit.

"I ask for the right to vote in this proceeding!" And she explained her logic: people who vote to elect a president should have a vote on his impeachment. As anticipated, she was unsuccessful, but once again Eleanor had found a way to tell the world about her cause.

Ever seeking ways to express the injustice the District suffered—"taxation without representation"—Eleanor continually devised fresh tactics. In 1999 she published a tax protest in her newsletter, providing the public with a copy of the letter she had attached to her personal federal income taxes. "My people will read that and some of them will do the same thing."

The warrior never let up. At seven or eight in the evening she usually left the office, with a quick stop on her way home, perhaps at a local banquet to say a few words, before arriving while Katherine was still up watching television or doing puzzles. When her mother appeared—no matter how tired—the two embraced.

"She is great, regardless of how bad her day is, she still comes in here and hugs her daughter," says her child-caretaker, Mrs. Vermell Howard. "Regardless of how her day is outside, she never brings it home. And that's what I love about her. No matter how tired she is, she'll do her little dance. Then she'll come to Katherine and she'll hug her. She's never too tired for that when she comes in that door. And the same thing with Johnny when he comes home to visit, he's just the same."

Close friends agree that Katherine is central to Eleanor's life. "I watched her with her daughter," says Maudine Cooper, president of the Greater Washington Urban League. "She brought her to one of our football games and I saw a side of her I haven't seen: she was motherly.

" 'Do you want something to eat.' 'Are you okay?' We don't see our politicians as human. I was a little surprised. You see Hercules pick a flower."

Eleanor says she is never sure how to deal publicly with Katherine.

"On one hand I don't have the least compunction talking about my child who's retarded. On the other hand, I have nothing but contempt for people who use their children politically.

"Recently I spoke at the National Christian Church, one of the great cathedral-like churches that President Johnson, Garfield and others attended. After a few words about the church, I said, 'I'm going to speak about my mother because it's Mother's Day. On this day mothers think about their children; my mother is a good mother because she is a good woman. And I strive to be a good mother to my twenty-eight-year-old daughter who has Down's syndrome.'

"I said it because I thought it was relevant. On Mother's Day. And of course whenever I've announced for Congress, I've had Katherine there. But I don't parade the fact that I have this retarded child or pretend to be some kind of poster mother."

Even with her demanding schedule, Eleanor drove herself to think creatively, accepting substantive and challenging local speaking engagements to push herself. "Being a legislator makes you think about race and many issues superficially because you wonder, "How should I vote?" You need to know quickly which side you are on. What you do at a given moment may not be the best long-term thing to do." Venues like the Brookings Institution guaranteed she would deeply contemplate a subject; she took local invitations whenever she could.

But while Eleanor conceptualized, strategized, and delivered all the goods she could to her city, every two years she had to run for reelection. On January 8, 2000, she opened her sixth campaign with a kickoff event at Howard University's School of Business auditorium.

Driving herself, with Katherine and Mrs. Howard in the backseat, Eleanor pulled up to the school's doors at 11:45 A.M., an hour later than she had planned, but still before the event's noon beginning. She was greeted enthusiastically outside by supporters. One man had waited to give her a letter; another, visibly awed, shook her hand, saying, "I never saw you up so close before," as his eyes drank her in. A TV cameraman followed her, backing up, with the camera trained on Eleanor as she walked in.

Katherine, who had developed suspicions of crowds, balked at the threshold. Eleanor coaxed Katherine firmly but patiently.

"There's food in there. It's a party."

When persuasion failed, she phoned Edward, scheduled to care for Katherine at his apartment later that day. But getting no answer she sent Katherine to the car with Mrs. Howard. Taking just a second, Eleanor gathered herself and strode inside, smiling broadly as she greeted supporters.

"I'm fine. Look at this!" In the lobby, tables with colorful balloons were set to register campaign volunteers. Upstairs, tables overflowed with food—water, soda, pretzels, nuts and other snacks—and blue "Eleanor! For Congress" T-shirts, buttons and bumper stickers.

By 12:20, the auditorium began to fill with an overwhelmingly African-American audience, many of them the middle-aged women who are the backbone of D.C. political activism. One dreadlocked woman sported a "Free DC" cap. James Forman, with other luminaries of an earlier civil rights movement, sat down front, and a sprinkling of graying whites scattered, clustering in small groups. Eleanor wore a bright red blouse, its collar coming smartly over her blue Eleanor! T-shirt. The mayor arrived, shaking hands; men hugged him while recorded music played "Order My Steps in Your Word, Dear Lord" and a gospel group, wearing "Eleanor!" T's over their white tops, filed in. Red, white and blue balloons—her colors—graced the stage, where Eleanor sat with a giant fifteen-foot "Norton" banner as backdrop.

"Welcome to Campaign 2000!" Willie Flowers, president of D.C. Young Democrats, said, opening a high-spirited introduction of "our hard-fighting congresswoman who leaves no stone unturned!" He highlighted the D.C. College Access Act, which meant that a local student could now attend a school like George Mason University in Virginia for five instead of fifteen thousand dollars. Eleanor had chosen Howard, the Young Democrats and the high school chorus to emphasize her prized achievement of the session.

"Lightning can strike, storms can hit, earthquakes can come, but the greatest force of nature is Eleanor Holmes Norton!" Mayor Anthony Williams called from the podium to her hard-core supporters. They roared; she laughed delightedly.

"She is a vibrant, extraordinary monument of living democracy," he continued, while she beamed. "Here is a woman without a vote who's managed to work with the federal government to pass a consensus budget, get the College Access Act, credit the University of the District of

Columbia, as it should, as an historically black college, getting millions of dollars . . ." he continued, trumpeting her accomplishments, calling after each one, "Who has gotten us this?"

"Eleanor Holmes Norton!"

"Who will lead the city?"

"Eleanor Holmes Norton!"

"She never gives up fighting! We're here to celebrate what she's done and what she'll do in the new century!"

"Eleanor Holmes Norton!" As the crowd chanted, Eleanor laughed with pleasure. This was her moment.

Councilwoman Sandy Allen spoke about Eleanor's style, one clearly beloved by her audience. "Sometimes Eleanor, you let it be known that being cool and proper is not the proper way. 'Yes, I am a woman but I'm leading the charge . . . and if you don't give me the vote on the floor, I'm going to bring my people to fight for the right to spend our taxes as we choose. I will not allow anyone to kill the people of the District of Columbia.' " Allen hit a nerve; the crowd exploded.

"Well, Eleanor," Allen promised, to cheers, "We are here for you!"

"What time is it?" she asked the crowd.

"Norton time!" they called back.

Council member Jack Evans, a tall white man, rose. "The Wilson building, she made it happen! She has the ability to exercise her clout on behalf of all of us. You've been a champion for us . . . We're here for you!"

Then Florence Pendleton, the shadow senator, an older black woman and enthusiastic speaker, broke it down. "One of the main reasons we need to send her back is she fights! On the screen and off the screen!" Cheers. "She's also a bridge builder. We need her help for full voting representation."

The crowd's enthusiasm was further fueled by the gospel ensemble, ten talented students from the Duke Ellington School, which Eleanor was seeking to affiliate with the Kennedy Center. Their director played his keyboard while proudly leading.

Donna Brazile rose to pay tribute, calling Eleanor "my political mother."

"Eleanor Holmes Norton is always there to lift me up. I'm going to take credit today for going over to Eleanor's house ten years ago and knocking on her door, and asking her to run.

"Whenever I cook, Eleanor listens and she eats." The crowd laughed. "For ten years I've been honored to serve as her chief of staff. She calls before seven A.M. and after 11:30 P.M., seven days a week. That's what it's like working for Eleanor Holmes Norton.

"She calls before seven to tell you she's on television at seven, watch it, she'll be calling back to hear what you thought. She does call back, right after seven, to see what you thought about it, what she could have done better. . . . That's what it's like working for Eleanor Holmes Norton!

"There's no such thing as a federal holiday, because people may need help. If you work for EHN you have to have a listed phone number, because *she's* listed.

"I never had to drive her. Eleanor is a fourth-generation Washingtonian. She knows her way around. I am a gentle giant compared to this hurricane-force volcanic person. She *can* cause the seasons to change on time.

"It's rare to find a leader who won't leave their district on junket . . . I can't ever book her on a plane. She's here. She'll bring home the bacon and anything else she can scrape out of Congress. Let them know we still want statehood and our rights!" Donna concluded, walking over to embrace Eleanor, who stood and took the mike.

"Donna brought tears to my eyes, because her sacrifices go unrewarded while I'm out front. So much of my success, for which I've gotten generous credit, is due to her.

"The Republicans took my vote but they couldn't take yours. As long as I have your vote, let us vow to win the full vote in the House that we seek in the courts right now."

The crowd was on its feet, cheering mightily.

"I will demand the vote because it is your vote, not mine. But I will never use the absence of the vote to not bring home what others bring to theirs. I was in the top 4 percent of members to pass bills in the 105th Congress. I produce legislation, and still I want my vote!

"With or without the vote, the IRS takes your money!" Her voice got deep and angry. "We pay our full fare as American citizens. It's time we got paid what we are owed as citizens of the nation's capital. So ready or not, Congress, here we come!"

Generations of disenfranchisement echoed, from the days when black citizens paid taxes for schools they couldn't use, or parks and municipal swimming pools they couldn't enter.

"D.C. is left to pick up the tab," Eleanor thundered, "for services D.C. residents provide to federal employees and tourists! Don't leave half a million people paying for services for the millions who use them!" The crowd was on its feet. The commuter tax was a burning issue.

"Congress insults us by taking your money while taking your vote.

"Your votes have been my sword and my shield that I wear on my lapel so I can walk . . ."

"YES!" the crowd cheered.

"Tall and proud . . ."

"YES!"

"Your votes . . ."

"YES!"

"Protect me and sustain me."

"YES!"

"Your votes."

The choir closed with the Edwin Hawkins gospel hit, "Oh Happy Day," as the crowd swayed, clapped and sang along with the chorus. People crowded up to Eleanor. They knew the campaigner would be reelected by a huge margin; yet she wondrously created an event that reenergized support. People embraced her, knowing she would work from dawn till way past dusk. This was her path, this was her choice. The crowd closed in on Eleanor. She was swallowed up by her people, who would continue to reelect their Warrior on the Hill.

CHAPTER 14

Mr. President: "Yes, Eleanor"

*I regard celebrity as one of the great defects of our time. It comes out of my egali-
tarian sense. So I don't pretend that I've met some crescendo. And everybody
ought to understand, "What more can you ask of me?"*
ELEANOR HOLMES NORTON, 2001

Reflecting on her role in "the century of equality," Eleanor muses, "a
lot had to do with your moment in time, and what that moment
gave you the opportunity to learn." But Eleanor took her opportunities
and chose to broaden chances for others. "In the black community, it is
expected," says John Lewis. "If you get a good education, there is a role
for you to play. You are almost automatically cast into leadership."

"In black families one child is usually selected to be 'the one,'"
Eleanor's cousin Dr. Warren Ashe says, reflecting his life as well as hers.
"The child does things whether he wants to or not. You take on challenges to build that preordained destiny, while underneath there is a
quietness you never let people see. Part of the evolution of black families is that 'the one' has to take the opportunity and run with it. That
individual becomes the hope and dreams of the family . . . When you are
'the one' and the pressure is there, you have to go on whether you're
bone tired or not.

"Eleanor has to keep that image on. I watch Eleanor. When she's not
in crowds she's very quiet, almost sad. Someone walks up, she plays the
role. A lot of that quiet comes from her mother.

"As years went by and her mother got older, the question came on,
'How can she do all she's required to do and take care of her mother?'"

When Vela's health failed during the summer of 1999, Eleanor struggled to meet her obligations; sister Portia lived in Georgia, Nellie in
California. Early in September Eleanor had to speak in Maine with Vice
President Gore; she called her cousin and asked him to watch out for
her mother.

"Her constituents don't care if her mother's dying," Dr. Ashe remarks sadly. "They want to know, 'What can you do for me?' All her life Eleanor's taken that leadership role. She's an admirable woman, with a great degree of sensitivity. She just keeps going."

"Eleanor has never demonstrated vulnerability," marvels Portia. "My mother was like that. She must have had feelings, but we didn't see them. When mother died though, Eleanor was vulnerable."

On Thursday, September 30, 1999, Vela Elizabeth Lynch Holmes, who had experienced virtually the entire twentieth century, passed away at the age of ninety. Her funeral took place five days later at St. George's Episcopal, her home church at 2nd and U Streets, NW.

On the morning of October 5, an open casket lay in the small chapel's foyer; a pink satin lining draped with white gauze surrounded the generous face, now haloed with silver hair. Potted palms and flowers crowded the space as mourners took their seats. Soon the small chapel was filled with people talking quietly: Vela's neighbors, old family friends, members of Congress and Eleanor's civil rights colleagues, like Dick Gregory, Dorothy Height and Julianne Malveaux. Her staff members, volunteers at the entryway amidst the forest of plants, handed out programs while Eleanor rushed to greet friends and attend to plants and ushers, making sure strangers didn't sit in family rows.

At noon an organ played, with the Twenty-third Psalm and two hymns: "A Mighty Fortress Is Our God" and "Amazing Grace." Reverend Vincent Powell Harris spoke warmly about his parishioner, a member for sixty-two years, lauding her many volunteer efforts. An avid reader, Mrs. Holmes was acutely attuned to current events, her television always tuned to CSPAN or Public Broadcasting when he visited.

The three daughters paid homage. Eleanor opened. "Vela and Coleman Holmes had their children in rapid succession and when the third was another girl, they quit, never looked back and spent the rest of their lives making the most of it—and of us.

"We learned without knowing we were being taught. All that was necessary was to watch her. When your mother and father are going to college and graduate school when you are little children, they need not preach the importance of education. When your mother raises her family while engaged in a full-time career, you become an instinctive feminist. We never had to be told to be somebody. We simply watched her become somebody. We never suffered the illusion that we were self-made women. We lived with the genuine article.

"Mother's personal qualities are more difficult to imitate," Eleanor's voice softened. "It was far easier to model her work habits and high standards than to develop her patience, her disposition. . . .

"What is one to do with a mother who grows more solicitous of you the older she gets? What you do is to be grateful to have had an extraordinary mother who lived a long life. What you do is to be mindful that Mother was like most people, whose most visible legacy is their children." She began to cry. "What you do is to recognize how much further you have to go to be a legacy worthy of Vela Elizabeth Holmes, our mother."

Portia, a former Howard dean of students, now a college president, described her mother as a master teacher. "I went to college for four years to learn to teach. When I graduated she sat with me for twenty minutes and taught me more, practically speaking, than I learned in four years." Later the thrifty Vela insisted, after Portia's first teaching paycheck, "Meet me at the corner" to bank the check, keeping only $50 to spend.

Nellie, a health care administrator, spoke last, invoking the image of geese flying in formation. "Mother was the goose at the head of our flock; her wings broke the wind for us."

After the daughters finished, four black altar men in white robes swung pots of incense in the medieval ritual. The service continued with "Precious Lord" and the congregants, holding the *Lift Every Voice and Sing Hymnal,* sang all four verses of "It Is Well with My Soul."

When mourners were dismissed, following the chants and swinging incense to the door of the church, they drove in a convoy past Eleanor's childhood Kenyon Street home to the Fort Lincoln Cemetery in Brentwood, Maryland. There, friends and family gathered around the sisters seated under a canopy as the priest sprinkled holy water on the casket.

"My father was cremated at his desire," Eleanor says evenly. "My mother said he had claustrophobia and didn't want to be buried. Aunt Selena, his sister who lived to be ninety, thought it was sacrilegious. Who did my mother think she was, doing this? But she did what *he* wanted.

"When we went to bury my mother, I went to see where his ashes were. We had my mother buried as close to him as possible. They're in a building where there's a stone block with the ashes, and Coleman S. Holmes is way up there in the sky."

Reflecting on the funeral that evening, Eleanor said, "I finally relented and let the casket go open. Portia wanted it, and only because she seemed to want it so badly did I relent. I'm sure that much of my sense of what should be done came not only from Mother but from my elegant father. He would have known that while this is a big thing in D.C., to go look down at somebody's dead face—'Aw, she's so pretty'— that's not the point. He would have understood why I wanted the casket closed. And Vela agreed."

The formal Eleanor surfaced in this most stressful of moments. Not only would she have preferred a closed casket but she wanted a traditional service, rather than having friends or relatives sing and speak. She insisted on keeping out that "self-indulgence."

"This is a fairly high Episcopal church. That's the one they belonged to, that's the church she loved. I'm not going to change that. You've got to first look to the person.

"I have Coleman's sense of propriety. Mother, of course, to the very end, did not have particularly elegant taste. She was still the farm girl. I was always taking a necklace off my mother."

But Eleanor missed the loving farm girl. The next evening she sat in her living room talking on the telephone, nestled into home. Eleanor still favored the antiques her father loved, but now she also had African-style baskets all over the house, and on her white couch Eleanor was framed by small African statues, a gourd and other African instruments.

"Tonight I didn't want to come home from the office," she acknowledged to Donna. "I feel lonely for the first time in my life. I don't want to be alone in the house." Typically, after allowing herself this moment of emotional indulgence Eleanor soon added, "I can't whine, my mother was ninety years old." But she instituted monthly conference calls with Nellie and Portia. Now that they were parentless, the three sisters pulled closer together.

Others had died as well. Six months before Eleanor had participated in a congressional tribute to Judge A. Leon Higginbotham, whose death in December 1998, at age seventy, closed a chapter in her own life.

"The man we commemorate on the floor this afternoon is a man of rare talent and humanity, an extraordinary American . . . one of the youngest men ever appointed to the bench, and one of the first African Americans ever appointed to the federal bench.

"But I must tell the members that this was not the kind of superlative that Judge Higginbotham was after in his life, the youngest or the blackest or the first of a kind. He spent his life being the best. . . .

"[He] understood and was dedicated to equality as a universal principle. He felt as deeply about women, for example, as for African Americans. He did not believe that the word or the idea of equality could be segmented."

Three weeks later she rose to honor another early hero, Dr. Dorothy Height, on the legendary leader's eighty-seventh birthday. She praised her early understanding that there "must be no cleavage between women's rights and African-American rights, between race and sex." As Eleanor celebrated the life of the president of the National Council of Negro Women, "one of America's great coalitions," she saluted qualities she exemplified as well as admired.

As Eleanor herself began to age, still hardheaded, still swearing at the closed-circuit television in her office as her colleagues "dropped grenades" in Congress, she was also changing.

The former Sunday school teacher returned to God after decades of rejection. Her whole adult life she'd avoided religion, associating it with conservatism and hypocrisy, used to rationalize slavery and segregation. Faith, as transmitted through organized religion, seemed "greatly flawed."

Now she says, "I believe that the notion that there is no God—or 'I don't know whether it's a God'—is flawed. The universe is so magnificent and we are such tiny parts of it that it is presumptuous to think we could understand how it all came together. Ultimately I approach God through my brain. That's the way I approach everything else. But I understand the very point of faith is that you can't explain everything. That's the essence of being human. There are things way beyond us.

"What is wonderful and extraordinary about Christianity is quite simply Jesus. What they made of it is a different story. Regardless of whether the miracles occurred, I can understand why people came to worship Jesus. His philosophy and humility are irresistible.

"And he was so human. When they were going to put him on the cross, 'Father, let this cup pass from me.' This always breaks me. Here's where the Christ is the human being like everybody else.

"I think of Christianity when I go on the House floor and hear people gay-bash or come forward with undiluted capitalism, where it is every person for himself. I try to imagine this man 2,000 years ago who came forward saying things that the times were ripe for, in a world where you were supposed to reap what you sowed. 'Eye for an eye, tooth for a tooth.' And here came this person with this notion of love. It was revolutionary."

Eleanor has also been changed by the tax debacle. The woman who could never be bothered to look at a bill became conscientious about personal finances.

"Eleanor called me the other day and told me I should lower my mortgage," reports the stunned Donna. "I said 'Huh?' This was a woman that I could not get involved in any discussion about finances a decade ago; now she's calling me."

"Interest rates are at their lowest point," Eleanor told her protégée. "You should refinance."

"What? I can't believe you're paying attention. What the hell happened to you?"

By the year 2000, most activists of the early sixties had taken some years off—to raise children, make a living or pursue personal interests. But not for any period of her life has Eleanor taken time simply for herself. "She goes all the way to California to make a speech," says Portia, "and spending the night is such a joy to her. But she doesn't stay." Even though Nellie lived in southern California, Eleanor had D.C. business awaiting.

"As my congresswoman, I give her an A-plus," says Donna, "As my boss I give her a C because she doesn't take vacations. Her flaw is that she would not take time out to reflect, to get away, to spend some of her capital that she's earned from District residents, to back off a little bit."

For years her friends called each other begging, "Get her to a party!" Says one Georgetown colleague, "We'd persuade her; she'd come for ten minutes at the end. She never relaxed. That personal life dimension seems not to exist."

Another friend who coaxed was Barbara Babcock. "We are alike in so many ways," says Eleanor. "She teaches law. I teach law. But Barbara always did know how to have fun while working hard; she knows better than I do."

Women alone, especially successful women, are often assumed to be lonely. But Eleanor asserts that the idea—power translates to loneliness—assumes she would want something else.

"There is no felt loneliness. That may be in part because of the activism in my life. And my childhood. I was very much off to myself. I had my own room; Nellie and Portia slept in the same room and were closer. So I'm not lonely. I'm more comfortable being alone. I like to be around people, but it doesn't occur to me that when I am alone I'm lonely."

Many friends, she fears, have given up on her. "Oh, 'She's too busy, why bother to call and invite her? She'll never come.' "

"You all shouldn't assume that I wouldn't go anywhere!" Eleanor reprimanded, now and then attending a weekend movie with Katherine and a friend. "When you go to a movie with Eleanor you have to eat before," one laughs. "After the movie you have to have argument time. She likes to argue the fine points over the popcorn; she gets loud and raucous." But it was hard for Eleanor to get away.

"I'm a workaholic," she admits. "It's not healthy; it does not lead to enough variety in life, and it's a real problem. Because life goes on. If you have invested so much in one single pursuit, you come to a point in your life: what do you do if you retire? You get old. It seems to me, as with everything, balance is important. And a workaholic is by definition unbalanced."

By the turn of the twenty-first century, Eleanor was beginning to shift, taking a week each summer in Oak Bluffs on Martha's Vineyard. Charlayne owned a house in the historically black seaside vacation town; Eleanor stayed nearby, reveling in the indulgence of reading in bed: "What I really miss is reading for pleasure. I had the whole week full of leisure."

Eleanor even began to change her attitude about money. Recognizing that she has enough for herself and for Katherine after her own death, Eleanor started buying nonessential goods. Occasionally.

"There's some Calvinistic way she has, real tight with a dollar," says

Charlayne. "I take her to the most expensive shop in Edgartown [Martha's Vineyard] and make her buy something. She fights me; it's very hard for her. But then when we get home she loves it and whispers, 'I'm so glad you made me buy it!' "

One summer at the Vineyard, Eleanor reluctantly paid an airplane change fee to stay a few more days. Acknowledging that it was hard to spend, she nonetheless relaxed over the coming days until her voice became mellow and sweet, revealing that gentle quality her cousin Warren Ashe had glimpsed. Entering empty time so her mind could simply float, she permitted a self seen by few to delicately unfold.

On other rare occasions Eleanor relaxed by dancing. Barbara Williams-Skinner recalls that on a black leadership retreat in Jamaica, with colleagues like Maya Angelou and Alexis Herman, Eleanor danced so long she closed the place down. "Most of the participants had seen Eleanor argue issues. They knew if she's on it, you better come prepared. And here she was, dancing to the band, staying out there longer than anybody. She shocked those who were used to seeing her in the seminar." Fervently moving to the beat, drenched in music, Eleanor released months of late night work hunched in her easy chair. It was joy.

On her return from lazy days at the Vineyard or a long evening's dancing, Eleanor jumped easily back into action. She retained every ounce of the drive she once described, almost growling, to her Georgetown colleague Emma Coleman Jordan, "You've got to get up every morning and you gotta want it! Really want it! " At the beginning of the new millennium she was hardly fading, ever ready to take on a fresh issue or doggedly reframe an old one.

"She's exceptionally consistent. She hasn't deviated in the last forty-five years," Antiochian Art Finch comments about the activist who has never given up on blacks, women, the people of "real-life Washington" or those of the world.

Characteristically, she associated herself with fresh causes. Just as she helped start an earlier movement to hasten apartheid's fall, in the new century she was one of the first public figures to expose slavery in Sudan. Haunted by the scant reports, she approached New Jersey Representative Donald Payne, a CBC colleague and senior member of the International Relations Committee who had visited Sudan. Asking him to co-lead a one-hour House floor discussion with her, the two described the genocidal war in southern Sudan, where pro-government militias enslaved thousands of Africans. And she applied her typical analysis. Leaving others to tell the horrific tales of rape and mutilation, and still others to buy the freedom of African slaves one by one, as groups of schoolchildren did, Eleanor laid bare the economic tangle: oil enabled the Sudanese government to force conversions and enslave. Later she spoke publicly, with other rights leaders and ex-slaves, about "the unspeakable tragedies"; then helped lead congressional efforts to ensure $1 billion U.S. food spread through non-Sudanese government channels, and legislation banning exploitative companies from U.S. markets.

Eleanor also participated every year in Washington's giant gay parade, which she walked instead of riding in the convertibles many politicians used. "A parade is for walking, to show your respect. Who am I? I'm no beauty queen or hero waving out of a car. This is not my parade, this is their parade. They're not celebrating me, I'm celebrating them.

"Now gays are organized the way blacks were organized. Because whoever is on the outside is who organizes . . . Women went through something of the same cycle. Every movement does. The labor movement did it the same way. Your issues peak. You are successful, and the movement itself becomes more diverse.

"We don't have black marches in D.C. anymore. We have fewer feminist marches. But we have umpteen gay marches. It's the people most excluded who need to march."

While taking up new challenges Eleanor never yielded on the central issue of the District: home rule, statehood and the congressional vote. She continued to work step-by-step toward the goal. At the close of 2000 she started another campaign, energizing Washingtonians to lobby Congress for the return of the floor vote that had been taken by Republicans. Calling together hundreds of citizens to rally in a meeting room of the Rayburn House office building, she was visibly moved by the turnout, with overflow crowds two weeks in a row.

"It's pretty lonely up there," she told her people, her voice breaking. "Thank you for being here with me. It's lonely up there all alone," she repeated, clearly unused to having her back covered. "Thank you. This is a moment I treasure personally."

After allowing herself to be moved by the show of support, Eleanor called out, "We have to go national to regain the vote they took from us. There is no time in the history of the country when people had a vote and had it taken back!"

Ever action-oriented, she emphasized there was some step each person could take toward statehood. "We've got to have milestones on the way. We can't swallow it all at once." Speaking directly to "our statehood friends," Eleanor emphasized the common denominator at this coalition, where grassroots Stand Up for Democracy activists mingled with more mainstream proponents like DC Vote and the progressive, civil liberties–oriented People for the American Way. Perhaps the only person in the city who could mobilize such a range of citizens, she begged for support in incremental steps.

"If they won't give us the whole enchilada we still don't have to let them beat up on us. It's such an insult," she told her people, "when attachments are put on our bills.

"This is America, my friends," her voice rose. "This isn't how we do it!

"How do you get Congress to vote on statehood? Street demonstrations aren't enough. You have to bite off a movement in chunks you can digest."

Just as Eleanor had instructed her classmates in high school assemblies how to organize ("have meetings in your home rooms") she directed this crowd. And she proposed one immediate chunk: getting back the limited delegate vote. The return of the vote she had in 1993 was "only a down payment on the full vote in the House and Senate. But it's a way to get everyone's attention. We need to use the next two years to go national, so we can let people know this is a civil rights issue!"

Using the contested 2000 presidential election as backdrop, she declared, "There are 10,000 disenfranchised black voters in Florida. But over 500,000 disenfranchised voters in Washington D.C.!"

Months later, the issue got national exposure with the help of the District's rebellious new license plates: "Taxation Without Representation," dreamed up by D.C. resident Sarah Shapiro. Now, the 25 million tourists visiting the capital each year go home better informed: in the heart of world democracy, "the last colony" is still denied congressional representation.

*   *   *

Whatever rights campaigns emerge in coming decades, many count on having Eleanor at their side. As Washingtonian June Johnson says, "We have different ideologies sometimes, but in terms of integrity, she has a heart. That's what I like about her the most. That means a hell of a lot." People know this woman with the long-haul commitment will keep leading the charge, from equal pay for female congressional custodians—recently paid a dollar less per hour than men—to rights bills, such as the first to ban racial profiling.

"She works hard, she prepares, she's smart and she believes," says Vernon Jordan. "You don't need much else." This woman who has had so many incarnations—civil rights champion, lawyer, government appointee, law professor and member of Congress—is gearing up for new battles. As former Antioch classmate David Crippens declares, "I'm waiting to see what she's going to do for her next act."

Professor Emma Jordan sums up her colleague, "She has the scars of a survivor and a pathbreaker, with an unusual set of strengths and weaknesses. The bottom line is so hugely impressive. You cannot take away her legacy."

Her full accounting is yet to come, for Eleanor is not done. Her current mission—full democracy for the District of Columbia, the home town bequeathed to her by Richard Holmes—is far from finished. Though the District has undergone a renaissance, with four years of surpluses, cash reserves and bond upgrades, the woman encouraged as a child to get the job done battles on. Meanwhile, "it is people like Eleanor who keep my eye on the prize," testifies Charlayne Hunter-Gault. "We all get involved in situations that test us, where our egos get involved. But when you are close to someone who is so pure, you don't get far from those principles. She's proud of what she does. She tells me, 'Girl, you should have seen them when I told them. . . .' But it's without ego." Laughing, Charlayne adds, "It's not humble, either."

On June 13, 2000, Eleanor received a sparkling sixty-third birthday gift. Vernon Jordan and Bill Clinton, then the president of the United States, gave her a fund-raising party at the Jordans' exquisite home in Northwest Washington.

Dressed in a soft green silk dress, Eleanor, forty-five minutes behind schedule, swept happily into the large-columned home. Soon the downstairs rooms were filled by waiters with trays of canapés and wine;

the well-dressed, well-heeled crowd exuded an excited buzz of anticipation. Right on schedule the president's advance team of dark-suited men sporting lapel pins swept through the four rooms and back patio; suddenly, the president stood silhouetted in the large doorway, hugging his hosts. Slowly, the tall man advanced through the crowded foyer, chatting warmly with each of the fifty guests, including Portia and her husband, before genially having his photo taken with every visitor.

After an hour of mingling, the president stood at one end of the richly carpeted living room with Jordan and Mayor Anthony Williams to pay tribute to Eleanor. Jordan opened, introducing Eleanor, whom he claimed he'd advised not to run for Congress. He had, he said, been wrong.

"Eleanor usually turns out to be right!" the handsome host acknowledged to laughter.

Next the mayor told Eleanor's fans, affectionately, that he "braced himself" for her calls. Finally the president took the microphone, joking about this coalition-builder, "If the Republicans liked me the way they like Eleanor, Congress would repeal the Twenty-second Amendment [limiting presidential terms]!" After the laughter subsided, he continued on a more serious note, honoring Eleanor's talents.

"Because she's been where she's been, it's been possible for me to be a pretty good friend ... of Washington, the most beautiful capital in the entire world," with "a rich and textured history that deserved to be nourished.

"But if she didn't have the enormous credibility she has in the Congress, among both Republicans and Democrats; and if she didn't have an idea a minute"—the crowd laughed delightedly—"then all these things that I have been able to do, I could not have done.

"Someone could write a whole chapter on my service as president to Washington, D.C. in two words: 'Yes, Eleanor.' And if it were to be four words it would have to be: 'Yes, Eleanor. Yes, Eleanor!' "

The audience erupted, as, 150 years after Richard Holmes made the trek to a precarious freedom, his beaming great-granddaughter was saluted by the president of the United States for continuing to expand it. The woman who'd already had her own long journey—sitting in her Dunbar classroom when the Supreme Court rendered its decision in *Brown* v. *Board of Education,* facing down lawless sheriffs in Mississippi, getting the tools she needed at Yale Law School, fighting unpopular free-speech battles for the ACLU, carving anti-white-flight strategies in New York, writing landmark guidelines at the EEOC, creating new legal subjects at Georgetown and defending her home city for eleven years— this woman was acknowledged as a force to be reckoned with. One to whom the only answer, even from the president, could only be, "Yes, Eleanor."

At the end of the evening a radiant Eleanor declared this the best birthday since her seven-year-old party, where she'd "made it happen." Appreciating the thoughtfulness of her old friend Vernon, his wife Anne, and the president, she closed out the late night curled in her big stuffed chair in the second-floor family room, happily ruminating on the elegant evening.

Then she shifted in the chair, stiffening.

"None of it will turn my head. Tomorrow is another day."

ACKNOWLEDGMENTS

I am grateful to EHN for allowing me intimate access, with no holds barred, to comb through a life. And to her staff, who have been unfailingly helpful, especially Donna Brazile, Jon Bouker, Sheila Bunn, Crystal Day, Cedric Hendricks, Julia Hudson, Cartwright Moore, Doxie McCoy, Matt Morrison and Joyce Patterson.

Thank you to the ninety-five interviewees who provided the heart of the book. Your generosity of time, depth of caring and insights about Eleanor were invaluable.

And to readers of chapters or entire drafts, thank you for gracious and sensitive readings: Barbara Babcock (project midwife), Hilary Cairns, Modupe Carpenter, Toni Gripper, Jewelle Gomez, Carole Johnson, Wendy Lichtman, Donna Korones, Malcolm Lester, Nancy Massey, Kenyatta Monroe, Betty Powell, Mardi Steinau, Gloria Steinem, Dorothy Wall, Lynn Wenzell, Jean Wiley and Maxine Wolfe.

I am grateful for my brilliant team: agent Sydelle Kramer, editor Tracy Sherrod, who lit a fire under the book when it fizzled, and Malaika Adero, who skillfully took over production midstream.

A special thanks to archivists Scott Sanders (Antioch), William Massa Jr. (Yale), Laura Bedard and Erin Rahne Kidwell (Georgetown Law Center), and Christine Marcone (Seeley G. Mudd Manuscripts, Princeton). And thanks to Yale administrators Linda Koch Lorimer, Xenia Shaffer and Elizabeth Stauderman; Eli Kilner, Hilary Cairns, Ian Manuel Urbina, Anna Ekindjian, Karen Mulhauser and Mardi Steinau for various research assistance; biographers Evelyn White, John Demilio, and the late Henry Mayer, for advice; Dorothy Stewart, for transcriptions; Julius Lester for telling me early on, "Find one story and stick to it," and Ruth King, Robert Collins, Morton Steinau and Barbara Steinau, for constant support.

Appreciation to the Lifebridge Foundation and the Thanks Be to Grandmother Winifred Foundation for research funds. And to Carole Johnson, for the idea and infinite patience. Thank you for your commitment to the book, to Eleanor and to me.

Rosemary Addy, September 5, 1999
Warren Ashe, February 28, 2000
Barbara Babcock, May 24 and October 6, 2000; April 15, 2001
Vic Basile, June 30, 1999
Laura Bedard, November 15, 2000
Ed Bing, March 30, 2000
Albert Blumrosen, October 9, 2000
Ruth Blumrosen, October 9, 2000
Jon Bouker, November 15, 16, 2000
Brazile, Donna, August 4 and September 25, 1999; May 14, 2001
Ed Brown, July 17, 2000
Steve Bumbaugh, April 9, 2000
Ed Brown, July 17, 2000
Dolores Brule, November 3, 1999
Shelley Eisenberg Chandhok, March 11, 2000
Mildred Coates, February 2, 2000
Maudine Cooper, December 11, 2000
David Crippens, March 11, 2000
Howard Croft, September 1, 1999
Courtland Cox, June 12, 2000
Preston David, August 3, 2000
The Honorable Thomas Davis, October 3, 2000
Bette Stubing Denich, April 17, 2000
Armand Derfner, May 18, 2000
Manuela Dobos, May 20, 2000
Robert Drynan, November 14, 2000
Marian Wright Edelman, July 27, 2000
Eleanor Elliot, January 18, 24, 2000
Marjorie Elliott, January 17, 2000
Walter Fauntroy, December 20, 2000
Arthur Finch, April 4, 2000
Charlotte Frank, September 7, 11, 2000
Ronnie Gilbert, January 28, 2000
Speaker Newt Gingrich, October 11, 2001
Alvin Golub, October 26, 2000
Jewelle Gomez, September 21, 2001
Lawrence Guyot, January 10, 2000
Nellie Hallomand, December 16, 1999
Peter Hambright, March 29, 2000
Stephanie Lynch Hayes, January 25, 2000
Cedric Hendricks, July 1, 1999

Neil Herring, May 15, 2000
Rachelle Horowitz, May 23, 2000
Natalie Howard, November 2, 1999
Vermell Howard, May 1, 2001
Julia Hudson, October 15, 2000
Charlayne Hunter-Gault, June 4, 2001
June Johnson, November 30, 2001
Emma Coleman Jordan, January 10, 2001
Vernon Jordan, December 3, 2000
Herschel Kaminsky, April 9, 2000
Myra Wesley King, January 20, 25, 2000
Dorie Ladner, May 17, 2000
Joyce Ladner, May 23, 2000
Gene Lebovics, July 24, 2000
Willie Leftwich, January 10, 2000
The Honorable John Lewis, December 18, 2000
Judith Lichtman, February 2, 2001
Judy Mage, May 5, 2000
Lucy Montgomery, February 25, 2000
Cartwright Moore, July 2, August 23 and September 24, 1999
Karen Mulhauser, November 18, 2000
Frances Nails, November 11 and December 2, 1999
Constance Newman, November 17, 2000
John Holmes Norton, October 16, 2001
Philip Pannell, September 27, 1999
Christine Philpot, March 27, October 15 and November 16, 2000
Mark Plotkin, December 15, 2000
Robert Press, April 3, 2000
Mary Preston, December 13, 2000
Rene Redwood, August 31, 1999
Inez Smith Reid, January 9 and May 24, 2000
Susan Deller Ross, December 12, 2000
Richard Schwab, April 4, 2000
Rochelle Schwab, April 4, 2000
Portia Holmes Shields, January 4 and February 18, 2000
Pauline Schneider, July 5, 2000
Nancy Schwerner, March 13, 2000
Steve Schwerner, March 13, 2000
Daniel Spicer, October 27, 1999
Judith Stein, June 1, 2000
Gloria Steinem, August 6, 2002
Donald Stewart, July 12, 2001
Mark Thompson, December 14, 2000

Brooke Trent, August 9, 2000
Daisy Murray Voigt, October 15, 2000
Annice Robinson Wagner, January 10, 2000
Ara Walls, November 3, 15, 1999
Eve Wilkins, October 23, 2000
Wendy W. Williams, November 27, 2000
Barbara Williams-Skinner, January 18, 2001
Judith A. Winston, October 10, 2000
Bette Woody, April 18, 2000
Patricia Ann Early Young, November 9, 1999
Electra Yourke, October 10, 2000

Interviews with Eleanor Holmes Norton
    1999: April 1, 2, 3; May 7, 8, 9; June 29; July 1, 2, 3, 4; October 6, 11, 17;
November 17. *2000:* January 7, 8, 9, 10, 11; March 1; April 6, 7, 8, 17, 21, 24; May
1, 8, 16; June 9, 10, 11, 12, 13; July 27; September 29, 30; October 1; November
11; December 1, 2, 3, 4, 5, 6. *2001:* February 12; March 19; May 11, 12, 13; June
27; October 14; November 11.

NOTES

Archives

Antioch College: Student Records, Publications
Freedmen's Bureau, Washington D.C.: Richard Holmes Records
Vela Elizabeth Lynch and Coleman Sterling Holmes Personal Papers
Moorland-Spingarn Research Center, Howard University: Civil Rights Documentation
Seeley G. Mudd Manuscript Library, Princeton: ACLU Papers
National Archives, Washington, D.C.: Family Records
New Haven Register: Library Archives
New York Times: Library Archives
Eleanor Holmes Norton Papers
Vermont Avenue Baptist Church: Founding Documents
Virginia Historical Society: Genealogical History
Washington Post: Library Archives
Yale University Graduate School: Student Records, Publications
Yale University Law School: Student Records, Publications

Abbreviations

AA=Antioch College Archives
EHNP=Eleanor Holmes Norton Papers
LAT= *Los Angeles Times*
NYP=*New York Post*
NYT=*New York Times*
SMM= Seeley G. Mudd Manuscript Library
WP=*Washington Post*
WS= *Washington Star*
WT=*Washington Times*
YUL=Yale Law School Records

Note: Unless otherwise cited, all EHN quotes are from author interviews, 1999–2001.

PROLOGUE

Holmes's escape from bondage in Virginia, part of Holmes family oral history known to all branches, is the sole fictional scene in *Fire in My Soul*. Composite details from Ira Berlin, "The Slaves' Changing World," *A History of the African American People,* (eds., James Oliver Horton and Lois E. Horton, New York: Smithmark Books, 1995); Berlin and Leslie S. Rowland, eds., *Families & Freedom: A Documentary History of African-American Kinship in the Civil War Era* (New York: The New Press, 1997); slave narratives in Julius Lester's *To Be a Slave* (New York:

Dial Books, 1968); James Mellon, *Bullwhip Days: The Slaves Remember* (New York: Weidenfeld and Nicolson, 1988); and Charles Perdue Jr., Thomas E. Barden and Robert K. Phillips, eds., *Weevils in the Wheat: Interviews with Virginia Ex-Slaves* (Charlottesville: University Press of Virginia, 1976).

CHAPTER 1: THE ANCESTORS

Background interviews: family members Vela Lynch Holmes, Lucy Holmes Montgomery, Myra Wesley King, Mildred Coates, Warren Ashe, Stephanie Lynch Hayes, Angela Echols, Ara Walls, Daniel Spicer, Dolores Lynch Brule, Portia Shields and Nellie Hallomand. Additionally, family friends Natalie Howard, Frances Nails and Patricia Early Young.

Other background texture from Donald G. Nieman, *To Set the Law in Motion: The Freedmen's Bureau and the Legal Rights of Blacks, 1865–1868* (Millwood, New York: KTO Press, 1979); the magnificent anthology edited by James Oliver Horton and Lois E. Horton, *A History of the African American People;* Mary Church Terrell's *A Colored Woman in a White World* (Washington D.C.: Ransdell, Inc., 1940); urban historian Howard Gillette Jr.'s comprehensive *Between Justice and Beauty: Race, Planning and the Failure of Urban Policy in Washington, D.C.* (Baltimore: Johns Hopkins University Press, 1995); and the venerable Constance McLaughlin Green's *Washington: A History of the Capital,* (Princeton: Princeton University Press, 1962).

11 **Author Charles Dickens** Gillette, p. 12.
11 **President Jefferson said** Ibid., p. 13.
11 **In the 1850s** Adam Platt, "The Rise of Imperial Washington," *Washington, D.C.,* Washington: Smithsonian Books, 1992.
11 **In the District, local newspapers** *National Intelligencer,* August 27, 1835. Neighboring Virginia had honored a law for almost fifty years requiring free blacks to leave the state within a year of achieving freedom. Gillette, p. 27. Often the unacknowledged offspring of whites, their status was ambiguous: neither slave nor citizen.
12 **In 1835, after** Gillette, p. 29.
13 **But incredibly, the government** Gillette, p. 42. Twenty years later, Chinese gold miners in California also faced taxes not levied on whites for similar work. Ronald Takaki, *A Different Mirror: A History of Multicultural America,* New York: Little, Brown and Company, 1993, p. 195.
13 **Richard Holmes continued** Marriage License, Richard Holmes and Lucy Ellen Jones, Witnessed by R. J. Meigs, Clerk, August 20, 1872. National Archives.
15 **Historian Constance** Green, vol. 2, p. 86.
17 **Mary Church Terrell** Condensation of descriptions in Terrell's autobiography, passim.
19 **With their middle-class** Jane Freundel Levey, "The Scurlock Studio," *Washington History,* 1:1, Spring, 1989, pp. 41-58. EHN describes butlers learning fine wines, porters picking up the manners of "cultured" whites, and government clerks, all considered middle class. Teachers, doctors and lawyers were a top layer. Class status was heavily influenced by education,

church attendance, manners, and stability of work and family life. Clayborne Carson, "A Season of Struggle," in Horton, p. 159.

26 **Upwardly mobile Washington** The color fixation was riveted in by the head start lighter people got "when they were house Negroes with kinship to the family," EHN says, "so they sometimes knew how to read and write when they got out." EHN's own ancestors exemplify the several faces of this "kinship." Great-uncle Alfred on her mother's side, the "different looking" son resulting from the rape of great-grandmother Emily Fitts by her owner, was sent to law school. On her father's side, great-grandmother Lucy Ellen Jones, the light-skinned daughter of another white owner and a slave, was dropped off in Washington as a young girl to fend for herself.

26 **After saying their vows** Reverend Joseph C. Mosselle, 1053 East Fayette St., Syracuse, New York. Marriage License, EHNP.

27 **Even white-owned stores** Marvin Caplan, "Eat Anywhere!" *Washington History*, 1:1, Spring, 1989, p. 29.

27 **Singer Lena Horne** Joe William Trotter Jr., "From Hard Times to Hope," in Horton, p. 142.

CHAPTER 2: A WARRIOR IS BORN

Background: EHN family papers, student materials and school newspapers; interviews with family members Portia Shields, Nellie Hallomand, Warren Ashe, Myra Wesley King, Mildred Coates, Dolores Lynch Brule, and Ara Walls; classmates Annice Robinson-Wagner, Inez Smith Reid and Willie Leftwich; neighbors Eleanor Elliott, Marjorie Elliott and Natalie Howard, and Vela Holmes's coworker Frances Nails.

Background sources for the period of Eleanor's childhood (1937–1955) included Jervis Anderson's "Dunbar High School" 1978 *New Yorker* article, Marian Anderson's autobiography, *My Lord, What a Morning* (New York: Viking Press, 1956), E. Franklin Frazier's *The Black Bourgeoisie* (New York: The Free Press, 1957), the Hortons' anthology and Gillette's *Between Justice and Beauty*, both mentioned in Chapter one background sources. Early civil rights history was additionally furnished by journalist Joanne Grant's biography of *Ella Baker* (New York: John Wiley & Sons, 1998), raised in the same North Carolina county as Vela Lynch Holmes.

29 **When Eleanor was two** Marian Anderson, pp. 184–206.

30 **Middle-class black parents** EHN quoted in *The Antiochian*, January 1969, page 7.

31 **One week later** Trotter, op cit., p. 150.

31 **The order also** EHN book review, Michael I. Sovern, "Legal Restraints on Racial Discrimination in Employment," *The American University Law Review*, 16:3, June 1967, p. 454.

43 **When Eleanor entered Banneker** Marvin Caplan, "Eat Anywhere!" *Washington History*, 1:1, Spring, 1989, pp. 25–39, for Thompson's Restaurant case.

46 **In an interview thirty years** Mary Joy Ostrovski, "Which Women Lead?" *Womennews*, December, 1978, p. 13.

51 **Dunbar was, in effect,** Quoted in Jervis Anderson, "Dunbar High School," *The New Yorker*, March 20, 1978, p. 10.

52 **During her second fall** The Washington D.C. Recorder of Deeds (Book 3202, p. 266; Book 10087, p. 542) shows Vela became sole owner of the 5th Street property, conveyed by Helen Latimer on November 12, 1953. Vela and middle daughter Portia would become co-owners of Coleman and Vela's final home at Iris Street, on April 6, 1971.

55 **Ten years later Eleanor** EHN, "Our Civil Rights Progress," *Sunday Herald Tribune*, March 15, 1964, p. 1.

CHAPTER 3: FAR FROM U STREET

Background interviews with Antioch classmates Ed Bing, David Crippens, Shelly Eisenberg Chandhok, Arthur Finch, Peter Hambright, Herschel Kaminsky, Bob Press, Richard Schwab, Rochelle Schwab, Nancy Schwerner, Steve Schwerner, Bette Stubing Denich, Bette Woody, and author recollections. Additional research on Antioch details is drawn from *The Antioch Record*, EHN student file and other college publications.

Background for the 1955–1960 civil rights history intercut with Eleanor's personal development was supplied by powerful firsthand accounts in Clayborne Carson et al., eds., *Eyes on the Prize* (New York: Penguin, 1991); Vicki Crawford, Jacqueline Anne Rouse and Barbara Woods, eds., *Women in the Civil Rights Movement* (Bloomington: Indiana University Press, 1993); *Negro Protest Thought in the Twentieth Century*, edited by Francis L. Broderick and August Meier (New York: Bobbs-Merrill, 1965); and Howell Raines's collection, *My Soul Is Rested* (New York: Putnam, 1977). Also several excellent histories: Taylor Branch's *Parting the Waters*: (New York: Simon and Schuster, 1988); Charles M. Payne's *I've Got the Light of Freedom* (Berkeley: University of California Press, 1995); Lerone Bennett Jr.'s classic, *Before the Mayflower* (New York: Penguin, 1982) and Jervis Anderson's biography *Bayard Rustin* (Berkeley: University of California Press, 1998).

59 **While not always honoring** Prominent Antioch educator Arthur Morgan refused Dr. Bette Woody's African-American father admission in the early twentieth century, saying "We wouldn't be able to place you in a co-op job." Interview with Woody, April 18, 2000.

64 **On a cool December** Darlene Clark Hine and Kathleen Thompson, *A Shining Thread of Hope: The History of Black Women in America*, New York: Broadway Books, 1998, pp. 273–276.

65 **Utilizing Ghandian philosophy** Bayard Rustin would shortly be expelled from King's inner circle because of his previous arrest as a gay man. Brian Freeman, *Civil Sex: The Life of Bayard Rustin*, Berkeley Repertory Theatre, Berkeley, California, March 2000.

66 **On November 13, 1956** Supreme Court ruling, reported in next day's *NYT*. Implementation occurred a month later.

66 **It was a defining** EHN, "30 Life Lessons from Sisters We Know and Love," *Essence*, May 2000.

68 **Her stunning** Lester Schulman, "Reviewer Lauds ATA Play Choice, High Level of Acting Displayed," *Antioch College Record*, May 8, 1956.

69 **In 1950, Hiss** James Thomas Gay, "1948: The Alger Hiss Spy Case," *American*

History, May/June, 1998; Robert G. Whalen, "Hiss and Chambers: Strange Story of Two Men," *NYT,* December 12, 1948.

71 **If you, our president,** Branch, p. 213.

82 **In the mid-fifties** Payne, p. 34.

82 **A Negro waitress** Carson version, *In Struggle: SNCC and the Black Awakening of the 1960s,* Cambridge: Harvard University Press, 1981, p. 10. Branch reports, "Fellows like you make our race look bad," op cit., p. 271.

82 **McCain later wrote** Carson et al., *Eyes on the Prize,* p. 115.

83 **In early March** Belinda Doty, "A 'March to Freedom' in Xenia," *Antioch College Record,* March 11, 1960.

84 **The ever-chilled** EHN Letter to unnamed interviewer, circa 1963. EHNP.

85 **It was then decided** Myron Gessner and Peter Gunn Montague, "Barber Issue Breaks! NAACP Takes Action," *Antioch College Record,* April 22, 1960.

CHAPTER 4: BALLOTS, BULLETS AND BOOKS

Background interviews: Yale classmates Christine Philpot, Neil Herring, Judith Stein, Armand Derfner, Inez Smith Reid, Marian Wright Edelman, Donald Stewart and Barbara Babcock; civil rights colleagues Lawrence Guyot, Courtland Cox, Rachelle Horowitz, Dorie Ladner, John Lewis and Joyce Ladner, Gloria Steinem and author recollections.

Background material was drawn from EHN student files, Yale publications of the early 1960s, the newspaper *New America* for which EHN wrote, and contemporaneous *New Haven Register* articles.

Civil rights participants' experiences were culled from author's memories and documentary histories mentioned in Chapter 3 notes; also the excellent collection of *New York Times* articles in *Black Protest in the Sixties,* edited by August Meier, Elliot Rudwick and John Bracey Jr. (New York: Markus Wiener, 1991) and Dick Cluster's anthology, *They Should Have Served That Cup of Coffee* (Boston: South End Press, 1979). Kay Mills's Hamer biography, *This Little Light of Mine* (New York: Plume, 1993) provided key details.

Additionally, the classics *When and Where I Enter: The Impact of Black Women on Race and Sex in America* by Paula Giddings (New York: Bantam, 1984), Taylor Branch's *Pillar of Fire* (New York: Simon and Schuster, 1998) and Clayborne Carson's *In Struggle: SNCC and the Black Awakening of the 1960s* (Cambridge: Harvard University Press) formed the backbone of the "factual" structure of civil rights events in the time period covered by this chapter: June 1960–June 1964.

89 **Thank God I'm a Negro** *Life Aims* paper, 1956. AA.

94 **By November** EHN letter to Antioch Dean of Students J. D. Dawson, November 30, 1960, AA.

95 **By spring she** EHN letter to Jesse Treichler, June 13, 1961. AA.

96 **I do miss** Ibid.

96 **She received a** Grant from the Foundation for Student and Youth Affairs.

97 **On August 17** EHN Letter to Neil Herring, August 17, 1961, in possession of Herring.

98 **When Eleanor returned** Fred Powledge, *Model City,* New York: Simon and Schuster, 1970.

99 **In October 1961,** Press Release, Rally and Sit-Out, October 6, 1961, typewritten copy, EHNP; and Eleanor Holmes, "New Haven 'Sits Out' for Housing, *New America,* October 27, 1961.

99 **The young advocate** *Yale News,* October 19, 1961, p. 2.

101 **The law partners** EHN Postcard to Treichler, circa 1963. AA.

101 **Eleanor, with a knack** Letter to Neil and Ethel Herring, dated June 30, 1062, with a P.S. written several days later. In possession of Neil Herring.

102 **"We dissipate** EHN Letter to Neil and Ethel Herring, July 23, 1960. In possession of Neil Herring.

105 **An iconoclastic** Fred Rodell, "Goodbye to Law Reviews," *Virginia Law Review,* 48: 2, 1962.

107 **Tracing its evolution** Murray in "An American Credo," *Common Ground,* Winter 1945, quoted in EHN unpublished paper, "World War II and the Beginning of Non-Violent Action in Civil Rights," May 1963. EHNP.

110 **Mississippi is a magic** EHN, "Mississippi Freedom Democratic Party," *New America,* April 14, 1964, p. 4.

110 **Its open violence** Payne, pp. 25–26.

110 **The fate of farmer** Chuck McDew, "Thou Shall Not Resist," in Bud and Ruth Schultz, eds., *It Did Happen Here: Recollections of Political Repression in America,* Berkeley: University of California Press, 1989.

110 **Less than 2 percent** Payne, p. 25.

113 **Ms. Hamer had barely** Mills, p. 60, corroborated by interviews with Dorie Ladner, Guyot and EHN, who elaborates: "That's how you humiliated people; make them beat their own."

113 **Attesting to his** Guyot adds, in interview: "I do not like some of the things that Eleanor has done politically, but I've always been struck by her essential brilliance and her sense of self, and I always liked her political fluidity . . . when she wants to be, she's tough as nails. She gives no quarter, she asks no quarter."

113 **Ms. Hamer would later** Mills, p. 120.

114 **At the end of June** EHN Postcard to Neil Herring, June 25, 1963. In Possession of Herring.

114 **After a month in the** EHN Postcard to Paul and Jesse Treichler, AA.

115 **On August 13, two** Branch, *Parting the Waters,* p. 861.

118 **At the Lincoln monument** Juan Williams, with Eyes on the Prize Production Team, *Eyes on the Prize: America's Civil Rights Years, 1954–1965,* New York: Penguin, 1987, pp. 197–205; Branch, *Parting the Waters,* pp. 876–83; Hine and Thompson, pp. 280–282.

119 **As Rustin later wrote** "The Meaning of the March on Washington," *Liberation,* VIII:8, October 1963, p. 11.

119 **A week later** Carole Denise McNair, age 11, and Carole Robinson, Cynthia Dianne Wesley, and Addie Mae Collins, all 14, were killed in the Sixteenth Street Baptist Church on September 15, 1963.

119 **By midwinter Eleanor** EHN Letter to Treichler, February 11. 1964. AA.

120 **Her application** EHN student file, YUL.

Chapter 5: A Pivotal Year

Background interviews: Yale classmates Barbara Babcock, Armand Derfner, Marian Wright Edelman, Gene Lebovic, Christine Philpot, Judith Stein; Rachelle Horowitz, SNCC workers Courtland Cox, Lawrence Guyot, June Johnson, Dorie and Joyce Ladner.

Background bibliographic research for this chapter included civil rights sources noted in the previous two chapters and several early feminist anthologies—Toni Cade's *The Black Woman: An Anthology* (New York: Signet, 1970); Gerda Lerner's *Black Women in White America: A Documentary History* (New York: Random House, 1972), Robin Morgan's *Sisterhood Is Powerful: An Anthology of Writings from the Women's Liberation Movement* (New York: Random House, 1970) and Barbara Smith's *Home Girls: A Black Feminist Anthology* (New York: Kitchen Table: Women of Color Press, 1983)—plus Susan Brownmiller's *In Our Time: Memoir of a Revolution* (New York: Dial Press, 1999) and Ruth Rosen's *The World Split Open* (New York: Viking, 2000).

122 **The brief made** "Brief Submitted by the Mississippi Freedom Democratic Party For the Consideration of Credentials Subcommittee of the Democratic National Committee, Credentials Committee of the Democratic National Convention, Delegates to the Democratic National Convention," Prepared by: Joseph L. Rauh Jr., assisted by Eleanor K. Holmes and H. Miles Jaffe.

123 **I shall never forget** EHN Remarks, Jewish Currents Dinner, NYC, May 19, 1974. EHNP.

124 **With tears welling** Mills, p. 121.

125 **Rustin said rejection** Rustin, "From Protest to Politics," *Commentary*, February 1965; Maurice Isserman, *The Other American: The Life of Michael Harrington*, New York: Public Affairs, 2000, p. 245.

126 **Ms. Hamer, near** Mills, pp. 120–121.

126 **In some countries** Hine and Thompson, p. 283.

129 **As it turns out** EHN letter to Treichler, December 13, 1963, AA.

130 **That was not the** A. Leon Higginbotham Jr., "The Dream with Its Back against the Wall," speech at Yale Alumni Weekend, Fall, 1989. *Yale Law Report*, Spring, 1990.

130 **A decade after her** Peggy Lamson, *In the Vanguard: Six American Women in Public Life*, Boston: Houghton Mifflin, 1979, p. 163.

130 **After she'd been in** EHN to Rostow, YUL.

130 **The job gave** EHN, "A. Leon Higginbotham: Master of All Trades," *Law & Inequality: A Journal of Theory and Practice*, IX:3 August 1991, p. 395.

Chapter 6: Free Speech

Background interviews: Antiochians Steve Schwerner and Judy Mage, friends Charlayne Hunter-Gault and Christine Philpot, Movement colleagues Ed Brown, Courtland Cox, Dorie Ladner, Joyce Ladner, and recollections by the author, who also lived in New York City during this period (1965-70)

Other background research was primarily in ACLU archives at the Seeley G. Mudd Manuscript Library, Princeton, and civil rights and feminist texts mentioned at the front of earlier chapter notes.

134 **The ACLU, cofounded** Gertrude Samuels, "The Fight for Civil Liberties Never Stays Won," NYT *Sunday Magazine,* June 19, 1966.

134 **The agency lobbied** When Eleanor was hired John D. Pemberton Jr., a Harvard-trained lawyer and Quaker, was executive director, Melvin Wulf was ACLU legal director and Aryeh Neier was New York chapter director.

135 **Under its rule** Coleman Sterling Homes, "The Constitution as Parent," term paper, circa 1930. EHNP.

139 **A special committee** Raines, p. 18.

139 **We cannot help** EHN letters, SMM.

140 **His alleged abuses** James Haskins, *Distinguished African American Political and Governmental Leaders,* Phoenix, Arizona: Oryx Press, 1999, p. 202.

140 **The venerable Chair** Inez Smith Reid, *"Together" Black Women,* New York: Emerson Hall Publishing, 1972, p. 145.

141 **Honoring constitutional** "Defender of Unpopular Causes," ACLU pamphlet profiling EHN, reprinted from January 1969 *Ebony.*

141 **The ACLU successfully filed** *Brandenburg* v. *Ohio,* 395 U.S. 444 (1969).

142 **Walking into court,** Jacqueline Trescott, "Eleanor Norton: A Fighter in the EEOC Chair," *WP,* June 22, 1977.

143 **For some whose** Ed Brown, for example, says in author interview, "We were young and full of vinegar. When Eleanor took that position most of us were confused and puzzled and, frankly, a little disappointed. . . . It did not sit well." Today, "Symbolically the idea that we end up defending those people who are most vicious and do irreparable harm to us is a very confusing message. In my viscera it still leaves a big lump in my throat."

143 **She understood that** Earl Warren was Supreme Court chief justice, 1953 to 1969.

144 **She told an interviewer** *The Antiochian,* January 1969, p. .7.

145 **Justice Marshall** The first black Supreme Court justice, appointed by President Lyndon Johnson, confirmed August 30, 1967.

145 **Although Justice Abe Fortas** Fred P. Graham, "High Court Limits Right to Ban Rallies," NYT, November 20, 1968, p. 1; *The United States Law Week,* Supreme Court Opinions, The Bureau of National Affairs, Inc., Washington, D.C., November 19, 1968, 37:19, p. 1.

145 **Surely the Warren** *The Antiochian,* January 1969, p. 7.

146 **On the one hand** Judy Michaelson, "Close-up: Law and Justice," *NYP,* October 30, 1968.

146 **And less than a** Ibid.

147 **Its first director** Giddings, p. 300.

147 **Roy Wilkins,** Marylin Bender, "Black Woman in Civil Rights," *NYT,* November 2, 1969.

148 **At the rally** "Liberation," The Talk of the Town, *The New Yorker,* September 5, 1970.

148 **Do black women want** EHN, *NYT,* April 18, 1969.

150 **(Graham would later** Interview, Terry Gross, *Fresh Air,* National Public Radio, re-aired July 17, 2001, just after Graham's death.

150 **But, Eleanor asked** EHN, "New Black Directions: A Reappraisal," *Civil Liberties,* 259, December 1968, p. 3.

150 **Should the black** Ibid., p. 3.

151 **The "tidy melodrama"** EHN, "Community Control: Strains in the Liberal Coalition," Presented at *Civil Liberties Clearing House,* Washington, D.C., March 20, 1969.

152 **One-tenth of the** Thomas R. Brooks, "A Strategist Without a Movement," NYT *Sunday Magazine,* February 16, 1969, p. 105.

152 **Rustin critiqued** Ibid., p. 105.

152 **To liberals who are fond** EHN, *Civil Liberties Clearing House,* op cit.

152 **Yet, as Eleanor lectured** Ibid.

153 **Each side** Draft of EHN speech to a New York Jewish organization, no venue noted, circa 1970, EHNP.

153 **Even fighting Shirley** Reid, p. 159.

CHAPTER 7: AN UNEXPECTED MOTHERHOOD

Background interviews: sister Portia Holmes Shields, Commission staffers and consultants Albert Blumrosen, Preston David, Charlotte Frank, Brooke Trent, Electra Yourke, and friends Barbara Babcock, Charlayne Hunter-Gault, Judy Mage, Christine Philpot and Judith Stein.

158 **It's only possible** Ivers Peterson, "Woman to Be Head of City Rights Unit," *NYT,* March 24, 1970.

158 **A very different challenge** EHN, *The Challenge of Equality: The Work of the New York City Commission on Human Rights,* 1970–1977, New York, May 1977.

158 **"Could we** Ibid.

160 **Eleanor had signed** *NYT* Ad, July 31, 1969.

160 **On Monday, March 23** Office of the Mayor, John V. Lindsay, City Hall, New York City, Press Release, Monday, March 23, 1970. EHNP.

160 **Munching on grapes** *NYT,* June 3, 1970, p. 91.

160 **Eleanor was quoted** Johanna Berkman, "The Insider," *NYT* Magazine, July 16, 1970.

160 **I trust you will be** Mayor Lindsay to EHN, July 16, 1970, EHNP.

166 **I sure never felt** Greta Walker, *Women Today,* New York: Hawthorn Books, 1975, p. 69.

171 **In 1962 Charlayne** John Sanders, *Black History Month Profile,* Bakersfield.com, 1998.

CHAPTER 8: MADAME COMMISSIONER

Background interviews: Commission staff and consultants Albert and Ruth Blumrosen, Preston David, Charlotte Frank, Brooke Trent and Electra Yourke, and friends Barbara Babcock, Charlayne Hunter-Gault, Judy Mage, and Christine Philpot.

Contemporary *New York Times* and *Post* articles, EHN papers, and rights texts cited above provided background for New York in the early 1970s, as did Vincent Cannato's *The Ungovernable City: John Lindsay and His Struggle to Save New York,* New York: Basic Books, 2001.

172 **One of her first** *NYT,* June 3, 1970.

173 **Two peoples, each of** EHN handwritten draft speech, circa early 1970s, EHNP.

173 **All of us who** Ibid.

174 **The legacy of** EHN, draft of Grand Council Speech, March 4, circa early 1970s, EHNP. This is basically what she told her staff, according to members who heard her.

176 **We finally decided** Fern Marja Eckman, "Woman in the News: Eleanor Holmes Norton," *NYP,* November 13, 1971, p. 23.

177 **Reasoning that it took** Reid, p. 32.

177 **Eleanor's personal stamp** *Women's Role in Contemporary Society: The Report of the New York City Commission on Human Rights,* New York: Avon Books, 1972.

178 **Eleanor's introduction prophetically** Ibid., p. 7.

178 **But Eleanor insisted** Edith F. Lynton, *Toward Better Jobs and Better Service in Household Work: A Report and Recommendations Based on a Conference on Household Work Held by the New York City Commission on Human Rights,* New York City Commission on Human Rights, 1972, p. 1.

178 **It is easy enough** Ibid., p. 7.

179 **In a year** Jacqueline Trescott, "Eleanor Norton: Rights' Thinking Person in Charge at EEOC," *WP,* June 22, 1977.

180 **All over America** Paul Tractenberg, ed. *Selection of Teachers and Supervisors in Urban School Systems: A Transcript of the Public Hearings Held Before the New York City Commission on Human Rights,* January 25–29, 1971, New York: Agathon Publication Services, 1972, p. 2.

180 **Under the Commission's mandate** Ibid., p. 1.

181 **After 140 experts** EHN, Preface, *Equal Employment Opportunities and the New York City Public Schools: An Analysis and Recommendations based on Public Hearings held January 25–29, 1971,* New York: The Public Education Association, 1971.

181 **Yet with words that** Similar doubts would later reverberate through other city departments, questioning relevance of hiring criteria to job performance.

181 **The overwhelming weight** Andrew H. Malcolm, "Rights Unit Seeks to Drop Teacher Examiners' Board," *NYT,* May 5, 1971.

181 **New York's Southern District** *Chance and Mercado v. Board of Examiners et al.*

181 **She attacked housing** Pamela G. Hollie, "Eleanor Holmes Norton: 'I'm a Natural-Born Advocate,' " *Juris Doctor,* April 1974, p. 46.

181 **When some blacks complained** Ibid., pp. 46–47.

187 **A storm of criticism** Reid, pp. 58–59.

187 **Dr. King, who agreed** Ken Auletta, "The Underclass—Part III," *The New Yorker,* November 30, 1981, p. 130.

187 **The furor was so great** Ibid., p. 128.

188 **She opened with** EHN Remarks, National Urban League, Atlanta, Georgia, Wednesday, July 30, 1975.

188 **Upon his retirement** *Congressional Record, House of Representatives,* May 15, 2000, Page H2977.

189 **In December, 1973, Shirley** Chisholm in *Newsweek,* December 17, 1973.

189 **Thirty-five years after** Francis Fox Piven, professor of political science, Graduate Center of the City University of New York believes Moynihan's research was "academically invalid," "shoddy," and paved the way for attacks on welfare; William Julius Wilson, professor of social policy at the Kennedy School of Harvard, considers Moynihan's work prophetic. Alan Wolfe, "Not the Ordinary Kind, in Politics or at Harvard," *NYT,* September 9, 2000, p. 19.

190 **When Mrs. Hamer died** EHN, "The Woman Who Changed the South: A Memory of Fannie Lou Hamer," *Ms.,* July 1977, p. 51.

191 **While "we're not romanticizing** Fern Marja Eckman, "On Another Offensive," *NYP,* undated clip, circa 1971, p. 23, EHNP.

191 **What the women's movement** EHN in Barbara Deckard, *The Women's Movement: Political, Socioeconomic and Psychological Issues,* New York: Harper & Row, 1975, p. 363.

191 **One would sue** Laura Kiernan, "Ex-Housekeeper Says EEOC Chief Owes Her $18,663 in Overtime," *WP,* December 4, 1980.

191 **But you do what** clipping fragment, "Eleanor Holmes Norton, Tuesday at Home," November 1974, EHNP.

192 **The obituary she wrote** Phrase repeated in funeral program, St. George's Episcopal Church, July 23, 1976.

192 **That fall, a peanut** Jimmy Carter, *Turning Point,* New York: Times Books, 1992, p. 196.

CHAPTER 9: BRAND-NEW LAW

Background interviews: EEOC staff and consultants Al Blumrosen, Ruth Blumrosen, Preston David, Charlotte Frank, Alvin Golub, Brooke Trent, Daisy Voigt, Eve Wilkins, Judith Winston and Electra Yourke; and Washington colleagues Barbara Babcock, Maudine Cooper, Rachelle Horowitz, Judith Lichtman, Constance Newman, Wendy Williams, and Barbara Williams Skinner.

Gillette's *Between Beauty and Justice* provided other major Washington background, as did *New York Times* and *Washington Post* archives and EEOC documents of the time.

193 **Brown, an old friend** Steven A. Holmes, *Ron Brown: An Uncommon Life,* New York: John Wiley & Sons, 2000, p. 82. Confirmed by interview with Rachelle Horowitz. Vernon Jordan disputes the belief that Brown was a serious contender.

194 **Vernon Jordan strongly backed** Ibid., pp. 82–85

194 **Her old friend Ron** Ibid., p. 84. Confirmed by EHN.

194 **I don't mind being** Claudia Dreyfus, "A Singular Woman: I Hope I'm Not a Token," *McCall,* October 1971.

194 **This time, Eleanor came** Eden Ross Lipson, "In the Carter Administration, Big Jobs for Young Lawyers," *NYT,* May 1, 1977.

194 **Jet and Ebony magazines** Bill Drummond, "Carter Opens New Doors to Top Black Appointees," *LAT,* December 12, 1977.

194 **District governance** Gillette, pp. 190–191.

195 **New York's Amsterdam** *NYP,* January 23, 1978.

195 **And the paper congratulated** *NYP,* March 26, 1977.

196 **How was she to overcome** "Job Opportunities Deemed Unequal," *WP,* July 3, 1978.

197 **The agency was a laughingstock** Jacqueline Trescott, "Eleanor Norton: Rights' Thinking Person in Charge at EEOC," *WP,* June 22, 1977, p. 7.

197 **Civil rights and women's** Patrick Oster, "Employment Unit's 'Chair' Made of Sturdy Stuff," *Chicago Sun-Times,* December 26, 1977, p. 10.

197 **The agency's repute** Senate Human Resources Committee record, Room 4232, Dirksen Senate Office Building, May 24, 1977.

197 **Reporters dubbed Eleanor** Oster, "Employment Unit's 'Chair' Made of Sturdy Stuff," *Chicago Sun-Times,* December 26, 1977, p. 10.

198 **You are going to see speed** Lamson, p. 175.

198 **Acknowledging no fear** Lynn Litterine, "'The Chair' Battles Racism and Sexism," *The Philadelphia Inquirer,* March 30, 1978.

198 **We all deal with fear** Fern Marja Eckman, "Woman in the News: Eleanor Holmes Norton," *NYP,* November 13, 1971, p. 23.

199 **By the time they left** Ernest Holsendolph, *NYT,* June 6, 1977, p. 45; EHN Speech to Washington Press Club, December 1, 1977, p. 8.

200 **Six weeks later** Testimony before the House Subcommittee on Employment Opportunities, July 27, 1977.

201 **Her management team started** EEOC: *The Transformation of an Agency,* Office of Public Affairs, EEOC, 2401 E Street, NW, Room 4202, Washington, D.C., July 1978.

201 **Early model office returns produced** Dennis A. Williams et al, "Cleaning Up a Mess," *Newsweek,* January 16, 1978, p. 26.

201 **Dollar benefits for complainants** EHN, "Justice and Efficiency in Dispute Systems," *Ohio State Journal on Dispute Resolution,* 5:2, 1990, p. 227.

201 **and the backlog in** "Job Opportunities Deemed Unequal," *WP,* July 3, 1978.

201 **Widely viewed as confident** Williams et al., "Cleaning Up a Mess," *Newsweek,* January 16, 1978., p. 26.

202 **Employees marched and chanted** "The Troubled Drive for Efficiency at the EEOC," *Business Week,* December 19, 1977, p. 90.

202 **Eleanor's solution was to** Lawrence Speiser, "A Look at Eleanor Holmes Norton," *District Lawyer: The Official Journal of the District of Columbia Bar,* V. 4, No. 1, August/September, 1979. EHN also said, "Agencies do not deserve the privilege of enforcing the law if they cannot settle this kind of [inter-ethnic] competition." "A Conversation with Commissioner EHN," June 19, 1979, at the American Enterprise Institute for Public Policy Research, Washington, D.C., EHNP.

202 **. . . set herself hiring goals** EEOC 12th and 13th *Annual Report,* January 21, 1981.

203 **People who knew Eleanor** Jacob Wortham, "EEOC: Has It Really Worked?" *Black Enterprise,* September 1977, p. 23.

203 **Six months after** Walter Pincus and T. R. Reid, "In Fine Print: Cut at FBI, Growth at Rights Office," *WP,* January 24, 1978.

203 **The following year** *Reorganization of EEOC Programs, Reorganization Plan No. 1 of 1978,* February 1978.

204 **Eleanor boasted to** Roger Wilkins, "Black Leaders: A New Approach at White House," *NYT,* December 19, 1977, p. 2.

204 **The advocacy community** Nancy Kreiter, "Reinventing the Equal Employment Opportunity Commission," *Women Employed,* Chicago, 1995.

205 **During the hearings to** Senate Human Resources Committee record, Room 4232, Dirksen Senate Office Building, May 24, 1977.

205 **In 1980 Ford Motor** Reed Abelson, "Anti-Bias Agency Is Short of Will and Cash," *NYT,* July 1, 2001, Money and Business, p. 1.

205 **We will choose targets on** Roger Wilkins, "New Legal Effort to End Job Discrimination," January 9, 1978, *NYT,* p. 18.

206 **By December she** Lyle Denniston, "EEOC Offers 'Reverse Discrimination' Guide," *WS,* December 21, 1977.

208 **By the time the guidelines** Joann Lublin, "Guideline-happy at the EEOC?" *WSJ,* August 28, 1980, p. 16.

209 **Yet even the bridge-builder** EHN, "Black Presidential Appointees," *The Urban League Review,* 1:9, Summer 1985, p. 106; also see EHN, "Black Legacy and Responsibilities," *New England Law Review,* 27:3, 1993.

210 **Speaking four days** Lamson, p. 182.

211 **She reminded an NAACP** EHN, Keynote Address to the NAACP Annual Convention, Portland, Oregon, July 5, 1978, EHNP.

211 **A day after the conference** Nathaniel Sheppard Jr., *NYT,* May 7, 1978, p. 30.

211 **But she would continue** *NYT,* July 3, 1978, p. 20.

211 **Life is about struggle** Lynn Litterine, " 'The Chair' Battles Racism and Sexism," *The Philadelphia Inquirer,* March 30, 1978.

212 **The armchair rule of mothers** Oster, "Employment Unit's 'Chair' Made of Sturdy Stuff," *Chicago Sun–Times,* December 26, 1977, p. 10.

215 **We must march** EHN, National Urban League Conference, Conrad Hilton Hotel, Chicago, July 25, 1979, EHNP.

215 **By 1980 Eleanor,** Data Black National Opinion Poll, *New York Amsterdam News,* July 19, 1980; in *The 1978 10th Anniversary World Almanac and Book of Facts,* November 16, 1977, four black women—EHN, Patricia Robert Harris, Coretta Scott King and Barbara Jordan—were among twenty-five "most influential American women."

CHAPTER 10: EXILE

Background interviews: Georgetown faculty Father Robert Drynan (letter), Emma Coleman Jordan, Susan Deller Ross and Wendy W. Williams; EHN's son John Norton; also colleagues and friends Barbara Babcock, Maudine R. Cooper, Lawrence Guyot, June Johnson, Vernon Jordan, Judith Lichtman, Constance Berry Newman, and Barbara Williams-Skinner.

For South African Embassy sit-in background: TransAfrica's Mwiza Muthali, the Honorable Reverend Fauntroy and personal correspondence from researcher Richard Knight. Washingtonian Steve Bumbaugh provided recollections (confirmed by EHN) of street incident with police, and again, author memories corroborated some details of EHN's life during the 1980s.

Most bibliographic research for this chapter took place in EHN papers, newspapers, and contemporary popular and legal periodicals.

218 **In fact, within six** Chris Benson, "Whatever Happened to Carter's Top Blacks?" *Ebony,* July 1981, vol. 36, p. 27.

218 **Senator Orrin Hatch** Chairman Hatch, R-Utah, Opening Statement before Senate Labor and Human Resources Committee During Oversight Hearings on EEOC, June 15, 1982.

218 **Despite years of glowing** Nancy Kreiter, "Reinventing the Equal Employment Opportunity Commission," *Women Employed,* Chicago, 1995, p. 3.

218 **. . . a series of GAO** Reports issued July 1981, October 1981 and June 1982.

218 **. . . alleged millions of** *NYT,* June 16, 1982.

218 **With her usual statistics** EHN letter to Senator Hatch, July 30, 1982, EHNP.

219 **Many civil rights** "Interview with Eleanor Norton," *Equal Opportunity,* 13:1, Fall, 1979, p. 16.

219 **Several years before** *The American Lawyer,* August 11, 1978, preview issue.

221 **Justice is assumed** EHN, "Justice and Efficiency in Dispute Systems," *Ohio State Journal on Dispute Resolution,* 5:2, 1990, p. 230.

221 **Yet she had seen** Ibid., p. 229.

223 **Once, arriving for** Equity Institute, where author was executive director, hosted the mid-eighties reception. Amherst, Massachusetts.

224 **Rallying women for** EHN, "Good-Bye ERA . . .Hello Equality," *Human Rights,* Section of Individual Rights and Responsibilities of the American Bar Association, 12: 1, Spring, 1984, p. 25.

224 **"Without free expression** EHN, Transcript of speech at Florida International, circa mid-eighties, EHNP.

224 **In a 1988** *Life* "Tough Talk on the Crippling of a Noble Cause—And Breaking Through Today's Barriers," *Life,* Spring, 1988, 11:5, p. 42.

224 **All that we have won,** EHN, "Commitment Makes a Difference," clip fragment, Milwaukee dateline, 1981, EHNP.

226 **"Welfare," she said then** "Tough Talk on the Crippling of a Noble Cause—and Breaking Through Today's Barriers," *Life,* Spring, 1988, 11:5, p. 43.

226 **Putting forward a solution** EHN, "Restoring the Traditional Black Family," *NYT Sunday Magazine,* June 2, 1985, p. 43.

226 **Two years later she** Committee on Policy for Racial Justice, *Black Initiative and Governmental Responsibility,* Washington, D.C.: Joint Center for Political Studies, 1987, p. 3.

228 **On December 2** "Protest Chronology," *WP,* November 27, 1985.

228 **Two months later, singer** Karlyn Barker, "Stevie Wonder Arrested in Apartheid Protest," *WP,* February 15, 1985.

229 **Eleanor said then** Kenneth Bredemeier and Michel Marriott, "Fauntroy Arrested in Embassy," *WP,* November 22, 1984.

229 **The sanctions movement would** Edward Walsh, "Sanctions Imposed on S. Africa as Senate Overrides Veto, 78–21," *WP,* October 3, 1986.

231 **In 1986 she wrote** EHN letter to Neil Herring, March 20, 1986. In possession of Herring.

232 **In May, 1989** EHN letter to Neil Herring, begun May 23, 1989, continued June 15, 1989, finished December 18, 1989. In possession of Herring.

232 **The final platform** Pam Maples, "Jackson Backers Win One, Lose One," *Rocky Mountain News,* June 26, 1988, p. 3; Michael Seele, "As a Bargainer,

O'Neill Professor Norton Helped Define the 1988 Democratic Campaign," *Boston College Biweekly,* March 16, 1989.

234 **Generally, I don't take** Linell Smith, "Eleanor Holmes Norton: A Life Crowded with the Issues of Our Time," *The Evening Sun,* April 26, 1988, p. E1.

235 **Featured as one of five** Bill Berry, "Husbands of Well-known Women," *Ebony,* April 1978.

235 **Friends suggest that** Orlando Patterson, *Rituals of Blood: Consequences of Slavery in Two American Centuries,* New York: Avon Books, 1998, details troubled African-American gender relations as one legacy of slavery; one friend references this. EHN, who agrees in interviews that black male-female relations are "all messed up" as a consequence of slavery, is unimpressed with any such application to Edward or their marriage.

236 **Over a rare** Letter from Wendy Williams, Patricia White and Susan Deller Ross, *WP,* October 30, 1990.

237 **Together they published** EHN and Edward W. Norton, "A Setback for Minority Businesses," *Legal Times,* 11:4, May 1, 1989.

237 **To a question once** Wendy Law-Yone, "Reflections," *WP,* November 22, 1979.

238 **Near the end of the decade** Letter to Neil Herring, December 1989, in Herring's possession.

238 **Overwhelmed and** In October 1989, Yale Law School Dean Guido Calabresi unveiled the portrait.

239 **Finally she finished** EHN, "Bargaining and the Ethic of Process," *New York University Law Review,* 64.3, June 1989.

239 **The government released** Sahn Venter, *Associated Press,* February 10, 1990.

239 **People ran by** Ibid.

240 **To counter revisionism** EHN, "At Liberty," *Constitution,* 1:5, Fall, 1989, p. 19. Speech at Mound City Bar Association annual dinner. *St. Louis Post-Dispatch,* June 25, 1989.

240 **Now maybe it was time** EHN, "Black Legacy and Responsibility," *New England Law Review,* 27:3, 1993, p. 689.

CHAPTER 11: AN ELECTION EXPLODES

Background interviews: Campaign workers Rosemary Addy, Vic Basile, Donna Brazile, Howard Croft, June Johnson, Cartwright Moore, Karen Mulhauser, Phillip Pannell, Mary Preston, Rene Redwood and Pauline Schneider; commentator Mark Plotkin; and Georgetown Law colleagues Emma Coleman Jordan and Wendy Williams.

Celia Morris's *Storming the Statehouse: Running for Governor with Ann Richards and Dianne Feinstein* (New York: Scribner, 1992) provided national texture on women candidates; *Washington Post* campaign articles and Gillette's *Between Justice and Beauty* gave Washington background.

244 **In 1990 Washington** Gillette, p. 201.

245 **Women were running** Morris, passim.

248 **Donna once bluntly** Robin Givhan, "Clearing the Decks at Gore Headquarters," *WP,* November 16, 1999, p. C1.

249 **Joe Rauh, the** Michael Abramowitz, "Rights Activist Norton May Run," *WP*, April 12, 1990.

249 **The *Washington Post* enthused** "D.C.'s Next Voice on the Hill," Editorial, *WP*, April 13, 1990.

250 **Before a diverse** R. H. Melton, "Norton Enters Race for Delegate," *WP*, May 6, 1990.

250 **Pro-choice organizations** Abramowitz, "Norton's Contributions Controversy," *WP*, July 26, 1990; Abramowitz, "Women's Groups Endorse Norton," *WP*, August 14, 1990.

251 **The D.C. Coalition of** Abramowitz, "Jarvis Contribution Leaves Some Fuming," *WP*, August 16, 1990.

253 **Contributors included** Abramowitz, "Norton Wins AFL-CIO Endorsement," *WP*, July 17, 1990.

254 **Kane contended that** Abramowitz, "Taking the Gloves Off," *WP*, July 9, 1990.

254 **Eleanor fired back** Ibid.

254 **On August 29, a *Post*** Abramowitz, Richard Morin, "Norton Leads Delegate Race," *WP*, August 29, 1990.

254 **A week later,** Melton, "Ray Begins $100,000 TV Blitz," *WP*, September 5, 1990.

255 **On September 7,** Abramowitz, "Rivals Label Norton Outsider," *WP*, September 7, 1990.

258 **Her disclosure** Abramowitz, "Norton's Husband Urges Voters Not to Punish Her," *WP*, September 11, 1990.

259 **The bill kept** Abramowitz, "Nortons Change Account of Failure to File Taxes," *WP*, October 27, 1990.

259 **The city sent** Ibid.

260 **The last thing we** Abramowitz, "Norton to Pay D.C. $25,000 in Delinquent Taxes," *WP*, September 8, 1990.

260 **Rival Sterling Tucker** Abramowitz, "Norton Filed No Returns for 1982–89," *WP*, September 9, 1990.

260 **Her numbers went** Steve Twomey, "Some Voters Rethinking Support for Norton," *WP*, September 10, 1990.

261 **I have a lifetime** Abramowitz, "Withholdings Will Cut Bill, Norton Says," *WP*, September 10, 1990.

261 **People were on** Ibid.

261 **No dirty tricks** Abramowitz and Steve Twomey, "Norton's Husband Urges Voters Not to Punish Her," *WP*, September 11, 1990.

262 **But it was a matter** Ibid.

262 **Over the next** Abramowitz, "Norton Was Late in Filing 1989 Federal Tax Return," *WP*, September 26, 1990.

262 **That day the *Post*,** Editorial, *WP*, September 10, 1990.

262 **As public criticism** Abramowitz, "Norton's Husband Urges Voters Not to Punish Her," *WP*, September 11, 1990.

266 **When all the votes** Abramowitz, "Norton Overcomes Last-Minute Crisis to Win," *WP*, September 12, 1990.

266 **She wanted to** Michael York, "Norton Tries to Win Back Support of White Voters," *WP*, September 13, 1990.

267 **Is someone who** Judy Mann, "Norton's Tarnished Image," *WP*, September 28, 1990.

267 **As September wore** Melton, "Norton to Make Tax Payment," *WP*, September 19, 1990.

268 **Her reaction to** Sam Smith, "Not Guilty by Association," *WP*, October 7, 1990.

268 **But Ward Three's** Melton, Abramowitz, "Second D.C. Candidate Didn't Pay Taxes," *WP*, September 25, 1990.

268 **Eleanor gained** Melton, "Barry Defends D.C. Tax System," *WP*, October 17, 1990.

269 **At the end of** Abramowitz, "Norton Would Take Big Pay Cut If She Wins," *WP*, October 29, 1990.

269 **On October 31** Inquiry initiated October 31, 1990; EHN response November 13, EHNP.

269 **A week before** Editorial, *WP*, October 31, 1990.

269 **Days before the** Twomey, "Norton and Singleton Take Off the Gloves in Lively Debates," *WP*, November 1, 1990.

270 **Even though I** Dorothy Gilliam, "Judging Norton by Her Record, *WP*, November 5, 1990.

270 **Washingtonians were out** Twomey, Morin, "Norton Holds Lead Tenuously," *WP*, November 2, 1990.

271 **I haven't talked to** Abramowitz, "Key Hill Democrats Offer Dixon Support on District Finances," *WP*, September 13, 1990.

271 **Let's give the** Ibid.

CHAPTER 12: WARRIOR ON THE HILL

Background interviews: The Honorables Tom Davis, Reverend Walter Fauntroy and John Lewis; other colleagues Maudine R. Cooper, Constance Berry Newman, Mark Plotkin, Mary Preston, Mark Thompson, Barbara Williams-Skinner; EHN staff Jon Bouker, Donna Brazile, Cedric Hendricks, Julia Hudson, Cartwright Moore and consultant Karen Mulhauser; SNCC colleagues Courtland Cox, Lawrence Guyot, June Johnson and Joyce Ladner; and Georgetown Law Center colleagues Emma Coleman Jordan and Susan Deller Ross.

A home rule framework was given by *Washington, D.C. in Transition: Reinventing Our Nation's Capital: A Summary of Research and Seminars of the Task Force on District of Columbia Governance, November 1996–April 1997* (Georgetown Public Policy Institute, Georgetown University, April 1997) and fleshed out by Jamin B. Raskin's, "Is This America? The District of Columbia and the Right to Vote," *Harvard Civil Rights–Civil Liberties Law Review*, 34:1, Winter 1999.

Background on women in Congress was provided by Clara Bingham, *Women on the Hill: Challenging the Culture of Congress* (New York: Random House, 1996); Barbara Boxer with Nicole Boxer, *Strangers in the Senate* (Washington D.C.: National Press Books, 1994); LaVerne McCain Gill, *African American Women in Congress* (New Brunswick: Rutgers University Press, 1997); Marjorie Margolies-Mezvinsky with Barbara Feinman, *A Woman's Place . . . The Freshmen Women Who Changed the Face of Congress* (New York: Crown, 1994); and Pat Schroeder's *24 Years of House Work. . . . and the Place Is Still a Mess: My Life in Politics* (Kansas City: Andrews McMeel, 1998).

273 **When Pat** Schroeder, p. 155.

276 **Six weeks after** *Jet,* March 25, 1991, v. 79, p. 14.

276 **He told the** *Post* Kent Jenkins Jr., "D.C. Delegate Norton Seeks Separation," *WP,* March 5, 1991, p. B1.

276 **For her part, Eleanor** Quoted in "Norton," *WT,* August 5, 1991, p. B4.

277 **The District's new Delegate** "Surprising Star," *WSJ,* May 10, 1991, p. 1.

280 **I'm burned out** "Norton," *WT,* August 5, 1991, p. B4.

281 **Eleanor had been drawn** Ibid., p. B4.

282 **Otherwise, she wrote** EHN, "Anita Hill and the Year of the Woman," *Race, Gender and Power in America: The Legacy of the Hill-Thomas Hearings,* eds. Anita Faye Hill and Emma Coleman Jordan, New York: Oxford University Press, 1995, p. 243.

282 **Eleanor ran to** Boxer, pp. 54–55. The following description of the standoff at the Senate doorway relies on her book as well as EHN.

284 **No one will believe** A grassroots network, African-American Women in Defense of Ourselves, sprang up within days and placed full-page ads, signed by 1,603 women, in the *New York Times* (November 17, 1991) and African-American newspapers all over the country. *NYT,* November 17, 1991, supplemented by recollections of Jewelle Gomez, one of the signers, in author interview. Also Lynne Olson, *Freedom's Daughters,* New York: Scribner, 2001, p. 381.

284 **She and Mayor Sharon** EHN, "The District's Belated Federal Payment," *WP,* June 11, 1991, p. 21; Gillette, p. 204.

285 **In a** *Wall Street* EHN, "Quota Scare Must Not Destroy Civil Rights Bill," *WSJ,* May 16, 1991, p. 17.

285 **After it failed** Economic Development Newsletter from EHN Congressional Office, March 1992.

286 **The** *New York Times* **concurred** Editorial, *NYT,* July 21, 1992.

287 **In a letter** EHN, "Sharing My Thoughts on a Difficult Decision," *Letter to Constituents,* November 1993.

287 **The point of seeking** Kent Jenkins Jr., "Norton Wavers on Seeking Vote on D.C. Statehood," *WP,* November 11, 1993, p. D9.

288 **Twenty-four people** Jenkins, "Statehood Push Redoubled as Vote Looms," *WP,* November 19, 1993, p. C1.

288 **Mr. Chairman,** EHN and subsequent quotes in debate, *Congressional Record, New Columbia Admission Act, House of Representatives,* November 20 and 21, 1993.

289 **Official Washington, the** The District's Statehood Constitutional Convention had completed a state constitution, subsequently approved by District voters and revised by Congress. Hilary Cairns, "Making D.C. a Livable City: Ideas for Governmental and Fiscal Reform," unpublished paper, Georgetown University, December 1996, p. 8.

291 **On Sunday, November 21** Jenkins, "House Turns Down Statehood for D.C.," *WP,* November 22, 1993, p. 1.

293 **Representatives might beat** EHN, Editorial, *WP,* October 8, 1992, p. 21.

CHAPTER 13: UNDER ATTACK

Background interviews: The Honorable Tom Davis, Speaker Newt Gingrich, Reverend Walter Fauntroy and John Lewis; staffers Donna Brazile and Cedrick

Hendricks; Antiochian and lawyer Art Finch; child-care aide Mrs. Vermell Howard; and friends and political colleagues Barbara Babcock, Charlayne Hunter-Gault, Lawrence Guyot, June Johnson, Mark Thompson and Barbara Williams-Skinner.

294 **The withdrawal of a vote,** "Delegate Voting: Norton Struggles to Get Floor Vote Back," *Constituent Newsletter,* Summer, 1995, p. 3.

295 **That hot August** Michael Janofsky, "Gingrich Beards the Lions at Capital Town Meeting," *NYT,* August 3, 1995, p. B10.

296 **The Speaker, joined** Howard Schneider, David A. Vise, "Gingrich Defends Vision for D.C. at Forum," *WP,* August 3, 1995, p. 1.

297 **She cooled his** "An Unexpected Guardian Angel," *The Economist,* August 19, 1995, v. 336, p. 23.

297 **On November 10, 1994** Vise and Schneider, "Norton Seeks $300 Million in Cuts," *WP,* November 10, 1994, p. 1.

297 **The District's annual federal receipts** Carol O'Cleireacain, "The Orphaned Capital: Adopting a Revenue Plan for the District of Columbia," *Policy Brief,* 11, Brookings Institution, January 1997.

298 **On February 16, 1995,** Vise and Schneider, "Norton Seeks Control Board," *WP,* February 17, 1995, p. 1.

298 **"Neither wanted** confirmed by Janofsky, "Congress Drafts Bill on Financial Overseers for Washington," *NYT,* February 17, 1995 p. 25.

298 **Eleanor, trying to resolve** "District, Congressional Leaders Voice Their Concerns and Hopes," *WP,* February 23, 1995, p. 10.

299 **People have called** Yolanda Woodlee, "Norton Balances Message to Get the Most for District," *WP,* March 29, 1995.

299 **Eleanor's old civil** Hamil R. Harris, "City Activists Condemn Control Board," *WP,* March 30, 1995, p. 7.

300 **The D.C. government has** John Dizard, "Capital Offense: Government Largesse Brought Washington to Its Knees," *National Review,* July 15, 1996, 48:13, p. 35.

300 **A *Post* poll** Yolanda Woodlee, "Norton Balances Message to Get the Most for District," *WP,* March 29, 1995, p. 1.

300 **And she won support** Maria Puente, "D.C. in a $722 Million Mess," *USA Today,* February 22, 1995, p. 3A.

302 **The Revitalization Act—taking** Jeff Itell and Fred Siegel, "From the Ramparts: The End of Street Politics," *The New Republic,* September 1, 1997, 217:9, p. 14.

302 **The Revitalization Act** Vise, "D.C. Rescue Agreement Strips Barry's Power," *WP,* July 31, 1997, p. 1.

302 **However, the new Act** Ibid.

302 **Many residents' worst** Vise, "Brimmer Takes Reins in Transfer of Power," *WP,* August 6, 1997, p. 1.

302 **An unelected "dictator"** "The Lady Who Shamed Marion Barry," *The Economist,* August 9, 1997, v. 344, p. 21.

302 **A group of protestors** Ibid.

302 **In a poignant** Vise and Michael Powell, "Woman in the Middle," *WP,* August 1, 1997, p. D1.

303 **Budget Deal Creates Heat** Janofsky, "Budget Deal Creates Heat for District of Columbia's Delegate," *NYT,* August 12, 1997, p. 12.
303 **while the *City Paper*** "Loose Lips," *Washington City Paper,* August 22–28, 1997.
303 **Eleanor wrote an explanatory** EHN, "It's Not the Package," *WP,* reprinted in EHN *Constituent Newsletter,* Fall, 1997, p. 2.
303 **In Congress Eleanor's** Vise and Powell, "Woman in the Middle," *WP,* August 1, 1997, p. D1.
309 **Driving herself** author observational notes of campaign launch. Howard University, January 8, 2000.

CHAPTER 14: MR. PRESIDENT: "YES, ELEANOR"

Background interviews: sister Dr. Portia Shields; cousin Dr. Warren Ashe; Georgetown colleagues Wendy Williams and Emma Coleman Jordan; friends Charlayne Hunter-Gault and Vernon Jordan, Antioch classmate David Crippens.

Author observations and notes provided background for Vela Lynch Holmes's funeral, the press conference on slavery in Sudan, the Give It Back! rally, and EHN birthday party at Vernon and Ann Jordan's home.

317 **The man we commemorate on the Floor** "Salute to A. Leon Higginbotham," *Congressional Record, House of Representatives,* March 3, 1999.
318 **Three weeks later** *Congressional Record, House of Representatives,* March 24, 1999.
321 **Characteristically, she associated herself** EHN, *American Anti-Slavery Group Press Conference on Slavery in Sudan,* Washington, D.C., September 28, 2000. Author notes.
322 **Later she spoke** EHN, Press Release, "Norton at Bipartisan Press Conference Calls for Major Initiative to End War and Slavery in Sudan," March 22, 2001.
322 **Calling together** Give It Back! rally, Rayburn House Office Building, December 5, 2000. Author notes.
324 **On June 13, 2000** Jordan home, Washington, D.C. Author notes.

INDEX

NOTE: EHN refers to Eleanor Holmes Norton. HRC refers to Human Rights Commission (New York City).